U-BOATS
OFF
BERMUDA

U-BOATS OFF BERMUDA

PATROL SUMMARIES AND MERCHANT
SHIP SURVIVORS LANDED IN
BERMUDA 1940-1944

ERIC WIBERG

FONTHILL

for men farfar John Åke Truls Wiberg, 1902–1963

entrepreneur, politician, philanthropist

Fonthill Media Language Policy

Fonthill Media publishes in the international English language market. One language edition is published worldwide. As there are minor differences in spelling and presentation, especially with regard to American English and British English, a policy is necessary to define which form of English to use. The Fonthill Policy is to use the form of English native to the author. Eric Wiberg was born and educated in the USA; therefore American English has been adopted in this publication.

Fonthill Media Limited
Fonthill Media LLC
www.fonthillmedia.com
office@fonthillmedia.com

First published in the United Kingdom and the United States of America 2017

British Library Cataloguing in Publication Data:
A catalogue record for this book is available from the British Library

Copyright © Eric Wiberg 2017

ISBN 978-1-78155-606-1

Typeset in 10.5pt on 13pt MinionPro
Printed and bound in England

MIX
Paper from
responsible sources
FSC® C013056

Acknowledgements

Thanks to Guðmundur Helgason and Rainer Kolbicz of Uboat.net, as well as stalwart Capt. Jerry Mason and his wife Charla of uboatarchive.net for their inestimable help. Dr. Axel Niestlé was an immense help in solving riddles of U-boat losses. Michael Constandy of Westmoreland Research and Robert Eller Pratt, cartographer, continue to do excellent work on archival research and map-making. In the UK, Simon Fowler, archivist, and in Bermuda, Ellen Hollis of the Bermuda National Archives were a huge help to me and very generous with their time and accurate in what they delivered. I am very grateful to my agent Alan Morell of Creative Management Partners for his continued support and sage counsel. Many thanks to Dr. Edward Harris, Executive Director of the National Museum of Bermuda, for graciously writing the Foreword.

Derek Waller was an authority over the disposition of *U-505* and the fates of number of other submarines. Cristiano d'Adamo and Platon Alexiades were both hugely helpful with respect to Italian submarines assigned to Bermuda either by the Axis or Allies. The U-Boot Museum of Germany and their staff were very helpful as was Doreen of the St. Paul's Parish in Bermuda. Sailing legend and mentor Warren Brown did not live to see this book, but would have enjoyed it. For his interest and enthusiasm for this project, I thank my son Felix and I hope one day to show him the wonders of Bermuda. As ever, I appreciate my family for their continued interest, enthusiasm and support, particularly my parents, siblings, and the many friends who continue tolerate the far-off topic of U-boats over the years.

By the same author

CONTENTS

Foreword

Bermuda, the nearest oceanic neighbor of the United States in the western North Atlantic, stands on a volcanic seamount some 640 miles due east of Cape Hatteras, North Carolina. In some aspects of the history of that country, tiny Bermuda has figured large, but has usually been written small, mostly due to a neglect of continental historians as it is out of sight, so to speak, over the horizon and yet a British territory. For one period, the present volume adds considerable insights into military activity around Bermuda in the Second World War in great and illuminating detail.

As the second British colony in this hemisphere, Bermuda can be credited with saving dozens of starving colonists at first, namely in May 1610 at the settlement of Jamestown in what would become the Commonwealth of Virginia, then engaging in cannibalism, as lately revealed in archaeological excavations at the site of James Fort. During the American Revolutionary War, to save the island from starvation, due to an edict of the Continental Congress, some Bermudians appropriated the Governor's supply of gunpowder and sent it to General Washington. The action resulted in the lifting of a shipping embargo against Bermuda, but not for other British possessions; it was apparently used at the Battle of Bunker Hill on 17 June 1775.

After that conflict, Bermuda became an imperial outpost, with the construction of a large dockyard for the warships of the Royal Navy and a series of fortifications to hold the island against an invasion by the new United States of America. In effect, with bases in the Canadian Maritimes and the British West Indies, Britain moved its western borders to an imaginary line between those two localities, with Bermuda being in the center and becoming the headquarters of the North America and West Indies Stations, sometimes said to be the 'Gibraltar of the West.' It was from this new station, established as a result of losing the harbors on the East Coast, that the British Fleet set forth to attack Washington during the War of 1812.

The Civil War (1861–65) again brought Bermuda into close connection with the United States, as it became, with Nassau in the Bahamas, a major transshipment center for goods from Britain destined for the Confederacy. While the South was a losing cause, the Bermudians made considerable amounts of money, being the

A parody of the quasi-occupation of Bermuda by Allied military officials. A diverse set of characters, from civilian to sailor and soldier, were painted by illustrator Floyd Davis in 1942. This shows the quayside and Front Street, Hamilton Harbour, in front of the Royal Bermuda Yacht Club. (*Life Magazine*)

middlemen of that commerce through the Northern blockade. It was during that period that significant changes took place in the design of armaments, and the current arms race had begun, signaling an end to the three centuries hegemony of the smoothbore cannon and the round cannonball with the introduction of rifled artillery firing elongated projectiles. The old 'wooden walls' of Britain's great Navy also gave way at this time to ships of iron and latterly steel, powered not by the vagaries of the wind but by the constancy of steam and ultimately oil. New fortifications were made at Bermuda to mirror those significant military changes, all into the early 1900s when Britain and the United States became allies in time for World War One (1914–18).

On 3 September 1939, Britain declared war on Germany and the last imperial fortification was placed on Bermuda, intended to keep German warships well at sea on any approach to the island. A couple of days prior, a lease had been signed between the United States and Bermuda for lands in the colony upon which US Forces could establish military bases, without being declared a belligerent by Germany. Two such entities were created on the island beginning in April 1941, for the United States would not join Britain in the war until Pearl Harbor was attacked in December of that year. Other bases were established in Argentia in Newfoundland and in the British West Indies, thus the United States reversed the order set up by the British in the early 1800s and extended its borders to an imaginary line 640 miles into the North Atlantic, plus air cover from those new stations.

The story of the US Bases at Bermuda during World War Two has yet to be writ large, although this tome does much to fill out an important aspect of the period. Covered are the activities of the U-boat divisions of the *Kriegsmarine*, the seaborne sector of the German military triangle of the *Wehrmacht* that included the land-based *Wehrmacht Heer* and the airborne Luftwaffe. Neither of the latter two forces presented much of a threat to Bermuda and the United States, although Kindley Field had all of its early buildings painted in camouflage against aerial bombardment.

As illustrated so well in this book, the main and serious threat in Bermuda-US waters was the submarine, the German U-boat, although the island itself was never attacked. Eric Wiberg's detailed work is the first comprehensive elucidation of U-boat activity in the Bermuda region and follows his substantial volume on similar movements around the Bahamas and the eastern frontier of the Caribbean Sea, with significant British oil sources from Trinidad. Thanks to his scholarship, the subject has now been forced to the surface and, like the *U-505*, which spent its last war year in captivity at Bermuda, is now ours to examine in all and every detail. This volume will encourage others to write the rest of the story of Bermuda in the Second World War, especially as it related to the other activities of the US Forces on the island.

Of course, submarines continue the military story of this sector of the North Atlantic, but the German threat was replaced after the war by the menace of boats from the communist USSR and here, Bermuda remained a major player into the end of the Cold War in 1995. The US Forces left Bermuda after fifty-four years, a loss to the island and, some might say, a loss in the defense of the United States and its allies of the North Atlantic Treaty Organization. Following this excellent campaign, Captain Wiberg might take on the perhaps more challenging task of forcing the story of Russian 'U-boats' to the surface and daylight of present times.

Edward Cecil Harris, MBE, JP, PHD, FSA
Executive Director
National Museum of Bermuda
3 September 2016

Chart depicting eighty Allied merchant ships attacked or sunk by German and Italian submarines around Bermuda between 24 January 1942 and 27 February 1943. The first of roughly 1,270 survivors landed in Bermuda from SS *Uskbridge* on 28 October 1940, and the last from the SS *Melbourne Star* on 10 June 1943. (*Robert Pratt, for the author*)

Introduction

By any standard, Bermuda is a small place. Its 1939 population was 30,814, its total land mass is 20.54 square miles, and though there are 150 islets, the archipelago is formed by seven main islands. During World War Two, Bermuda served as a kind of air craft carrier—a strategically located offshore port. Indeed, the Fleet Air Arms' Royal Naval Air Station was named HMS *Malabar*, as though it were a ship. Bermuda was not the first territory or 'stone frigate' to receive the designation—remote Tristan de Cunha (HMS *Atlantic Isle*), Bahrain (HMS *Juffair*), and others (HMS *Ascension*) have as well.

If the Canadian Maritimes and the north-east Caribbean form the jaws leading to the underbelly of the United States East Coast, then Bermuda sits squarely in the middle of the path. Alongside a single Italian submarine, 142 German U-boats used the routes north and south of Bermuda to invade American and Caribbean waters and transit homeward, starting in early 1942 and ending in the summer of 1944. Over the course of more than 1,000 patrol days, these submarines essentially besieged little Bermuda, cutting off the islands' merchant marine supplies to the extent that local historians say the lack of foodstuffs arriving for horses hastened the ascension of the automobile there.[1]

The 1939 Declaration of Panama established a neutrality zone extending 300 nautical miles from US territories, prohibiting the warships of belligerent nations from entering it. This of course was pierced after Adolf Hitler declared war on the United States in December 1941, a few days after Pearl Harbor. Still, the Americans and their Allies in the Bahamas and other Caribbean colonies were not expecting German (or Italian) attacks that first winter, and nor, by any objective standard, were they prepared for them (a situation resulting in a blame game derisively called the Battle of Washington).[2]

Whereas the rumors that an Axis submarine shelled Mona Island between Hispaniola and Puerto Rico on 3 March 1942 were unfounded, the historical record is replete with multiple attacks much more alarming. German U-boats attacked the sea lanes off the Panama Canal, causing such a stir that two Allied subs—the *Dorado* and the French *Surcouf*—were sunk by friendly fire. No Italian submarine approached as close to the coast of the United States as the *Enrico Tazzoli*, which returned home between Bermuda and the US mainland. Had it not been disabled at the time, history might have paid more attention. As it was, the submarine returned to Europe, its exploits relatively unknown to the Allies, and was sunk soon thereafter. German subs laid mines in the approaches to most of the major ports between Boston and San Juan, Puerto Rico, including in the US Gulf. They landed saboteurs in Florida, New York, Maine, New Brunswick, and the Gulf of Saint Lawrence. In fact, German submarines penetrated the Red Sea, the Persian Gulf, Indonesia, the Pacific to Japan, Australia, and even New Zealand. Early in the war, their surface raiders captured a Norwegian whaling fleet in the Antarctic and crossed between Europe and the Pacific in the Arctic seas above the Soviet Union. The question with respect to German submarines, raiders, blockade-runners and supply submarines was not what they did, but what they did not manage to do.

The Germans wanted to fulfill Admiral Karl Dönitz's, and Hitler's, vision of domination of the seas. Britannia may have ruled the waves, but beneath them the Axis controlled the battle, at least until Black May of 1943, when Allies turned the tides and Dönitz recalled his wolf-packs. As one German sub commander wryly put it, he worked for the largest ship-scrapping effort in world history. The Germans alone accounted for 2,779 vessels and over fourteen million gross registered tons of Allied shipping sent to the bottom. During 1942, they destroyed over six million tons.

The Axis goals in the Western Hemisphere were two-fold: cut off the supply of oil (tankers) from the US Gulf and Venezuela to Halifax, where it was being protectively convoyed to the UK, and to sink Allied ships faster than the Allies could rebuild them. They very nearly succeeded, since in the winter and spring of 1942, they were sinking an average of a tanker every ten hours. Due to a lack of convoys, escorts, air cover, and signals intelligence, coupled with lights (including lighthouses) blazing from shore, German commanders would actually choose which type of ship to expend their valuable torpedoes on. They could afford not only to let smaller prey pass, but also to linger at the site of an attack for hours, to both ensure the victim was finished off, and to interact with survivors, gain intelligence, and provide assistance if needed. It was indeed a fairly unique theater of war in that regard, to the extent that Germans called early 1942 in the Americas the second happy time, recalling the outbreak of war when pickings were relatively easy and safe.

The Germans also made extraordinary gains over Allied ship production from September 1939 to spring 1943, after which improved intelligence, detection, sub-sea bombing techniques, sonar, hunter-killer groups, the elimination of supply U-boats, and improvements in the range, capacity and sub-detection capabilities (radar) on airplanes sealed their doom, finally with the closing of the air gap over the North Atlantic between Canada and Europe. The nail in the Axis' coffin was the mass-production by American industrialists like Henry J. Kaiser of the Liberty Ship, a wonder of assembly-line output, resulting in ships being launched less than a week after having their keels laid, a feat not achieved before or since. This was all made easier by an American workforce sheltered from the war, access to raw material which ships carried around Bermuda to the US, nationalization of shipyards by the Maritime Administration, and a keen workforce, much of it supplemented by women.

During World War Two, Bermuda not only sent forth convoys, escorts, and aviators to attack or evade submarines, it also welcomed over twelve hundred survivors from wrecked merchant marine, Royal Canadian Navy, and US Navy survivors to its shores. There were fifteen sailors buried in Bermuda between 1940 and 1944, perished in accidents aboard eleven Allied ships. Overall, nearly 4,657 Allied sailors were thrown into the ocean by German or Italian submarine attack around Bermuda. Of those, 1,208 (roughly a quarter) perished, the balance finding safety ashore, mostly by drifting for days in lifeboats and being rescued, but some of them by being retrieved from the water by Bermuda-based aircraft.

This is the story of the nearly 100 Allied ships which deposited hapless and distressed mariners ashore in Bermuda between 1939 and 1945, particularly those whose ships were sunk. There were nearly eighty merchant marine ships sent to the bottom by U-boats in a 450-mile radius around the island. They represent nearly half a million tons of shipping destroyed or attacked—474,795 gross registered tons. About a dozen voyages were destined for Bermuda or originated there, and their loss, particularly of passenger ships, was keenly felt by the island's population. Bermudians were forced to realize that despite their relative proximity to the mainland of America, they were in many ways cut off by sea. Some vessels, like the merchant ship *Anna* and its escort the irascible navy tug USS *Owl* encountered the enemy more than once, as did seasoned aviators based in Bermuda who managed to sink two German subs. One of the pilots, killed in action weeks later in Europe, never received the recognition due him. When the Germans found their targets at Cape Hatteras—nicknamed Torpedo Junction—tapering off, they intentionally moved their depredations east towards Bermuda to catch vessels using that route to avoid the lethal capes, keeping the Allies tasked with hunting them perennially off balance.

This is not a study of the social, political or even military situation on Bermuda in World War Two—there are others (including Jonathan Land Evans) who have covered that topic in great detail.[3] In this study, Bermuda is seen as a pivotal hub around which the activities of over 200 vessels—submarines and merchant ships— revolved. One could even think of Bermuda as a rescue ship—a highly welcome destination and landing spot for desperate survivors cast into the North Atlantic and its often-cold waters. Most of them were quickly packed off to serve on other vessels in other theaters of the war, also fraught with danger. For most of them, their cherished days in Bermuda were uniquely restful ones.

There are many tempting distractions from the core story of U-boats versus merchant ships in and around Bermuda in World War Two. There were the early convoys that sent forth the famously brave men of the escort the *Jervis Bay*, attacks by the breakout German Panzerschiff the *Deutschland* 400 miles to the east in October of 1939, the accelerated construction of a naval air station and Naval

Operating Base, the arrival of Sir Winston Churchill and the Duke and Duchess of Windsor in transit, the capture of suspected spies on merchant ships, the harboring of the captured and highly secret *U-505* on the island, the enabling of a small army of censors, and the utilization of six French as well as eight Italian submarines for testing by Allied ships in Bermuda and the mainland. But they all lead away from the core tale, which is submarines and their victims off the island, and survivor's resultant arrival on it.

It is precisely because of the relative invisibility of these victims—the fact that the attacks all occurred hundreds of miles from land and were unseen by anyone except the participants—that the author strives to have these stories heard. That men and women of all races and religions—crew from the Far East and India, passengers from Europe, and North and South America, made it ashore in Bermuda is extraordinary. A coterie of women who ran various benevolent organizations graciously opened their homes to the survivors, as did hoteliers and the indefatigable Dickie Tucker, who founded both the Bermuda Sailors' Home and the Guild of the Holy Compassion. This is their story.

U-boats off Bermuda deals also with U-boat attacks and survivor stories from Bahamas and New England. In that sense, Bermuda is pivotal. The area covered herein is roughly 400,000 square nautical miles, and since the Bahamas area covered one million, there is some overlap in vessels. However, aside from survivors who found themselves taken from Bermuda to New England, there is little overlap with New England. Canada, New York, Cape Hatteras, the Gulf of Mexico, and the Caribbean are not covered because other authors have already ably done so. By contrast, the topic of the war in Bermudian waters has not been addressed, and nor was it likely to be.

The reasons this story has not been told are manifold: we do not tend to move activities which were far beyond our horizon of sight and knowledge into the forefront unless it is done for us; the loss of half a million tons of shipping and over 2,000 Allied sailors represented a black eye for the Allies; Bermuda was essentially 'out there'—a colony of Great Britain, not a country of its own, distant and afar from any neighbors; and finally, the story of the German and Italian exploits have been unheralded for the simple reason that for a time it represented an Allied loss, and to the victor goes the privilege, generally, of telling the tale. This particular tale will remain no longer omitted or overlooked, and this book aspires to add another 400,000 square miles to the vast and yet growing lexicon of World War Two.

The goal of this book is to both inform and perhaps to inspire empathy not only for the mostly civilian victims of Axis submarine attack, but also for the indubitably brave Axis submariners who were attacked with increasing and fatal ferocity towards the end of the war. Without U-boats attacking, there would be no stories of stoic Allied response and survival. The German and Italian stories bear telling. There were 143 Axis submarine patrols to the area resulting in attacks on eighty Allied vessels, including one naval ship (USS *Gannet*). The most intense period of attacks was between January and August 1942, and the German offensives during this period were named Operation Drumbeat (*Paukenschlag*) and Operation New Land (*Neuland*). The Italian submarine sailed for the Betasom Flotilla, a joint venture between the Germans and Italians based in Bordeaux, France. *U-505* was not on a patrol when it came to Bermuda in June 1944; it had been captured and was taken to the island in secrecy for analysis.

Operation *Paukenshlag* (literally timpani, or drum beat), was ordered by Adolf Hitler shortly after Germany declared war on the United States. In order to reach the US coast off New England, New York, the Virginia Capes, and Cape Hatteras, the most direct route took the submarines through the Bermuda region. This applied to their return voyages to bases mostly in France as well. *En route* to and from the US, the subs, of course, continued to sink lone shipping targets. Overall, these attacks were devastating on the largely undefended US coastline: 609 ships of 3.1 million tons—roughly twenty-five percent of all Allied merchant ship losses in the war—were sunk at a cost of twenty-two Axis U-boat losses. In the Bermuda region, eighty ships were lost at a cost of two enemy submarines (*U-158* and *U-84*). The first wave of Drumbeat boats—the larger Type IXs—departed France on 18 December 1941 and arrived off Bermuda starting on 20 January 1942. During a few weeks, Hardegen in *U-123* sank seven ships, Kals in *U-130* sank six, Zapp in *U-66* sank five, Bleichrodt in *U-109* sank four and Folkers in *U-125* sank a single ship.

There were five waves of Operation Drumbeat. Operation New Land, which followed, was aimed more to the south and the Caribbean, but the U-boats still skirted Bermuda. These included the smaller, more maneuverable Type VII submarines. Looking at a composite chart of all Axis submarine patrols around Bermuda, it is clear most of them were heading to or from Cape Hatteras, the Straits of Florida, the Windward Passage, the Bahamas, and Caribbean. Patrols to the Bermuda area lasted for thirty-two months, from January 1942 to August 1944, with 11 months in that period during which no patrols began. The last patrol began 24 August 1944. Subs entered the region in pairs on nineteen occasions. The busiest single month for patrol commencement was April 1942, with twenty-five patrols begun that month—almost one a day. The most active single day was 28 April 1942, during which there were fourteen Axis submarines patrolling the waters around Bermuda.

Who were these submariners who attacked the vulnerable underbelly of the new world so persistently, and then dispersed for other more fruitful waters—like the bauxite route of north-eastern South America—as quickly as they arrived? The average commander departed and returned to France, spend just over one week in aggregate in Bermudian waters per patrol, was thirty years of age, and sank ten ships of 50,000 gross tons over his career. The longest patrol in the area around Bermuda was by Hans-Ludwig Witt in *U-129* and lasted twenty-four days.

There were only two U-boat commanders who patrolled the Bermuda region three times; Horst Uphoff in *U-84*, who was sunk by Allied aircraft south of Bermuda on 7 August 1943; and Reinhard Suhren (known as Teddy), in *U-564*.

There were twenty-nine skippers who made two patrols to the region, among whom Erwin Rostin in *U-158* and his crew, who were lost west of Bermuda on 30 June 1942, also to Allied aircraft based in Bermuda. Overall, there were 108 individual U-boat commanders, indicating that thirty-five submarines came back for multiple patrols.

The ranks used to categorize U-boat commanders were those they attained at the end of their careers. There were seventy-one commanders with the rank of *Kapitänleutnant* and forty-eight who were ranked *Korvettenkapitän*. Eleven attained the rank of *Oberleutnant zur See* and one of *Oberleutnant zur See (R)*. Nine were *Fregattenkapitän* and only one (Heinz-Ehler Beucke) was *Kapitän zur See*. Di Cossato, the only Italian commander, was ranked *Capitano di Corvetta*. Erich Topp in (among others) *U-552* sank the most ships during his overall career; thirty-five ships for 197,460 tons, followed by Heinrich Lehmann-Willenbrock in *U-96*, who sank twenty-seven ships of 194,989 tons. Georg Lassen of *U-160* sank twenty-six of 156,082, followed by Heinrich Bleichrodt of *U-109*, who sank twenty-four ships of 151,260 tons. At the other end of the spectrum, Rupprecht Stock in *U-214* sank a single ship of 200 tons, and twelve other skippers did not sink any ships at all over the course of their careers.

Certain commanders achieved multiple attacks in the Bermuda region. Di Cossato of the *Enrico Tazzoli*, Scholtz of *U-108*, Hardegen of *U-123*, and Schnee of *U-201* all attacked five ships. Bleichrodt in *U-109* and Rostin in *U-158* attacked four each in the region. The most decorated commander to patrol Bermuda was Reinhard Suhren, with the Knight's Cross with Oak Leaves and Crossed Swords with the War Merit Cross 2nd Class with Swords added in 1944 and the U-boat War Badge with Diamonds in March 1942. Erich Topp of *U-552* also earned the Knight's Cross with Oak Leaves and Crossed Swords and the U-boat War Badge with Diamonds. Otto von Bülow of *U-404* received the Knight's Cross with Oak Leaves, as well as the U-boat War Badge with Diamonds and the War Merit Cross 2nd Class with Swords.

Di Cossato was awarded his armed service's highest decoration: a Gold Medal of Military Valor, as well as two silver medals for bravery. He also had an Italian Navy submarine named after him in 1980. Kurt Diggins of *U-458* was awarded the Italian Medal in Bronze for Military Valor. Overall, sixty-one out of the skippers were awarded Knight's Cross in some iteration. The balance received a variety of awards and additions to the Knight's Cross, including Wounded Badge in Silver with U-boat Front Clasp, Iron Cross First Class, U-boat War Badge 1939, Iron Cross 2nd Class, and German Cross in Gold.

Overwhelmingly, most of the boats—sixty-eight out of 143—were Type VIIC, followed by the Type IXC, of which there were forty-two. There were thirteen IXB, eight IXC/40, and six VIIB and three VIID types. There were three milk cow-type tanker subs of the XIV type and one Italian of the *Calvi* Class. Overall, there were eight classifications of sub; however, three were iterations of the VII type (seventy-seven overall) and three types of the IX class (sixty-three overall). It is noteworthy that the submarines did not necessarily have the same commanders for each patrol.

There was a total of nine different flotillas represented by the submarines which attacked the region. However, membership in a flotilla did not necessarily determine which ports the subs sailed to or from, as they moved from base to base, flotilla to flotilla, and repositioned. Members of the 10th U-boat Flotilla, for example, sailed from St. Nazaire, Lorient, Kiel, Helgoland, Kristiansand, and La Pallice. There were forty-one submarines in the 2nd U-boat Flotilla, twenty-five in the 1st, twenty-three in the 10th, and twenty in the 7th. The 3rd U-boat Flotilla was represented by eighteen U-boats, the 6th U-boat Flotilla by seven, the 9th by five, and the 12th—the tanker boats- by two. The lone Italian submarine sailed for the Betasom Flotilla ('*Beta*' is for Bordeaux and '*Som*' for *Sommergibili*, the Italian word for submarine).

Most of the Axis submarines which patrolled Bermuda—fifty-two—left from Lorient. Thirty-one departed from St. Nazaire, and twenty-nine from Brest. A further thirteen left from La Pallice (near La Rochelle) and two departed from Bordeaux. A dozen departed from Kiel in Germany, two from the island base of Helgoland, and two left from Kristiansand in Norway, using their patrol to the Americas to reposition from the Baltic to French ports. Lorient was the lead port for the U-boats to return to after their patrols, with fifty-four submarines going there, followed by thirty to St. Nazaire, and twenty-three to Brest. There were nineteen U-boats sunk or captured. La Pallice had thirteen U-boats return there following Bermuda patrols, Flensburg two, Bordeaux two, and El Ferrol (in neutral Spain) one. Three subs were sunk in the Bay of Biscay en route to France, three off Cape Hatteras, and one each off Panama, Virginia, Key West, New Orleans, the Azores, Cuba, Haiti, and Halifax.

The age ranges of the commanders of submarine patrols around Bermuda were between twenty-three (Offermann and Carlsen) and forty-seven (Wolfbauer, who had fought in World War One). There were sixty-three commanders killed in the line of duty or otherwise—one committed suicide rather than face execution, and another dove from the conning tower and struck a saddle tank. This study does not account for whether commanders became Prisoners of War during or after the conflict, only whether they survived the war. Perhaps the most striking statistic is that there are estimated to be, at the time of writing in May 2017, thirteen commanders who could possibly still be alive. They are: Carlsen, Petersen, Lauterbach-Emden, Stock, Markworth, Wissmann, Wintermeyer, Hardegen, Siegmann, Geissler, Schulze, Schutze, and Borchert. It is well known that the Axis submariners, particularly German U-boat officers and sailors, suffered death rates of roughly 66 percent over the war—the highest such ratio experienced on either side by any branch of the services. This compares with the merchant mariner's death rate of twenty-five percent in Bermuda. Though only a small fraction of U-boat mariners perished in the Bermuda sphere; most of them were killed while positioning to or from the region, or on later patrols.

October 1940:
SS *Uskbridge* and HMCS *Margaree*

SS *Uskbridge*

The British steamship the *Uskbridge* was built in 1940 by Burntisland Shipbuilding Company, Burntisland West Dock, Scotland, across from Edinburgh. Her keel was laid on 21 September 1939, she was launched as hull number 236 on 8 April 1940, and delivered on 22 June that year. The ship weighed 2,715 gross registered tons (GRT, the standard measurement) and could carry 4,500 tons of cargo. Her dimensions were 324 feet in length, 45.2 feet in width, and 20.6 feet in depth.[1]

The ship's owners were the Uskport Steamship Company Limited of Newport, Wales, which was a subsidiary of Richard W. Jones and Company, Dock Street, Newport, Monmouthshire. Usk is a town roughly 14 miles north-east of Newport after which all three other ships in the fleet (the *Uskside*, the *Uskmouth*, and the *Uskport*) were named. In October 1940, the *Uksbridge* loaded 4,000 tons of anthracite coal to be discharged in Montreal that fall. She loaded in Swansea, Wales, and proceeded to Liverpool to the north in order to join a transatlantic convoy.

On her first and final voyage, the *Uskbridge* sailed in Convoy OB 228, departing Liverpool on 13 October 1940, and dispersed four days later on the 17th. The convoy consisted of forty merchant ships and four naval escorts. Of these, the *Bonheur* (British, 5,327 tons) was sunk by *U-138* under Wolfgang Lüth on the 15th. The *British Glory* (British, 6,992 tons) was also torpedoed by *U-138*; however, it was towed back to the Clyde River, Scotland. On 17 October, *U-93* under Claus Korth sank the Norwegian steamer the *Dokka* of 1,168 tons with the loss of ten lives; seven survived. The following day, the straggler the *Sandsend*, a British steamer of 3,612 tons, was sunk by *U-48* under Heinrich Bleichrodt. It was a grim tally for the nascent convoy, and the *Uskbridge* would be among the casualties.[2]

There were twenty-nine men aboard the *Uskbridge* on her maiden voyage, all under the command of Captain Wilfred Breckon Smith, aged forty-three, supported in part by his Second Officer, Frederick John Bettridge, aged twenty-five. In the early hours of 17 October, the *Uskbridge* was roughly 180 nautical miles south of Iceland. It was a 'fine moonlit night,' though doubtlessly cold in October. At 2.39 a.m.

Kapitänleutnant Claus Korth in command of the German submarine *U-93* fired a G7e-type torpedo into Convoy OB 228, not sure exactly where it would detonate. In fact, it missed his intended target and hit the *Uskbridge* on the starboard side instead. As the impact was most felt beneath the ship's bridge or wheelhouse, where Captain Smith and Second Officer Bettridge were standing, they were both killed. The Chief Officer was also on the bridge, but managed to survive.

The starboard bridge wing was sheared off, and the torpedo blew a hole in the side of the *Uskbridge* 'big enough to drive a bus through.' Survivors related that the water thrown up by the explosion reached as high as the vessel's main mast. Water swirling around on deck and through the passageways in the ship's accommodation areas made some of the sailors think that their ship was already doomed; however, it stayed afloat for many hours. One sailor related that he was on the Monkey Island, on watch above the bridge, at the time of impact. He noted:

> After the blow, I saw spars falling about me. It dazed me and it took me a few minutes to come to. I thought I was in the ocean at first, but when I realized I was still aboard I went down off there. I heard somebody shouting. It was the wheelman [Quartermaster], who was crawling out of the wheelhouse. He was covered in blood. I helped him down to the life boat as best I could and eventually got him into it. … [I] had only one thought; we had one thing to do—get the boats out.[3]

The radio operator later told a reporter his perspective on events:

> I was sitting there with the 'phones to my ears … and suddenly I heard a ringing sound but did not hear an explosion. You see, our cabin is closed in. Then I felt a lurch, which shot me to one side. At that moment, I did not believe we were hit, but afterwards it came to my mind that it must have been a torpedo. [None of the crew or the officers had seen a submarine]. I put on my lifebelt and prepared to lend a hand to the others, which I did.[4]

The twenty-one-year-old third officer told of being in his cabin at the time. He tried to collect some keepsakes and 'ran about in circles for a few seconds… then I made for the alleyway. I had to fight my way out like a wild cat. A rush of water swept me up like a trout going upstream.' There was enough time for the twenty-seven survivors to get away from the *Uskbridge* in two boats. There were ten men in one boat and sixteen in the other. The quartermaster, who had been steering at the time of impact, had his face badly cut by flying glass. The chief officer had apparently been blown off the bridge and was fortuitously retrieved from the water by another ship, probably on account of new flashing red lights worn on life vests which were equipped with waterproof batteries.

The men in one of the boats agreed to return to their stricken mothership in order to look for Captain Smith, the missing chief officer, and Second Officer Bettridge.

Though they did indeed return to the steamship at great peril to themselves (as their rescue ships in the convoy were plodding away and *U-93* still lurked in the area), they could find no trace of the missing men. As the engine room had not been hit, the *Uskbridge*'s lights were still on.

The third officer said that though 'there was a bit of shouting, there was absolutely no panic at all. As a matter of fact, in our lifeboat ... there was a good deal of joking and laughing. ... somebody would crack a joke and we would all have a good laugh.' Six of the men in one of the lifeboats were taken aboard the *Montreal City*, a 3,066-ton British steamer built in 1920 and owned by Charles Hill and Sons, Bristol—across the Bristol Channel from Newport, where the *Uskbridge* was registered. They were presumably taken to Montreal, where the *Uskbridge* was destined.

The twenty-one men left in the *Uksbridge*'s lifeboats were picked up by another ship in the convoy, the Dutch steamer the *Katwijk*. Built in 1921, this 1,589-ton steamer was owned by the Erhardt and Dekkers firm of Rotterdam. She was 253.5 feet long, 38.2 feet wide, and 16.11 feet deep.

Badly disabled, the *Uskbridge* straggled out of the convoy and *U-93* was able to catch up with the stricken vessel ten hours later. At 1.36 p.m., Korth sent a second torpedo into the *Uskbridge*; this was a *coup de grâce*, and she quickly sank. At some point, perhaps when the ships were safely clear from the immediate danger of torpedoing, the *Katwijk*'s master transferred his twenty-one charges to the steamer the *Cristales*. This may have been for a number of reasons: insufficient food and accommodation for the extra passengers, or simply a destination that did not suit the survivors.

The *Cristales* was a 5,389-ton steamship built by Cammell Laird and Company Limited, Birkenhead, UK in 1926. Her owners were the Elders and Fyffes Limited firm of Covent Garden, London, and her homeport was Liverpool. The ship's dimensions were 400.3 feet long, 51.5 feet wide, and 26.9 feet deep. She was capable of an impressive 13.5 knots, which may have been another reason why the survivors were transferred from the 8.5-knot *Katwijk*—she could get them to safety considerably faster.[5]

The *Cristales* arrived in St. George's, Bermuda on Monday, 28 October 1940, after a passage of roughly twelve days (depending on where and when she picked up her twenty-one passengers from the *Katwijk*). The *Cristales*' Master in May 1942 was Captain Hugh Roberts. A local reporter wrote that 'Upon arrival here, the crew were brought to the Sailor's Home by a special train,' indicating that they were landed to the north-east, in St. George's and taken by the Bermuda Railway to the capital, Hamilton. Once in Bermuda, the officers were separated from the men, as was customary, particularly in British colonies and on British ships at the time. The sixteen sailors and engine room staff were accommodated at the Bermuda Sailor's Home, and the five officers were put up at a private home named 'Gladwyn,' listed in the present day as a residence of the King Edward VII Memorial Hospital.[6]

The *New York Times* of 29 October 1940 reported the landing of the *Uskbridge*'s survivors in Bermuda and that the captain had been lost; however, with wartime censorship, it could only conclude the short piece by noting that 'The ship, the name of which has not been revealed, was said to have been commissioned in June of this year.'[7] A reporter for the Bermuda *The Royal Gazette and Colonist* visited the Sailor's Home to interview some of the men and officers. They caught some of the sailors inside playing billiards and others 'out on the gallery.' The twenty-one-year-old third officer spoke with the reporter, as did a member of the bridge watch when the *Uskbridge* was first struck.

Captain Warren Brown of Bermuda wrote that 'I was thirteen at the time. Survivors were looked after by The Bermuda Sailor's Home. Their address is now 22 Richmond Road, Hamilton.'[8] The *Cristales* was torpedoed in Convoy ONS 92, south of Greenland by *U-124* under Johann Mohr on 12 May 1942. All of her complement of eighty-two merchant mariners, gunners, and passengers were rescued by HMSC *Shediac* (K 110) as well as USCGC *Spencer* (WPG 36) and landed at St. John's Newfoundland and Boston respectively. The *Montreal City*, under Captain Edward R. W. Chanter, which rescued six of the *Uskbridge* survivors, was subsequently sunk by *U-591* under Hans-Jürgen Zetzsche south of Greenland and east of Newfoundland on 21 December 1942. The *Katwijk* was renamed SS *Etna* early in 1954; she ran aground and was wrecked in Scotland on 19 January of that year.[9]

Over his career, Korth sank a total of thirteen ships of 54,584 tons, as well as a warship, another ship damaged and another a total constructive loss. Claus Korth survived the war, having moved to training positions ashore in 1942. He spent six months as a POW in Allied captivity. Between 1955 and 1970, he returned to the *Bundesmarine*—Germany's post-war navy. He lived until the age of seventy-six, passing away in Kiel in 1988.[10]

HMCS *Margaree*

The survivors of a convoy collision that the Royal Canadian Navy ship HMCS *Margaree* suffered early in its career resulted in them being landed in Bermuda. The *Margaree* was built as the British destroyer HMS *Diana* in 1931; on 6 September 1940, she was transferred in London from British to Canadian control to compensate for the earlier loss due to collision of HMCS *Fraser* off France with the loss of forty-five Canadian lives. Many officers and men who survived the *Fraser* sinking were serving aboard the *Margaree*, which was named for a Canadian river, when it was rammed and sunk in Convoy OL 8, bound from the UK to Canada roughly 300 miles west of Ireland. Her commander was J. W. Roy of Halifax. On 22 October 1940, in heavy rain and reduced visibility, the larger ship, the *Port Fairy*, cut off the bow of the warship, with the result that 142 Canadian sailors were drowned—the largest single casualty in the Royal Canadian Navy at that time. The destroyer escort was not meant to have ventured among the cargo ships. It was Roy's first destroyer command; he left a post in headquarters in Halifax to assume it.

After the collision, the forward section, which held most of the sailors yet had the least bulkheads, immediately sank with 140 men in it. The aft section, by contrast, remained afloat for at least twelve hours. Lines were thrown from the *Port Fairy* to the aft section of the *Margaree*, and men pulled the two ships together manually in rough weather. Then, three ladders were lowered from the rescuing vessel. A man and a 'boy seaman' named Alfred Jones of Cloverdale, British Columbia, perished while climbing up the side of the rescuing *Port Fairy* when they fell and were crushed between the ships. Thus, thirty-four out of 176 men were pulled out alive.[11]

Canadian journalists in Bermuda observed that 'survivors of the *Fraser* sinking gained the warm safety of this Bermuda port after the *Margaree* disaster.' They arrived on 31 October, and would 'soon be returned to Canada,' in time for Christmas.[12] The Royal Canadian Navy issued a brief statement saying that both ships had been proceeding without lights in the stormy North Atlantic at around midnight in a submarine zone when the casualty occurred. It was also reported that 'A Royal Canadian naval officer ... was being brought to Bermuda to help authorities ... with the investigation.'[13] In Bermuda, Lieutenant William M. Landymore of Brantford, Ontario, spoke with journalists, describing how after the collision, on the aft part 'there was no noise at all.'[14]

The British flagged *Port Fairy* was a refrigerated ship built in 1928 and weighed 8,337 gross registered tons. Her next port of call was Bermuda, at which she called late in October, depositing the six officers and twenty-eight enlisted men. The ship was laden with ammunition and the convoy was a high-speed one. Gunners from the merchant ship fired on the aft hulk of the *Margaree*, setting it afire. Of the 142 sailors lost, eighty-six of them had served on the *Fraser*. One newspaper observed how 'The loss of the two destroyers by collision in four months was a bitter blow to the Canadian navy and the large loss of lives was a shock to all at home.'

HMCS *Margaree*'s career as a Canadian ship had lasted just over six weeks. Canadian Prime Minister Mackenzie King eulogized to the nation from Ottawa on 28 October that 'the names of the brave officers and men who perished with their distinguished commander in the performance of their duty at sea will live in the grateful memory of their country.'[15]

September 1939–20 January 1942: One U-boat

Returning from his celebrated opening attacks of Operation Drumbeat off New York and Cape Hatteras, Reinhard Hardegen in *U-123*, decided to swing south and perform an exploratory sail-past of Bermuda on his way home. He entered the region from the west-north-west on 20 January 1942, and skimmed very close to Bermuda on the 22nd, before exiting the area to the east-north-east on the 24th. It is one of half a dozen patrols to come so close to the island that the commander undoubtedly utilized the lighthouses of Bermuda as a navigational 'fix.'[1]

On this patrol, Hardegen sank nine ships (the *Cyclops*, the *Nornesss*, the *Coimbra*, the *Nordana*, the *City of Atlanta*, the *Malay*, the *Ciltivaira*, the *Culebra*, and the *Pan Norway*) of 57,627-tons, including one damaged, since 12 January. His was the first U-boat of World War Two to attack the US coast; in World War One, not only had U-boats done so, but one of them, *U-53*, spent the afternoon of 7 October 1916 hosting officers of the neutral US Navy in Newport before sinking six Allied ships off Nantucket.[2]

U-123 began its patrol on 23 December 1941 in Lorient, and ended it in the same port on 9 February 1942. On 19 January, the submarine was chased by a Norwegian whaling factory ship, the *Kosmos II*. It was a close call, but *U-123* was able to outrun its erstwhile quarry before aircraft called in by the Norwegians could arrive and cause permanent damage. The final two ships were sunk north-east of Bermuda. On 27 January, Hardegen vectored in the Greek *Mount Etna* to retrieve survivors of the *Pan Norway* that he had sunk two days previously.

Hardegen's incursion off Bermuda occurred just over one and a half months following the Japanese attacks on Pearl Harbor and the US entry into the war. Hardegen achieved the rank of *Korvettenkapitän*, though at the time, he was *Kapitänleutnant*. Over his career, he sank twenty-one ships for a total of 112,447 gross registered tons and damaged four others for 32,516 GRT—he also sank one warship and damaged another. On 23 April 1942, following this patrol he was awarded the Knight's Cross with Oak Leaves, and later the U-boat badge with Diamonds. A member of the crew of 1933 at the Naval Academy (*Marineschule*) in Mürwik, eastern Germany, he was thirty at the time.

SS *City of Birmingham*, the passenger ship with by far the most people on board when arriving in Bermuda. Of the 381 passengers, nine perished; the survivors strained the local civilian and military infrastructure on the island. (*Steamship Historical Society, sshsa.org*)

Hardegen began his career in the naval air force, but injuries sustained when he crashed as a pilot brought him to the U-boat arm in November 1939, at the outset of the war. Hardagen's patrols feature prominently in books such as *Operation Drumbeat* by Michael Gannon, *Torpedo Junction* by Homer Hickam, and *The Führer's U-boats in American Waters* by Gary Gentile, who accused Hardegen of doctoring his log.[3] By all accounts, Hardegen is a personable and likeable commander and veteran—he was said to have tied the shoelaces of an old merchant mariner who visited him to meet the man who sank his ship.

Hardegen corresponded with his victims, and took part in two particularly tragic sinkings: that of the only battle-tested armed merchant cruiser which the Americans put forth, the *Atik* (AK 101 aka the *Caroline*), in which all members of the US Navy crew and one of Hardegen's crew perished on a stormy night; and the *Muskogee*, whose desperate survivors were photographed by Hardegen's crew but never seen alive again (photos from a German magazine surfaced in a POW camp for Allies and survived the war). In many ways, Reinhard Hardegen has come to personify Operation Drumbeat's audacious initial attacks on the US eastern seaboard.[4]

24 January 1942: SS *Empire Wildebeeste*

The British steamship the *Empire Wildebeeste* was owned by the Ministry of War Transport and operated by George Nisbet and Company Limited of the UK. She was built as the *West Ekonk* in seventy-three workdays and launched on 22 June 1918. The ship was 5,631 gross tons and had 8,554 deadweight tons capacity. Her overall length was 409.5 feet, beam 54.2 feet, and her Curtis-geared steam turbine engine turned a single propeller, giving the ship 11.5 knots when built, and 9.5 knots by early 1942. Her builders were Skinner and Eddy of Seattle Washington, and she was yard number twenty-five. At the time, she was listed as the ninth-fastest-constructed ship in the world. Her cost was $1,776,468. Between 1918 and 1919, she crossed the Atlantic three times for the US Naval Overseas Transportation Service.[1]

From mid-June 1919, the *West Ekonk* was allocated to the US Shipping Board and performed a number of voyages for them and Atlantic Transport Line between New York and Baltimore, her base, before being laid up in Norfolk. In 1924, the ship sailed out of Los Angeles before being sold in 1933 to the Lykes Brothers Steamship Company.[2] The Ministry of War Transport of the UK purchased her in 1940, taking delivery in Savannah in October.[3] In the two years or so under British control, the *Empire Wildebeeste* as she was now known (named for the Afrikaans for 'wild beast', an ox-like African antelope prized by hunters), experienced numerous breakdowns. In Halifax, on 9 December 1940, her boiler condensers were repaired for a day, then again in January 1941 in Liverpool; her compass also broke while in convoy between both ports. The ship was officially renamed in February 1941 in the UK. After surviving a transatlantic convoy in which five ships were sunk nearby, in mid-May more repairs were initiated in Newcastle, UK—those took two weeks. On 29 June, she experienced steering gear damage, which took a week to repair in Baltimore.

Then, in the summer, repairs in the Bristol Channel, UK, took another two weeks, from 11 to 22 August. After leaving St. John's Newfoundland for Hull on 11 October, the ship had to put back for repairs on the 18th. Finally, on 28 October in Sydney, Nova Scotia, she underwent more engine repairs, which were completed the following day, but had to put back to Sydney from 5 to 10 November. Then, in

Hull, she went in for repairs from the 11 to 24 December 1941. By that time, the ship had completed three transatlantic convoys.

The *Empire Wildebeeste* began its final voyage from Liverpool in position thirteen in Convoy ON 53 on 1 January 1942, then from Loch Ewe and around the north end of Scotland on 5 January. She was bound for Baltimore but straggled behind the convoy before it was dispersed on 19 January, and made its way independently. The problem was that the convoy ran into severe weather east of Iceland on 10 January. The weather reached hurricane force. Despite this, the ship managed to stay in contact with the convoy commodore until 17 January, but the fierce conditions lasted for ten days, by which time all the vessels were scattered. During this time, the ship labored into north-west winds, making only six knots.[4]

The ship's complement was led by Captain Hugh Cameron Stewart, who was described by a journalist as 'A short stocky Scotsman with a constitution of iron and a jaw symbolic of Britain's famous bulldog.'[5] Captain Stewart appears to have survived, by his own admission, two notable sinkings in the North Atlantic earlier in the war. The first was the sinking of the British *Cheyenne* on 15 September 1939, less than two weeks after the outbreak of war. The tanker was sunk by *U-53* under Ernst-Günter Heinicke. Fortunately, HMS *Mackay* (D 70) was on hand to drive off the submarine, and the Norwegian *Ida Bakke* picked up thity-seven survivors out of forty-three and landed them at Baltimore, near Cork, Ireland.

In the second incident, Captain Stewart was sailing as first officer of the British *Blairmore* whose men rescued survivors of the HMS *Penzance* (L 28), sunk by *U-37* under Victoer Oehrn on 24 August 1940. The following day, the *Blairmore* itself was also sunk by the same submarine. Thirty-six of the complement of forty-one along with seven survivors of the HMS *Penzance* were rescued by the Swedish ship *Eknaren* and taken to neutral waters and Baltimore. Captain Stewart was no stranger to enemy action and survival at sea.

Captain Stewart was responsible for four naval gunners, six army gunners, and thirty-three officers and men in the British merchant marine. There was a total of forty-three men on board; most of whom were British. Fifty-seven-year-old Cook Joaquin Cardoso was Portuguese and had served in that country's navy for over two decades. Robert Owen Skelton, an ordinary seaman, was only seventeen, and Charles Wilson, the galley boy, was only sixteen. Other teens included Ted Templeman, fireman, and Richard Hamill, known simply as a sailor, aged eighteen. These last five were to perish, as was Carmelo Fenech of Malta, a fifty-year-old greaser.[6]

The *Empire Wildebeeste* was sailing in ballast, which consisted of 2,500 tons of slag, 800 tons of oil, 500 tons of salt water, and some 300 tons of fresh water. The vessel was armed with a 4-inch gun, one Bofors gun, twin-Marlin machine guns, two single Marlins, four parachute rockets, kites, and snowflake rockets. By the morning of Saturday, 24 January 1942, the ship was east of Halifax and roughly equidistant (480 nautical miles) from Bermuda and Cape Cod.

Twenty-seven-year-old *Kapitänleutnant* Hermann Rasch and his men in the German submarine *U-106* had left Lorient on 3 January. Three weeks into their patrol, they had not encountered or sunk any vessels, and the fifty or so men were no doubt keen to start doing so. With the slow-moving steamer, they had found their prey. Rasch spotted the *Empire Wildebeeste* at 7.26 p.m. on Friday, 23 January. He then went into pursuit that would last five hours, until 12.39 a.m. on the 24th.[7] Rasch had just been ordered to proceed to the coast of the US between New York and Cape Hatteras. Captain Stewart noted:

> We received a message from the Admiralty giving us new positions to pass through. I steered for the first position but found I was a little bit South, so I altered course to made for the next given position which was directly on the track for Cape Henry. I was very close to this position when at 0100 A.T.S. on 24th January … we were struck by a torpedo in the starboard side of the bow in the chain locker about 30 feet from the bow.

Thus, orders from very different masters in two European capitals led two enemy vessels right into each other between Bermuda and the mainland.

Captain Stewart continues: 'I was in the chart room at the time, and a tremendous column of water was thrown up, flooding the chart room. The second officer was on watch at the time and stated that he saw a flash, but did not notice any smoke or smell of cordite.' The ship had been zigzagging; however, once the moon set, Stewart felt confident enough to set a straight course of 258 degrees at 12.30 a.m. After all, the very first wave of U-boats was just arriving off the American coast and most merchant skippers did not know about them. The ship's speed was 11.5 knots. Indeed, Rasch in *U-106* observed that his intended victim was maintaining 'course west.' He had not completed his attack yet.

The force of the explosion, though it was in the bow, threw out the gear clutch on the main engines, stopping it immediately. Slowly, the *Empire Wildebeeste* settled down by the bow. Captain Stewart noted that the Number One hold flooded on top of its 300 tons of ballast, suggesting that the bulkhead had burst. The radio operator immediately transmitted a message, which was picked up on shore. Initially, a Canadian station picked up the message and asked the operator to switch to 800-meter wavelength so that shore stations could direction-find off the signal; this was done from New Jersey. The *Enemy Action Diary* for the Eastern Sea Frontier reads:

> At 0104 Direction Finder Station Cape Henlopen intercepted following message which they immediately relayed to District Headquarters 4ND [Fourth Naval District], Inshore Patrol, Cape May, and Coast Guard, "SS *WILDEBEESTE* torpedoed…. At 0458 GMT.

Rasch, in the submarine nearby, also heard the same message, thus enabling him to identify his victim.

Though Captain Stewart and his officers remained calm on the bridge, a form of group hysteria gripped some of the younger and less experienced seamen. Stewart writes that 'Some of the crew rushed to the forward port boat and let go one of the falls and the boat was left hanging by one fall.' He ordered another group to remain calm but abandon ship, 'but some of the men were rather excited. Nine men got into the forward starboard boat which drifted away quickly and was soon out of sight.' Meanwhile, the other starboard boat, further aft, was successfully launched with seventeen men.

While more men were preparing to board this boat, another torpedo struck the ship, this time on the opposite, or port side, in the way of the Number Four deep tank (fourth hatch back from the bow). The struck at about 1.30 a.m., about fifty minutes after the initial attack. The torpedo managed to penetrate the tank before exploding; when it did, it ruptured the bulkhead in front of the engine room, flooding the machinery space and ending any hope that the ship could propel itself out of its predicament. It also injured the wireless officer, who remained at his station and suffered bruises and a cut to his lip.

The second officer was working on lowering the portside lifeboat when he witnessed the torpedo streaking towards the ship, its wake probably illuminated by Gulf Stream phosphorescence. All of the men who were already in the port lifeboat were thrown out of it, however fifteen of them managed to clamber back into it. The captain and three other officers then joined these men and cast off. Since there were only fifteen men in the starboard lifeboat which had been stored aft, the skipper transferred two men to it, so that there were seventeen in each boat, plus nine in the boat that had already drifted off, meaning that all forty-three men—including the engine room crew—had managed to escape the stricken ship. At about 1.45 a.m., twenty minutes after the second torpedo, a third and final explosion ripped into the *Empire Wildebeeste*, sealing its doom. Though some sources say this may have been the boilers exploding, Captain Stewart is clear on the point that 'a third torpedo struck the ship in the engine room. We all saw a flash as the torpedo struck and heard a very load explosion. The ship settled and quickly sank at 0205 A.T.S.'

Now came the open-water survival component for the Allied sailors. For Rasch and his men, it was off to further hunting; within two days, she had sunk the *Traveller*, and within a week from that, the *Rochester*, the *Amerikaland*, and the *Opawa*. Captain Stewart prided himself on keeping the lifeboats prepared for exactly this contingency. He connected the two lifeboats with a heaving line. The chief officer took command of the other boat. The Associated Press reported that 'As they drifted through the bitterly cold [January] night a portable radio brought along by one of the men was turned on and ironically the first thing they heard was a New York station broadcasting a furrier's announcement: "Now is the time to buy your winter coats."' The likelihood of a crewman bringing a functioning radio, which was able to receive a signal from New York, nearly 1,000 miles away, will be for the reader to judge. Captain Stewart makes no mention of the contraption.

Once daylight broke—about four hours after the ship sank—they sighted the other lifeboat. The skipper recognized Harold Fenton, a twenty-year-old Navy DEMS (defensively equipped merchant ship) gunner and an army gunner named William F. Lanfear. With despair in his retelling, Captain Stewart observed that 'we soon lost sight of them as they had their sail up and tacked away from us, and they have not been seen or heard of since.' He postulated that Joaquin Cardoso, the Portuguese Cook, 'must have taken charge of the sailing.' Stewart goes on about how well stocked the lifeboats were; fitted with dodgers and a protection hood, with red bunting sewn into the sails, they had ample flares (which he disparaged) as well as water tanks under the seats, pemmican (meat paste), chocolate, and malted milk tablets.

Fortunately for the men of the *Empire Wildebeeste* at 11.20 a.m. on their first morning in the boats a Royal Canadian Air Force Catalina aircraft found them. As Stewart observed, it 'flew over us and circled around us all day until about 4.30 p.m. when he dropped a life jacket with two containers of flares and a note attached. The note said that a corvette would pick us up the following morning around 9 p.m.' According to a Bermuda journalist after the fact, 'the pilot swooped down so low that a message dropped practically alongside the lifeboats, asking the men if they required blankets and food.' Despite Captain Stewart's belief that a single plane held station above him for most of the day, 'A few hours after the plane left, a number of other planes soon were circling overhead.'

With spirits no doubt buoyed by the news, the men must have passed a reasonably comfortable night. The conditions were described as 'light' winds and 'slight swell.' However, by 9.30 a.m. the following morning, there was still no sign of the corvette. Stewart lit one of the flares from the Catalina and was very pleased with the result, as they popped out smoke and balls of fire alternately, 'like a Roman candle.' By 10.30 a.m., there was still no ship, so more flares were lit. At 11.30 a.m., 'as there was still no sign of help coming to us,' wrote Stewart, 'I lighted and hoisted a smoke flair to the masthead. Afterwards I tied a yellow weather protection suit to the masthead.'[8] Then, success—what every shipwrecked sailor dreams of:

> At 12.45 I fired another smoke flare and about 13.30 [exactly 36 hours after the attack], we sighted a ship, which proved to be USS *LANG*. The *LANG* had not seen our smoke flares but was attracted by the yellow suit, which was flying from the mast. This was not the Corvette, which the Catalina had said was coming to our assistance. This Destroyer ....had been patrolling some 500 miles away and had picked up our W/T signals. He had rushed to our position in order to hunt the submarine and had been in the area about 12 hours before he sighted our boats.

The USS *Lang* (DD 399) was built by the Federal Shipbuilding and Dry Dock Company in 1937–1938, and commissioned into the US navy as a Benham-class destroyer on 30 March 1939. The ship's dimensions were: 2,250-tons displacement, 340.9 feet long, 35.6 feet wide, and 12.1 feet draft. The ship could reach 38.5 knots and cruise for 6,500 miles. Her first commander was Felix L. Johnson. In 1939, she escorted President Roosevelt to Canada and in 1941 was assigned work in the Caribbean and off Bermuda. On board as assistant to executive officer was Pemberton Southard, twenty-three years old, who kept a detailed record of the ship's report on the subsequent rescue.

The *Lang*'s commander at the time was Lieutenant Erskine Austin Seay. On 1 February, he filed a detailed and lengthy report to his commanding officers in New York, accounting for his and the *Lang*'s activities relative to the *Empire Wildebeeste* between 24 and 28 January. On 21 January, while *en route* from Halifax to Bermuda, the *Lang* was relieved of escort duties by HMS *Duke of York* and made for Bermuda. At 1.25 a.m. on the 24th, the *Lang* intercepted a relay of the *Empire Wildebeeste*'s SSS signal, indicating, in the fog of war, that two vessels were in distress and giving two positions. Seay correctly adjudged the proper latitude and longitude, and reasoning that the *Lang* 'could reach the second torpedoed vessel in less time than a ship based at Bermuda would be able to,' he set a course for the ship, 410 miles away and bearing just north of west from the *Lang*'s position, which was east-north-east of the casualty. Speed was brought to 24 knots.

Five hours later, shore stations confirmed that Seay's hunch was correct about the position of the casualty. Three hours later, a refueling tanker ship named the USS *Sapelo* informed the *Lang* that the tanker could give the destroyer 40,000 gallons of fuel oil. The *Lang*'s ETA on site would be just before midnight. Then the *Lang* received a report from aircraft that two lifeboats were spotted, roughly 24 nautical miles north of the sinking. The destroyer began a crisscross search in the night-time, with visibility only two miles, which not surprisingly turned up nothing. The *Sapelo* also began a search pattern.

At dawn, the *Sapelo* and the *Lang* rendezvoused and determined the set and drift of the current (1.5 knots to the north-east, or 68 degrees true) with wind of about 15 knots from the north-west. On that basis, the *Lang* set out to the east and north of the ship's reported position, the search of the actual position during the night having turned up 'no debris, oil slicks, or any indication' of a wreck.

On the turn of the fourth leg search at [1.10 p.m.] on course 270 degrees True a makeshift signal consisting of a pair of trousers hung on an oar was sighted by a lookout at a distance of about four miles. Upon further approach two small boats could be seen lashed together, which proved to be the survivors of the SS *EMPIRE WILDEBEESTE*.... 47 miles from position reported.

Seay continues: 'At [1.25 p.m.] the survivors were taken aboard and both boats scuttled. One man was brought aboard in a stretcher, suffering from diabetes. Some 20 minutes later a life raft was sighted without occupants.' He goes on to recount how difficult it is to see a lifeboat in a running sea as 'the boats were visible approximately 10 seconds per minute at a range of 600 yards.' Aside from the diabetic, the *Lang* men treated the radio operator for multiple contusions and another man for 'cancroid of penis,' a 'social disease.'[9]

The thirty-four men were well looked after aboard the large navy ship, with the four senior officers eating and sleeping in the wardroom, the other five officers in the chief petty officer's quarters, and the regular crew bunking in the forward crew quarters and eating with the US Navy crew. Seay notes:

> It is believed they were quite comfortable considering that they had lost practically everything they possessed aboard the torpedoed ship. Clothing and toiletry articles were distributed to the survivors. The crew of the *LANG* was very generous in providing the survivors with their own clothing.[10]

Captain Stewart informed Lieutenant Seay about how the nine men in the missing boat 'had left the ship previous to orders to disembark, without an officer and that the missing boat had a dip-lug sail rig with a red bunting.' As the *Lang* was low on fuel, it succeeded after several tries to connect to the *Sapelo*, which provided the destroyer with 26,310 gallons of fuel oil—all that was left. The *Sapelo* also transferred medical supplies for the injured or sick men. Though noting that planes were searching for the nine-man boat on 24 and 25 January, the *Lang*'s people never saw the aircraft. On the 26th, the *Lang* was ordered to search until dusk and then return to Bermuda, which it did. No sign of the nine-man boat was ever found. As Seay noted, 'the search was unsuccessful,' though of course he had found the majority of the crew.[11]

At 8 p.m. on the 27th, the search was broken off and the destroyer headed back to Bermuda. After anchoring in Hamilton Harbor, the British merchant sailors and gunners were held on board the *Lang* while intelligence officers from the British Admiralty as well as the US Naval Operating Base interrogated them.[12] The British arranged to receive their compatriots, and an ambulance was made available for the diabetic case. By about 3 p.m. on the 28th, a British motor launch brought the thirty-four remaining men ashore, their saga afloat ended for the time being. A Bermuda-based journalist noted:

> All survivors were treated royally aboard the American warship. The captain added that the treatment extended to himself and his men by the personnel of the United States destroyer was exceptional … "They couldn't do enough for us and, believe me, we are all very grateful to them." Soon after their arrival here, officers and crewmembers were fitted out with complete outfits of clothing. It was also understood that the captain cabled his company for money to pay the men while they were being sheltered in these islands. All the officers had a word of praise for Mr. L. N. Tucker, M.B.E., Superintendent of the Bermuda Sailor's Home, for the interest he had taken in their welfare.[13]

On shore, the crew was separated. The 'naval men' (the gunners) were sent to HMS *Malabar*—a navy facility on the south-west of the island. The army gunners went up to St. George's Island to the east, and the twenty-six merchant sailors from the fourth service were put up at the American House and the Bermuda Sailor's Home, run by Dickie Tucker. Captain Warren Brown wrote:

> Many survivors were put up at Westmeath guest house. I met many of them as the building belonged to Stanley Conyers, and his son was one of my best friends. As a consequence I was often over there. Also the Ladies' Hospitality Organization Bermuda. Although not mentioned, my mother and father and a Mrs. Bridges carried out most of the work in looking after the sailors. I spent many an evening there helping my parents. We also always had at least two sailors staying at our house. They usually did not say a great deal about their role, as everything was always hush, hush.[14]

Captain Stewart expressed his hope—or at least his optimism—that the nine men in the other boat would survive, despite their failed search in the *Lang*. He told the journalist that the boat 'was still adrift in the Atlantic,' but that 'he feels they will be all right and probably will be landed at some Eastern port along the United States coast.'[15] The article goes on to say that survivors of the *Empire Wildebeeste* crew, still concerned about the fate of their nine shipmates, attended the funerals of four engineering crew from another merchant ship, the *British Tenacity*, who had been burned essentially to death by a boiler explosion on 28 January.

The *British Tenacity* put into Bermuda's Number Seven wharf on 30 January with two bodies and six badly burned men, of whom two died in King Edward VII Memorial Hospital on the island. The funeral, held at St. Paul's Church in Paget, was officiated by the Venerable Henry Marriott, (Archdeacon of Bermuda from 1925–1951), and other dignitaries. The men were laid to rest in the sailor's plot at the churchyard. The victim's ages were twenty-one, thirty-two, thirty-four, and forty-eight.[16]

Captain Stewart of the *Empire Wildebeeste* wrote:

> We were 800 miles from Cape Henry when we were picked up, but were landed at Bermuda on Wednesday morning, 28th January, as the destroyer was ordered there after her search. After we were picked up the USS *LANG* searched throughout the day for the third boat, but nothing was seen of it. We were very well treated on board the *LANG* and everything possible was done for us. It was one of the newest ships and the whole crew were very efficient and keen.[17]

4

26–30 January 1942: Four U-boats

Korvettenkapitän Richard Zapp brought *U-66* north of Bermuda from east to west for four days, starting on 27 January. Entering north-west of the island, Zapp headed due east, passing north of Bermuda on the 27th, and east out of the area on the 29th. Along with *U-123* and *U-125*, *U-66* was the first wave of Operation Drumbeat U-boats to reach the US. Before arriving off Bermuda, Zapp sank the US ship *Allan Jackson* and the Canadian passenger ship *Lady Hawkins* of 7,988 tons on 18 and 19 January respectively. Out of 300 people on board, only ninety-six survived. Then, *U-66* sank the US-flagged *Norvana*, followed by the British *Empire Gem* and the American *Venore* on 24 January, before heading east and back to Lorient, which it reached on 10 February 1942, having set out on Christmas Day 1941 for the 2nd U-boat Flotilla.[1]

Richard Zapp was born in 1904 and a member of the Crew of 1926. He began the war in naval anti-aircraft and joined U-boat training in April 1940, and *U-46* before commissioning *U-166* in January 1941. After sea service, he commanded the 3rd U-boat Flotilla and a naval regiment named after him in La Rochelle until the surrender. He was a POW until July 1947. Zapp was awarded the Knight's Cross in April 1942, not long after this patrol and others to the Caribbean.[2] Over five patrols of 264 days, Zapp sank or damaged seventeen ships of 118,702 tons. He lived until 1964 and the age of sixty. *U-66* was sunk under a different commander west of the Cape Verde Island by depth charges, ramming, and gunfire from aircraft flying off of the USS *Block Island* and the destroyer USS *Buckley* on 6 May 1944—thirty-six of her crew survived, twenty-four perished.

Korvettenkapitän Ernst Kals led the next patrol into the area; he was a veteran skipper of thirty-four years at the time. He brought *U-130* north of Bermuda from west to east, starting on 29 January when the boat penetrated the region to the north-west. Kals headed east until the 22nd and a point several hundred miles north of Bermuda. Then he cruised south-east until the 4 February and eastwards out of the area on the 6th at a point north-east of the island. During this patrol, *U-130* joined *U-66*, *U-109*, *U-123* and *U-125* as part of Operation Drumbeat.[3] The patrol began in Lorient on 27 December 1941, and on 1 January, the boat was detected by an RAF plane, but escaped two depth charges. Off Cape Breton in Canada, *U-130* sank the Norwegian *Frisco* and the Panamanian *Friar Rock*. During another attack the sub was chased off by a US destroyer. Off New York, on 21 January, Kals sank the Norwegian *Alexandra Hoegh* and then the Panamanian ship *Olympic* off Hatteras the following day.

On the 25th, *U-130* sank the Norwegian *Veranger*, then the American *Francis E. Powell* and finally the US-flagged *Halo*. North of Bermuda, on the way back to France, *U-130* refueled *U-109* on the 4 February, just north-east of the island. In the Bay of Biscay, *U-130* had another rendezvous, this time with *U-587* on 18 February to bring home five ditched German aviators rescued by *U-587*. She arrived in Lorient on 25 February 1942. Born in 1905 and a member of the Crew of 1924, Kals obtained the rank of *Kapitän zur See* in 1944, following which he was awarded the Knight's Cross. He began his career as a sea cadet, ending it with a tally of seventeen ships sunk for 111,249 GRT, three auxiliary war ship sunk for roughly 35,000 tons, and another ship sunk for just shy of 7,000. Kals went on to command the 2nd U-boat Flotilla in Lorient from January 1943 to the end of the war—in retribution, the French detained him for three years. He lived until seventy-four years old, dying in Emden Germany in 1979.

U-107, under *Oberleutnant zur See* Harald Gelhaus, passed north of Bermuda heading west to the Virginia Capes and Hatteras, then passed eastbound about three weeks later. This was the second wave of three U-boats behind the first wave of five boats, which attacked on 13 January 1942. *U-107* attacked in concert with *U-106* and *U-103* as the first wave withdrew eastwards, to maintain a continuous presence off Hatteras. The patrol to the box north of Bermuda began on 30 January 1942, and resulted in the sinking of the *San Arcadio*, a British tanker of 7,419 tons, on the 31st.

U-107 motored west and left the Bermuda zone on 3 February, to return bound eastwards for France on the 15th. While off the US coast, he sank the *Major Wheeler*, an American vessel of 3,431 tons, on 6 February. On 16 February, the boat transferred some fuel to *U-564* under Teddy Suhren, north of Bermuda. When north-east of Bermuda Gelhaus and his team damaged the *Egda*, a Norwegian ship of 10,068 tons operating in Convoy ON-65 on 21 February south-east of Canada's Sable Island. The patrol began in Lorient from the 2nd U-boat Flotilla on 7 January 1942 and ended there on 7 March. Born in 1915 in Göttingen, Gelhaus began his career on the light cruiser *Karlsruhe* and battleship *Gneisenau* in 1938, before moving to U-boats the following year. He was in the class of 1935. Over ten patrols, Gelhaus spent 425 patrol days and sank or damaged an impressive nineteen ships of 110,411 tons. In March 1943, he earned the Knight's Cross to supplement an Iron Cross, and the U-boat Front Clasp in October 1944. Following command of *U-107*, in June 1943, he became a commander of U-boat Operations in the Eastern Baltic, joined Naval High Command in the North Sea in April 1945, and was detained by the Allies until August 1945. He died in December 1997 at eighty-two years old.[4]

Kapitänleutnant Ulrich Folkers brought *U-125*, a Type IXC boat of the 2nd U-boat Flotilla in Lorient, north of Bermuda between 30 January and 2 February 1942. It was a straight course west to east from Hatteras back to base, passing north of Bermuda on 1 February and north-east out of the region on the 2nd. Folkers was twenty-seven at the time. This patrol began in Lorient for the 2nd U-boat Flotilla on 18 December 1942. On the way west, Folkers followed Convoy HG 76 west of Portugal, but was chased away by escorts. During this patrol, Folkers fired at the grounded ship the *Olney*, but no detonation was heard. It then sank the US freighter the *West Ivis* east of Hatteras on the 26th, three days before transiting Bermuda. The sub returned to Lorient on 23 February. Folker's other victims included the *Lammot du Pont*, an American steamer sunk south-east of Bermuda.

A member of the crew of 1934, Folkers obtained the Knight's Cross on 27 March 1943; he was killed just over a month later, on 6 May in the North Atlantic, when the boat was scuttled with the entire crew after being hammered by British destroyers.[5] His total tonnage was seventeen ships for 82,873 gross registered tons. Along with Kals and Hardegen, Folkers was one of the first wave of five U-boat skippers to attack the Americas in Operation Drumbeat.[6] He had been in the U-boat service since April 1940 and served under 'Nico' Clausen on *U-37*.

31 January 1942: SS *San Arcadio*

The British tanker the *San Arcadio* was built by Harland and Wolff Limited of Govan, Glasgow in April 1935. Yard number 938, she was 7,419 gross registered tons, could carry 11,275 tons of petroleum, was 465 feet long, 60 feet wide, and 19 feet deep. An eight-cylinder diesel engine turned one propeller with 3,500 bhp to achieve a speed of 12 knots.[1] The ship was armed with a four-inch gun, a 12-pound gun, two Hotchkiss machine guns, two Lewis machine guns, and a single strip Lewis. The *San Arcadio* was also equipped with degaussing equipment as a defense against mines.[2]

The ship was owned by the Eagle Oil and Shipping Company Limited of Finsbury Circus, London. There were twenty tankers in the fleet, all beginning with the prefix 'San.'[3] The Texas newspaper *Port Arthur News* covered her sailing from the Gulf of Mexico to the UK on 9 January 1939. The *San Antonio Light* of 10 December 1939 reported that she arrived via Convoy HFX 14 at Corpus Christi, Texas. It noted that Captain Flynn would 'never know until twenty-four hours after they sail from the port here where the convoy will be located.' The ship participated in thirty-nine convoys during World War Two, many of them between Liverpool and Halifax.[4] In December 1941, she left Liverpool in Convoy ON 42, bound westwards. The convoy was dispersed and she proceeded independently for Houston to load oil for the UK via Halifax.

There were fifty men aboard the *San Arcadio* on her final voyage, of whom five were Royal Navy or army gunners. The master was Captain Walter Frederick Flynn, aged forty-one. He was supported by Chief Officer William Thomas Douglas (thirty-four), and Second Officer Clement Jerwood (twenty-four). The Third Officer was Joseph Ross Stephen and the First Radio Officer was George Wilfrid Watson. Mess Room Boy William Whyte was only fifteen years of age, and cadets Victor Byron Pitt and Roye William Patrick were each eighteen. The sixth engineer officer was William Boyd Docherty, aged nineteen.[5]

After arriving in Houston in January 1942, the *San Arcadio* loaded 9,900 tons of petroleum product—6,600 tons of gas oil and 3,300 tons of lubricating oil. On Thursday, 22 January, the ship sailed for Halifax where it intended to join a convoy back to the UK. On the following Wednesday, 28 January, the ship was struck by such severe weather that it broke off zigzagging. The ship and men weathered the storm for three days, and finally, on Saturday, 31 January, they were able to resume zigzagging at 10 a.m. local time.[6]

Twenty minutes after resuming the defensive maneuver, the ship was struck by a torpedo fired by the German navy commander Harald Gelhaus, twenty-six years of age, in command of the submarine *U-107*. At about 10.45 a.m. the torpedo struck aft near the Number One tank, about 300 feet from the bow and on the starboard side. The ship was then about 340 nautical miles north-east of Bermuda, and 330 nautical miles south-east of Nantucket. There was a heavy ocean swell at the time, with a wind from the north-north-west at about 20 knots. The ship had been steering north-east and making about 10 knots.

Prior to the attack, the merchant sailors had been warned that there were enemy submarines in the area, but all of the danger zones were at least 300 miles from their position, and they did not see the submarine before they were attacked. The explosion was so muted that Third Officer Stephens and others at first thought they had been hit by another strong wave and lurched. First Radio Officer Watson was thrown from his chair on impact. Stephens, who was on the starboard bridge wing, saw a flame burst from the impact site, which lasted five to ten seconds, but no column of water.

Lubricating oil was splattered all over the ship and into the ocean. The flying bridge was shoved to one side and some of the starboard deck bulged upwards. The engines stopped. Five seconds after the first torpedo, while flames still shot up from the first impact, a second torpedo penetrated the *San Arcadio* near the pump room, also on the starboard side. This one hit just ahead of the bridge, between tanks Number Five and Number Six. According to Stephens, it seemed as though the ship's back had been broken. He believed that the Number Five tank was empty of cargo.

The second torpedo brought down the two derricks, which were blown off the foremast and to the port side. Lookouts did not see a track from either missile. Adding to the confusion the loud steam-operated whistle jammed on and could not be shut off. Captain Flynn ordered the radio officer to transmit the ship's position for fifteen minutes on the emergency set, as the ship's radials had been brought down by the explosions. Stephens carried the position to him. Then, the word was passed around to abandon ship, though he didn't hear the order directly from the captain.

One of the davits on the after-deck lifeboat Number Three jammed—the forward davit was bent, so that the boat was suspended by the bow, with its stern submerged. Three men had been thrown into the ocean when this happened, however two of them grabbed the pilot ladder and climbed back on board. The third man clung to the boat's stern. As launching the forward raft would crush the men in the water, some officers and men released the after raft. When it drifted away with no one on it, Third Officer Stephens jumped on board, a distance of about four vertical feet.

Meanwhile, the men managed to clear away two of the port side lifeboats and one of the starboard boats. Although there was a heavy swell, the oil leaking from the ship smoothed the sea surface. The last ones off the ship were the captain and radio operator. One of the able-bodied seamen ran forward to the ship's forecastle after being swamped in the after lifeboat and clambering up the pilot ladder. Captain Flynn and Radio Operator Watson were looking for him, then dove into the sea, where they swam to a raft. The AB decided to swim to them, but he removed his life jacket. Though he jumped in and almost made it to the raft, his strength gave out and he drowned. His companion AB climbed back into the damaged Number Three boat and drifted away, to be rescued by the second mate, Jerwood. Second Radio Officer Francis Joseph McAree, twenty and Stephens were on a raft from which they were plucked by a boat with only six men in it. They pulled clear of the ship. Captain Flynn was in bad shape when rescued, however all forty-nine of the men, barring the AB who drowned, were now in boats a safe distance from the *San Arcadio*. It was about an hour after the initial attack.

An hour later, at 12.20 p.m. Gelhaus brought *U-107* to the surface. The Allied sailors could not see much of the submarine because of the distance and the rough sea and it was low in the water. *U-107*'s men pumped twenty-four shells towards the ship from the deck gun, however none registered hits.[7] When this failed to sink her, Gelhaus lined up a *coup de grâce* torpedo which finally broke the vessel's back. The sub's men continued shelling the ship until the magazine exploded; she then broke into two pieces and caught fire. The bow floated vertically and the stern floated away. By midnight, the flames had disappeared; at sunrise, there was no trace of her.

During the night, the three lifeboats managed to stay together by stringing a line, or painter, between them, and running sea anchors off their bows and sterns. There were twenty men each in two boats and a total of nine, including two gunners, in Third Officer Stephens boat. Fortunately Stephens could rely on the skill of a Scottish Highlander who had grown up on boats: Seaman John Campbell. When their sea anchor parted, Campbell fashioned a new one from a grapnel anchor and canvas, to form a mushroom-like shape. Stephens wrote:

> We found it more effective than our original sea anchor. … His boat knowledge proved invaluable. It was his good seamanship, which was in a great measure responsible for the boat weathering the first few days of bad weather. Before doing anything I always asked his advice.[8]

Indeed, it appears likely that the other boats, with more than twice as many men and without the kind of expertise that Campbell brought to Stephens' boat, probably foundered during the bad weather of the second night. At 2 p.m. on the second day, Second Officer Jerwood's boat broke free from the others in the rising weather. At 4 p.m., Stephens' sea anchor broke and Campbell replaced it. Not only were the large ocean swells threatening to swamp the boats, but there was a tropical deluge of rain as well. It took two men to man the helm in such weather, and only Stephens, Campbell, and a storekeeper named Golightly were able to carry out the task.

Food and water were rationed, and four men were kept under the cover forward, though the lifeboat was down by the head, meaning water was collecting there. Two men were kept amidships, working the primitive rotary bilge pump, as the hose was only long enough to reach the nearby side of the boat. The other three men stayed by the helm. The men were thirsty and so they supplemented the 30 gallons with which the boat was equipped with fresh rainwater. The breakers were kept forward and aft to protect them from infusion with salt water.

In the first five days, they were only able to sail about thirty hours towards the south-west. They calculated they must be 300 miles from land, yet they had no tools to estimate longitude. The men persisted with their routines, rations, and vigilance for nearly a week. Then, at 4 p.m. on Wednesday, 11 February, salvation came from the sky. As Stephens said, 'it was a calm day with a light swell and no wind, and we were drifting as much as sailing.' They were 240 nautical miles south south-east of where the *San Arcadio* sank and 160 nautical miles north-east of Bermuda.

Unbeknown to the survivors, their rescuers assumed they were a U-boat and actually dived in for an attack. The airplane's identifying number was 74-P7 and it flew for the 74th Squadron, based in Bermuda. The pilot was US Navy Lieutenant Joseph Abraham Jaap. Lt. Jaap's son wrote that Jaap 'thought he had spotted a German submarine and began a run. When he got over them he realized it was a life raft. At that time, there was a significant sea state and he was afraid if he landed they would all be lost, but he had no choice.'[9]

Stephens relates that 'The flying boat alighted on the water close to the boat and we pulled over to him. [We] got on board...' Jaap's son continues: 'After they got the sailors aboard he had difficulty getting airborne. The waves kept knocking the plane down. Finally, after a few "Our Fathers" he took off. During the war, *Life Magazine* commissioned some war artists to paint pictures of World War Two events. His rescue was picked and the painting "Rescue off Bermuda" was in *Life Magazine* and now is at the museum in Pensacola,' in Florida. The artist was Floyd Davis.[10]

Stephens carries on the narrative of the rescue: '[We] were taken to Bermuda. In the 'plane we were given only a little water to drink, as the crew of the aircraft had received wireless instructions from Bermuda that they were not to give us food of any kind.' He describes landing at 6 p.m.[11] All nine men were taken to King Edward VII Memorial Hospital and treated for swollen feet 'and general weakness.' He said that the men 'had salt water sores on their bodies and limbs.'[12]

Apparently, Golightly, a pillar of support to Stephens, had recently undergone surgery for the piles, and during the voyage 'his strength finally gave out'; however, he remained upbeat and never complained, and was a role model for the other sailors and gunners. Stephens said that four men were discharged from hospital and that the other four were held back for varying periods.

This brings up a contradiction in Stephens' account: he is consistently emphatic that eight men total were in the boat (starting with he and one other man being rescued by a boat with only six men in it). However, all other accounts—by the US Navy, by the press, and a list of forty-one dead—refer to nine men being rescued by Lt. Jaap. The contradiction remains unresolved, except that of all witnesses, Stephens ought

Nine survivors of the British SS *San Arcadio* being rescued from the air at sea on 11 February, 1942. US Navy Lieutenant Joseph Abraham Jaap and crew in Squadron VP-74, plane P-7 boldly landed on the water. Jaap's son tells how 'he had difficulty getting airborne. The waves kept knocking the plane down. Finally, after a few "Our Fathers" he took off'. The merchant sailors had been in a life boat for twelve days and were hospitalized on arrival. (*Life Magazine*)

to have known how many were in his boat. The only explanation is that Stephens was referring to the eight other men in the boat, or in the hospital, besides himself.

The British Admiralty War Diary for Foreign Stations of 11 February states that 'U.S. Naval plane picked up 9 survivors from SS *SAN ARCADIO*. Senior survivor is 3rd Officer J. R. Stephens who states that he believes they are only survivors.'[13] A CP Cable story of 14 February was headlined 'Plane Rescues U-boat Victims', and leads with 'Nine survivors, rescued from their lifeboat by a United States plane which made a daring landing in the Atlantic 160 miles off Bermuda, said yesterday an enemy U-boat fired two torpedoes into their British tanker off the American coast… Jan. 31.'[14] The wire story continues: 'the men said 40 of their ship-mates escaped from the tanker into other boats. One other member of the ship's crew was drowned while leaving the ship.' The article goes on to say that all survivors were British. The local Bermudian papers do not appear to have covered the arrival of these men, perhaps because the group was small, perhaps because they were landed by the military and not a civilian ship, or simply because they were one of the first batches of survivors to land and censorship applied. The *San Arcadio* survivors were only the second batch, after those of the *Empire Wildebeeste* landed just over two weeks before, to be landed in the colony from ships sunk nearby.

1 February 1942:
Merchant Sailors Buried in Bermuda

Fifteen merchant sailors from eleven ships were buried in Bermuda during World War Two. Their graves were generously provided by the Guild of the Holy Compassion at St. Paul's of Paget. James Clarke of the SS *Winamac* was buried on 20 August, 1940, followed by St. Clair Cummings from the SS *Magician* on 19 April 1941. Ten days later, he was joined by Carl Olafsen of the SS *Alcoa Leader*, and three months after that, William Pigett of the SS *Laguna* was buried on the island.

Then came the tragedy of the SS *British Tenacity*, from which six men were landed on the island, two of them already dead. A total of four men were buried: Harold Ransom, William Kelley, J. McIntosh, and Joshua Brewer, all in a procession on 31 January 1942, during the start of U-boat hostilities around the island. Since survivors of the *Empire Wildebeeste* were on the island at the time, they participated in the funeral procession.[1] The service was attended by dignitaries. The *British Tenacity* was built for the British Tanker Company (Anglo-Persian Oil Company, which later became BP), by Swan, Hunter and Wigham Richardson Limited of Newcastle in 1939. She was 8,439 gross tons and left Belfast Lough, Ireland bound for Aruba on 13 January, 1942, having left Avonmouth on the 9th.[2]

Due to an explosion at sea on 28 January, the ship pulled unexpectedly into Bermuda on the 30th and disembarked those injured and killed in the accident. The tanker remained in Bermuda for roughly three weeks for surveys and repairs to be carried out, as well as for the dead to be buried and the injured hospitalized at the King Edward VII Memorial Hospital, where two out of six were saved. On 22 February, the ship sailed from Bermuda, arriving in Kingston Jamaica on the 25th, and finally Aruba to load kerosene on the 27th. True to her name, *British Tenacity* survived the war, going on to be scrapped in 1959.

The victims of the *British Tenacity* were followed a year later by the interment of Charles Davis of the SS *Herman Winters* on 25 January 1943, and John Wilkin of the SS *Ocean Vesper* on 16 June that same year. Finally, Norman Leslie Lakey of the SS *Sangara* was laid to rest there on 20 February 1944. Lakey was chief officer of the *Sangara* who had died the day before. Aged thirty-five, his wife Elizabeth Currie Lakey lived in Tuffnell Park, London. His father was William Coulson Lakey.[3]

3 February–12 March 1942:
Twenty U-boats

U-109 under *Kapitänleutnant* Heinrich 'Ajax' Bleichrodt, aged thirty-two, entered the area on 3 February 1942 north-north-west of Bermuda, heading south-east. On the 6th, the boat turned to port and headed off in a north-easterly direction, exiting the region north-east of Bermuda on the 8th. *U-109* was one of five boats in the first Drumbeat wave, and began its patrol for the 2nd U-boat Flotilla off Newfoundland. On 19 January, Bleichrodt fired six torpedoes at a single ship; however, all missed and the vessel escaped. Then, on the 23rd, she sank the British ship *Thirlby* of 4,887 tons off Cape Sable, Canada.

Closer to Bermuda, *U-109* sank the British ship *Tacoma Star* on 1 February. Then, on the 4th, she was refueled by the homeward-bound *U-130* north of Bermuda. On the 5th, while north of the island, she sank the British tanker *Montrolite* of 11,309 tons and, the following day, the *Halcyon* of Panama, of 3,531 tons. It took 300 rounds of gunfire to sink the *Halcyon*. *U-109* left the region on the 8th and returned to Lorient on 23 February, having begun the patrol on 27 December 1941.

Ajax Bleichrodt graduated in the crew of 1933 and was a *Kapitänleutnant* at the time, achieving *Korvettenkapitän* late in 1943. His decorations include the Knight's Cross early in the war—in October 1940, followed by an addition of the Oak Leaves in September 1942 and the U-boat War Badge with Diamonds a month later. In January 1945, he was given the War Merit Cross Second Class with Swords. His total tonnage was an impressive twenty-four ships of 151,260 tons, plus a warship of 1,060 tons and two ships damaged for 11,684 GRT. *U-109*, on its fifth of nine patrols, was sailing from and to Lorient for the 2nd U-boat Flotilla. The patrol began on 25 March and ended on 3 June.[1]

Early in his career, Bliechrodt served on both the *Gorch Foch* and the *Admiral Hipper*, moving to U-boats in October 1939. He also served as first watch officer (second in command) of *U-564* under Teddy Suhren.[2] In one patrol as commander of *U-48* in 1940, he sank eight ships of 43,106 tons. Moving ashore in July 1943, he went on to command the 27th and 22nd U-boat training flotillas. He lived until 1977, passing away in Munich at the age of sixty-seven.[3]

Like *U-107* and *U-103*, *U-106* under *Oberleutnant zur See* Hermann Rasch merely dipped into the area to the north of Bermuda while westbound back to Lorient between 4 and 6 February 1942. The patrol started off Newfoundland, and Rasch moved south off the Chesapeake Bay area in late January. On the way south, *U-106* sank the *Empire Wildebeeste*. This attack occurred north-east of Bermuda. While leaving the Bermuda area, *U-106* sank the 10,354 British ship *Opawa*, also north-east of Bermuda, on 6 February. The patrol began on 3 January 1942 with the 2nd U-boat Flotilla and ended, also in Lorient, on 22 February.

Rasch was a member of the Crew of 1934 and was twenty-seven at the time of this patrol, having been born in Wilhelmshaven in 1914. He began his naval career on the sail training ship *Albert Leo Schlageter* in 1939 in the North Sea and moved to U-boats the following year, initially as a staff officer and then in minesweeping. As a member of the Naval High Command at the time of Germany's surrender, he was imprisoned until July 1946. Rasch lived until the age of fifty-nine, dying in 1974.

Over his career, Rasch accrued 308 patrol days between October 1941 and April 1943, all of them on *U-106*. During that time, he managed to sink or damage fourteen ships of 91,438 tons. For this he was awarded the Knight's Cross in December of 1942. One of his later victims would be the Canadian passenger liner *Lady Drake*, sunk in the vicinity of, and bound to, Bermuda. Between 24 December 1941 and 8 January 1942, *U-128* was supplied and provisioned. Her torpedoes were all offloaded, checked, and re-loaded. A lighter (barge) came along side and pumped diesel oil aboard, and provisions were loaded for an extended patrol to the Americas. On 8 January, a minesweeper and two patrol boats escorted her into the Bay of Biscay, starting at 11 a.m. The crossing of the Atlantic was apparently uneventful, probably punctuated by a series of diving drills.

Beginning on 13 February, Heyse came quite close to the south-east coast of Bermuda, perhaps using St. David's Light located there as a navigational 'fix'; given his later experience of being attacked by aircraft from Bermuda, he would do well to give the island a wider berth. On 14 February, *U-128* turned south for a day, then turned back east-south-east, leaving the area briefly on the 15th and performing some kind of patrol line south of Bermuda. On the 15th, the boat reversed course and motored due west for the next four days, passing north of Abaco and Grand Bahama and arriving off the coast of Florida near Cape Canaveral on 18 February. The sub motored north-east towards Bermuda on the 6th, and 7th, when it was attacked by aircraft. This patrol began in Lorient on 8 January, and ended there on 23 March 1942.

Kapitänleutnant Ulrich Heyse was born in Berlin-Friedenau on 27 September 1906; he was aged thirty-five at the time of *U-128*'s commissioning, he lived to 1970 and the age of sixty-four. A member of the Crew of 1933, he sank twelve ships for 83,639 tons over his career, which is the same tally for *U-128* since he was one of only two commanders of the sub and the only one to confirm sinking enemy ships on her. Ulrich Heyse rose from *Offiziersanwärter* in 1933 to *Korvettenkapitän* on 1 April 1943. Having served in the merchant marine, he then went to the surface fleet of the *Kriegsmarine*, serving on the destroyer the *Theodor Riedel*. During 1939–1940, Heyse undertook an impressive twelve patrols on the *Riedel* before transferring to U-boats in July. His first U-boat was *U-37*, which he led on one short patrol as *Kommandantenschüler* (commander-in-training). Over his career, he served 311 war patrol days over five war patrols.[4]

In 1940, Heyse was awarded the Iron Cross 2nd Class, and the day he returned from the Bermuda patrol, this was increased to 1st Class. The same day, he also received the U-boat War Badge of 1939. Roughly half a year later, based on a reported tonnage of 98,000 tons (actually, it was 83,639 that is not as much of an exaggeration as some other skippers'), he received the Knight's Cross, one of the highest awards of the German military, making him a Knight of the *Wehrmacht*. To give an idea of the rarity of this award, he was only the 143rd recipient in the *Kriegsmarine* and the seventy-eighth in the U-boat arm at the time he received it. A year after his return from Bermuda, in March 1943, and after two patrols to Brazil, Heyse moved ashore to become an instructor in U-boat learning divisions called *Unterseeboots-lehrdivision*. Two years later, in March 1945, he rose to command the 32nd (training) U-boat Flotilla. The war would end within two months and Heyse would survive it.

The patrol of *U-432* under *Kapitänleutnant* Heinz-Otto Schultze entered the Bermuda region on 8 February 1942 westbound for the area of Cape Hatteras. Overall, the submarine was near Bermuda for eight days—five inbound and three further north outbound. The first leg lasted from 8 to 12 February, the second, eastbound, from 1 to 3 March. The patrol began in La Pallice, where it

USS *Owl*, which went to the rescue of numerous Allied ships around Bermuda, including the *Victoria*, the *Anna*, the *Freden*, the *Lady Drake*, the *Lady Nelson*, the *West Notus*, the *Maldonado*, and the *West Notus*, earning her officers and crew numerous accolades.

sailed for the 3rd U-boat Flotilla, on 21 January and returned to the same base in France on 16 March 1942.

The submarine was part of the third wave of Drumbeat boats, arriving as *U-106*, *U-107*, and *U-103* were heading back to Europe.[5] Before arriving north of Bermuda, *U-432* escorted the German blockade-runner the *Doggerbank* safely into the Atlantic, and then refueled from an inbound U-boat in early February. Initially, the sub approached the Americas around Nova Scotia before heading south. While off the coast of the United States, but not in the vicinity of Bermuda, *U-432* sank several ships: the neutral Brazilian *Buarque*, the *Olinda*, the *Miraflores*, the *Norlavore*, and the *Marore*, which was sunk two days before the sub re-entered the area around Bermuda.

Schultze was born in Kiel in 1915 and was part of the Crew of 1934. He joined U-boats early (in 1937) and commanded four of them—*U-4*, *U-141*, *U-432*, and *U-849*—for a total of 325 patrol days. His father Otto Schultze sank fifty-two ships of 129,540 tons with *U-63* during World War One. Overall, the younger Schultze sank or damaged twenty-two ships of 83,657 tons, for which he was awarded the Knight's Cross in July 1942. He was killed when *U-849* was sunk west of the Congo River estuary, West Africa, on 25 November 1943. Heinz-Otto Schultze was twenty-eight at the time.

Kapitänleutnant Teddy Suhren entered the Bermuda area on 8 February 1942, and sank two ships during eight days in the region. Heading west to Hatteras, *U-564* sank the 11,401-ton Canadian freighter *Victolite* north-west of Bermuda on 11 February, and left the region the following day. Returning on the 15th, Suhren managed to damage the tanker the *Opalia* (British, 6,195 tons) with gunfire north of Bermuda on the 16th. The same day, *U-564* received fuel from *U-107* north of Bermuda. Then, the following day, the sub left the area heading east to Brest, where it was part of the 1st U-boat Flotilla. The patrol began in La Pallice on 18 January, and ended in Brest on 6 March.

Suhren is the author of an autobiography named *Ace of Aces*, and his exploits are well documented during his other patrols to Bermuda. In an extraordinarily successful career, he attacked twenty-three ships and sank or damaged 125,351 tons of Allied shipping. He served aboard *U-564* from June 1941 to July 1942, for 284 patrol days. Later in the war, he served as commander of U-boats in Norway and then the North Sea. Born in Taunus in 1916, he lived until 1984 and the age of sixty-eight, dying in Hamburg where he had become a businessman. *Ace of Aces* makes for enlightening and entertaining reading, and Suhren's leadership style and personality could be justifiably described as a maverick.[6]

U-98 under *Kapitänleutnant* Robert Gysae merely dipped into the region north-east of Bermuda for three days between 7 and 9 February 1942. Most of the patrol was off Newfoundland and Nova Scotia. Sailing for the 7th U-boat Flotilla, *U-98* left St. Nazaire, France on 18 January 1942 and returned there on 27 February. During that time, Gysae managed to sink the British steamship the *Biela* of 5,298 tons north of the Bermuda area.

Robert Gysae was born in 1911 and had just turned thirty-one at the outset of the patrol. A member of the Crew of 1931, he was older than most of his contemporaries that attacked the Americas. His naval career began with the torpedo boat T-107 before he joined U-boats in 1940. From 1944, he joined a naval anti-tank regiment and then served as senior officer in minesweeping. He lived until seventy-eight years, dying in 1989. Overall in his career, he sank twenty-five ships and damaged one for a total of 149,403 tons. He was awarded the Knight's Cross before this patrol, on 31 December 1941, to which the Oak Leaves were added in May 1943; the U-boat Front Clasp was given in October 1944.

Kapitänleutnant Werner Winter led the submarine on a patrol which would take it for four days along the north-east quadrant of the Bermuda region. On 9 February, *U-103* approached Bermuda from the north, then turned east for three days between the 10th and 12th. By the 13th, the sub was leaving the area, bound back to Lorient, where it sailed for the 2nd U-boat Flotilla. It arrived back on 1 March. During the patrol, *U-103* sank the *W. L. Steed* and the *San Gil* off Delaware and Maryland on 2 and 4 February respectively. Then, it sank the *India Arrow* and the *China Arrow*, both off the coasts of New York and Delaware. Winter would go on to lead several patrols to the region. Born in Hamburg in 1912, he was a member of the Crew of 1930. He joined U-boats in 1935 and skippered both *U-22* and *U-103* for a total of 209 days. During the period between September 1939 and July 1942, he sank fifteen ships of 78,302 tons, for which he earned the Knight's Cross in June 1942. On being ordered ashore, Winter served as a staff officer in Brest, where he was captured when that bastion surrendered in 1944. Later released, he lived until 1972 and the age of sixty.

Korvettenkapitän Hans-Georg Friedrich 'Fritz' Poske brought *U-504* on a complex patrol south-east and south-west of Bermuda for twelve days, beginning on 13 February 1942, thereafter patrolling off Florida and the Bahamas. Entering the area to the east-south-east of the island, *U-504* headed west until the 17th, when it exited for Cape Canaveral. Poske returned to the region on 6 March to the south-west of the island, initially heading east until the 9th. Then, the boat reversed course, patrolling off the Gulf Stream, and doubled back westwards until the 11th. Finally, *U-503* dipped south and exited the region on 12 March 1942. *U-504* was mistakenly given credit for sinking the British ship *Manaqui* of 2,802 tons east of the Caribbean; however, it actually sank the *Stangarth* north of the islands, and the Italian submarine *Morosini* sank the *Manaqui* on or about 15 March.

The patrol began on 25 January 1942 in league with the third wave of Drumbeat boats. After sinking the *Mamura*, the Allied authorities were made aware of the boat's presence and, on 28 February, a US aircraft from Key West attacked what it thought was a sub, but what was in fact a whale. Fritz Poske went on to become a *Kapitän zur See* and was awarded the U-boat War Badge 1939 and the Iron Cross First Class immediately after this patrol, then the Knight's Cross in November 1942. Born in October 1904, he was thirty-seven and thus one of the older skippers of those that patrolled the Bermudian waters. His career tally over 264 patrol days on four missions was fifteen ships sunk worth 78,123 tons and a 7,176-ton ship damaged.

Poske began his naval career in the class of 1923 before serving on cruisers and a torpedo boat, joining U-boats in 1940. At the time of his first command he (unusually) did not have command experience. He became Chief of Staff for Marine Infantry towards the end of the war, was imprisoned by the British for nearly a year, rejoined the German Navy in 1951, and lived until 1984, dying near Bonn at seventy-nine years of age. The patrol of *U-108* north of Bermuda was short but very busy, with a ship sunk every other day. The submarine was commanded by *Korvettenkapitän* Klaus Scholtz, aged thirty-three, from Magdeburg, Germany, who had earned the Knight's Cross just over a month before. *U-108* was part of the second wave sent to maintain Operation Drumbeat, along with *U-103*, *U-106* and *U-107*. *U-108* entered the area north-west of Bermuda and heading east on 15 February 1942. The following day, it sank the *Ramapo*, Panamanian flag, of 2,968 tons. After a dog-leg to the south-east on the 17th, Scholtz resumed course for Lorient and the next day sank the *Somme*, a British ship of 5,265 tons north-east of Bermuda. It left the region the same day—18 February. This patrol for the 2nd U-boat Flotilla began in Lorient on 8 January and ended there on 4 March 1942. While off the Hatteras area, Scholtz and his men sank the *Ocean Venture*, the *Tolosa* and the *Blink*, the latter ship just west of the Bermuda region. A member of the 1927 Naval Academy Crew, Scholtz entered the U-boat arm in 1939.

His Knight's Cross was supplemented with the Oak Leaves in December 1941. Overall, Scholtz underwent eight patrols, all in *U-108*, between February 1941 and July 1942, for a total of 361 patrol days. Over his career, he sank twenty-five ships worth 128,190 tons. One of them in April 1941 was the British Armed Merchant Cruiser *Rajputana*, in the Straits of Denmark. In September 1944, Scholtz was captured whilst commander of the 12th U-boat Flotilla in Bordeaux and held until April 1946. After the war, he joined the *Bundesmarine* and was base commander in several locations, including Kiel and Wilhelmshaven. By 1966, he was *Kapitän zur See* and he passed away at age seventy-nine in 1987.

On 24 February 1942, *U-653* under *Kapitänleutnant* Gerhard Feiler arrived north-east of Bermuda heading west towards the US coast. After motoring three days west the submarine found and sank the Norwegian ship *Leif* of 1,582 tons at the midway point between Bermuda and Cape Hatteras. Finding no other victims along the mainland coast, the boat returned on 7 March, heading east for three days, and exited the region on 9 March 1942, having spent a total of nine days in the area. The patrol began at the 1st U-boat Flotilla base in Brest on 31 January 1942 and ended there on 30 March.

Feiler was thirty-two at the time, having been born in Breslau in 1909. A member of the Crew of 1934, he served on the destroyer the *Karl Galster* between 1938 and 1940 before joining U-boats in July of that year. He commanded *U-653* between 1941 and 1943. Over seven patrols in the same sub for 412 patrol days, he managed to attack five ships worth 9,382 tons—less than stellar results when compared with his colleagues in the same timeframe. He was awarded the German Cross in Gold in 1944. Gerhard Feiler lived until 1990.

Kapitänleutnant Ernst Bauer spent ten days in the Bermuda region both inbound and outbound, beginning on 26 February 1942. The sub entered the area east-south-east of Bermuda on a south-westerly course and exited south of the island on 3 March. Coming back from its patrol, it re-entered south-south-west of the island on a straight north-easterly course, passed south-east of Bermuda on the 17th and exited the following day, returning to Lorient for the 2nd U-boat Flotilla on 29 March 1942. On 1 March, when he entered the area midway from Bermuda to Anegada, Bauer sank the *Gunny*, the *Mariana*, the *Barbara*, the *Cardonia*, the *Esso Bolivar* (in the Windward Passage), the *Hanseat*, the *Texan Olga*, and the *Colabee* (damaged)—all within the area of the Bahamas or its border with Haiti and Cuba. This patrol yielded a highly impressive tally of seven ships sunk for 32,955 tons and two damaged for 15,907 in the space of less than two weeks. Bauer was a highly successful commander who built on these sinkings to amass twenty-four ships sunk for 111,564 tons, one warship (albeit one being carried by a transport ship) of 450 tons, and five ships damaged for over 38,000 GRT damaged in his career.

The patrol began on 2 February 1942 in Lorient and ended there on 29 March. During this patrol, he was awarded the Knight's Cross and this was embellished in April 1945 with the War Merit Cross First Class with Swords. He began his naval career in the Crew of 1933, and after a stint on the cruiser the *Konigsberg* joined the U-boat arm in 1938. After successes in the Caribbean and West Africa, he became a training officer and survived the war, rejoining the navy in 1955 and living until 1988 at age seventy-four as a *Kapitän zur See*.

The Type IXC submarine *U-502* under *Kapitänleutnant* Jürgen von Rosenstiel only entered the region long enough to transit the south-east corner of the box around Bermuda. Entering on 1 March heading north-east for base, *U-502* nipped the area and left the following day, returning to Lorient for the 2nd U-boat Flotilla on 16 March. *U-502* was part of Operation Neuland. During this patrol, it attacked the waters off Aruba and off Venezuela, managing to sink three tankers: the *Tia Juana*, the *Monogas*, and the *San Nicolas*. Then, on 16 February, it and *U-67* bombarded the refineries of Aruba with only limited success. Other victims during this patrol were the *Kongsgaard*, the *Thalia*, and the *Sun*. *U-502* was to return to the Caribbean on its next patrol during which it was sunk with all hands, on 5 July. Later, on another patrol, *U-502* had the dubious distinction of being the first U-boat to fall victim to two Allied anti-submarine warfare weapons—the Wellington bomber (commanded by Pilot Officer Howell) and the Leigh Light, which was switched on as the plane barreled in at night, blinding the gun crews on the submarine. The attack took place near La Rochelle on 6 July 1942; all fifty-two crew were killed.

A member of the Crew of 1933, von Rosenstiel was born on 23 November 1912 and was twenty-nine at the time of these attacks. Though he probably would have received higher decorations had he survived this extraordinarily successful patrol, he perished with the U-boat War Badge of 1939. Initially serving on the training ship *Schlesien*, von Rosenstiel joined U-boats in 1940. His total of 179 sea days on four patrols and fourteen ships of 78,843 tons were all achieved aboard *U-502*.

U-96 under *Kapitänleutnant* Heinrich Lehmann-Willenbrock merely dipped into the area north of Bermuda between 1 and 3 March 1942. Sailing for the 7th U-boat Flotilla, the sub patrolled mainly off Nova Scotia as far south as Cape Cod and south from there. Successes included sinking the *Empire Seal*, the *Lake Osweya*, the *Torungen*, the *Kars*, and the *Tyr* outside the Bermuda area. The patrol began in St. Nazaire on 31 January and ended there on 23 March. Lehmann-Willenbrock was thirty at the time and a member of the Crew of 1931. Already a holder of the Knight's Cross with Oak Leaves, he commanded four submarines over his career: *U-8*, *U-5*, *U-256*, and *U-502*. His early experience included a stint as watch officer of the *Horst Wessel*, a sail training ship. He entered the U-boat arm in 1940. Over his career, Lehmann-Willenbrock accrued 327 patrol days in ten patrols, sinking or damaging twenty-seven ships of 194,989 tons up until the *Tyr*. After that, he was assigned commander of the 9th U-boat Flotilla, then, after managing to escape the siege of Brest for Norway in a damaged U-boat, the 11th U-boat Flotilla based there.

Before the surrender, Lehmann-Willenbrock was a watch officer on the new boat *U-3524*. He was detained after the war he was freed in March 1946. He served in the merchant marine and daringly rescued fifty-seven men from a burning Brazilian freighter. Between 1969 and 1979, he skippered the German nuclear research ship the *Otto Hahn*. Lehmann-Willenbrock was a consultant for the film *Das Boot* and lived until 1986, passing away in Bremen at the age of seventy-four.

U-155 under the command of Adolf Cornelius Piening both entered and exited the area midway Bermuda-Anegada, spending a total of nineteen days in the Bermuda region. Firstly, *U-155* arrived off the north-east corner of a box around Bermuda on 2 March 1942 and headed west-south-west. Passing north of the island on the 4th, it left the region north-west of Bermuda on the 6th. After a busy patrol, *U-155* re-entered eastbound on 11 March, passed north of the island the following day, and exited north-east on the 13th. The patrol originated in Kiel on 7 February for the 10th U-boat Flotilla and ended in Lorient on 27 March.

U-155, a Type IXC boat, began its offensive patrol off Newfoundland by attacking Convoy ONS 67 on 22 February, sinking the British tanker the *Adellen* of 7,984 tons and the Norwegian *Sama* of 1,799 tons. *U-588*, *U-587*, and *U-158* operated in coordination against the convoy. On 7 March, *U-155* was further south, off Hatteras, and sank the Brazilian *Arabutan* of 7,874 tons. Three days later, and a day before entering the Bermuda region an officer, First Watch Officer *Oberleutnant zur See* Gert Rentrop, was lost overboard during a storm. Accountable for twenty-five ships for a very impressive total of 126,664 GRT, as well as a warship (HMS *Avenger*) of 13,785 tons sunk and an auxiliary warship of 6,736 tons damaged, Piening had already earned the Knight's Cross. He was thirty-two at the time of this patrol; he lived until 1984 and the age of seventy-three. During the closing weeks of World War Two, while in command of *U-255*, he mined the approaches to St. Nazaire against an Allied attack and spent until 1947 in captivity. He rejoined the *Bundesmarine* in 1956 for thirteen years and achieved the rank of *Kapitän zur See*. A special route to avoid Allied aircraft in the Bay of Biscay became known as the Piening route, since he is acknowledged to have perfected it. He achieved 459 days at sea on eight patrols over his career after initially serving on the cruiser the *Deutschland* and *U-48*.[7]

Kapitänleutnant Werner Hartenstein brought *U-156* for a mere brush with the Bermuda region on a patrol that was predominantly spent in the Bahamas and Caribbean. On 2 March, *U-156* merely skimmed the far south-eastern corner of the Bermuda region on a patrol that began in Lorient for the 2nd U-boat Flotilla on 19 January 1942 and ended there on 17 March. It was part of the first wave of five U-boats in the *Neuland* operation, including *U-67, U-129, U-161,* and *U-502.* *U-156* was the first one to return to France. On the afternoon of 16 February, the boat withstood an attack by an American 'A' 20 bomber off Aruba.

Werner Hartenstein was thirty-three years of age at the time of his patrol, a member of the class of 1928 and a *Korvettenkapitän*. During the patrol, he was awarded the German Cross in Gold and was to earn the Knight's Cross by year's end. He was killed at age thirty-five on 8 March 1943 in an attack on his submarine east of Barbados, following five patrols of 294 days. Before joining the U-boat arm in March 1942, he completed sixty-five patrols in torpedo boats. On this patrol, he additionally sank the *Pedernales*, the *Oranjestad*, the *Arkansas*, the *Delplata*, and the *La Carrier*, for a total patrol tonnage of 22,723 sunk (five ships) and 10,769 tons from two ships damaged. His total career tally was twenty ships for 97,504 GRT and three more damaged for 18,811, plus a damaged 1,190-ton warship.

U-158 under *Kapitänleutnant* Erwin Rostin spent eight days in the Bermuda zone, starting on 1 March 1942, when he sank the *Finnanger* between Bermuda and Nova Scotia. The *Finnanger* was a Norwegian tanker of 9,551 tons out of Convoy ONS 67. On the way to the US east coast, *U-158*, which had left from Helgoland, Germany on 7 February, pursued convoy ONS 67 off Canada. Rostin was an aggressive commander and managed to sink the *Empire Celt* and the *Diloma* on 24 February. After sinking the *Finnanger* and transiting north and west of Bermuda from 1 to 6 March, *U-158* sank the *Caribsea*, the *John D. Gill*, the *Olean*, and the *Ario* as far south as the Carolinas. Then, the submarine returned to the waters north of Bermuda on the 16th, heading east-north-east until the 19th when it left the region. *U-158* arrived in its new 4th U-boat Flotilla base of Lorient on 31 March 1942. Erwin Rostin was a member of the Crew of 1933 and thirty-four years of age at the time. His earliest commands were of minesweepers M 98 and M 21 before he joined U-boats in March 1941. A daring and highly accomplished commander, he was awarded the Knight's Cross on 28 June 1942, merely two days before being attacked by a Bermudian-based aircraft and sinking north-west of Bermuda. As commander of *U-158*, he racked up 111 patrol days in two patrols during which he attacked nineteen ships of 116,585 tons.

U-588 under *Kapitänleutnant* Victor Vogel dipped into the area north-east of Bermuda between 2 and 5 March 1942, *en route* to patrol the Jersey Shore between New York and Delaware. Between Bermuda and Cape Sable, Canada, the submarine sank the British ship *Carperby* of 4,890 tons, from convoy ON 66 on 1 March. The following day, it entered the Bermuda area, turned south-west, then west on the 3rd; on the 4th, it turned north-west. Off the US coast, it attacked a ship believed to be the British steamer the *Consuelo*, then sank the 6,676-ton *Gulftrade* near Atlantic City on the 10th. Sailing for the 6th U-boat Flotilla from Lorient, the sub left on 12 February and returned to St. Nazaire on 27 March 1942. Victor Vogel was born in 1912 and was twenty-nine at the time. His four patrols of 130 days were all aboard *U-588*, which was sunk with all hands, on 31 July 1942 off Canada. Originally, he had served in anti-submarine and mine-sweeping roles before joining U-boats in March 1941. His career total of ships sunk or damaged was nine ships for 44,623 tons.

Carlo Fecia di Cossato, aboard the submarine the *Enrico Tazzoli*, began its patrol on 2 February, sailing for the Betasom Flotilla. Her assigned area was to the east of Florida and the Bahamas; as she was so busy sinking ships, she would never have the need to approach Florida directly. The *Tazzoli* was the first Italian sub sent to the region. On the way to the patrol area, she encountered and fired three torpedoes at the 8,017-ton British tanker the *Rapana* in daylight on 3 March. Due to interference from the sea conditions, they all missed. Three days later, on 6 March, the *Tazzoli* came upon the 1,406-ton Dutch steamer the *Astrea* and sank her. Later that same day, the *Tazzoli* destroyed the Norwegian tanker the *Tonsbergfjord*. There is evidence of the sinking in a photo of the *Tazzoli* crew displaying the *Tonsbergfjord*'s life ring on the conning tower.

The *Montevideo* was sunk on 8 March—she was a 5,785-ton steamship from Uruguay that had been built in Italy (ironically) as the *Adamello* in 1920. Claims that the neutral ship was sunk by Germans inflamed anti-German nationalism in Uruguay and led to protests and that country's eventual abandonment of its neutrality. Uruguay's neutrality had crucially allowed the Germans to seek refuge there after the Battle of the River Plate earlier in the war on the cruiser the *Graf Spee*.

The *Tazzoli*'s next three attacks were the *Cygnet* off San Salvador on 10 March, the British *Daytonian* off Abaco on the 13th, and the *Athelqueen*, a large British tanker in ballast, also off Abaco on the 15th. As the *Tazzoli* had its starboard torpedo tubes damaged in the attack on the *Athelqueen*, it was forced to break off the patrol and make back for Bordeaux.[8] Its arrival and passage up the Gironde estuary, was photographed with crew lining the rails, its impressive girth on display, and the damage visible. She arrived on 31 March, culminating in one of the most successful single missions to the region and of the war as a whole, with a ship attacked on average every day of the week for a period. The submarine returned to base on 2 February 1943.[9]

After roughly four years in submarines, di Cossato was transferred back to torpedo boats. He assumed command of the *Aliseo* in the Mediterranean. The *Tazzoli*, meanwhile, was stripped of its armament to enable it to serve as a supply boat to Japan. It left Bordeaux on 16 May 1943, loaded with 165 tons of material. The following day, communication with the submarine was lost. It is likely that the USS *Mackenzie* sank the submarine by a depth-charge attack on either 16 or 22 May. As a result, all the officers and crew of the *Enrico Tazzoli* remained on eternal patrol.[10]

The loss of his former crewmates so soon after he left them made di Cossato distraught. He suffered severely from what might today be called survivor's guilt. Nevertheless, he again proved himself a dashing and capable commander when aboard the *Aliseo*, in an extremely fluid situation; in September 1943, he sank a number of German ships escaping the port of Bastia on the island of Corsica. However, he was overtaken by events larger than himself. The Italian navy surrendered, and as a consequence, officers were no longer required to swear allegiance to the king, but rather to the new government. Di Cossato could not accept those terms, and refused to serve. For this, he was imprisoned and ignored.

Then, the royal court would not receive him in Naples. To a man whose family had fought for noble causes for generations, and whose busy life had been devoted to the same goals, it was too much for him. Unable to reunite with his family in the north due to the fighting there, and unwilling to take up arms with the Allies, he became deeply depressed. The authorities were unsure exactly what to do with di Cossato. From Naples, in the last letter to his mother, dated August 21st 1944, he wrote: 'For months I have been thinking about my sailors of the *Tazzoli* who are honourably on the bottom of the sea, and I think that my place is with them.' Carlo Fecia di Cossato took his own life the day he wrote his final letter, which he ended with the instructions: 'Hug Father and sisters, and to you, Mother, all of my deep, untouched love. In this moment, I feel very close to you and you all and I am sure that you will not condemn me.'[11]

U-332 under *Kapitänleutnant* Johannes Liebe patrolled north of Bermuda for ten days, not sinking anything in the region but doing so off the US coast. Originally, the patrol began in the waters of Newfoundland before Liebe headed south across the Gulf Stream. The Bermuda incursion began on 8 March to the north-east. *U-332* headed south-west to a point north-west of Bermuda on the 11th, then motored away to the north on the 12th. Off the US, it sank the US schooner the *Albert F. Paul* east of Hatteras killing all the men on board as well as the ship's dog, on the 13th. That evening, *U-332* sank the *Trepca*, a Yugoslavian freighter, off Cape Henry. By this point the boat was very low on diesel and had only six days to attack the area off the US capes.

On 16 March, Liebe attacked the large tanker *Australia* and while waiting to finish it off was detected by the USCG *Dione*, a Coast Guard cutter, which attacked with depth charges. *U-332* managed to escape, returning to the Bermuda area on the 23rd after sinking the *Liberator* on the 19th east of Hatteras. On 25 March, the sub took a dog-leg south-east to the north-east of Bermuda before resuming its course homeward for La Pallice. The submarine was part of the 3rd U-boat Flotilla and began its patrol on 17 February, ending it on 10 April 1942.

Born in Saxony in 1913, Liebe was a member of the Crew of 1933. His first assignment was on a naval airfield before he gained command of the school boat *U-6* in 1940, having joined U-boats late in 1939. Then, he served aboard *U-48* under Schultze, a renowned skipper. Liebe served 277 patrol days on five patrols, all of them aboard *U-332*. Over his career, he managed to sink eight ships of 46,729 tons. He was detained for several months in 1945, and passed away in 1982 at the age of sixty-nine.

Kapitänleutnant Johann 'Jochen' Mohr took *U-124* westbound and eastbound for Hatteras via Bermuda between 12 and 27 March. Starting well to the north-east, *U-124* headed west from 12 to 14 March 1942; on that day, north-north-west of Bermuda, he sank the British 7,209-ton tanker the *British Resource*. Then, two days later, he exited the area bound for Hatteras. Off Hatteras, *U-124* sank the Honduran banana ship the *Ceiba* on the 17th. Mohr returned on the 24th, this time eastbound, and also north of Bermuda. Starting on the 24th, the boat headed first north-east then east, passing north of the island on the 26th and out of the region on the 27th. The patrol began in Lorient on 21 February for the 2nd U-boat Flotilla and ended there on 10 April. His other victims included the *Ceiba*, the *Acme*, the *Kassandra Louloudis*, the *E. M. Clark*, the *Papoose*, and the *W. E. Hutton*, all sunk, and damage to the *Esso Nashville*, the *Atlantic Sun* (11,355 tons damaged), and the *Naeco*.

This patrol began on 21 February 1942 in Lorient and ended in the same port. Mohr returned to base on 10 April. Aged twenty-five at the time, he was awarded the Knight's Cross during the patrol. Eight or so months later, the Oak Leaves would be added. His career total included twenty-seven ships sunk for 129,976 GRT, two warships sunk for 5,775 tons and the three aforementioned ships damaged on this patrol. The *Atlantic Sun* was ultimately sunk by *U-607* in the central North Atlantic on 15 February 1943, nearly a full year later. In April 1943, Mohr was promoted to *Kovettenkapitän;* the following day, he was killed in the central Atlantic when the British corvette HMS *Stonecrop* and sloop HMS *Black Swan* attacked west of Oporto Portugal, destroying the sub with all hands. His other great success was against a convoy, ONS 92; Mohr began and ended his career on a single boat, *U-124*, on which he served under Georg-Wilhelm Schulz. During his return voyage, he reported his success to Admiral Dönitz in verse, expressing the giddy sentiment of the second happy time, which U-boat skippers found to their disbelief on attacking the largely undefended US east coast in early 1942.[12]

14 March 1942: MV *British Resource*

The motor tanker the *British Resource* was built by the Greenock Dockyard Company in Scotland and launched two days before Christmas in 1930 as yard number 421. She was registered to London and owned by the British Tanker Company of that city. Her dimensions were 440.6 feet stem to stern, 59.4 feet wide, and 32.9 feet deep. Her tonnage was 7,209 registered tons. Her modern oil-fueled engine generated 653 net horsepower and was built by J. G. Kincaid and Company Ltd.[1] On 25 July 1939, she ran aground at Busrah in Abadan, but was pulled off. Between the outset of war in September 1939 and March 1942, the *British Resource* had a busy time of it. In 1939, she called at Mombasa, Cape Town, Freetown, and Dakar, all in Africa, then discharged in Liverpool over Christmas. Unfortunately, on 18 October, she collided with the British ship *Celtic Star* and two men were killed. From there, she called at Texas, Bermuda, the UK, Cape Town, the Middle East, West Africa, and various ports in the UK. Aside from engine trouble in September 1940 and September 1941, she seems to have had no other problems.

In early 1941, she called at Aruba, Bermuda again, and several British ports. From there, it travelled to Texas and Halifax, then back to the UK, sailing independently. One of her earlier wartime voyages, she left New York on 31 May 1941. She sailed for Halifax in Convoy HX 131 carrying benzene. She used the loading port at Baltimore in July 1941. At the end of 1941, she loaded in Texas again and returned to the UK via Halifax. Overall, the *British Resource* participated in convoys OB 124, BHX 42, SL 50, OB 287, HX 131, and EN 3.[2]

On her final voyage, the *British Resource* left the River Mersey (Liverpool) on 8 February 1942 in ballast for Curacao. There, she loaded a cargo of what Captain James Kennedy described as 10,000 tons of 'petrol and Aviation spirit'—highly flammable and deadly liquid. She was armed with a 4-inch gun, a 12-pound gun, and several machine guns (two Lewis, two Twin Hotchkiss, and two Single Hotchkiss). The ship was also equipped with two P. A. C. parachute rockets. The human complement consisted of fifty-one persons, of whom forty-three were British merchant mariners and eight were gunners—four naval gunners and four military or army gunners.[3]

It is worth noting how young many of the *British Resource*'s crew were. Those twenty or under included apprentice Bernard Allison (aged sixteen), apprentice Keith Charles Finn (aged nineteen), deck boy Norman Hartnell (aged seventeen), cabin boy Dougall Hoyle (aged seventeen, who had gone to sea when a boy in his village had given him a white feather, symbol of cowardice), able seaman Arthur Ernest Jones (aged twenty), carpenter Ronald Patrick Jordan (aged nineteen), assistant steward Alexander McLeod (aged nineteen), and ordinary seaman George W. Newstead (aged eighteen). Other crewmen included ordinary seaman John Owen (aged eighteen), Second Radio Officer John Eric Robinson (aged eighteen), cook Leslie Saunders (aged nineteen), and cabin boy Robert Strathie (aged eighteen). Perhaps most poignant were the two sons of the Manaley family of London, steward Hugh Manaley (aged seventeen), and his younger brother assistant steward Charlie Ramsey Manaley (aged fifteen). All of the crew were British, except chief officer Patrick John Broderick (age thirty-three), who was South African, and Percy Donald Duncan Melvin (aged twenty-one) was from Canada.[4]

The *British Resource* arrived in Curaçao early in March, and she departed the island at 10 a.m. on Wednesday the 4th, bound for Halifax. Ten days later, at about 3 p.m. on Saturday, 14 March 1942, the ship was 225 north-north-west of Bermuda, 485 miles south-east of New York and roughly 500 miles south of Halifax. Mohr was watching, as he wrote in his war diary:

> Two masts in sight bearing 225°T, 14 nm away. Maneuvered ahead to the north. Tanker zigzags regularly, no long legs. Speed 11 knots. Dived on general course line.... Double shot, range 1,000 meters, 1st hit: after edge of forecastle, 2nd hit: forward mast. Tanker settles forward deeper and stops. Port lifeboat was put to the water.[5]

Captain Kennedy later wrote that 'We were making a speed of 11 knots zigzagging day and night as ordered, changing the pattern every two hours. I received no submarine warnings and was not expecting to be attacked.' The ship was on course six degrees north when suddenly two torpedoes struck them from *U-124* under Mohr. Visibility was good, winds were described as light and variable, and the sea was calm. Though Mohr says that torpedoes hit the 'after edge of the forecastle' as well as the 'forward mast,' Captain Kennedy says a single torpedo 'struck in the Fore Deep Hold on the Starboard side.' He continues:

> There was a violent explosion and a considerable amount of water and oil from the bunkers was thrown up. No flash or flame seen. The ship settled down rapidly by the head so I 'phoned the Chief Engineer [William Alfred Corlett, aged fifty], who was in the engine room to put the engines full speed ahead and then come on deck. Together we entered the pump room forward and opened the sea valves to try and restore a little of our lost buoyancy by running down Nos. 1 and 2 tanks. The submarine periscope was sighted about five cables on the starboard beam so we immediately engaged him with the 4-inch aft. I gave the helmsman a course to bring our stern to the submarine.[6]

Second Officer Samuel John Rennels, aged twenty-seven, led the gun crew. Kennedy says that he 'took charge of the guns when the *British Resource* was torpedoed and fired on the submarine until he and the gun's crew were eventually forced away from their stations by the flames and were compelled to jump overboard in an attempt to save their lives.' Mohr writes: 'Anti-submarine armament recognized 3 cannons (about 5 cm) on forecastle, forward walkway and stern walkway. 1 cannon (15 cm or 10.5 cm) on stern. Stern cannon was manned and fired in the direction of the periscope. No impacts heard.'

Captain Kennedy continues:

> By now the engines had stopped, having lost the fuel oil suction owing to the ship being so far down by the head. As we were now a sitting target I ordered No.4 boat to be lowered and the Chief Officer and 30 men abandoned ship in this boat. At 15:03 a second torpedo struck the ship in the way of No. 6 tank, starboard side, throwing a huge column of blazing benzene high into the air, setting the ship on fire from the fore mast, right aft. The water on both sides was immediately covered with burning benzene.

Kennedy then had the tragic duty to relate that despite his efforts to save his men at the cost of his own life, the opposite in fact happened: 'In spite of the port boat being 250 feet away from the ship it was filled with burning benzene and being a metal boat it soon melted. The occupants must have perished immediately.'

Mohr continues: '*Coup de grâce*, range = 700 meters. Hit between after mast and engine room. Munitions locker exploded. At the same moment, the entire ship is in flames. 800-meter high smoke column, 200-meter-high flames. On board munitions explode at short intervals.' The ship 'blew up, spewing flames 600 feet into the sky.' There were however at least six men still alive on the mortally stricken ship. Captain Kennedy describes all this frenetic activity taking place between 3 p.m. and a second shot at 3.03 p.m.—three minutes. Mohr provide a more realistic time frame of fifteen minutes, between when the first two shots were fired, and when the *coup de grâce* or second round was fired.[7]

Kennedy was on the bridge with the helmsman and two radio operators, one of whom was Neil Murray Coleman, third radio officer. He wrote:

> I ordered these three men to make for the forecastle head—the only portion of the ship not enveloped in flames.... After throwing the codes overboard [he] followed these men, jumping onto the deck and up through the fore peak hatch. I saw none of the crew on the way, and on reaching the forecastle head saw that the three men had already jumped overboard. I found a torn life jacket which I took with me then I slipped into the water from the anchor which was already awash and swam after them just as the burning flames met on the water round the bow of the ship. All this happened in two or three crowded minutes.[8]

Mohr continues in his KTB entry:

> Surfaced. Name on stern: BRITISH R.... London. From construction (normal stern, straight bow, pole masts between bridge and after mast) identified as

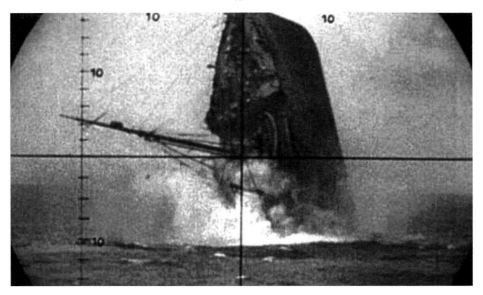

The destruction of another Allied ship by a German U-boat, as seen through the commander's periscope. This is one of 2,779 Allied victims out of over fourteen million tons sunk by the Germans in World War Two alone. Often the destruction of ships took mere minutes, jettisoning ill-prepared sailors into dark, cold waters with very short life expectancy. (*Jak P. Mallmann Showell*)

'BRITISH RESOURCE' 7209 GRT, loaded. Tanker still floats on burning oil. In hours will be totally burned and sink. In the vicinity rafts and one lifeboat also burned. Four swimming people seen. Continued westerly transit. Reloaded.[9]

Meanwhile, Kennedy and his companions swam to windward to avoid the burning benzene. He recognized Second Officer Rennels among the men in the water, as well as some of the gun crew and some engineers.

Suddenly the submarine surfaced off the port quarter and began taking photographs of the blazing ship. The men nearby began swimming towards the submarine in an attempt to board it, but as they got within reach they were brutally waved away and the submarine went full speed ahead and steamed through them…. The crew were all young and fair and the men in the water told me that they were speaking in German.

It was a tragic evening for Kennedy and his companions:

One by one, the crew reached the limit of their endurance, lowered their heads and slowly dropped astern [of the drifting ship]. I bumped into several of my men—doubtless some of the crew of the Port lifeboat—I turned two of them over but they were beyond recognition, the flames had done their work only too well. Their lifejackets were burnt and useless, so I passed on.[10]

The pathetic cavalcade of survivors continued to slowly paddle and wade after their flaming ship. After roughly three hours, the sun began to set. Kennedy spotted an object low in the water behind the ship. Due to its distance from him, it would require his exerting possibly the last of his strength to reach it, but he took the risk. Arriving at it, exhausted, he discovered that it was was 'the remains of a burnt out and partly submerged raft. The raft was still smouldering but we managed to put the fire out and thankfully crawled on to it, very tired indeed.'

By shouting into the falling evening Kennedy and the senior radio officer were able to attract the attention of three more men, including Third Radio Officer Coleman and the helmsman. He wrote 'we eargerly helped them on board, making them cover the splits in the barrel with their bodies to keep the water out. The heat was intense but it kept the water warm and for that we were thankful.' Meanwhile, Mohr wrote in the war diary 'Last fiery glow of the burning oil out of sight in the north-east.' Indeed, Kennedy records that the *British Resource* finally sank at 4 a.m. on Sunday, 15 March, 'still a blazing mass and the water continued to burn for another hour, then the wind blew the pall of smoke away and the sky cleared.'

Fortunately for the forlorn men, who numbered less than five out of the ship's original complement of fifty-one (in all, forty-six men perished), the Allies had received their SOS and quickly dispatched help. By 8 p.m., some five hours after the attack, Kennedy wrote that 'a large American flying boat arrived and dropped a number of flares and signalled with a flashlight. We took the red glass of our lifejacket lights and signalled back to him. This 'plane circled for about 4 hours and then giving us a parting greeting flew off.' This must have been an immense boost to the men's morale, particularly considering the trauma they had both witnessed and experienced.[11]

Indeed, the coordinated US and British response to the *British Resource* casualty was immediate, strident, and highly effective. First word of the attack was recorded at 3.27 p.m. in the Headquarters of the Fifth Naval District in Nofolk. It records simply 'SSS from SS British Resource giving position.' The Enemy Action Diary for the Eastern Sea Frontier records at 3.38 p.m., during the actual attack, that 'British Resource... sent an SSS [submarine sighted and/or attack]. This position is approximately 160 miles N by W from Bermuda.' The Naval Operating Base in Bermuda war diary for 13 March records:

> At 1900 an SSS was received from a British tanker 200 miles North of Bermuda. The night patrol plane immediately was sent to the secene. Two hours later plane reported tanker on fire, and nearby survivors identified by dim flashing light [life jacket lights described by Captain Kennedy]. Corvette *CLARKIA* ordered to proceed out, pick up survivors and attack submarine. Plane continued to guard survivors through the night and searched for submarine which was twice located on the surface and presumably driven down.[12]

Despite this latter entry, Mohr makes no mention of having been attacked or driven down by airplanes. Kennedy picks up the narrative:

At 1000 the 'plane returned, we waved an oilskin coat and they saw it and came and circled low over us. The 'plane then flew off and returned again shortly after noon, dropping a sleeping bag supported by lifebelts and a dinghy. The sleeping bag contained bread, water, butter, a can of corn and some cigarettes. They signalled to us the cheering message that a ship was coming.

The NOB Bermuda diary corroborates this, on Sunday, 15 March, recording that 'Additional planes were sent to the scene at daylight. Corvette *CLARKIA* reached scene in afternoon and picked up Captain and four other survivors from a raft. Planes covered *CLARKIA* and continued search for submarine, but no further contact was made. All others on tanker believed lost.'[13]

It would seem the reason a plane did not try to land and rescue the men right away at first light was because there was a heavy sea running. Mohr, though he was heading west, records conditions that morning as: 'heavy rain and thunder squalls, summer lightening, short large sea.' Also it appears that the Allied naval forces didn't want just to rescue survivors, but to attack the submarine which was the root cause of the casualty. Kennedy relates his elation and sudden rescue:

At [8 p.m.] just before dark the 'plane returned and signalled that a corvette was on her way, and almost immediately HMS *CLARKIA* steamed over to us and picked us up, taking us to Bermuda where we arrived on the 16th March. We were all very tired and suffering from burns but were very thankful to see the land again.

NOB Bermuda's diary for Monday, 16 March reads:

HMS corvette *CLARKIA* entered the port with the five survivors of the British tanker…. The *CLARKIA* was ordered to turn over the survivors to the Royal Navy. Royal Navy (Commodore-in-Charge, H.M. Dockyard) agreed to make necessary report to immigration authorities and to the Shipping Master in the Colonial Secretary's office.[14]

The Commodore-in-Charge at the time is thought to have been either Admiral Sir C. E. Kennedy-Purvis, KCB (outgoing in 1942) or Vice Admiral Sir Alban T. B. Curteis, KCB (incoming).

The commander of HMS *Clarkia* was Lieutenant Frederick John Gwynn Jones, RD, RNR, and he had quite an extraordinary time rescuing merchant sailors of varioius nationalities during the early part of the war. Jones commanded the *Clarkia* (K 88) between 4 April 1940 and 30 August 1942, and rescued 143 sailors from six ships: forty-five from the *Accra*, thirty-two from the *Vinemoor* (off the UK in 1940), sixteen from the Norwegian *Brandanger*, five from the *Empire Citizen* both off Iceland in 1941, five from the *British Resource*, and thirty from the *British Consul* off Trinidad in August, eleven days before he handed over command of the *Clarkia* and assumed command of HMS *Mansfield* (G 76). While in command of HMS *Rowley* (K 560), Jones was given partial credit for sinking *U-1208* in the English Channel on 27 February 1945.[15]

Unlike almost every other merchant marine casualty from which Allied sailors were landed in Bermuda, the Bermuda National Archives have been unable to locate local news stories about the survivors of the *British Resource* when they landed on the island. The probable reasons for this are three-fold: the survivors were landed by a Royal Navy ship and not another merchant ship; they were few in number and thus would have had a muted impact locally; and, given the dastardly and horrific way in which so many men died—ablaze in burning benzene, run over by an enemy U-boat, or simply drowned from exhaustion—it is unlikely that the naval authorities wished to publish such demoralizing accounts.

Insurer Lloyd's of London did however recognize two of the *British Resource*'s officers for exemplary conduct. Their War Medal for Bravery at Sea was instigated in 1940 to honor 'seafarers who performed acts of exceptional courage at sea.' In the course of World War Two, only 541 were awarded, and two of them went to the men of the *British Resource*: first radio officer Clark, aged thirty-one, and third radio officer Niel Murray Coleman, who survived with Kennedy. Without those two men staying at their post when most of their colleagues had abandoned ship, it was unlikely that rescue would have come so swiftly, if at all.[16]

Coleman and Kennedy were further honored by the King with the title 'Officer of the Civil Division of the Most Excellent Order of the British Empire [OBE].' The citation recounts the loss of the ship, the thirty men in the lifeboat, the remaining men's terrifying dash to the bow through flames, and a harrowing twenty-six hours on a frail life raft. Specifically, the citation reads:

> The Third Radio Officer [Coleman] showed great bravery and devotion to duty. He remained in the Wireless Room and held a broken wire in position while distress messages were transmitted. He did not leave until forced to do so by the enveloping flames.

As for Captain Kennedy, the citation reads: 'The Master displayed outstanding courage throughout. He did his best to fight the submarine and tried to safeguard the lives of the crew by getting the majority away in a boat at an early stage.'[17]

Meanwhile, back in the UK, young Tony Jordan, aged eleven, waited for his older brother Ron to return home from the *British Resource*. Tony, who had withstood the bombings of Coventry, was devastated by the loss of his sibling, but still erected a plaque with the names of both Ronald Patrick Jordan, carpenter, and commander Georg-Wilhelm Schulz of *U-124* on a bench at the British Museum of Road Transport. Apparently, Ron was drafted aboard the *British Resource* when Captain Kennedy was short a carpenter, but when war broke out, he was forbidden by wartime laws from leaving the ship. Peter Manaley lost two brothers aboard the *British Resource*: Charley aged fifteen and Hugh aged seventeen. Peter's son Rick writes 'My mum said that my dad was eight years old at the time and it was on his mind all his life.'[18]

16 March 1942: One U-boat

U-94 under *Oberleutnant zur See* Otto Ites only crossed north of Bermuda from west to east for three days between 16 and 18 March 1942. The sub came down from the waters of Canada and transited Bermuda between the US east coast and Canada. It was sailing with the 7th U-boat Flotilla and left St. Nazaire on 12 February. *En route* to Canada, it encountered convoy ON 67, and was directed to the location with several other boats. On the way, *U-94* sank the *Empire Hail*, a British ship.

After patrolling off Nova Scotia, Ites moved to the US east coast, sinking the trawler HMS *Northern Princess*, on loan to the Americans, off New Jersey on 7 February. On the 9th, she sank the *Cayru* of Brazil, and two days later, the Norwegian *Hvosleff* east of New York and Chesapeake respectively. After passing north of Bermuda, the homebound *U-94* was vectored by *U-203* towards convoy ON 77 east of Newfoundland. *U-94* damaged the *Imperial Transport*, a British tanker, which was towed to St. John's. The sub returned to St. Nazaire on 2 April 1942.

During this patrol, Otto Ites was awarded the Knight's Cross. Born in 1918, he was in the Crew of 1936 and turned twenty-four a week before the patrol began. Initially, he served aboard torpedo boats the *Kondor* and the *Albatross*, joining U-boats in October 1938. He went on to command *U-146* as well as *U-94*, from which he was captured in the Windward Passage off Haiti on 28 August 1942 when the HMCS *Oakville* rammed her. He was released in May 1946. Over seven patrols, Ites served for 235 patrol days and managed to attack or sink sixteen ships of 84,904 tons. Ites became a dentist after the war, then returned to the navy where he led the destroyer *Z2*.[1] When he retired in 1977, his rank was *Konteradmiral*. He passed away where he was born, in Norden, Ostfriesland in 1982 at the age of sixty-three.[2]

20 March 1942: SS *Oakmar*

The US-flagged steamship the *Oakmar* was built as yard number thirty-three by the Mitsui Bussan K. K. shipbuilders in Tamano, Japan in July 1920. Her original name was the *Eastern Exporter*, and she was commissioned for the United States Shipping Board. She was 385 feet long, 51 feet wide, and 34 feet deep. Her gross registered tonnage was 5,766 and a triple expansion steam engine developed 554 net horsepower, propelling the ship's steel hull at 10 knots when built.[1]

In 1923, the *Eastern Exporter* was sold to the Garland Steamship Corporation of New York. She was renamed the SS *William Campion*. In 1927, the Calmar Steamship Company Inc., also of New York, purchased the ship and renamed her the *Oakmar*. Calmar was a subsidiary of Bethlehem Steel and operated from 1920 to 1970. In the spring of 1942, the *Oakmar* found itself on passage between Calcutta and Boston via Trinidad and Cape Town for bunkers. Her cargo was manganese ore, rubber, and burlap. The thirty-six men on board were under the command of Captain Nolan Eugene Fleming, aged forty-four. There was a passenger working his way between India and the US named Herbert L. Jernigan. There was a total of thirty-six men aboard *Oakmar*.

According to an eighteen-year-old oiler among the crew named Erio Pearson from Galveston, Texas, on the passage between Trinidad and Boston, the ship evaded no fewer than four other German or Italian submarines in recent days. He said that 'Every time a sub would get near us the captain would order full speed ahead. We got away four times.'[2] Their luck was to run out on Friday, 20 March 1942. On that day, the ship was 310 nautical miles north-west of Bermuda and 300 nautical miles south south-east of Nantucket. The *Oakmar* was heading 342 degrees north-north-west true at 11.5 knots. At 2 p.m., it was still daylight and the ship was zigzagging. The ship was not armed and nor were there lookouts, though those on deck were described as 'alert.'

There was a ship about five miles ahead of the *Oakmar* heading from right to left of them. This vessel turned out to be the Dutch motor vessel the *Talisse*; her captain reported witnessing the attack on the *Oakmar* when he arrived in New York some days later. Built in 1930 and owned by the Netherlands Steamship Company of Amsterdam, the vessel was 8,169 GRT, 490 feet long, 62.2 feet wide and 29 feet deep.[3]

Conditions were bad—there was a very heavy sea running and the wind was blowing Force Seven or Eight, and so a fresh gale of 35 to 40 knots was blowing from the north-west; visibility was good. Suddenly at 2.10 p.m., the men spotted a surfacing submarine off the starboard quarter, heading towards them at least 10 knots—some said as fast at 16 knots. The submarine was the German U-boat *U-71* under *Kapitänleutnant* Walter Flachsenberg (soon to be promoted to *Korvettenkapitän*). They had entered the area north-west of Bermuda heading east on 2 April. The day before, the sub had sunk the *Eastmoor*, a British ship of 5,812 tons. While patrolling the east coast of the US from Hatteras to New York, *U-71* sank the *Ranja* on 17 March.

Walter Flachsenberg was born in 1908 and a member of the Crew of 1929, making him thirty-three years of age at the time of the patrol. He served with naval artillery from 1939 to 1940, when he joined the U-boat arm. The weather was so rough that Flachsenberg did not want to risk an initial submerged torpedo attack, preferring instead to disable his unarmed quarry with machine gun fire. Captain Fleming was a bold spirit, and turned the wheel hard to port to out-run his attacker.

Fleming had the radio operator immediately send an SSS signal, and it was acknowledged by at least five shore stations. The radio operator gave the noon position, course and speed. At 2.48 p.m., the Headquarters of the US Navy's Fifth Naval District in Norfolk recorded the *Oakmar*'s SSS, 'intercept on distress frequency.' The Eastern Sea Frontier Enemy Action Diary recorded that the *Oakmar* was 'being pursued by a submarine' at 7.30 p.m.[4]

It seemed the *Oakmar* might have a chance of outrunning *U-71* until the U-boat opened fire with a pom-pom anti-aircraft gun located in the conning tower. The first shot tore into the bridge wing, the second landed in the chart room, and the third ended up on the deck. Captain Fleming presumed that these were warning shots, and he ordered the *Oakmar* stopped and the ship abandoned. He sent the ship's confidential papers overboard in a weighted bag, lest they end up in enemy hands.

Thirty men managed to get away in the starboard lifeboat, including the passenger. However, two men leapt into the water and, because it was so rough, the men in the lifeboats could not save them. Captain Fleming and three other men—four in total—were seen launching the port lifeboat. The thirty men in the large lifeboat were very impressed by the 'unusual stability' of the U-boat. They observed that 'The *OAKMAR* was bobbing around "like a cork" while the submarine cut across 10 to 15 foot waves in a 6 or 7-point north-west wind on an apparently even keel.' When *U-71* was only 100 yards away from the *Oakmar*, it began firing 'in spurts' at the ship. Over the next fifteen minutes, some thirty to forty shells were observed to have been sent at the merchant vessel. The Allied survivors thought they could read 'SB118' on the side of the conning tower, and they saw four men on the tower.[5]

After failing to sink the ship with gunfire alone, Flachsenberg opted to fire torpedoes. At 2.20 p.m., he fired the first torpedo, but it deviated in the heavy seas and missed. At 2.39 p.m., *U-71* sent a second torpedo at the *Oakmar*; this one hit just forward of the bridge. It had the effect of making the ship sink by the bows within a matter of minutes. The survivors in lifeboats, struggling to stay afloat, were unaware that torpedoes had been used. Flachsenberg never interacted with them. The sub motored away, submerged and unseen.

The chief engineer and third officer marveled at the gunnery of the enemy submarine in such adverse seas. They reported to the US Naval Intelligence:

> In a heavy sea, the submarine was able to fire several shorts from it pom-pom, but sought the lee of the vessel before commencing destructive firing. … It seems remarkable that so much damage was done with a deck gun in such heavy seas. The third officer of the vessel, who was for several years in the Coast Guard, stated that he had never launched a lifeboat in such high seas.[6]

These men also felt that had the *Oakmar* been armed they might have been able to keep *U-71* submerged and perhaps avoided being sunk. Probably Flachsenberg only surfaced after ascertaining that the ship was unarmed and could not counter attack.

Meanwhile, according to the Naval Operating Base in Bermuda records, a craft named *R6* was sent to 'proceed to assist *OAKMAR* and attack enemy forces.' The twenty-eight US sailors and two Norwegians in the large lifeboat did not know this. They were facing a very rough night ahead of them on the open seas. It would be too dangerous for the *Talisse* to turn back and rescue them; they were on their own. To make matters worse, the side of the lifeboat had been smashed while it was being lowered. An oiler from Maybrook, New York named James Stickney, thirty-two years old and 220 pounds, later told a reported how 'We found pieces of wood and some tools in the boat. We salvaged timber from the sea and pulled nails from drifting planks, and fixed up our boat.' Another member of the lifeboat crew, William Teffner, aged twenty-seven and also an oiler, from Landsdowne, Maryland, said that 'some of the fellows in the boat didn't even have their pants. They just had life preservers and pajamas.'[7] It must have been bitterly cold in the North Atlantic in mid-March.

Of the four men in the port lifeboat, struggling in the seas without enough men to man the oars, all were lost. Additionaly, two men died in the heavy seas while trying to escape the doomed ship. The names of all lost were: Captain Fleming, first assistant engineer Floyd Thomas Ireland, messman Robert Eugene Lang, steward Cyril Alexander Ogle, messman Elmer Dewitt Richardson, and able seaman John Wise Hartley. For the thirty other men, their ordeal in the open boats only lasted over two days, or fifty-four hours to be exact. At around 8 p.m. on Sunday 2 March, they managed to attract the attention of a Greek steamship named the *Stavros*, which was sailing for the neutral Swiss government.

The *Stavros* of 4,853 tons was built in 1925 by Furness Shipbuilding in the UK and in 1942 was owned by the Kassos Steam Navigation Company, Ltd. of Syra, Greece. In March 1942, she was on charter to the Swiss government. Her previous names were the *Ashleigh* and the *Kingston Hill*. The *Stavros* arrived in Hamilton, Bermuda at 5 p.m. on Tuesday, 24 March. Two of the crew were hospitalized on the island. The commandant of the NOB base in Bermuda, Admiral James, contacted the US Consul General on the island regarding processing and repatriating the twenty-eight Americans and two Norwegians. Most likely the survivors were put up in the Bermuda Sailor's Home and in local residences—*The Royal Gazette and Colonist Daily* did not record their arrival. Twenty-nine of the survivors— one of them remained behind in Bermuda to recuperate in hospital—flew to La Guardia Airport in New York on a Pan American Clipper aircraft. They arrived on Wednesday, 1 April. Once there, they were interviewed by the Office of Naval Intelligence and some of them—Pearson, Jernigan the passenger, and Stickney—by an Associated Press reporter, who sent the item out under the title 'Beat Four Subs, Sunk by a Fifth.'[8]

U-71 followed the *Oakmar* sinking with a successful attack on the *Dixie Arrow*, but the sub was chased off by the USS *Tarbell*, resulting in a depth charge attack. On the 31st, Flachsenberg found and sank the British ship the *San Gerardo* between New York and Bermuda. *U-71* sailed with the 7th U-boat Flotilla from St. Nazaire on 23 February, and returned to La Pallice on 20 April 1942. Flachsenberg lived until 1994, aged eighty-six.

The *Stavros* had an interesting war. Less than two months after rescuing the *Oakmar* men, she was herself attacked, by *U-593* under Gerd Kelbling. In the morning of 14 May 1942, Kelbling put a torpedo into the mid-section of the ship south-east of New York before realizing it was sailing under neutral Swiss markings, at which point the U-boat broke off the attack. The *Stavros* was salvaged, repaired, and placed back in service. It survived the war, was sold to Costa Rica in 1953, Panama in 1960, then Japan for breaking up in 1962.[9]

21 March–15 April 1942:
Fourteen U-boats

U-105 under *Fregattenkapit*än Heinrich Schuch patrolled north of Bermuda for twelve days between 21 March and 1 April 1942. It was one of eleven subs assigned to the fourth wave of Operation Drumbeat. It left Lorient as part of the 2nd U-boat Flotilla on 25 February and entered the region north-east of Bermuda westbound on 21 March. It proceeded west then south-west, performed a dog-leg and sank the British tanker the *Narragansett* of 10,389 tons on the 25th. Then, it proceeded north-west until the 27th, when it sank the Norwegian ship the *Svenør* north-west of Bermuda. Earlier that day, it attacked a ship with a torpedo and heard a detonation, however no confirmed damage or sinking has been attributed to this attack, and the Eastern Sea Frontier Enemy Action Diary (US) is silent as to ships reporting an attack in this location.[1] *U-105* then headed east until 1 April, exiting just north of where it had entered. It returned to Lorient on 15 April.

Schuch was born in 1906 and was a member of the Crew of 1925, making him thirty-five years of age at the time. From 1938 to September 1939, he commanded *U-37*. His other command aside from *U-105* was *U-154*. He moved ashore in 1945 as a Head of the Weapons Division until the surrender. Overall, he was responsible for sinking seven ships of 39,187 tons, three of them from *U-154*. Schuch received no decorations. He died in 1968 at the age of sixty-one.[2]

On 6 April, Reinhard Hardegen on the famous 'one two three' boat, *U-123* returned for one devastating week. After skirting Newfoundland and Hatteras, the boat entered the region to the north of Bermuda both eastbound and westbound. North-east of Bermuda on 21 March 1942, *U-123* entered the area heading west. On the 22nd, it sank the US tanker the *Muskogee* of 7,034 tons; this was followed, two days later, with the British ship the *Empire Steel* of 8,138 tons.

Two days after coming south from the Carolinas to off the Georgia coast, he damaged the 7,989-ton tanker the *Esso Baton Rouge* and the 9,264-ton *Oklahoma*. Proceeding south along the eastern coast of Florida to a position some 30 miles off West End Grand Bahama, he sank in quick succession the *Esparta* on the following day (9 April), then the tanker the *Gulfamerica* off Jacksonville two days later. Immediately following this attack, the boat was pinned down by an Allied plane and ships in an attack, which would have led to the destruction of the U-boat by more persistent foes in almost any other theater at the time. To these successes, he added the American-flagged *Leslie*, and the *Korlsholm*, a Swedish ship that began the war detained off Morocco. Given that Hardegen sank the *Alcoa Guide en route* home and the *Liebre* to and off Hatteras, his tally for one patrol was eight ships sunk for 39,917 and three damaged for 24,310 tons. On the way home, *U-123* again transmitted Bermuda, this time eastbound from 16 April until the 20th, beginning to the north-west, going north of the island on the 18th, and exiting to the north-east. In the Bay of Biscay, *U-123* met with *U-107*, which was outbound to exchange a codebook and information. *U-123* returned to Lorient on 2 May 1942.[3]

Oberleutnant zur See Georg Lassen entered the area north of Bermuda on 21 March 1942, heading south-west. Overall, the submarine was in the area for ten days, transiting westbound and eastbound. On the first leg, the sub spent five days, exiting north-west of Bermuda towards Hatteras on the 26th. On the return patrol *U-160* re-entered the region on 12 April and motored on a straight course north-east, exiting north-east of Bermuda on 15 April. The patrol for the 10th U-boat Flotilla began in Helgoland on 1 March and ended in its new base in Lorient on 28 April 1942. The patrol began off Newfoundland but pushed south to the US capes. The day after leaving Bermuda astern, on 27 March, Lassen found and sank the *Equipoise*. Off Hatteras *U-160* then sank the *City of New York* on 29th and the *Rio Blanco* on 1 April. Five days later, it damaged the *Bidwell*. On the 9th, the *Malchace* was sunk, followed by the *Ulysses* on the 11th—the ship was *en route* from Australia, carrying evacuees from Japanese attacks in South-east Asia. A day later, *U-160* re-entered the area around Bermuda in a straight trajectory to Lorient.[4]

Born in 1915, Lassen was a member of the Crew of 1935. He began U-boat training in April 1939 and went on to command *U-29*, without conducting war patrols on it. After 328 patrol days on four war patrols, he sank or damaged thirty-one ships of 190,501 tons. For this, he was awarded the Knight's Cross in August 1942, the Oak Leaves in March 1942 and the U-boat War Badge with Diamonds in October 1944. He passed away in 2012 on Mallorca at the age of ninety-six.

U-202 under *Kapitänleutnant* Hans-Heinz Linder entered the area north of Bermuda on 1 April 1942, heading west and south-west by increments until the 6th. At that point the sub turned south, then east from 7 to 10 April, when it exited the region. Sailing for the 1st U-boat Flotilla, *U-202* left on 1 March 1942 as part of the fourth wave of Drumbeat boats aimed at Hatteras and surrounding targets.[5] On 22 March, she encountered and sank the *Athelviscount*, a British ship of 8,882 tons north-east of Bermuda and some 700 miles south-east of Sable Island, Canada. Moving west, the boat sank the British ship the *Loch Don* of 5,249 tons roughly 500 miles north-north-east of Bermuda. On returning towards Europe after the 6th, the submarine was refueled by the U-tanker *U-A* west of the Azores.

Linder was born in 1913 and turned twenty-nine during this patrol. Part of the Crew of 1933, he served as on *U-18* and *U-96* under Lehmann-Willenbrock. In

March 1941, he took command of *U-202*, on which he served for six patrols and 236 patrol days up to September 1942. His total tally was seven ships sunk, for 33,693 tons in aggregate, including the *City of Birmingham* near Bermuda. In late fall 1942, he moved ashore to naval staff duties, and he died on 10 September 1944 at age thirty-one. *U-71* under *Kapitänleutnant* Walter Flachsenberg entered the area north-west of Bermuda heading east on 2 April. The sub had sunk the *Eastmoor*, a British ship of 5,812 tons, the day before. While patrolling the east coast of the US from Hatteras to New York, *U-71* sank the *Ranja* on 17 March followed by the *Oakmar* on the 20th. On the 31st, Flachsenberg found and sank the British ship the *San Gerardo* between New York and Bermuda.

Kapitänleutnant Heinz Hirsacker brought his command, *U-572* on a relatively long patrol north of Bermuda between 3 and 26 April 1942—totaling fifteen days. The sub entered the Bermuda area on 3 April, and the following day the British tanker the *Ensis* of 6,207 tons, which was damaged by gunfire and 20-mm shells. The patrol started off of Newfoundland then went south between Bermuda and the mainland. For over two weeks, the submarine patrolled north-west of Bermuda. During that time, she sank the Panamanian *Desert Light* of 2,368 tons on the 16th, off Virginia, followed by the British *Empire Dryden* of 7,164 tons north north-west of Bermuda on the 20th. The U-tanker *U-459* refueled *U-572* 500 miles north-east of the island. This patrol began for the 3rd U-boat Flotilla on 14 March 1942 in Brest and ended there on 14 May.

Hirsacker was born in 1914 and was a member of the Crew of 1934. He received the U-boat War Badge of 1939. In his early career, he served aboard *U-36* in 1937 and then *U-64* under Schulz and later aboard *U-124* under the same commander. He took over *U-572* in May 1941. Following a number of lackluster patrols and one in which he fabricated the log and remained submerged most of the time, Hirsacker was court-martialed in Paris while being re-assigned to destroyers the *Hans Lody* and the *Z33*. Found guilty of cowardice and sentenced to death, Hirsacker chose to take his own life instead, which he did on 24 April 1943. Over six patrols and 267 patrol days, he sank three ships of 14,813 tons and damaged another of 6,207 for a total of 21,020 tons, all of them in early to mid 1942, and three of them on this patrol.

U-571 under *Kapitänleutnant* Helmut Möhlmann entered the area north of Bermuda on 5 April 1942 for a three-day incursion in which it sank the Norwegian tanker *Koll* on the 6th north-north-west of Bermuda. This was followed by a return voyage across the north of Bermuda from west to east, between 19 and 22 April. The boat sailed for the 3rd U-boat Flotilla on 10 March from La Pallice and returned there on 7 May 1942. Originally, Möhlmann headed for the waters of Newfoundland before heading south to the area off Hatteras, which she reached on about 26 March. On the 29th, the sub sank the British ship the *Hertford* of 10,932 tons, then the *Koll* of 10,044 tons on 6 April, and the *Margaret*, 3,352 tons off Hatteras. *U-571* rendezvoused with *U-459* on 21 April, which would have placed it north of Bermuda at the time—it is more likely that the refueling took place about 25 April and closer to 500 miles north-east of Bermuda.

Born in Kiel in 1913, Möhlmann was a member of the Crew of 1933. Early in his career, which began as a cadet, he served aboard the light cruiser the *Nürnberg* and later the torpedo boat the *Luchs*, joining U-boats in 1940. In that capacity, he served on *U-143*, a training boat, and *U-52* before commissioning *U-571*. Möhlmann's tally was 344 patrol days in eight patrols, all of them on *U-571*. Between August 1941 and July 1942, he sank or damaged eight ships of 58,563 tons.[6]

After his seagoing career, he moved to the U-boat headquarters staff, and the Naval Academy in Berlin. This was followed by command of the 14th U-boat Flotilla in Narvik Norway from 1944 to war's end, after which he was imprisoned for four months. He was awarded the Knight's Cross in April 1943 and the U-boat Front Clasp in September 1944. He died in 1977 at the age of sixty-three.

Kapitänleutnant Hans Ostermann brought his submarine *U-754* briefly into the Bermuda area between 5 and 8 April 1942—just long enough to sink the Norwegian tanker the *Kollskegg* of 9,858 tons on the 6th. Aside from this, it was a highly successful patrol in which he also sank the British tanker the *British Prudence* off Newfoundland and St. Pierre. Following this Canadian foray, the sub moved off the Hatteras area in the end of March. There, it attacked three barges and their tug with gunfire before sinking the *Barnegat* and the *Alleghany* (both barges) and the tug the *Menominee*, and damaging the barge the *Ontario*.

Thereafter, on 1 April, Oestermann sank the tanker *Tiger* off Virginia, followed two days later by the *Otho*. After sinking the *Kollskegg U-754* returned for Brest, where it was based for the 5th U-boat Flotilla. The patrol began 7 March and ended on 25 April 1942. Born in 1913, Oestermann was a member of the Crew of 1933 and turned twenty-nine during this patrol. He would drown within the year, the victim of Allied anti-submarine efforts north-east of Boston. Early in his career, Oestermann served aboard the destroyer the *Hermann Shoemann* before joining U-boats in July 1940. His only boat before commissioning *U-754* was *U-151*. Overall, he accrued 135 patrol days in three war-going patrols and sank or damaged 14 ships of 56,149 tons. He received no decorations before being sunk by a Royal Canadian Air Force Hudson on 31 July 1942.

Oberleutnant zur See Eberhard Greger brought his command, *U-85* into the Bermuda area on 6 April, on route to being sunk off Hatteras a week or so later. The incursion began north-east of Bermuda up to the 7th, then there is a dog-leg south towards Bermuda, a change of course westward on the 8th, and then more westward progress to the 9th, when the boat exited the theater for the US coast. *U-85* sailed for the 3rd U-boat Flotilla in La Pallice on 21 March 1942. On 10 April, *U-85* is believed to have sunk the *Christian Knudsen*, a Norwegian tanker of 4,904 tons near the US coast. Then, USS *Roper* made radar contact with *U-85* east of Roanoke Island, Virginia and the destroyer went in for an attack.

The submarine's torpedo attack missed the mark and the *Roper* caught the surfaced sub in a searchlight and heavy gunfire, which killed the sub's gun crew. Jittery US crew depth-charged the waters around thirty-one survivors, and some of the bodies were too badly maimed by machine gun fire to be retrieved. Sixteen of the sub's crew went down with their boat—the first U-boat sunk by a US Navy ship in World War Two. Greger was born in 1915 in the Netherlands and joined the Crew of 1935. After serving aboard the destroyer the *Wolfgang Zenker* he moved to U-boats in October 1939 and served aboard *U-110* and *U-30*. Between August 1941 and March 1942, he served 137 days on four patrols aboard *U-85*. His total tally was three ships sunk for 15,060 tons. Greger received no decorations. He was twenty-six years of age when killed.

Kapitänleutnant Erich Topp brought *U-552* into the Bermuda region on a straight line of four days north of the island. During the submarine's return from the US coast off Hatteras *U-552* entered the area north-west of Bermuda on 11 April and motored north-east until leaving on 14 April 1942. While he did not sink vessels during his tangent north of Bermuda, Topp managed to attack seven ships during this patrol: the *Ocana*, the *David H. Atwater*, the *Byron D. Benson*, the *British Splendour*, the whale factory ship the *Lancing*, the *Atlas*, and the *Tamaulipas*. Except for the *Ocana* sinking which occurred outbound, these attacks occurred off Hatteras between 25 March and 10 April 1942—the last, the *Tamaulipas,* occurred a day before his voyage back to France for the 7th U-boat Flotilla out of St. Nazaire. The patrol began on 7 March as one of eleven U-boats comprising the fourth wave of Drumbeat. It ended on 27 April 1942.

Born in Hannover in 1914, Topp was a member of the Crew of 1934. After a stint on the light cruiser the *Karlsruhe*, he joined U-boats in October 1937. He joined *U-46*, then *U-57*, and finally *U-552* which was known as the 'Red Devil Boat.' He accrued 352 patrol days between July 1940 and July 1942, sinking a highly impressive thirty-six ships of 198,650 tons and a further four ships damaged for 32,317 tons. Topp is, along with Hardegen and Suhren, one of the better-known U-boat commanders. He moved ashore as commander of the 27th U-boat Flotilla and wrote battle instructions for new U-boat commanders. At war's end, he was in command of *U-2513* off Horten Norway; he also commanded the XXI Elektro boat *U-3010*. After a stint as an architect following the war, he rejoined the navy and served with NATO, retiring in 1969 as a *Konteradmiral*. He passed away the day after Christmas in 2005 at the age of ninety-one.

Kapitänleutnant Günther Heydemann spent nearly three weeks between 11 and 30 April 1942 in the area north and north-west of Bermuda. The only result of this patrol was the sinking of the American ship *Robin Hood* of 6,887 tons by combined torpedo and gunfire on the 16th north-west of Bermuda at the outside of the sub's patrol area. Starting on the 11th, Heydemann moved south-west until the 15th, then north, then west, south, and south-east, reaching its closest point to Bermuda on 24 April. From there, the boat proceeded north and north-east along a similar track it had arrived with. *U-575* sailed for the 7th U-boat Flotilla out of St. Nazaire on 24 March and returned there on 14 May 1942.[7]

Heydemann was born in 1914 and was a Crew of 1933. His first stints were aboard the *Schlesien* and the *Schleswig-Holstein*, then he joined U-boats in April 1940. After serving on the *U-69* under Metzler, he commissioned *U-575* in mid-1941. Over eight patrols, he accrued 395 patrol days and sank or damaged eight ships of 48,920 tons. He received the Knight's Cross in July of 1943, after which he moved ashore to command the 23rd and 25th U-boat training flotillas until the war's end. Günther Heydemann died in 1986 at age seventy-one.

Oberleutnant zur See Ludwig Forster brought *U-654* on a complicated nineteen-day patrol literally around Bermuda, passing so close to the island on 29 April 1942 that he must have seen St. David's or Gibbs Hill lights. On 10 April, *U-654* entered north-east of the island and headed west for five days until 14 April. Less than a week later, on the 20th, the boat approached from the west going north-east and sank the *Steel Maker* (US flagged, 6,176 tons) and then the same day the *Agra* (Swedish, 4,569 tons). Before leaving the *Steel Maker*, Forster promised the merchant skipper that the sub would radio the survivors' position; however, he failed to do so and two men died in the lifeboat voyage. The following day, Forster changed course heading south until the 22nd to a point just west-north-west of Bermuda. Then he headed west for two days, south until the 25th, and due east until 28 April. At that point, *U-654* turned north to pass very close to the east of Bermuda, and then north-north-west until 1 May. Thereafter, Forster opted to head north-east until 3 May at which point he exited the region to the north-east of the island.

At the time, and for the balance of his career, Ludwig Forster's rank was *Oberleutnant zur See*. He achieved the Iron Cross Second Class on the first month of the war, and was killed on 22 August 1942 north of Colon, Panama. All forty-four men were killed when a US B 18 Digby aircraft attacked the submarine. Aside from the successes on this patrol, he sank a 900-ton Allied warship in a total of four patrols of 162 sea days. The Type VIIC boat *U-582* was brought into the region for a near-record twenty days by its commander, *Kapitänleutnant* Werner Schulte. The sub patrolled to the north-east of Bermuda from 13 April until the 26th, then went south-east of the island, south-west, and finally west on 2 May. There were several sharp changes (that resembled zigzags). *U-582* headed west-north-west from the 13th to the 19th, passing close north of Bermuda on the 17th. Then, it turned east from the 20th to the 23rd, then south-west to a point east of Bermuda on the 27th. For two days, it motored south-east, then west to the 30th, then north-east to pass again close to the east of the island. Thereafter, it turned west and exited the region heading towards Hatteras on 2 May 1942.

Having begun its patrol on 19 March, intending to escort the German blockade-runner the *Rio Grande* from Japan into Europe, the boat instead patrolled to the west. Towards the end of April, *U-582* was refueled by *U-459* roughly 500 miles north-east of Bermuda, which would explain its proximity to that island. There were no ships struck by Schulte on this patrol, which ended in Brest on 24 May 1942. *U-582* sailed from and to Brest, where it was based with the 1st U-boat Flotilla. Its only commander was *Korvettenkapitän* Schulte, whose career total was six ships sunk for 38,826 GRT and one 46-ton warship lost aboard a transport ship sunk.

Schulte was not able to engage any Allied ships during this sixty-seven-day patrol, which ranged from off Nova Scotia to Hatteras south to Bermuda.

Werner Schulte was born in Kiel on 7 November 1912 and joined the *Kriegsmaine* in 1937 as the 'A' Crew of that year. After serving on the *Köningsberg*, he moved ashore to a staff position in Norway. He joined U-boats in October 1940. As part of his training, he served under Robert Gysae on *U-98*. He took the sub on four patrols and sank six ships with her. His promotion from *Kapitänleutnant* to *Korvettenkapitän* was posthumous, as Schulte was killed with forty-six others when *U-582* was found and sunk by Catalina aircraft on 5 October 1942, off the south-west of Iceland.

Kapitänleutnant Rolf Mützelburg brought *U-203* across the northern portion of Bermuda homeward bound between 15 and 18 April 1942. It was a straight line from south-west to north-east. The boat sailed for the 1st U-boat Flotilla in Brest on 12 March and returned there on 30 April. It was in the fourth wave of Drumbeat boats. Along the way to the Cape Hatteras area, *U-203* was refueled by the U-boat tanker U-A on about 23 March in the vicinity of the Azores. Along the US seaboard, U-203 had four successes: the *San Delfino* on 10 April, the *Harry F. Sinclair Jr.* the following day (it was repaired), then *Stanvac Melbourne* the day after that, and finally the *Empire Thrush* off Cape Hatteras on the 14th—the day before it returned via northern Bermuda. Mützelburg was born in 1913 in Kiel and was twenty-eight at the time of this patrol. He served on minesweepers for two years and joined U-boats in October 1939. Early experience was obtained on *U-10* and *U-100* under Schepke before he commissioned *U-203* in February 1941. In July 1942, he earned the Knight's Cross with Oak Leaves. Aboard *U-203*, he served 242 days on eight patrols and managed to sink or damage twenty-two ships worth 99,013 tons. His life was cut short on 11 September 1942 when he fatally dove from the conning tower.[8]

16 April 1942: SS *Robin Hood*

The US-flagged steamship the *Robin Hood* was built by the Skinner and Eddy Corporation of Seattle in December 1919 as yard number 73. She was commissioned and built for the US Shipping Board. She was 6,887 gross registered tons, 425 feet long, 55 feet wide and 33.5 feet deep. The ship was propelled by a steam turbine General Electric engine that developed 637 net horsepower and propelled the steel hull at 10.5 knots. In the spring of 1942, the *Robin Hood* was owned by Seas Shipping Company, Inc. of Corlandet Street, New York. The firm was also known as the Robin Line. At the outset of World War Two, the firm had eleven ships, all but one of them beginning with the name Robin. They were in a service from New York to Baltimore, Cape Town and Mombasa, East Africa.[1]

According to *The Oakland Tribune* of 28 April 1925, the ship was then operated by the Argonaut Line and was making great speed between Baltimore and Oakland with mostly steel and iron products. Argonaut Line was a division of the American South African Line of 26 Beaver Street, New York. Their main route was to the Pacific.[2] In March 1927, the *Robin Hood* was back in Oakland, according to the *Tribune* of 21 March 1927. Her captain was named McKenzie and she carried a general cargo from Baltimore to Parr Terminal. By 1927, the ship was owned by the Robin Line. The ship was bound as far north as British Columbia, then back to the US east coast via the Panama Canal. Her call was newsworthy enough that in both instances, they were accompanied by photos.[3]

During World War Two, but before the US was directly involved, the *Robin Hood* was reported sighting 'a suspicious vessel under Swedish colours' on 12 November 1942 in the South Atlantic. This turned out to be the SS *Tisnaren* laden with Allied airplanes but the British took note of the report and sank HMS *Devonshire* to investigate.[4] In March 1942, the *Robin Hood* loaded a cargo of 8,725 light tons. This included 4,500 tons of chrome ore, 800 tons of asbestos, and general cargo including sisal, skins, wood, gold and copper concentrates, liquor, cocoa, and wolfram ore. Her draft forward was 27 feet and aft 28 feet.

The *Robin Hood* loaded in East Africa and proceeded to Boston via Cape Town and Trinidad for bunkers. The voyage went uneventfully except that on 9 April it sent a radio message about another suspicious vessel in the North Atlantic, possibly compromising her own position in doing so. The ship was unarmed, so there were no gunners aboard, and there were only two lifeboats. It is not known whether there were rafts aboard, but since there is no mention of them it can be assumed there were none. On her final voyage the ship's master was Captain John A. O'Pray. There were thirty-seven men under him. All of them were US citizens except for able bodied seaman Frederick C. Pedersen of Denmark and second cook Pedro A. Peralta of the Philippines. There were also two passengers on board, named Hall M. Newhall and George Davis, so the total number of persons on board was forty.

The ship left Trinidad on Tuesday, 7 April, with orders to pass east of Grenada and Barbados, then 'NW to 32-01 N, 66-45 W; N. to 39-01 N, 66-45 W.' On the night of Wednesday, 15 April 1942, she was approaching its destination, as it was 210 nautical miles south-east of Nantucket and 395 nautical miles north-west of Bermuda. Her course at the time was 343 degrees true north-north-west, and Captain O'Pray was adhering to the British zigzag patterns eleven and thirty-four. Speed was 10.7 knots through the water. It was a dark and cloudless night, with south-westerly winds in the 14 to 20 knot range, a choppy sea, and lots of phosphorus in the ship's wake. There were two lookouts, one on each wing of the bridge, with Third Officer Richard T. Chapin manning the starboard bridge wing.

Unbeknown to them, the *Robin Hood* was being stalked by *U-575* under Günther Heydemann. At 9.42 p.m., O'Pray was in the chart room on the bridge when Second Officers Curtis W. Denton called him to say that a torpedo fired from astern had just passed along the starboard side close by. O'Pray ordered a hard turn to port, but then another torpedo struck the side at the Number Three hatch. This caused the boiler room to explode and filled the air with cordite and steam. Some of the crew believed that a third torpedo struck 50 feet behind the first; however, others believed that the concussion was actually the ship tearing apart as a result of the first blow. The trauma to the ship's hull was so extreme that it 'lifted the deck and folded it over', as well as blowing out hatches one and two forward and knocking down the foremast.

Within a minute of the first torpedo strike, seawater covered the well deck and the ship rapidly began to sink. Also, debris from the explosions forward sent metal shards raining down on deck, giving the impression that the ship was being fired on by shells. According to several sailors the forward mast in particular shattered and rained debris down on deck: '...there was a great deal of gear raining down on deck from the shattered mast, but they did not observe any shell hits.'

Subsequent interviewers commented on the 'nervous condition of the master compared with the composed bearing of the crew members, especially that of an ex-British naval rating of 4 years' experience, 1914–1918,' and that 'It is believed that the vessel was sunk as the result of a single torpedo explosion, causing the vessel to break amidships and that there was no shelling by the submarine.' Captain O'Pray had radio operator Benjamin Pinz send the rather vague message 'SOS POSITION UNKNOWN,' however since the aerials were down it is doubtful whether this message was received ashore (it was not). In any event, O'Pray did not enjoy a strong working relationship with Pinz, who along with messman Adolph P. Moses 'had been trouble makers on the voyage prior to the attack, grumbling at and criticizing the orders received from their officers.' O'Pray did manage to send the confidential codes overboard in a weighted canvas bag.[5]

O'Pray claims that he saw 'no more than a vague outline of the submarine' off the starboard side. He also reported two submarines signaling each other, though this report was discounted by interviewers. Though O'Pray was convinced his ship was attacked by two submarines, no one else on board was so convinced. In any event, a submarine shone a searchlight on the ship, possibly to learn its name. The second mate (Denton) felt it was a carbide lamp. Subsequent interviewers noted that 'In the darkness and excitement the description of the submarine is lacking in details.'[6]

As the starboard lifeboat was smashed, twenty-six men out of a complement of forty (twenty-four sailors including the two passengers) managed to get away in the port lifeboat. The boat got away at 9.45 p.m. and two minutes later, at 9.47 p.m., The *Robin Hood* broke in half just forward of the Number Three cargo hold and sank. According to O'Pray, he was 'blown off bridge and hauled into lifeboat.' This might account for, or have contributed to, his nerves. Up until that point, she had been settling on an even keel. Once broken in two, the bow raised then sank, and the stern briefly floated with the poop raised in the air before it too sank. The submarine motored off at 9.50 p.m., without Heydemann having interacted with the survivors.

On board the boat the mutinous behavior of some elements of the crew (Pinz and Moses) continued to harass the already-stressed O'Pray: 'Considerable difficulty was experienced in handling the boat the first night due to a smashed rudder and the failure of messman Adolfph Moses and radio operator Benjamin Pinz to obey orders and remain quiet in the boat.' Fortunately with the rising of a warm sun the situation improved: '….a steering oar and sail were rigged and these crew members brought under control.' It would be over a week before help arrived. During that time, O'Pray managed to keep morale high and rationed his supplies well. As for the fate of the fourteen sailors and officers left behind, little is known. Unless they managed to get away in a damaged lifeboat or life raft, they would have been either killed in the explosion or drowned when the ship sank. Apparently distracted by the broken rudder and the heavy seas, the twenty-six men in the other lifeboat did not linger to determine their fate.

Among the dead, the most senior was Third Officer Richard T. Chapin, followed by bosun John Mulligan. There was an able-bodied seaman (Isias Enduzy), two ordinary seamen (Freitag and Ramirez), 1st, 2nd and 4th assistant engineers (Seaman, Allen, and Lindley), oiler (Caronias), two firemen (Glemby and Nickersen), a wiper named Hoffman, chief cook Wright, and messman Sherrad. The three engineers were almost certainly killed in the engine room when the boiler room exploded.[7]

After seven days, twelve hours, and forty-five minutes, the US Navy destroyer USS *Greer* came upon the men in the lifeboat. The transformation of morale in the boat was considerable as the *Greer*'s commander reported:

> It was notable at the time the survivors were recovered that the condition of the boat was very good and that discipline of the crew was excellent. It was considered that the Master, Captain John A. O'Pray is deserving of special credit for the manner in which he conducted this crowded lifeboat. He stated that about five day's rations and three days' water supply was on hand when rescued.[8]

The USS *Greer*, DD 145, was under command of Lieutenant Commander L. H. Frost. In the fall of 1941, she fired on a German ship three months before the US officially entered World War Two, in what became known as the '*Greer* incident.' About seven weeks earlier, the destroyer rescued thirteen men from the merchant ship the *Equipoise* on 1 March 1942. The ship had been sunk by *U-160* off Cape Henry on 27 February. USS *Greer* was built by William Cramp and Sons Ship and Engine Building in Philadelphia; it launched on 1 August 1918 as part of the Wickes-class. She was decommissioned (laid up) between 1922 and 1930 and between 1937 and 1939.

According to the *Greer*'s War Diary of Thursday, 23 April, at 10.06 a.m., she 'Sighted flare ahead and small boat with sail up. Proceeded to investigate.' At 10.20 a.m., she 'Approached boat and picked up twenty-six survivors from torpedoed ship SS *ROBIN HOOD*.' At 10.30 a.m., she 'Shelled lifeboat and destroyed it.' At noon, they received orders from the Commandant of Bermuda, Admiral James, to make for that island. The position where the *Greer* rescued the *Robin Hood* survivors was roughly 50 miles west south-west of where the ship had been sunk. It was roughly 300 nautical miles north north-west of Bermuda. At 3.40 p.m., the *Greer* informed Bermuda that their ETA was the following day and that two of the merchant sailors would require medical attention.

At 1.12 p.m. on Friday, 24 April, the *Greer*'s men sighted Bermuda. Just after noon they were sighted by two US Navy planes and exchanged the password signals. At 3.16 p.m., the ship entered the mine-swept channel to Bermuda and at 3.52 p.m., she moored alongside USS *Altair*. By 4.30 p.m., all twenty-six survivors of the *Robin Hood* had been transferred 'to United States Authorities in Hamilton, Bermuda.' *The Oakland Tribune* reported that the *Robin Hood* men (the ship's name had to be censored) were 'safe in port today after spending eight days in a lifeboat,' based on an Associated Press wire story that went out from Hamilton on 25 April.[9] The *New York Times* scooped the story on 24 April, publishing it the following day.

Saying that the group was the third landed on the island in as many days (the others were from the *Agra* (thirty-three men), and the *Derryheen* (eight men) landed 22 April), *The Times* noted that 'Three were hospitalized and two were placed in the infirmary in the Sailors' Home. The men did not suffer a water shortage, but were without food for several days before they were picked up, their biscuits having been damaged by sea water....' The article continues: 'Some of the men were described as "in very bad shape." Most of them are suffering from swollen feet. It is understood that the men who were lost died in the lifeboat.'[10] This last statement contradicts the notion that twenty-six men entered the lifeboat at the time of the attack and twenty-six exited it—all alive—in Bermuda, and that at least three men died in the explosion in the engine room.

The one newspaper with best access to survivors was *The Bermuda Gazettte and Colonist Daily*, which reported:

> The latest band of men to weather the ordeal of a torpedoing have undergoing extreme hardship and are in worse shape than the other crews brought to the islands on Wednesday. They were eight days at sea in a lifeboat, and when picked up were in a weak condition. Upon their arrival here, three of the men were sent to the King Edward VII memorial Hospital and two were placed in the infirmary at the Bermuda Sailor's Home. It was only recently that the infirmary wing was made ready. It has been a godsend ... Most of the men's water and biscuits were lost overboard during their struggle in the lifeboat against heavy seas. They suffered no dire shortage of water but were without food for several days. ... Most of the men needed immediate rest and sustenance. However some of them were dancing at the Naval Recreation Rooms last night, none the worse for their ordeal.[11]

17–19 April 1942: Four U-boats

Kapitänleutnant Heinrich Bleichrodt brought *U-109* on its second patrol to Bermuda for ten days in total, starting on 17 April and ending on 17 May. Firstly, *U-109* headed west, starting at a point north-east of Bermuda, until the 19th and 20th, when it turned south. It then continued west until 21 May when it exited the area for Hatteras. On his voyage inbound, Bleichrodt sank the *Harpagon* north of Bermuda on 20 April—she was a British ship of 5,719 tons. On the very same day as Schacht, *U-109* under Bleichrodt, aged thirty-two, headed from Savannah to Bermuda on 26 April and exiting the same way on 30 May 1942. He sank two ships off the coast of Miami: the *La Paz* of British registry and the *Laertes* of Dutch flag, on 1 and 3 May respectively. Bliechrodt's total for this patrol was three ships of 18,092 tons. The *La Paz*, however, was merely damaged for 6,548 tons.

Bleichrodt graduated in the crew of 1933. His decorations include the Knight's Cross early in the war followed by an addition of the Oak Leaves in September 1942 and the U-boat War Badge with Diamonds a month later. In January 1945, he was given the War Merit Cross Second Class with Swords. His total tonnage was an impressive twenty-four ships of 151,260 tons, plus a warship of 1,060 tons and two ships damaged for 11,684 GRT. *U-109*, on its fifth of nine patrols, was sailing from and to Lorient for the 2nd U-boat Flotilla. The patrol began on 25 March and ended on 3 June.[1] Early in his career, Bleichrodt served on both the *Gorch Foch* and the *Admiral Hipper*, moving to U-boats in October 1939. He also served as first watch officer of *U-564* under Teddy Suhren. In one patrol as commander of *U-48* in 1940, he sank eight ships of 43,106 tons. Moving ashore in July 1943, he went on to command the 27th and 22nd U-boat training flotillas. He lived until 1977, passing away in Munich at the age of sixty-seven.

Adalbert 'Adi' Schnee led the next patrol into the region on 17 April 1942, remaining between Hatteras and Bermuda for most of eighteen days. The day after arriving north-east of Bermuda, *U-201* torpedoed the neutral Argentinian ship the *Victoria*, a tanker of 7,417 tons. The ship did not sink; her crew re-boarded her and took it to New York, where the US authorities eventually requisitioned it. On 21 April, Schnee sank the Norwegian *Bris* of 2,027 tons east of Bermuda and, two days later, the British-flagged *Derryheen* of 7,217 tons as well as the US-flagged *San Jacinto* of 6,069 tons the following day. For the next four days, the sub headed north then west towards Hatteras, leaving the region on 27 April. The *San Jacinto* was noteworthy in that it was a steam passenger ship carrying 183 persons (104 of them passengers), of whom fourteen were killed. The 169 survivors included thirty-two women and children huddled together on rafts and boats then sent an SOS via portable radio the following day. They were picked up on 23 April and landed on the next day in Norfolk. The *Derryheen* sinking was remarkable inasmuch as the gun crew of the merchant ship managed to fire back at the submarine, though it might be a stretch to call it a duel.

U-201, a Type IXC boat sailing in the 1st U-boat Flotilla out of Brest, was on its sixth of nine war patrols. On 23 April, Schnee left the region with a patrol total of three ships sunk for 5,313 and one of 7,417 damaged. However, the *Victoria* was towed into port by destroyers, which rescued the crew. The patrol began in Brest on 24 March 1942 and ended there on 21 May. On the way home, *U-201* again transited north of Bermuda, this time without sinking any ships. On 3 May, Schnee came east from Hatteras and then north-east, all to the north-west of Bermuda. Heading north until the 5th, he then turned east until 7 May, when it left the area to the north-east of the island. Schnee was a member of Crew 34; twenty-eight years of age at the time, he survived the war, dying in Hamburg in 1982 at the age of sixty-eight. Following this patrol, he was awarded Knight's Cross with Oak Leaves, a rare distinction. His total tally was twenty-one ships for 90,189 GRT, two auxiliary war ships for 5,700 tons, and three ships damaged for nearly 29,000 tons. He had begun his U-boat career in May 1937 and served under 'Silent Otto' Kretschmer aboard *U-23*. Moving ashore after his 7th patrol, Schnee led operations against convoys. The symbol for his boat was a snowman with a Knight's Cross around its neck, which was painted on the conning tower—this is because Schnee means snow in German. Following retirement from a commercial job in Germany, he directed a sailing school on the Mediterranean island of Elba, where Napoleon had been incarcerated in previous wars.[2]

Kapitänleutnant Freiherr Sigfried von Forstner entered the region on the Type VIIC boat *U-402* for a short incursion in the north-west quadrant on 25 April 1942. He was cruising off the Carolinas, actually closer to Bermuda, when he turned south for a day until the 26th. On 28 April, he turned north-east when still just east of Savannah. That evening, he ducked out of the region after four days, heading back to the Cape Hatteras area. The following day, *U-402* was sighted by Lieutenant (junior grade) Robert A. Proctor roughly twenty miles south of Cape Lookout, in the Carolinas. Having been vectored to the submarine by radar, the US Navy PBY Catalina aircraft swooped in to drop four depth charges, but the submarine escaped.[3]

Two days after that, *U-402* located and sank the Soviet ship *Ashkhabad* of 5,284 tons, followed on 2 May by sinking the USS *Cythera*, a yacht converted to patrol duties by the Americans and named PY 26 for Patrol Yacht. She was 602 tons, and von Forstner imprisoned two captives from her. Before entering the Bermuda region, *U-402* had sunk the *Empire Progress* of the UK on 13 April. She weighted 5,249 tons and contributed to von Forstner's overall career total of fourteen ships sunk of 70,434 tons, not including the *Cythera*.

U-402's patrol began on 26 March and ended in St. Nazaire, where it was based with the 3rd U-boat Flotilla, on 29 May 1942. *U-402*'s only commander was von Forstner, who took her on eight patrols totalling 349 days, right up to her demise on 13 October 1943 when she was destroyed with all hands by aircraft from the escort carrier USS *Card* in the Central Atlantic. Von Forstner was promoted to *Korvettenkapitän* a year after his incursion into the Bermuda and earned the Knight's Cross in February of that year. He was a member of the Crew of 1930 before serving on the *Nürnberg* during the first year of the war. He joined U-boats in April 1940 and served under the ace Kretschmer on *U-99* before commissioning his own boat, *U-402*. Thirty-one years of age when he dipped into the area, he was thirty-three when killed, having been born in Hannover on 19 September 1910.

Kapitänleutnant Hans-Dieter Heinicke brought his command *U-576* north-east of Bermuda starting on 19 April 1942 for four days. During that time, he managed to sink the US freighter *Pipestone County* of 5,102 tons north of Bermuda on 21 April. *U-576*'s patrol into the region looks like a horseshoe, as the sub motored south-west, then west, then north-west out of the area on 22 April. *U-576* sailed for the 7th U-boat Flotilla in St. Nazaire on 29 March. It was acting in concert with a group of at least eight U-boats whose purpose it was to determine whether ships were using routes away from the US mainland, to catch, intercept, and sink them. The other boats in the group were *U-135*, *U-213*, *U-404*, *U-432*, *U-455*, *U-566*, and *U-653*.

After waiting several days, most boats moved closer to the coast; however, Heinicke stuck further out and damaged the *Tropic Star*, which was ironically carrying survivors of his earlier attack on the *Pipestone County*. The latter attack occurred on 24 April south of Nantucket; the *Tropic Star* managed to make it to Boston despite the torpedo hit, which was a dud, saving the survivors the ignominy of being torpedoed twice by the same submarine. Several days later, *U-576* struck for a third time, this time sinking the Norwegian *Taborfjell* of 1,339 tons east of Cape Cod on 30 April. On 1 May, the sub tried to attack a troop convoy but Allied aircraft protected the precious shipment 80 miles from Cape Sable, Canada, so *U-576* resumed its course back to France, where it arrived on 16 May 1942.

Hans-Dieter Heinicke was born in 1913 and celebrated his twenty-ninth birthday two days after his return to France. It was to be his last, as *U-576* was caught by USS *Unicoi* and two Kingfisher aircraft off Cape Hatteras on 15 July that summer; all forty-five men on board the submarine perished. Heinicke was a member of the Crew of 1933 and served as watch officer of the U-boat tender *Wiechsel* in 1939 and 1940, at which point he began U-boat training. He served on *U-73* and helped commission *U-576*, the only boat he served on and on which he accrued 163 patrol days over five missions. His career tally was six ships sunk or damaged for 34,907 ton. Hienicke received no decorations over his career.[4]

20 April 1942:
SS *Agra* and SS *Empire Dryden*

SS *Agra*

The Swedish diesel motor ship *Agra* was built by Götaverken A/B, in Göteborg, Sweden, in 1925—she was the 389th vessel built by them. In 1933, Götaverken was the busiest shipyard of the world measured in launched gross tons. The ship's owners at the time of her demise were the Swedish East Asiatic Company (*Svenska Ostasiatiska Kompaniet* A/B), also of Göteborg. The SEAC, as it was known in English, was founded by members of the Wallenberg and Brostrom families with help from the Swedish Government in 1907 and lasted until 1978.[1]

The *Agra* was 4,659 GRT, making her a mid-sized vessel capable of carrying 7,905 deadweight tons of cargo. She was propelled by twin diesel engines of 625 net horsepower, which provided 12.5 knots of speed. Her dimensions were 392 feet in length, 52.5 feet wide, and 25 foot deep. The funnel of the Swedish East Asiatic Company was yellow, with a blue circle and three crowns inside of it, surrounded on each corner by one of the letters 'S.O.A.K.' in dark blue.[2] At the time of her loss, the *Agra* was sailing under British Admiralty routing instructions.

The *Agra* left Philadelphia on 18 April 1942, bound for Alexandria via Cape Town and Suez. Her cargo consisted of 6,666 tons' worth of nitrate, tanks, beer, airplanes, truck chassis,' machinery, benzene, and gasoline. Some of the cargo was carried in twenty cases on deck. The only armament was the Captain's .45 automatic pistol and another hand gun for shooting fish with, as well as thirty-six-year-old Captain Sture Selander's dog, which was named Garbo. In addition to the regular crew of thirty-nine men of mostly Swedes, the *Agra* carried seven members of the American Field Service who were going, some of them from the mid-West, to drive ambulances at the North African front. These young men included Carl Adam, aged twenty, and James Atkins, twenty-one, both of Madison Wisconsin, as well as Jacob Vollrath, nineteen, of Sheboygan, Wisconsin.[3] Adams parents were Reverend and Mrs. Oscar M. Adam of Madison. The other volunteers were Grafton Fay, William Eberhart, Peter Brooks, and George Lyon.[4] Fay and Brooks were from the Boston area—Brooks graduated from Harvard in the class of 1940. His parents were the Gordon Brooks' of Brookline.

Grafton Fay, twenty-eight, was from Westwood, Massachusetts and was the group leader. He graduated from Milton Academy and was in the class of 1933 at Lenox School. In March 1940, he married Mary Armory Eliot of Chestnut Hill.[5] In an article about his experience after the war, Carl Adam wrote that he was a copy editor at *The Daily Cardinal* newspaper in Madison, having graduated from the University of Wisconsin there, when an article about the American Field Service crossed his desk. He filled out the application attached to the press announcement; by April 1942, he arrived in New York ready to deploy to Egypt, where he would eventually end up in charge of public relations with his unit of the French army as well as an editor of an overseas service magazine.[6]

The merchant marine officers and crew consisted of thirty-two men who were mostly Swedish, but included an Australian third engineer, two Norwegians, one Dutchman, a Dane, a Belgian, a Latvian, and an Irishman.[7] The chief mate, Odd Graaf, and the chief engineer, Henry Granber, were both Swedish. On the evening of Monday, 20 April, *Agra* was proceeding on a course of 235 degrees, and making 11 knots, with a north-westerly wind from astern. The ship was painted wartime gray, had no Swedish or neutral markings on its side, and was not flying an ensign. The captain was set to resume a zigzag course. In the words of Carl Adam, 'the sun was shining and the ocean was comparatively quiet, although the winds was blowing.'[8] There were lookouts—two on the bridge and one in the crow's nest—but none of them were equipped with binoculars.

The ship had motored 400 miles south-east of Cape May at the entrance to the Delaware River and was only 225 nautical miles north-north-west of Bermuda. In the words of Carl Adam, 'our ship was unarmed and not convoyed, and although there had been a submarine watch posted earlier in the day, the captain had relaxed his vigilance.' Captain Selander was not above using the young volunteers to stand lookout duty, as Adam continues:

About 3 p.m. the second day out, Peter Brooks, my watch partner, and I were told to stand down after one hour of a two-hour stint on the bridge, looking for the telltale 'feather' of a submarine periscope. We were supposedly far enough east on our sixteen-thousand-mile journey, by way of the Cape of Good Hope in South Africa, to be relatively safe. Pete and I decided to continue a chess match on the starboard second deck. I was two games behind. We were in full uniform and wearing trench coats from our watch stint. The others, in rolled up shirtsleeves, were playing cards in the dining salon. Two and one-half hours after our watch, at 5.30 p.m., without warning, a torpedo slammed into our port side amidships. It sounded like someone whacking an overturned dishpan with a brass drumstick. I watched stupefied momentarily as a beautiful, orange-red wall of flame fingered its way a hundred feet up a curtain of blue sky. Then I ran for my lifejacket, reposing in my cabin because we 'were out of the sub belt,' and a precaution-packed musette bag of emergency items, then dashed for my lifeboat being launched. I left my typewriter and camera.

The torpedo is believed to have been fired from 3,000 to 4,000 yards off the port side. It was sent from *U-654* under *Oberleutnant zur See* Ludwig Forster, aged twenty-six, who sank 18,655 tons worth of Allied shipping. Forster had sunk the American 6,176-ton steamship *Steelmaker* earlier on the same day. He then rendezvoused with *U-572* under *Kapitänleutnant* Heinz Hirsacker who had also sunk a ship earlier in the same day—the *Empire Dryden*, British, of 7,164 tons. For whatever reason, when he saw the smoke of a new steamship—the *Agra*, it turned out—he graciously vectored his colleague Forster to the new prey. Forster needed no further invitation and 'ran off at high speed to the east' according to his attack diary, or KTB. When he finally spotted the ship, Forster wrote 'comes in sight out of a rain squall. Coming exactly towards me.' At 4.20 p.m., *U-654* dived for attack. At 4.23 p.m., Forster fired a double torpedo shot from tubes one and two. According to him, 'both torpedoes hit.' He said he aimed for 'the bridge and after mast' and 'two torpedoes shot because cargo observed to consist of barrels.'[9]

The torpedo penetrated on the port side of the *Agra* between Number Four hold and the engine room and 'the damage appeared to be deep in the ship. Flames were seen coming from Number Five hold. The ship listed to port and plunged stern first.'[10] There were an additional 116 pounds of aviation fuel stored on deck, which appears to have ignited. Captain Selander was busy in the last few minutes of his life. He ensured that the radio operator transmitted four 'SSS' messages, for 'submarine sighted surfaced'; however, there was no acknowledgement from shore, and the naval officials have no records of having received the transmissions.[11] Selander threw the confidential codes overboard so that they would not be captured by the enemy, but then he rushed below to save his dog Garbo. As the ship only remained afloat for about 3.5 minutes, Adam is convinced that this act of compassion cost the captain his life. A reporter for *The Royal Gazette and Colonist Daily* was told by survivors that Selander 'was still on the bridge directing orders to his crew to save themselves' up to the last minutes.[12]

Selander was not the only one to perish in the next few minutes. The Australian Third Engineer George Rogers never made it out of the ship—he was not seen from the time of impact. Crewmates and fellow Swedes, Lars Larson, steward, Hugo Anderson, electrician, Bertil Gustavson, motorman, and Julian Bogarth, a Belgian able-bodied seaman, all went down with the *Agra* or were drowned as the benzene and gasoline spread rapidly across the ocean around the ship.[13] According to the Mansfield Ohio *New Journal* on 24 April, survivors told authorities in Bermuda that 'no explosion occurred when the torpedo struck, but burning oil gushed from the freighter in a steady stream, lighting up the surface of the water for some time and burning several of the survivors while they were swimming around waiting to be taken into the lifeboat.' Adam added that 'only one of our 22-foot lifeboats, each accommodating twenty persons, could be launched, along with three rafts, one of which was afire. The ship slid under the water stern first in three and one—half minutes in a sea of blazing diesel fuel.'

According to Adam, 'flames were shooting out of the hole caused by the torpedo, and the ship was listing badly. I raced to a lifeboat, which was launched with considerable difficulty. For a time it was feared that the lifeboat would be sucked into the whirlpool caused by the sinking ship. ... There was no panic on board as the freighter listed and began to sink.' An article in the Lima, Ohio *News* of 24 April relates that 'one lifeboat and one raft burned up in the water, but twenty-six men finally got into another lifeboat and eventually they were able to take an additional seven from a raft.' This is corroborated by a Bermudian journalist, who transcribed that 'two lifeboats were launched, but one caught fire as flaming oil spurted from the hole in the ship's side made from the torpedo.'[14]

Adam continued: 'After the lifeboat reached the water, its passengers rowed toward the Italian submarine which had risen to the surface.' This was a misunderstanding based on the fog of war and the perception that the submarine's officers spoke with Italian, rather than German accents. In fact, the survivors confirmed seeing a white elephant emblem on the submarine, which was the logo employed by Forster and *U-654* and no other World War Two submarine, German or Italian. This and the German logbook confirm that *U-654* indeed sank the *Agra* that day. Forster wrote 'Surfaced. Sinking observed... AGRA, 4,569 tons coming from Philadelphia, cargo benzene in barrels.'[15] Grafton Fay, leader of the American Field Service team, picks up the narrative thus: 'Most of us jumped into the water. The submarine rose out of the water and moved towards the lifeboat, which was pulling away from our rapidly sinking ship. About six officers, all cleanly shaven and immaculately dressed in uniform, came on deck and asked the name of the ship, its destination tonnage and cargo. They were polite but firm, and spoke perfect English.'

'After they had recorded the information members of the crew pointed out the forms of struggling passengers in the water for the lifeboat to pick up. They were a little higher out of the water and could spot us better than the occupants of the lifeboat.' Meanwhile, the oil kept burning on the surface of the sea for some time, singeing some of the men who had jumped overboard and were swimming around waiting to be picked up. Two of the passengers were in the choppy seas for over an hour before a lifeboat reached them and dragged them to safety, while a member of the freighter's crew was picked up after the vessel had disappeared beneath the waves.

The one question that Forster's officers omitted to ask was the nationality of the *Agra*—though Sweden was neutral, clearly the purpose of her voyage was to deliver war materiel to Africa, in this case for the British military. The Swedes seem to have thought the Germans were 'definitely Italian, judging from the commander's accent and appearance. Although he spoke English, he had a decided Italian accent.' In contrast, Adam and Fay concur that the enemy spoke impeccable English. Adam, who kept a log while in the lifeboat, says that Forster 'promised to radio our location, which he did not do, and, after saluting smartly, re-entered the submarine.' Forster was described wearing an 'unusually high peaked cap' resembling an 'air force or overseas cap' over a blue or olive-green uniform (it was after all getting dark). The six men on the conning tower were described as clean-shaven, though their patrol had begun in Brest over a month before, and shaving was unusual on patrol, with limited fresh water.

The submarine was described as painted a dark green or gray (it was gray) and the paint appeared freshly applied. The men agreed that a cable stretched from the conning tower to the stern of the sub but were divided as to whether another (radio) cable ran to the bow (it did). Most of the men noticed the prominent white elephant's head on the tower. After ten minutes, *U-654* motored off to the west at 12 knots, and was swallowed by the night, leaving the twenty-six merchant sailors and seven young Americans bobbing in the swells aboard a lifeboat and a raft. The *Agra* would be Forster's last successful attack as *U-654* was sunk with the loss of all hands-on 22 August that year by a B 18 Digby bomber off Panama. The *Agra* had its revenge of sorts—later that night, Forster discovered that 'starboard diesel suddenly can not run at over 400 RPM. Later examination shows damaged propeller blade. Probably from pieces of wreckage.' As his reference book showed that the *Agra* was a Swedish vessel, Forster decided he must send a message to U-boat headquarters (B.d.U.) in France, so he did so, emphasizing that the ship had 'no markings' showing neutrality.

It was not yet 6 p.m. and Adam described the waves as reaching 15 feet. Fay described their night in the lifeboat as uncomfortable more than dangerous: 'We didn't have much trouble in the lifeboat except for cramped quarters, darkness and spray. The boat was supplied with food and water sufficient to feed us three weeks,' he wrote after the incident. The *Lima News* related that 'Their lifeboat was well stocked with provisions and the only discomforts resulted from wet blankets, minor cuts and bruises sustained from flying debris at the time of the torpedoing, and the minor burns from the flaming oil. No one was seriously hurt.'[16] Adam kept a log and told a reporter that during the night the men 'took turns at the oars during the next 16 ½ hours.' Adam relates that 'the sea was rough, rain fell, and most of the passengers became violently ill.' Those on shore admit to 'all but two of the men being seasick. Spray whipped over the sides of the boat…. Water in the bottom of the boat was over their ankles, to add to their discomfort; I prayed once or twice during the long night in the lifeboats, especially when it appeared that those aboard a raft strapped to the boat appeared in danger of breaking loose, which meant almost sure death for those clinging to it.'

According to Adam's diary, they were picked up at 8.47 a.m. on the morning of Tuesday, 21 April. Fay writes:

About 5 a.m. while still in total darkness, we decided to fire a flare. By good fortune, a Norwegian freighter spotted the flare and changed its course to investigate, although we couldn't see her then. Nearly two hours later we made out the dint outline of the Norwegian just as she began heading away from us. We immediately set off several flares and then the ship found us.

The ship was named the *Tercero*, which means 'third' in Spanish. At 4,415 tons and built in 1925, the *Tercero* had been managed from Oslo before Norway was occupied by the Germans. 'Both Fay and Brooks were emphatic in their praise of the officers of the Norwegian vessel. They reduced speed and stopped in sub-infested waters for nearly two hours to pick us up, Fay declared.' Here Fay's account is aligned with Adam's, who said at 8.47 a.m. all the men were aboard the Norwegian ship. The official survivors' statements record that 'six of crew including master lost on ship— all others including passengers picked up on 21 April 1942 at 9.30 a.m. by Norwegian SS *Tercero* 15 miles east position of attack and taken to Bermuda.'[17]

Fay writes that 'After getting aboard, we got underway again about 9 a.m. and at 1 p.m. a submarine was sighted. She had apparently been following us. The Norwegian had guns and the gun crews opened up with them. None of the passengers could see anything and while the guns kept blazing away, the vessel changed course and put on extra speed.' It is not known which submarine, if any was sighted by the Norwegians, but it must have been *U-654*.

Once safely on board the Norwegian ship, Captain Simon Holme went out of his way to look after his new charges: 'They were all given dry clothing immediately and, as some of the Swedish sailors remarked… plenty of warm food.' Chief Officer Graaf remarked that 'the rescue vessel showed excellent seamanship in effecting the rescue, having ploughed through submarine infested waters for hours in order to get the shipwrecked men to safety,' as well as having maneuvered alongside a small lifeboat without crushing it in a heavy seaway.

The *Tercero* deviated from its intended course to both rescue and deposit the survivors ashore. The *Tercero* left New York for Buenos Aires on 19 April, a day after the *Agra* left Philadelphia. She called at Bermuda in order to deposit the survivors on 22 April, and resumed her southward passage to South America on the following day. The *Tercero* people discharged their passengers in St. George's, on the north-east coast of Bermuda, quite a distance from the capital, Hamilton. Immediately on arrival 'most of the men on landing…. Complained of the bitter cold as they wallowed about in mounting waves….some of them showing slight burns on their hands, nostrils and the sides of their heads where their hair had been singed.'

The men then embarked on 'what Adam described as the slowest train he ever travelled upon, appropriately called 'The Flying Snail'.[18] Though the actual radio messages are not recorded in the war diaries of either the US or United Kingdom, the British Admiralty logged the loss of the *Agra* on 23 April thus: 'AGRA sunk by S/M [submarine] 20/4… C.Bs. [codebooks] went down with ship which [was] not boarded by enemy.' The information was given by First Officer Graaf and was sent by the Commander in Charge, Bermuda to Admiralty at 5.52 p.m. on the 23rd.

The men were able to spend from Wednesday 22nd to Tuesday 28th in Bermuda, recuperating. The officers and American passengers were accommodated on their first night at the American House. The merchant marine crew were put up at the Bermuda Sailor's Home.[19] For at least one of the men—a US volunteer—it was not his first visit to the islands, as he had been to Bermuda on his honeymoon with his wife two years earlier. The next morning both British and United States naval officials interviewed them. According to another Mansfield, Ohio paper, 'Thirty-three survivors of a Swedish freighter rested in Bermuda homes provided for them by the American Red Cross....'[20] The Bermudian papers were more specific, writing that by Thursday 'Mr. Alonzo Cornell, American Red Cross Director at Bermuda, distributed articles to each survivor. In the afternoon, Mr. Cornell had the passengers outfitted. One of them told *The Royal Gazette and Colonist* that he lost all his belongings, including his wallet which contained $35.'

Adam made a beeline to the Western Union offices not so much to contact his parents (he said 'at no time during his experiences at sea ... did he feel in danger of death'), but to file a story of the sinking with his former employer, the *Cardinal* newspaper. Normally spaces on the Pan American Airlines Clipper flying boats were reserved for 'essential torpedoed ships engineers and captains.' The seven young American volunteers were included in the roster of officers and they made it back to New York in a matter of hours instead of wartime weeks if they had waited to go by sea. The Swedish officers were interviewed at US Third naval district headquarters in at 30 Church Street, New York City by C. C. Vickery, Lieutenant Commander, US Navy Reserve, and Francis T. Carmody, Agent, District Intelligence Office on 28 April.[21] The crew then reported to the British naval authorities in New York as well as to the Swedish Consulate in New York, who kept careful lists of survivors and missing.[22] On arrival in New York young Carl Adam contacted his parents in Wisconsin. 'I returned home with 67 cents,' he writes, 'my field service uniform, coat and knapsack and the clothing issued by the British military.' After a visit back home, he and his university mates persevered in their efforts to be assigned to North Africa. Adam departed a second time in June, reached Suez and Alexandria in September and by October was in the thick of the battle of El Alamein. For over three years he followed armies through North Africa and southern and northern Europe.

In what might serve as the obituary for the *Agra*, at 9.45 a.m. on Wednesday, 29 April—nearly a week after the British published their intelligence—the loss of the ship and details of her survivor's rescue was printed in the Eastern Sea Frontier's Enemy Action Diary. On that very day, *U-654* passed within 20 miles of Bermuda, patrolling on its way back to France—the submarine's close shave went undetected and unchallenged.

SS *Empire Dryden*

The *Empire Dryden* was a British steamship of 7,164 tons, which was completed in February 1942 and lost in April of the same year, just over two months later, north of Bermuda. She was built by William Doxford and Sons Limited of Sunderland,

England as yard number 682. Though built for the Ministry of War Transport, the ship was owned by Sir R. Ropner & Company, Limited (known as Pool Shipping) of West Hartlepool, Sunderland.[23] Her dimensions were 443 feet long, 56.4 feet wide, and 35.4 feet deep. Her triple-expansion steam engine developed 511 net horsepower and propelled the ship at between 10 and 11.5 knots. It was built by Fairfield and Company Limited of Glasgow.

The *Empire Dryden*'s only master was Captain Robert Powley, aged thirty-five.[24] Her chief officer was Christopher Thomas Valentine, also British. In fact, all fifty-one men on board the ship were British. They included gunner John Edward Snary, and two other DEMS or 'Defensively Equipped Merchant Ship' Gunners; John Raymond Brown, aged ninteen and Dennis Brooks, twenty. There were a handful of other teenagers on board, including ship's boy Patrick Connor, galley boy John Colin Garrigan, sailor Thomas Hanlon, third radio officer Victor Leonard Longley, and sailor John Mason. There was a total of six gunners (two army and four navy) and 45 merchant sailors. The gunners were responsible for maintaining and firing a four-inch gun, another 20-milimeter gun and four machine guns as well as an Oerlikon, four PAC rockets, one Gymbal projector, and several kite rockets.

The *Empire Dryden* began her maiden voyage on 27 February 1942 when she left Sunderland and joined Convoy FN 642, bound for Methil, Fife, Scotland. From there, she joined Convoy EN 53, arriving in Oban, Scotland on 4 March, thence to Loch Ewe and Liverpool. The ship had no cargo at this point. On 9 March, the *Empire Dryden* sailed from Liverpool in Convoy ON 74 and arrived in Halifax on 25 March. There were 47 merchant ships and 10 escorts in this convoy. The convoy Commodore was Rear-Admiral F. B. Watson on the *Hopetarn*.[25]

From Halifax, the *Empire Dryden* steamed to Boston in Convoy XB 5 between 27 and 29 March. She utilized the Cape Cod Canal to sail independently for New York, where it arrived on 1 April. In New York Harbor, the ship loaded 7,100 tons of general cargo including grain, military stores, and explosives destined for the Allied forces fighting Rommel's army in North Africa. Her route was to Cape Town, then Alexandria via the Red Sea and the Suez Canal. On Friday 17 April at 5.30 p.m., the *Empire Dryden* began her first laden voyage, heading on a course that would take her east of Bermuda per voyage instructions. At dawn on Sunday, 19 April, about 350 nautical miles south-east of New York and halfway to Bermuda, the *Empire Dryden* came upon a lifeboat with the twenty-one survivors of the torpedoed and damaged Argentinian neutral ship *Victoria*, which had been attacked by *U-201* under Adalbert Schnee the previous day and (prematurely it turned out) abandoned.[26]

Just as Captain Powley was preparing to retrieve the men, his lookouts spotted the USS *Owl* (AM 2), a US Navy tug which had been towing a barge to Bermuda. The *Owl* then retrieved the men from the *Victoria*'s lifeboat and set about salvaging the ship, which was towed to New York, arriving 21 April. If they were not already, then the men of the *Empire Dryden* were now highly aware of the risk of U-boat attack, as they resumed their course to the southwards.

Then, at 4 p.m. on the 19th, when just north of the island, those instructions were changed. Naval Control in Ottawa, Canada decreed that the ship was now to pass to the west of Bermuda. It took the Radio Officers on board roughly an hour to decode the signal. At about 5 p.m., the course was altered a significant 30 degrees to starboard, to south-south-west.

Roughly four hours later, at 8.55 p.m. the same day, the *Empire Dryden* was 195 nautical miles north-north-west of Bermuda. At a speed of 10.5 knots, the ship was completely blacked out, her 'red duster' British ensign was flying, and the radio had not been used since leaving New York (except to receive signals). The weather was fine and visibility reported as good. According to Chief Officer Rixham the *Empire Dryden* was not zigzagging; however, to the Germans observing her movements from a periscope nearby (since sunset around 6.30 p.m.), she was.[27]

There were four lookouts: one in the crow's nest high above the deck on one of the ship's three masts, two on the gun platform at the stern, and between one or two officers in the bridge. They did not see a submarine in the dark, nor did they observe any torpedoes. The ship had unwittingly put herself in the sights of *U-572* under the command of *Kapitänleutnant* Heinz Hirsacker. Here is what happened next according to the official attack log (KTB) of the German submarine. At 6.45 p.m.:

Large freighter in sight bearing 330°T. Target angle 40°. Enemy bow left. General course 220°. Speed 8 knots. Freighter has 3 large king posts. Held contact on the freighter up to darkness. He zigzags 20-30° to port and starboard. From 02.00 hours I am positioned ahead of the freighter. After a new zigzag to port I initiate from the starboard side, and shoot at range 600 meters a three-fan. Target angle 90°, bow right.

At 9.06 p.m.:

Fan is fired at 03.06 hours. After 40 seconds running time a hit on the bridge. Freighter breaks apart (in the center). Foreship sinks immediately. Stern still floats. On the stern, a there is work by floodlight. But 12 minutes later the aftership also sinks. Stern stands high out and then sinks quickly. Two boats with anchor lanterns remain. Sunk steamer was type 'POELAU'.[28]

From the perspective of the men on the ship, there was a 'dull explosion' as, by their good fortune the torpedo struck about 15 to 20 feet under the water line in a cargo hold loaded with grain. It missed the hold carrying explosives. Two of the three torpedoes fired failed to find their mark, whizzing harmlessly beyond the ship. Third Officer Thomas William Money, aged twenty-six, 'reported seeing a flash and a tremendous column of water thrown up. It was too dark to see if any hatches were blown up or if there was any deck damaged.'

Immediately, the radio officers sent off an SSS signal for 'submarine sighted on surface' with the ship's position and name; however, the message was not acknowledged by shore or ship stations and, indeed, it does not appear in the Eastern Sea Frontier Enemy Action Diary.[29] The nearby Germans heard only three garbled SSS messages. The *Empire Dryden* men would be on their own if they could survive long enough to get into their boats; even the radio transmitter meant for the lifeboat was 'washed off the bridge and smashed by the column of water from the explosion.' The torpedo hit on the starboard side, behind the Number Two-cargo hatch and cut the bow of the ship off, as Hirsacker had observed. Back on the still-floating and still-moving stern section, there was frantic activity. Captain Powley, realizing the ship only had minutes to float, ordered a general abandon ship. The team from the engine department took this literally and left the engine room before stopping the engines.

At the time the torpedo struck, First Officer Rixham was in the pantry and he felt the explosion beneath him. He quickly made the boat deck, grabbing a life jacket and torch along the way. He discovered that the forward most lifeboats on the starboard side were completely destroyed. In the excitement, he dashed to the aft starboard boat and lowered it by knocking out some chocks; however, he then realized that the ship was still making forward speed—he said it had been going 11 knots at the time of the attack.

Seeing a fully lit but abandoned engine room, he tried to use a lever on the boat deck to stop the engines, but the spindle bent and jammed in his hands. Together with some other shipmates, they were able to slow down the engines to the point that boats could be launched. Third Officer Money was in charge of the boat and when Rixham finally stepped into it, the ship was so low in the water that he merely stepped horizontally into the boat, which was full of sailors and gunners.[30]

Meanwhile, on the port side Captain Powley managed to launch the forward jolly boat, which was smaller than conventional lifeboats. Second Officer David Scott Whittet, aged twenty-five, organized and successfully launched the port aft lifeboat, which was a motorboat. The men used their torches to stay in contact with one another. Shortly thereafter, the aft section of the young disemboweled *Empire Dryden* sank to the ocean floor, roughly seven minutes after the attack began.

Onboard the *U-572*, Hirsacker was smug. He observed at 10 p.m. local time:

Approximately 9000 GRT. Name not determined. On the 600-meter wave only garbled sss ... heard 3 times. Attack weather was good. Sea 1–2. Dark night. Boat positioned for attack against a dark rain cloud. Success report sent.[31]

All fifty-one of the men on board the *Empire Dryden* were able to get safely off the ship, with no serious injuries reported. They had been most fortunate, though less so than the men from the *Victoria* earlier that day, whose ship survived. Some of the men claimed that they saw two submarines half a mile apart signaling each other; one off the starboard bow (which had in fact fallen off) and one of the port quarter. Most likely they were witnessing the different boats trying to signal each other. They said the U-boat remained in the vicinity for forty-five minutes, but did not approach them or interact with any of the survivors, which is consistent with the KTB. Rixham did say that they could hear the engine of the submarine running, which is creditable as there is no record that the motor in the motor lifeboat was ever used.

Since it has significant bearing on who survived and who didn't, the division of boats and allocation of men from boat to boat can be described in the actual words of First Officer Rixham:

> When daylight came on the 20 April the three boats got together. The 2nd Officer changed into the small boat and the Captain transferred into the motor lifeboat. Some of the men from my boat were transferred into the small boat and I remained in my lifeboat with twenty-eight men. It was agreed that the boast should keep together if possible and to steer W. S. W. … By noon the small life boat was making too much water and was unable to keep up with the two large boats, so the men from this boat were divided between the two life boats and the small boat was abandoned after taking out all water and provisions. After this transfer, the master has twenty-six men in his boat and there were twenty-five men in my boat.[32]

The twenty-five men were composed of three gunners and twenty-two merchant seamen; among them was Fireman and Trimmer James Swinburn. For over two weeks, the men struggled against calms and storms. On the second day adrift, Rixham's boat lost contact with the captain's; however, they reunited on Wednesday 22 April. Calm settled over the sea from 1 p.m. that day until the next morning, when a strong gale of wind and waves set upon them, separating the boats for the last time. From 10.30 a.m. on Thursday the 23rd until 6.30 a.m. on Saturday the 25th, Rixham streamed a sea anchor, which worked until they pulled it in after the storm to find the canvas had been ripped off and only a metal ring remained. It is believed, after the fact and with no other explanation, that Captain Powley and the twenty-five other men in his boat were overturned during the same storm and perished.

The men then set a double-reefed (partially rolled-in) sail and set course westwards. Two hours later, they unfurled the rest of the sail and started making good headway. For two days, until Monday the 27th, they sailed, and then were becalmed. They began the voyage with 30 gallons of fresh water and a good supply of malted tablets, Pemmican (meat paste), and biscuits; this provided a generous allowance of 8 ounces of fresh water per man per day, later reduced to 4 ounces. Frustratingly, the men remained becalmed for over a week, until 11.45 a.m. on Tuesday, 5 May, when they saw their first ship. At that time, they had only enough water for one more day. Rixham wrote that 'The weather was very hot during the day, but at night it was very cold.'

The men's feet had begun to swell during the water immersion of the storm; however, by massaging them with oil and with the kind ministrations of Second

(Assistant) Steward James Charkley Dutton, the swelling was kept in check. Rixham described Dutton as 'a valuable asset' who 'looked after the stores and water in the boat and attended to the men's feet and health…. being at all times resourceful and cheerful.' He also singled out Whittet, Bosun Norman Saunders, and Able Seaman David Henry Donnelly for being upbeat and of assistance to him, particularly when a number of the other men became lethargic and despondent while drifting.

Fortunately for the men in the lifeboat, the ship they sighted was the 5,861-ton US passenger and cargo steamer the *City of Birmingham*, registered to Savannah and on a regular run between that port and Hamilton. Her master was Captain Lewis Percy Borum. Rixham mistakenly described her as the *City of Bermuda*. On sighting her, he wrote that 'we immediately burned smoke floats, red flares, and a life jacket soaked in oil.' Such unusual efforts to attract attention probably saved their lives, as the ship was a good ten miles away at the time. Indeed, it took over an hour for the ship to reach the lifeboat, but by 1.08 p.m., all twenty-five men were aboard the medium-sized liner.[33]

Their position was a bit south of a direct track from Savannah to Bermuda, being 215 nautical miles south-east of Savannah. Rixham proudly notes that they had managed to sail 450 miles over sixteen days. In fact, from the location of the sinking to rescue it was more like 630 miles. This would mean that the lifeboat averaged roughly 1.6 knots during their ordeal, which makes sense considering that much of the time they were merely drifting without adequate wind to propel them. Rixham relates their rescue:

> The working side doors …were opened in order to pick us up and the crew were able to reach down to the boat and help us on board. We felt more or less alright in the boat but as soon as we got on board the rescuing ship our legs collapsed. We were treated very well on board … [it] was a passenger vessel and carried a doctor. Mattresses were laid on the floor of the music room and we were immediately put to bed. They gave us small drinks of water at 15 minute intervals followed by apples, oranges, and ice cream in small quantities and spread over a long period.[34]

Under the heading 'Survivor Arrivals Here Elicit Wide Sympathy', a journalist from *The Royal Gazette and Colonist Daily*, of Saturday, 9 May, relates for the public a thumbnail sketch of the loss of the *Empire Dryden* and the rescue of her survivors. As for the others, Rixham optimistically notes '…those landed here yesterday stated that the remainder are still unaccounted for, although there is every likelihood that they were picked up.' There is a factual error made by either the survivors or the journalist, who writes '….on the day the ship [*Empire Dryden*] was torpedoed they had picked up a group of survivors from another vessel [*Victoria*].' As we have seen, USS *Owl* and not the *Empire Dryden* picked up the *Victoria* survivors.[35]

As they had been on the *City of Birmingham*, the men of the *Empire Dryden* were graciously looked after ashore in Bermuda:

Among the men brought here, only two were taken to hospital, this being merely for examination. The rescued officers are being accommodated in private homes, with the remainder of the crew at the Bermuda Sailor's Home, now filled to capacity. Rescued seamen housed there are being provided with beds in the games room. The majority of the men in the second survivor's group had lost most of their clothing, some landing merely in shirts and pants and wearing bedroom slippers. However, it was learned that by noon today the entire group will be outfitted.

The *City of Birmingham* was sunk by *U-202* under Hans-Heinz Linder two months later, on 1 July 1942. Out of her complement of 381 passengers and crew, all but nine survived, rescued by the USS *Stansbury* and taken to Bermuda.[36]

First Officer Rixham was awarded by his government. In May 1942, he was made a Member of the Civil Division of the Most Excellent Order of the British Empire (MBE). The citation reads:

The Chief Officer displayed great courage throughout. When the ship was hit, he made every effort to stop the engines by means of the deck controls and he was among the last to leave the ship. Taking charge of one of the boats, he made a voyage of sixteen days before being picked up. It was due mainly to his skill and leadership that the twenty-five occupants were brought to safety.[37]

21 April 1942: Two U-boats

Kapitänleutnant Heinrich Zimmermann in command of *U-136* entered the area only briefly from off the US coast near Cape Hatteras on 21 April 1942. On the 22nd, the boat penetrated to within a few hundred miles of Bermuda to the north-west, then returned west and then north, exiting the area the following day. The submarine sailed for the 6th U-boat Flotilla and left St. Nazaire on 24 March 1942. *U-136*'s patrol began off Newfoundland before continuing to Hatteras, where the sub sank the US tanker the *Axtell J. Byles* of 8,955 tons on 19 April. Zimmermann had actually been aiming for the USCGC *Dione*, but hit the tanker instead. Both the *Dione* and US Navy aircraft counterattacked to no effect.[1]

While north-west of Bermuda, *U-136* sank the British motor ship the *Empire Drum* of 7,244 tons on 24 April. Closer to shore on the 28th, she sank the Dutch steamer the *Arundo* of 5,163 tons south of New York. On the way home, also via Canada, *U-136* sank the 300-ton Canadian schooner the *Mildred Pauline* off Nova Scotia. Zimmermann and his men returned to St. Nazaire on 20 May 1942. Zimmermann was born in 1907 and was a member of the Crew of 1933. His early responsibilities included command of the 7th Minesweeping Flotilla in 1939–1940. He joined U-boats in 1941 and took command of *U-136* in August of that year. On 11 June 1942, the sub was caught by the Free French destroyer the *Leopard*, HMS *Spey*, and HMS *Pelican*, and was sunk with all forty-five hands off the Madeira Islands. Over three patrols, Zimmermann accrued 108 sea days and accounted for eight ships sunk or damaged of 34,454 tons. He received no decorations.[2]

Kapitänleutnant Walter Schug brought *U-86* into the area north-west of Bermuda for a five-day incursion starting on 21 April. Motoring due south-west, he left the region the following day, only to return from the Hatteras area on 28 April 1942. He motored east for a day, turned north on the 29th, and exited the region north-west of Bermuda *en route* to base on the 30th. *U-86* sailed for the 1st U-boat Flotilla out of Brest on 25 March 1942 as part of the fifth wave of Drumbeat boats to attack the US. Schug returned to base on 26 May 1942 without having sunk or damaged any ships.

Walter Schug was born in 1910 and was a member of the Crew of 1934. Originally, he served in the Naval Artillery Division and then with Naval Assault Troops before joining U-boat training in April 1940. He served as watch officer of *U-74* before commissioning *U-86* in July of 1941. Over eight patrols, he accrued 415 days and sank or damaged four ships worth 18,241 tons. Schug and his entire compliment of fifty men were killed by HMS *Tumult* and HMS *Rocket* east of the Azores on 29 November 1943. Schug received no decorations in his career.

22 April 1942: SS *Derryheen*

The SS *Derryheen* was one of the only merchant vessels stricken by U-boats in the region whose survivors were rescued on the open ocean by a Bermuda-based airplane. Built in 1942 by the Burntisland Shipbuilding Company Limited of Scotland, she was 420 feet long by 58 feet, and weighted 7,217 gross registered tons.[1] She was owned by McCowen and Gross Limited, London. The *Derryheen*'s crew of fifty-one men were led by Captain Harold Richardson.[2] She left Norfolk on her maiden cargo-carrying voyage on 19 April bound for Cape Town. Her cargo consisted of 11,036 tons of general cargo, which included 6,400 tons of military stores among them beer, trucks, and nitrates, destined ultimately to aiding the war in North Africa via Middle-East ports. Her original port of departure was Philadelphia.[3] According to Captain Richardson, he was ordered to divert his course several days out of Norfolk; however, the ship never received or followed those instructions. Instead, at 3 a.m. local time, *U-201* commanded by Adalbert Schnee, caught up with her in an abrupt manner.[4]

The weather was described as 'fine and clear but very dark' by the captain, who had just taken off his work clothes for the first time during the three-day passage, on 22 April. The ship's course was east-south-east or 150 degrees and her speed 11.75 knots when she was struck on the port side. A G7e torpedo penetrated the aft part of the ship by way of the Number Five hold, setting fire to the cargo of nitrates stored there and filling the air with an acrid smell of cordite and burning nitrates. Since the torpedo struck directly beneath the naval gunner's quarters (the ship was armed with guns manned by eight military gunners), their bunks collapsed on one another like pancakes. All four of the navy and four army gunners just managed to pry themselves out of the single exit to their Spartan accommodations.[5]

The crew acted with commendable order in the circumstances and within ten minutes managed to launch all four lifeboats. Captain Richardson yelled down the hatch for the engine room staff to abandon ship, and the engineer assured the master that the engines had been secured. However, they had not been, so the chief went below to do so himself. Up until then, the engines had been racing even though the propeller shaft was broken. All three boats except for Number One were cast off, with the latter standing by to collect Captain Richardson. Seeing that the ship was fiercely afire, the entire crew were off from the ship within twelve minutes.

At that time, a second torpedo slammed into the mid-ships port side and sent a column of water in the air. According to Captain Richardson, 'it was noisier than the first torpedo, but not nearly as loud an explosion as I expected.' Though they could not see *U-201* prowling nearby, they could 'distinctly hear her engines close to the boat.' Though the crew hoped to re-board their ship and send a Mayday for a tug to come out and tow the burning hulk to shore, the second torpedo accomplished its sender's objectives; at 3.30 a.m., the *Derryheen* sank.

Thus began an interesting and varied survival struggle from one to twelve days for fifty-one men in four boats for between one and twelve days. Boats with motors found that the engines did not work (their magnetos had been soaked), the smaller boats with only eight persons fared better than their larger cousins in that a boat load were literally air-lifted out in the days before helicopters, and the men ended up as far apart as Havana and eastern Florida. At dawn, the master divided the crew—eight each in the smaller boats and seventeen each in the larger lifeboats. They agreed to steer west-south-west towards the Carolinas. In order to get the emergency rations out of the rafts, they had to chop the rafts up.[6]

At noon on the same day—22 April—an Allied airplane spotted their smoke floats; after circling around, dropping its two bombs into the sea to free up weight, it landed on the surface of the sea. The captain selflessly suggested that eight men from the third mate's small boat be rescued; they were.[7] However, when the plane returned, the water was too rough. Unable to speak to the plane via the emergency transmitter, it flew off, not to return. *The Royal Gazette and Colonist Daily* of 24 April 1942 goes into great detail regarding the *Derryheen* survivors, even saying one of them had survived the *Altmark* affair, in which an Allied ship (renamed the *Altmark*) was captured as a prize by Germans and was recaptured in neutral Norwegian waters by an Allied naval ship.[8]

The following day, 23 April, the weather was blustery with a strong wind and rough seas. The line between the captain and first mate's boat was separated by the seas. The chief officer tried to signal by whistle, but the men in the Captain's boat were too busy bailing out to interpret the signals. By that night, the Captain's boat was riding with a sea anchor and the boats had been separated for good. Though the other two boats had engines, the motors were unusable. The master had again selflessly taken the smallest boat and the only one left with no engine.

Fortune shone on him, however. On the 24th, the weather was 'fine and clear, with a fresh wind blowing enabling us to sail well.' The next day, the wind abated, causing them to row. That morning, the chief engineer pointed out a bottle floating nearby to the captain, who wrote that 'as I turned around to look at it I saw two masts and a funnel of a ship on the horizon which appeared to be coming towards us.' The lifeboat crew set sail to attract attention; however, the observant master of the ship, a British motor ship called variously the *Lobos* and the *Globo* (master's statements), had seen the broken up liferafts 20 miles from the sinking and had posted extra lookouts.[9, 10]

The *Lobos* was heading south for the Straits of Florida and took the men to Havana.[11] There, they learned that the two other boats and their occupants had all been saved. Apparently, they were 'picked up within 60 miles of the coast by local patrol vessels. One boat was ten days and the other eleven days adrift before being rescued.' Given the spring temperatures and the exposure the men endured, there is a poignant medical or humanitarian request for clothing to be ready. On 25 April, a Dutch ship, the *Roode Zee* is confirmed to have been off the Carolina coast specifically looking for more *Derryheen* boats.[12, 13]

On 2 May, sixteen men were spotted by US Naval Ensign K. R. Peachee in a PBY aircraft, who vectored an American PBM Mariner aircraft which rescued the men and landed them in Banana River Naval Air Station, Florida by 2 p.m. the same day.[14] This was the *Derryheen*'s large boat under Second Officer John Stuart Burgess. The same day, a dozen *Derryheen* men were rescued by HMS *Polyanthus* and taken to Charleston; this was the second large lifeboat under Chief Officer Harold Ingledew.[15, 16, 17] In the *Supplement to the London Gazette* of 5 January 1943, the captain, Harold Ingledew Esq., chief officer and Second Officer John Stuart Burgess, Esq., were specifically cited for their outstanding seamanship.[18]

It had been an unusual ordeal afloat for the men, who obviously kept their heads. The varied landings of the survivors—an airport, a beach, and a city—demonstrate the vagaries experienced even by members of the same crew.[19] Often, men from different boats found themselves mixed in with the crews of even other ships on the high seas.[20] These mid-ocean mixings (called the 'extraordinary meetings of the stragglers club' by one wry humorist) are often a boon to the survivors but a challenge to those documenting the ultimate dispensation of the crews.[21] In the case of all fifty-one of the *Derryheen*'s crew, all was well that ended well.

23–24 April 1942: Three U-boats

Korvettenkapitän Klaus Scholtz brought his sub *U-108* into the area north-east of Bermuda for a deadly twelve-day transit starting on 22 April 1942. Three days later, he sank the *Modesta*, noteworthy as the ship sank closer to Bermuda in World War Two than any other. The *Modesta* was British, weighed 9,925 tons, and was sunk by both torpedo and gunfire. A day after Schacht and Bleichrodt, Klaus Scholtz came in *U-108*; he entered just east of St. David's Light on 27 April 1942, heading south-south-west as far as a point of Anegada, essentially skimming the eastern fringe of the area before turning north-north-west on the 30th and heading into the Turks & Caicos Passage. On the 29th, he sank the US tanker the *Mobiloil* halfway between Puerto Rico and Bermuda. He went on to patrol the area around Inagua and Caicos for over a week, during which he sank the *Abgara* on 6 May. Off the extreme north-west coast of Haiti—between Cape Mole and Inagua—he sank the *Afoundria*, chasing it towards the shore.[1]

On this patrol, thirty-four-year-old Scholtz would add the *Modesta* and the Norwegian *Norland* from convoy ON 93 for a total tonnage sunk of 31,340 on one patrol in five ships. The patrol began on 30 March 1942 and ended, also in Lorient, on 1 June. *U-108* sailed for the 2nd U-boat Flotilla. On the way it was refueled by *U-459* between Azores and Bermuda on 22 April. The sub returned to Lorient on 1 June 1942. In September 1942, a few months after returning from his patrol to the Inagua area, he was granted the prestigious Knight's Cross with Oak Leaves. A member of the crew of 1927, Scholtz began his career on torpedo boats and joined U-boats in April 1940. In October 1942, he moved ashore to command the 12th U-boat Flotilla in Bordeaux, where the Italian flotilla Betasom was based. When Bordeaux fell, Scholtz and 220 men tried to literally walk to Germany but were captured and held by Americans for one and a half years. He rejoined the first the Naval Armed Guard (*Bundesgrenzschutz*, or Federal Frontier Guard) and then in 1956 the German Navy (*Bundesmarine*) between 1953 and 1966, when he retired as *Kapitän zur See*. Klaus Scholtz lived until the age of seventy-nine, passing in 1987.[2]

The next patrol to the region was led by Walther Kölle, whose submarine, *U-154* was to return to the area several times in the course of the war. In the Bermuda theater, *U-154* merely transited between 23 and 26 April 1942, without sinking any ships. From a point south-west of the island, the sub headed north-east, bound for base, and exited east of the island on the 26th. The submarine left Lorient, where it sailed for the 2nd U-boat Flotilla on 11 March, returning there on 9 May 1942. The bulk of Kölle's patrol was in the Bahamas area starting by heading from north of Anegada into the Mona Passage, during which he sank two Allied ships, the Puerto Rican tanker the *Comol Rico* and the US-flagged *Catahoula* on the 4th and 5th respectively. On 6 April, Kölle entered the Mona Passage.

On this patrol, *U-154* sank five ships (including the *Delvalle* and the *Empire Amethyst* in the Caribbean) worth 28,715 tons—an impressive tally and in some ways close to his last. Aged thirty-four at the time (he would live to 1992 and the age of eighty-four), Kölle's career total included only two other ships (the *Tillie Lykes* and the *Lalita*), bringing his total to seven ships for 31,352 tons. He achieved *Fregattenkapitän* in March 1945 and was not decorated. His three patrols for 164 days were all on *U-154*. Kölle had earlier survived the scuttling of the *Graf Spee* off Uruguay and rose to senior naval officer of the Flushing base before joining U-boats in November 1940. His patrols to the region lasted sixty and eighty days respectively, with the following patrol to Mexico and the Caribbean. He surrendered command of *U-154* to Heinrich Shuch after his third patrol and moved ashore to staff positions.[3]

Teddy Suhren led his second incursion north of Bermuda lasting nine days in *U-564*, starting on 24 April 1942. He patrolled west for five days until the 29th, then exited north-west of the island. After a highly successful mission to the Florida Straits, he returned on 23 May, also north-west of Bermuda, heading north-east and leaving on the 26th. The patrol lasted between 4 April and 6 June 1942 and was mounted two days after the simultaneous arrival of three boats. *U-564* was able to replenish her fuel from *U-459* outbound 500 miles north-east of Bermuda on or around 27 April.[4] On 3 May, he sank the *Ocean Venus*, weighing 7,174 tons, of British registry, and the following day her compatriot, the *Eclipse* of 9,767 tons. Sailing in convoy ON 87, the ship was only damaged and returned to service. The following day, Suhren also damaged the *Delisle*, an American freighter of 3,478 tons, also off Florida. On 8 May, the *Ohioan* steamed its last mile before encountering *U-564* and the next day, the *Lubrafol* of Panama registry and 7,138 tons was sunk in the region.[5]

Commenting on the absence of anti-submarine-warfare (ASW) defenses and the lights not only of Miami but Great Isaac in the Bahamas shining, Suhren proceeded south in the Straits of Florida until he encountered the and sank the *Potrero del Llano*, a Mexican tanker of 4,000 tons whose flag he claims to have mistaken for the Italian. This sinking pushed Mexico considerably closer to declaring war against Germany, which it did mere weeks later. On 22 May, he exited the area just west of Bermuda and returned to Brest, one of the early commanders to be based from that port. The boat was subsequently lost in the Bay of Biscay under a different commander.

25 April 1942: SS *Modesta*

The British steamship the *Modesta* was built by Sir John Priestman and Company of Southwick, Sunderland, England in 1917. Originally, she was owned by Furness Withy Company Limited's Gulf Line Limited and was British-flagged. From 1920, the ship was owned by A/S Ivarans Rederi (Ivar Anders Christensen) in Oslo before being sold in 1926 to Leeston Shipping Company Limited (Chubb and Holley) of London. Then in 1933 she was sold to J. W. Paulin of Viborg, Finland. At the time of her loss in March 1942 the owners were the Euxine Shipping Company, Limited of 88 Leadenhall Street, London and her operators were the Ministry of War Transport.[1]

The *Modesta* was 3,830 gross tons, and could carry 6,250 deadweight tons of cargo. Her dimensions were 357.9 feet long, 50.10 feet wide, and 21.6 feet deep. Her single triple-expansion engine developed 319 net horsepower and could propel the ship at 9.5 knots. On 27 November 1920, the *Modesta* was listed as being in distress off the Orkney Islands, North Sea, while on a voyage between Philadelphia and Bergen, Norway. She was owned by the Gulf Line Limited at the time. In January 1921, the vessel is said to have brought two passengers (emigrants) to Ellis Island, New York, and one more in November of that year.[2] She is listed as arriving in New York on 25 October 1940 as a Finnish steamship.

In 1941, the Finnish ship was taken over by the UK. Specifically, according to the British *War Cabinet Resume*, on the night of 4–5 June 1941, a British 'trawler on patrol intercepted the Finnish SS *Modesta* (3,830 tons) and sent her into Kirkwall under armed guard.'[3] There, the ship was taken over and sent to sea under the British flag. On 5 March 1942, the harbor master of Portland Maine allowed the *Modesta* to remain in port for an extra night before sailing, placing the ship in the north-east US in the spring of 1942.

The master on the *Modesta*'s final voyage was Captain James Robertson Murray, aged fifty.[4] Under him were forty men including three naval gunners and two army gunners. There were at least three teenagers in the merchant crew: mess room boy Robert Borthwick, assistant cook Johnstone Harvey, and sailor Donald John MacLeod, all nineteen. There were also three Trinidadians, who possibly signed on as recently as the *Modesta*'s call there on this voyage: fireman Cyril Lashley, aged twenty-four, fireman Clement Sealy, aged twenty-three, and fireman Lewis Waldron, aged thirty-seven. The ship was armed with a four-inch gun, two twin Marlin machine guns, two

Lewis machine guns, four P. A. C. rockets, and a variety of kites. During the voyage from Trinidad and St. Thomas, Virgin Islands to New York, her anti-mine degaussing equipment was turned off. The ship loaded 5,800 tons of bauxite, which was used for the aluminum industry, and sailed from St. Thomas on Friday, 17 April 1942.

All went well until the early morning of Saturday, 25 April. At that point, the ship was 100 nautical miles north-east of Bermuda and 900 nautical miles north of St. Thomas. The weather was partly rough, with winds fresh from the east at over 25 knots and a rough sea. It was quite overcast and visibility was low. At about 11.12 p.m. on Friday, 24 April, *Fregattenkapitän* Klaus Scholtz in command of the German submarine *U-108* fired a torpedo from Tube II from 1,200 meters at the *Modesta*; however, his aim was thrown off by the pale moonlight in and out of the clouds.[5] The relatively small size of the target as well as the yawing of the submarine in the seas combined to make the torpedo miss; however, the lookouts on the *Modesta* did not see either the torpedo or the submarine.

Second Officer John Dewar was pacing the port bridge. His lookout duties supplemented another lookout on the bridge as well as a gunner aft at the gun. At 2.15 a.m., Scholtz took another shot, this one from Tube IV at 500 meters. It detonated against the side of the *Modesta* after just two minutes and twenty-nine seconds. Dewar tells what happened next, at 2.15 a.m.:

> I was crossing the bridge to speak to the look-out man, there was a violent explosion in the way of No. 3 hatch amidships. I saw a flash and a lot of water and debris was thrown up. There was a nauseating smell of bauxite and the hatches and beams were flying everywhere. It was very difficult to see anything in the ensuing confusion.[6]

However, the radio operator was able to get off an SSS message, which the U-boat was able to intercept and identify the victim with. Scholtz took pains to count the number of masts, funnel, hatches, etc. and mark them in his war diary.

Amid this chaos, Dewar managed to don a life jacket and regroup with some of the men on the boat deck below. Fortunately, the chief engineer was able to stop the engines from the emergency levers on the boat deck, as those in the engine room had been destroyed. However, as the men milled around looking for ways to escape the first mate, 'who was very excited by this time, kept shouting to the crew to jump overboard.' This added to the confusion and threatened to permeate panic among the crew. Efforts to lower two lifeboats were only partially successful. When the forward falls of the starboard boat were let go too quickly, the boat hung helplessly by the stern, dumping two men and much of the survival gear (like oars) into the water, while at the same time partially filling the boat with seawater. Apparently, only one man was in each boat as they got away.

The ship meanwhile took on a heel and began to settle rapidly. Seeing both boats drifting away astern, Dewar jumped into the water in his life vest. He swam towards the starboard boat and was pulled into it by two firemen, a steward, and a gunner. They saw a light and presumed it was the port lifeboat; however, it was *U-108* cruising among the wreckage on the surface. Five minutes after the attack, the ship was sinking rapidly by the bow. The *Modesta* finally turned its stern into the air and sank at 2.20 a.m. *U-108* submerged to re-load torpedo tubes and head for Bermuda, without interacting with the desperate survivors scattered about in the water. In the starboard lifeboat the situation looked grim. The boat was waterlogged and all the oars except two had been washed overboard, as well as the sea anchor. They did have a pump and a bucket, which the steward and gunner put to immediate use bailing the boat. The original five men then picked up another gunner and a mess room boy. Sighting a raft with no lights they paddled over to it and found the chief engineer. They took him aboard the boat and stripped the raft of water and food, which had also been lost from the lifeboat.

After some time, they met with the port lifeboat, which was also in a waterlogged state and towing a raft. They learned that Third Mate John McLeod had managed to cut the port lifeboat adrift and had then used it to pick up a number of men from the water. Using a torch to communicate, Second Officer Dewar took charge of the group, the captain not being among the survivors. Dewar instructed the third mate to stay within hailing distance during the night. It became clear that the port lifeboat was in far worse condition than Dewar's, so all the men, water, and provisions were transferred to the starboard boat, and the other vessels were cast adrift. While it was still night, the men in the remaining boat heard shouting and discovered six men holding onto the *Modesta*'s wooden topmast. Fortuitously, they also found a fireman clinging to a hatch cover as well as a sailor on another hatch. By that time, there were a total of twenty-four survivors in the boat, from a complement of forty-one. When daylight came, they searched the horizon for any other survivors and then, regretfully, set a course for the south-west towards Bermuda, leaving their seventeen crewmates, officers, gunners, and sailors, to their fates.

Due to the heavy seas, sailing was difficult. Since the mast had been lost, the men jury-rigged an oar and employed a boat hook as a yard and the dodger as a sail. Conditions were very cold as the wind blew strongly. As the seas sloshed aboard, the men were bailing continuously. Under these trying conditions, the twenty-four men carried on through Saturday the 25th and into Sunday, 26 April. On Sunday, the sun came out; though the seas continued rough, the fact they were able to dry out their soaked clothes and blankets cheered the men considerably. Many of them were very thinly clad, and six of them had no pants at all. At 10.00 a.m., while sailing westwards, the men saw two US Navy airplanes overhead. The planes must have seen the red-colored hood of the lifeboat, as they crossed above the boat. Dewar thinks that in the roughly forty hours since they had left the ship the lifeboat had covered some 70 nautical miles.

This is borne out by the Eastern Sea Frontier Enemy Action Diary for 26 April, which states 'Bermuda reports planes sighted lifeboats 25 miles east of Bermuda. Plane guided "*BELGIAN AIRMAN*" to scene. .... Planes will continue search other possible survivors at dawn.'[7] If the survivors were 100 miles from Bermuda when sunk and 25 miles away when rescued, then they covered 75 miles towards their destination. The War Diary of US Naval Operating Base Bermuda for the same day records that 'The survivors were located by two of our patrol planes yesterday off Bermuda, and rescued by the S. S. *BELGIAN AIRMAN*, directed to the scene by one plane, while the other circled over the survivors.' An hour after sighting the planes, at 11 a.m. on Sunday the 26th, the twenty-four *Modesta* men sighted a steamer approaching them cautiously. It was the *Belgian Airman*, a Belgian government ship of 6,959 tons that was having a very difficult voyage. In bad weather, one of the ship's life rafts had been swept away along with part of its deck cargo. The ship had been deviated by the weather off its usual track, enabling it to be quickly found by the planes and diverted to the scene of the *Modes*ta survivors—their trials benefiting the survivors.

The *Belgian Airman* was only delivered in February 1942 as the *Empire Ballantyne* before the British Ministry of War Transport transferred the ship to the Belgian government, who gave it the new name. The ship was 433 feet long, 56.3 feet wide, and 34.3 feet deep, and propelled by a single diesel engine of 490 net horsepower, which gave it 12 knots speed. It was built by Harland and Wolff Limited of Belfast, Northern Ireland and Glasgow. The Master of the *Belgian Airman* (believed to have been Captain E. Cailloux) skillfully brought his ship alongside the lifeboat and his men put over pilot ladders to enable the survivors, including the injured, to clamber up the side of the ship.[8] Dewar notes that 'we were treated extremely well.' Given their proximity to Bermuda, they were able to be landed in St. George's at 4 p.m. the same day, Sunday the 26th.

In Bermuda, volunteers and aid workers were working around the clock to accommodate survivors from numerous ships sunk around the island. The *Herald-American* in Syracuse New York of Sunday, 26 April 1942 titled a piece '67 Reach Bermuda from 3 Lost Ships.'[9] These were thirty-three men from the Swedish *Agra*, which landed on Wednesday, 22 April, after drifting two days; eight men from the British *Derryheen*, which landed the same day after drifting for a day; and twenty-six men from the US freighter the *Robin Hood*, who had been adrift for nine days and landed on Saturday, 25 April, a day before the *Modesta* men arrived. The *Bradford Era*, a Pennsylvania newspaper, reported on Monday the 28th:

> Spotted by aircraft and rescued by ship, survivors of an Allied merchant vessel torpedoed off Bermuda have been landed at nearby St. George's. The seamen reported their captain was among 14 [*sic*] believed lost. Seven officers were among the survivors.[10]

The most accurate reporting came, understandably, from the ground in Bermuda. On Monday, 27 April, *The Royal Gazette and Colonist Daily* in Hamilton described the plight of the *Modesta* survivors in great detail under a title 'More Survivors Landed Here After Torpedoing: British Seamen 4th Group Rescued in Five Days.' It states:

> The intensity of the submarine warfare in Atlantic waters has become a grim reality here. It is increasingly so to the many who are now tendering the wants of the seamen. Their number increases because of the heavy demands for accommodation, nursing and care. There are now 91 men in Bermuda who have escaped being the victims of the U-boat menace.[11]

The article, which takes two columns, continues: 'The Naval Recreation Rooms in Hamilton have taken survivors from the last two groups [the *Robin Hood* and the *Modesta*] and are now turning their facilities over to the care of these men.' Caregivers 'quickly prepared themselves for the emergency. Boiling water was made ready and food was cooked. Over the week-end they had brought comfort to the survivors they already were domiciling.' Though the American House and Bermuda Sailor's Homes, recently enlarged with an infirmary, were 'taxed to beyond their capacity', they fit six *Modesta* men and one officer. Eleven of the *Modesta* men were in the Naval Recreation Rooms' dormitories in Hamilton. Five of the seven officers were put up in private homes in Hamilton, one was in the home of Mrs. Leland Barnes in St. George's, and the seventh was at the American House. Third Officer McLeod is said by Dewar to have been placed in hospital; however, he must have been released to coalesce in a private home shortly thereafter. Six of the crew were placed in the new infirmary of the Bermuda Sailor's Home.

The author is sympathetic to the men's plight, describing their ordeal; they noted:

Some of the survivors had only managed to abandon ship with a minimum of clothing, and this added to their miseries. Those in the engine room found themselves one moment in warm waters and the next in the icy sea. Six of the men reached St. George's minus their trousers. They were blue with the cold and suffering from exposure. One seaman had a badly injured foot.

The article was highly laudatory of the volunteers as well as hospital staff:

While awaiting transportation [from St. George's to Hamilton], 11 of their number were given attention at the St. George's Sailor's Home, where Mrs. Barnes provided clothing and sustenance, in a very short time. Her efforts and those who assisted her were typical of the sympathy, which is felt by everybody here. It is not possible to mention all the acts of kindness, which are being performed. The staff of the King Edward VII Memorial Hospital, burdened as they are, have taken on new responsibilities with an undiminished vigor and they deserve a hearty commendation.

The newspaper notes that with the arrival of the *Agra* and the *Derryheen* survivors 'the Bermuda Railway Company operated its first night train (a special) to bring the survivors to Hamilton.'

An inquiry was held in Bermuda in which Second Mate Dewar, the chief engineer, and the first mate (who had generated some panic during the abandonment of the *Modesta*) were all interviewed. The *Modesta* survivors were brought back to the UK by the converted troop ship *Durban Castle* under the command of Captain R. C. T. Harris. Also on board were eight survivors of the British merchant ship the *Derryheen*. The *Durban Castle* was built in 1938 by Harland and Wolff of Belfast. She was 17,382 gross registered ton, 594.7 feet long, 76.4 feet wide, and could achieve an

Overflight of Convoy safely entering Bermuda's sheltered waters, as painted by Floyd Davis in 1942. In the foreground is Grassy Bay, and the Royal Navy Dockyard rises to the left, with Spanish Point to the right. In the middle a narrow channel was, with the exigencies of war, blasted through the coral. (*Life Magazine*)

impressive 18.5 knots of speed. Built for passenger service around Africa, the ship was converted to a troop ship in 1939 and helped evacuate the King of Greece and his entourage to Egypt in 1941.[12]

While *en route* back to Europe, the twenty-four survivors would have passed over or close to the spot where seventeen of their colleagues had perished that April morning. These included Captain Murray, teens Borthwick, Harvey, and MacLeod, and the three Trinidadians, Lashley, Sealy, and Waldron, who left three children alive at the time and one not yet born as well as a widow.[13] Nine of the dead were in their twenties: first radio officer Thomas Bentley Holcroft, Lashley, bosun George McCondach, ordinary seaman Hugh McFarlane, greaser V. Murray, fireman Reynold Prince, ordinary seaman James Scott, Sealy, and fireman Herman Simon.[14]

Late in the evening of Saturday the 25th, *U-108* observed two airplanes several times. These were most likely rescue planes sent out from Naval Operating Base Bermuda to look for *Modesta* survivors. Late in the same night, the submarine came so close to Bermuda that the skipper could observe Mount Hill Light bearing 315 degrees from 17 miles away. Scholtz also recorded in his war diary that he could clearly see the lights of Hamilton at around midnight. The *Belgian Airman* was sunk off Hatteras by *U-857* under Rudolf Premauer while on a voyage from Houston to Antwerp via New York. All but one of the forty-seven men on board survived. It was 14 April 1945, with only weeks left in the war between Germany and the Allies.

25–27 April 1942: Four U-boats

Oberleutnant zur See Horst Uphoff brought his command *U-84* into the area north of Bermuda from north-west to north-east between 25 and 29 April 1942. He was only on the fringe of the region for five days before heading north-east back to Europe. The boat sailed for the 1st U-boat Flotilla in Brest on 16 March for US waters as part of Operation Drumbeat. On 2 April, *U-84* had a rendezvous with the *milchkuh U-A* east of Newfoundland.[1] Proceeding to the waters east of New York, *U-86* managed to sink the Yugoslavian steamship the *Nemanza* of 5,226 tons, then went further south to Hatteras. On 21 May, *U-84* sank the Panamanian steamer the *Chenango* of 3,014 tons before moving east to an area off Bermuda. The submarine arrived back in Brest on 14 May 1942.[2]

Horst Uphoff was born in 1916 and a member of the Crew of 1935. Early in his naval career he was watch officer of the U-boat depot ship *Donau* up to 1939, when he enrolled in U-boat courses. Uphoff served as a watch officer of *U-46* under Sohler and Endrass. Commissioning *U-84* in April 1941, he led that sub until both were destroyed south of Bermuda on 7 August 1943 by aircraft from Bermuda. He was twenty-six at the time. Over nine patrols, Uphoff accrued 461 days and sank or damaged seven ships of 37,081 tons. He was awarded the German Cross in Gold posthumously in 1944, having received the Iron Cross First Class while alive.

Korvettenkapitän Wilhelm Schulze in *U-98* entered the area north of Bermuda on 25 April to contribute nine days of patrols to that area before leaving on 22 May 1942. On the 25th, he entered east-north-east of the island, patrolling west for four days until the 28th, when he exited north-west of the island bound for Hatteras. Then on 18 May, *U-98* returned, heading south-west towards the island until the following day, when he changed course and motored north-east for France until the 22nd, when the submarine exited the area north-east of Bermuda. *U-98* was refueled by *U-459* north-east of Bermuda on 27 April, but on that date, the sub was very near the island, so it was probably north-east of Bermuda on about 23–24 April. The patrol lasted from 31 March to 6 June, beginning and ending in St. Nazaire, where *U-98* was based for the 7th U-boat Flotilla. Three German U-boats entered the region on 28 April 1942: *U-333*, *U-98* under Schulze, and *U-506* under Würdemann; all entered from either south or west of Bermuda and made for the east coast of Florida before returning. Next across the imaginary line was Schulze in *U-98*, a VIIC type U-boat on its seventh of nine patrols for the 7th U-boat Flotilla out of St. Nazaire. The trajectory of this patrol indicates a skipper who is fastidious about following his cruising orders: from a point roughly midway between the Carolinas and Bermuda the boat made a bee-line for Cape Canaveral, then made a 90-degree turn to the north, sailing past Jacksonville and Savannah before taking another such turn, and then another, with the effect that a box is drawn off those ports. This patrol began in St. Nazaire on 31 March 1942 and ended there on 6 June. *U-98* was refueled by *U-459* around 27 April, roughly 500 miles north-east of Bermuda.

Wilhelm Schultze was ranked *Korvettenkapitän* in September 1942 and retired without decorations after two patrols of 130 days. Born in July 1909, he was a member of the crew of 1928. His career total was the damage of the US Armed Merchant Cruiser (AMC) the *Bold* by mines on 10 August 1942—she weighed 185 tons. Contrasted with the long list of kills that some submarine commanders achieved, Schultze's career demonstrates that success was by no means a given. For a large number of U-boat commanders, patrols consisted of staring at a hard, grey horizon wishing for an enemy ship to sail across it, and hearing of the accolades pouring upon more successful colleagues. This patrol is also a harbinger of things to come, as the only enemy sighted in over two months was the attacker, in the form of British aircraft, and not an Allied merchant marine victim.

Kapitänleutnant Peter-Erich 'Ali' Cremer brought *U-333* to the Bermuda area a day after its predecessor *U-98* on 26 April 1942 for a patrol of seven days ending on 12 May. In that time, *U-333* entered to the north-east of the island, headed west for a day until the 27th, then south-east till the 28th, then due west to the 29th, at which point it exited the region. On 10 May, the sub returned homeward bound from the same position, and headed north-east, passing north of Bermuda the following day. Then, it motored north-east and out of the area on 12 May. The patrol ended in La Pallice also on 26 May. Early in the patrol, the sub was bombed from the air and badly shaken but escaped. The boat left La Pallice (near La Rochelle) in France on 30 March 1942 and was refueled by *U-459*, like *U-98* before it, about 500 miles north-east of Bermuda, on 22 April.

A week after refueling, *U-333* sighted the tanker the *British Prestige* of 7,106 tons and pursued her into the evening of 30 April. Cremer fired a salvo of two torpedoes, which missed. While the U-boat crew were preparing a second spread, the tanker turned hard upon her and ran over *U-333*, badly damaging the sub's bridge casing, bow, and conning tower. On 1 May, the crew undertook what repairs they could and continued the patrol heading southwards to Florida. Cremer spent thirteen days in the region and exited several hundred miles west of Bermuda on the 10 May, leaving in his wake the hulks of four victims: the *Java Arrow*, the *Amazone*, the *Halsey* (all sunk on the same day—6 May off the coast of Florida), and the *Clan Skene* (sunk offshore on the 10th). Cremer's total tonnage for this patrol was 21,923. The patrol ended on 26 May in La Pallice.

Ali Cremer, a member of the class of 1932, was one of the more memorable of the U-boat skippers, in part because he penned a readable book about his career exploits entitled *U-boat Commander*, and he lived until the age of eighty-one, dying in 1992 in Hamburg. Immediately following this patrol, he was awarded the Knight's Cross, going on to win the Wounded Badge in Silver and the U-boat front clasp. His career tally was six ships sunk for 26,873 tons, one warship damaged for 925 tons, and the *Java Arrow* damaged for 8,327 tons. At the time of his raid on the US, he was a *Kapitänleutnant*, being promoted to *Korvettenkapitän* in July 1944. He served in command of *U-333* for five patrols between 25 August 1941 and 19 July 1944. Cremer had studied law for roughly three years at the time he joined the Navy in 1932, and his admission was accelerated by the loss of the school training ship the *Niobe* that year.[3] He served aboard the cruiser the *Deutschland* until the rank of *Leutnant* and, in 1940, transferred to U-boats. The boat's symbol was three fishes (for the three threes in its number) and Cremer's first command was accomplished without prior combat experience.[4]

Among the notable incidents in Cremer's career were the sinking of the German blockade-runner *Spreewald* due to a mis-communication, and an injury off West Africa, which necessitated a replacement skipper for the boat and three months of hospitalization for Cremer. His crew considered him their 'best life insurance.' After over a year on Dönitz's staff, in late 1944 Cremer took command of *U-2519*, a Type-XXI electric U-boat, in an effort to regain supremacy in the face of decimation of the U-boats by Allies. A personal account of Cremer and the Florida man who helped rescue survivors of the *Java Arrow* off Jacksonville and the friendship between them that developed after war is recounted in the book *Different Battles* by Rody Johnson.[5]

Kapitänleutnant Hellmut Rathke motored on his final war patrol just north of Bermuda, from east to west, starting on 27 April 1942. He sailed for the 3rd U-boat Flotilla in St. Nazaire on 7 April. Later that month, the boat was refueled by *U-459* to the north-east of Bermuda.[6] *U-352* then motored for Hatteras, passing north of Bermuda on 28, 29, and 30 April. Many sources—including Wynn, Gentile, and Hickam—discredit *U-352* and Rathke with the botched attack on the Swedish freighter the *Freden* on 5 May 1942 off Hatteras.[7, 8, 9] However, closer examination of the war diary of the submarine *U-202* under Adalbert Schnee confirms that, from location and precise attack details, the attack could only have been by Schnee, who was convinced that the *Freden* was a decoy ship or Armed Merchant Cruiser, such as the Germans deployed in great numbers (the British and Americans called them Q-Ships). Wynn writes that the attack was 'an amazing story of ineptitude on both sides' since the Swedes repeatedly abandoned and re-boarded their ship before it was even struck.[10]

The war log of *U-352* did not survive, as the U-boat was detected and sunk by the US Coast Guard cutter the *Icarus* on 7 May off Hatteras in shallow water. Sixteen of the Germans were killed in the attack, and thirty-three were imprisoned in Charleston after a delay in pulling them from the water; one of those subsequently died. Rathke was made a Prisoner of War until 17 May 1946. Perhaps surprisingly, he was not successful in convincing the Allies that he had not indeed attacked the *Freden*, possibly because he had tried to sink several ships—including the *Icarus*, without success on the same patrol. Rathke was born in East Prussia in 1910 and was thirty-two at the time of this patrol. He served in the Crew of 1930 and became leader of the Torpedo School in Mürwik, leading to a staff officer role. He began training for U-boats in April 1941 and commissioned *U-352* in August 1941. Over two patrols, he accrued seventy-six patrol days and did not sink any ships. His sole decoration was an Iron Cross 2nd Class. Rathke died in October 2001 at the age of seventy in Flensburg.[11]

1 May 1942: SV *James E. Newsom*

The four-masted schooner the *James E. Newsom* was built by the East Coast Company of Boothbay, Maine and launched on 23 August 1919. She weighed 707 gross tons (629 net tons) and was crewed by eight men on average. The vessel's length overall was 180.4 feet, the beam was 36.2 feet, and depth 14.9 feet. Her port of registry was Boston. The ship wasted no time in getting down to business, as she arrived in Boston to load lumber in the Mystic River for Buenos Aires the very day after being launched. In 1921, she sailed from Windsor, Nova Scotia to New York in late November with eight crew.[1] In 1923, she again visited from Nova Scotia as well as from the Dominican Republic, also with eight persons aboard, and in April 1924, she arrived from Walton, Nova Scotia.[2]

Author Ingrid Grenon, in her 2010 book *Lost Maine Coastal Schooners: From Glory Days to Ghost Ships*, writes of the *Newsom*:

Two major shipyards in Boothbay, the Atlantic Coast Company and the East Coast Company, were formed in 1917 and used exclusively for building and repairing large coastal schooners. …the East Coast Company backers included the mayor of Somerville, Massachusetts, and turned out five four-masted schooners. One of these schooners was the four-master *James E. Newsom*….serving the Crowell and Thurlow fleet. She was named after Boston fruit and produce merchant James E. Newsom and christened by his daughter, Miss Thelma Moss Newsom. The *Newsom* had an interesting and lengthy career; her first cargo consisted of 700,000 feet of lumber.

Spending years ranging up and down the East Coast, early in 1926 the Florida real estate boom found her aground off Miami heavily loaded with 710,000 feet of lumber and lightly damaged. After she went aground again and part of her cargo was removed, a squall came up and battered the craft, driving her ashore. With the seas raging over her decks and part of her hull in splinters, the crew decided to abandon ship. A testament to her robust construction, she was towed away and repaired. The *Newsom* grounded a few more times, was involved in a collision and lost her rudder in a storm, but she was able to weather those unfortunate mishaps.[3]

During the Miami grounding, 'The channel was blocked for one day until harbor officials ordered the ship towed to sea, over protest of the *Newsom*'s master, who contended that with assistance he could make port.'[4] Another grounding was upon Little Gull Island at the eastern entrance to Long Island Sound.[5] The schooner was bound from Halifax to New York and was pulled free by the US Coast Guard Cutter *Algonquin*, based in nearby New London, Connecticut. On 18 January 1921, she sailed from Moss Point, Mississippi for San Juan. Then, as related by witnesses:

> On the night of April 14th, 1921, at four minutes past 11 o'clock, the four-masted American schooner *James E. Newsom*, bound north with a full cargo of lumber and manned by the master (accompanied by his wife) and a crew of seven men, struck the Bluefish Lump Shoal at the extreme tip of Cape Lookout, N. C.[6]

The author James S. Beaman goes on to relate how the captain, his wife, and crew abandoned ship that day and were looked after by the Coast Guard crew at the Cape Lookout Lighthouse:

> Exactly at 5.25 a.m. on this memorable Friday, April 15th, 1921, the lookout in the tower sighted a sail coming just over the horizon from an easterly direction. As it neared, he made a mental note that the vessel sighted was a four masted schooner and gave no further thought to it, at the time, as she appeared to be in no distress and making good headway before a gentle breeze, bearing in for the Cape. From time to time, as he routinely scanned the sea with his powerful binoculars, the lookout would let his gaze rest momentarily upon the now nearer-approaching schooner. In one of these brief moments of inspection the thought came to him that while this particular vessel appeared to be shipshape and her behavior normal in every way... No single human form was to be seen anywhere upon her decks or in her rigging. No helmsman stood at her wheel, no lookout was in her bow. The only visible, animate thing about her was a lone white seagull, which flapped its extended wings in rhythmic beat at main mast height, a few yards before her bow.
>
> Presently, now sailing beautifully, with a bone in her teeth, before the strengthened breeze, the schooner approached near enough to land to excite the interest of those about the station other than the lookout. The master of the James E. Newsom, with his wife at his side, had taken his stand on the beach near the water's edge. Members of his crew and several Coast Guardsmen stood just behind them. Nearer and nearer the sailor-less ship drew to the, by now, thoroughly awed and silent group. For it was plainly evident to all whom watched that this schooner was the James E. Newsom, last seen by them wedged fast upon the shoal of Bluefish Lump.
>
> As if in heed to some unspoken command the stately sailing vessel, when she had almost reached land, veered slightly from her course and with graceful movements, as the wind slackened in her sails, brought her keel gently to rest upon the pebbly beach—one might, almost literally, say at the feet of her master.[7]

As witnesses were able to piece together what happened they realized that the ship had managed to wriggle itself free with the incoming and outgoing tides and fluctuating winds, then drift through dangerous shoals until it grounded improbably in front of the lighthouse, its sails having been left set, tantamount to a vehicle being left with its engines on and in gear… Only two sails were damaged.

In 1928, the *James E. Newsom* was sold to new owners, namely Zwicker Geldert Shipping Company Limited; she was reflagged to Canada and registered to Halifax. Her name was changed to the *D. Geldert*, but only from 1931 to 1935, after which it reverted to the *James E. Newsom* but remained under Geldert ownership. During a voyage from Halifax to Preston, England, in August 1937, Chief Mate Archie Geldert broke one of his legs when just seventeen hours out of their homeport. His relative Captain Dawson Geldert made splints and set the fracture. On landing in the United Kingdom the mate had the use of both legs, and the Captain received congratulations from physicians who examined the patient.[8] There is an interesting story from 1927 about these two men, each sea captains and brothers, who lived apart from each other for three decades:

> New York—Dawson Geldert and Archibald Geldert, Nova Scotian brothers, are sea captains, like their father, his six brothers, his father and his grandfather. After 30 years Captains Dawson and Archibald met for the first time when the four-masted schooners *Cutty Sark* and *Arthur H. Zwicker* were parked in the same creek in Brooklyn.

During World War Two, the *Newsom* transited New York City on 2 December 1939 outbound, then arrived on 29 August 1940.[9] On 28 October 1941, she was to sail; however, the lack of wind delayed departure until 30 October. In the fateful spring of 1942, the *Newsom* loaded salt on Grand Turk, Turks and Caicos, and delivered its cargo safely to Barbados, where it loaded molasses, setting off for St. Johns, intending to pass east of Bermuda. At the end of April, she passed about 270 nautical miles east of Bermuda. At sunrise on Friday, 1 May 1942, the schooner was 330 miles from Bermuda, double that from Newfoundland.

Meanwhile, the German submarine *U-69* under *Oberleutnant zur See* Ulrich Gräf, aged twenty-six, was having a very social patrol, which began in St. Nazaire on 12 April 1942. Ten days into the patrol, the submarine had to pass on a neutral Spanish ship. On the 25th, he was advised that 'Operations off America with the long routes pays only if every boat mercilessly exhausts its chances of success within the few days in the operations area allowed to him by his fuel.' Later that day, *U-69*'s men sighted *U-761* under Möhlmann and 'exchanged experiences.'

Three days later, on 28 April, *U-69* encountered *U-594* under Hoffman and *U-572* under Hirsacker. They were all in a rendezvous north-east of Bermuda to receive fuel from *U-459* under Wilamowitz. *U-459* was one of the milk cow tanker submarines designed to refuel attack U-boats and enable them to penetrate distant Allied waters for longer periods of time. The next day, *U-558* under Krech joined the group. During this time, supplies and fuel were exchanged between the boats, as well as intelligence. The *U-69* took on 32 cubic meters of diesel by 29 April.[10]

Two days later, at 5.54 a.m., Gräf observed: 'Sailing vessel in sight bearing 140°T, 4 masted schooner, course 5°, 6 knots. Maneuvered ahead to port. The white sails are very difficult to distinguish against with the hazy horizon.' Less than an hour later, Gunther Krech in *U-558* re-appeared, and the two subs exchanged recognition signals. Within ten minutes, Krech's U-boat is out of sight. Gräf is then free to concentrate on his attack on the sailboat, which is the *James E. Newsom*—his description of the ship having four masts and her position at that time confirms this. At 9.17 a.m., Gräf records: 'Crash dive! Am too close, however, am positioned ahead, decide to attack submerged. Surfaced. Because after 15 minutes not in sight. In sight directly astern, target angle 0°, very hard to distinguish. Dived for submerged attack. Sailor has no lookout, gives an innocent impression.' The conditions at the time were mild—wind about 5–10 knots; 1,011 millibars on the barometer; seas 1–3 feet; and medium, hazy visibility. Gräf does not appear to have been in a rush to attack. At 11.27 a.m., he 'surfaced for armed attack, after which I ran in his wake for a while.' Seeing a German submarine surface behind them and speed up for an artillery attack must have been a terrifying sight for the civilian crew of the *James E. Newsom*. They did not have to wait long, however, as a minute later, the men on *U-69* opened fire from a range of about 650 feet.

Gräf records that 'Crew (nine men) go to the boats. Sailing vessel darts in the wind. Name: "*JAMES E. NEWSOM*", homeport Halifax, 671 GRT. Sunk with full sails.' Altogether, it took *U-69*'s gunners fifty-four incendiary shells of 8.8 cm, twelve explosive shells of 8.8 cm, and sixty machine gun rounds of C/30 ammunition to destroy and sink the *Newsom*. Here are the reasons that Gräf gave:

> Sea state 3, the gun crew was continuously under water. During the firing 2 men went overboard, went back at AK and fished them out. The 2-meter high freeboard of the enemy. Zero mark of the barrel attachment was already broken at the first salvos. 10 shells went overboard, because people could hold on badly.[11]

He continues: 'Cargo and port of destination could not be determined from the crew. Course lead to the Cabot Strait'—in fact, the *Newsom* was headed to St. John's Newfoundland, but he was not far off. The sub commander concludes his analysis with: 'The incendiary ammunition had no effect. The wood ship hull began to glow for a few seconds then was put out by the washing over water.' He adds that he feels he's done about enough in the Bermuda area, noting: 'On the basis of messages from Scholtz of 30 April and Forster of 1 April there is no traffic in the Bermudas and increased fuel consumption by the pursuit of the sailor, ordered direct transit to the ordered attack area.' With that, *U-69* sailed out of the region.[12]

In 1937, the *Newsom*'s skipper was Captain Dawson Geldert, and the mate was Archie Geldert. In July 1937, Captain Dawson's daughter Marion Geldert, a student at Dalhousie University, crossed the Atlantic and back aboard her. This would have been the same crossing during which her uncle Archie broke his leg. Since the ship had been owned by Zwicker Geldert Shipping Co. Ltd., it is safe to assume that there was at least one officer named Geldert aboard her, and even that a Geldert was her master, very possibly Dawson Geldert himself. According to his obituary, Captain Dawson Geldert had sold the *James E. Newsom* in Barbados and planned to sail aboard her back to Canada, where he was to retire in Lunenberg:

> Captain Geldert retired from the sea when he sold his four-master, the *James Newsom*, while she was in port in Barbados, to enjoy the rest of his life in his home town which had seen little of him during his long life at sea. On her first trip out of Barbados under new ownership, the *Newsom* was sunk by a submarine and Captain Geldert counted this among his many close calls during his sea-going days.

Finally, when Captain Geldert died in July of 1945, he was sixty-four years of age. According to the local papers, the *James E. Newsom* skipper was sixty-two years old on arrival in May 1942. All indications are that Captain Dawson Geldert was in command of the *James E. Newsom*, which he no longer owned at the time of the ship's demise. For one week, between midday Friday, 1 May, and Thursday, 7 May (six nights and seven days), eight rugged Canadians and one West Indian crew sailed their lifeboat 330 miles from where they sank to Bermuda. This means that they averaged an impressive 2.2 knots. The voyage is testament to not only tenacity and determination, but also navigational accuracy. From interviews with survivors within twenty-four hours of their arrival by a Bermudian journalist, we know that a Bermuda-based airplane spotted the *Newsom*'s single lifeboat. Though Gräf said that he saw the men 'go to the boats' (plural), they must have transferred to a single boat afterwards. The plane called on the US Navy, also based at a Naval Operating Base in Bermuda, to go to their aid. On Thursday, 7 May, 'the office of the Commandant of the US Naval Operating Base released the following announcement: "A small group of survivors, British subjects, were brought in today by one of the Unites States naval vessels and turned over to the British Naval authorities."' The journalist notes that Captain Geldert 'was closeted for about an hour with an official at the [Sailor's] Home after he arrived.'

The first-hand witness described how 'considering their ordeal [they] were in reasonably good condition although suffering in varying degrees from severe salt water and sun burns, in addition to exposure. None of them was a hospital case.' When they were taken to the Sailor's Home, presumably from the St. David's or St. George's area, 'they carried with them bundles of clothing and personal belongings which somehow had escaped the sinking and the days at sea in the small craft.' They even had 'a suitcase [that] had become crushed by the handling it had received.' The men were given a dry pair of clothes, pajamas, and slippers. 'A few of the older men had grown beards—one of them had particularly black whiskers while a couple of very young men looked almost clean-shaven.'

The journalist goes on to describe Captain Geldert's interactions with the crew: 'he was plainly respected and liked by those under him. …when he came into the circle of the crew they were particularly solicitous about his condition. But the ruddy-faced captain, of slight build, was primarily concerned that the men were comfortable.' There was only one bath at the Sailor's Home and they all waited their turn patiently. When asked by Mrs. Darby if he did not mind waiting, one sailor replied 'I certainly don't. I'm lucky to be here having a bath.' After they had been bathed and clothed, the men were taken to in Hamilton 'for a solid meal.'[13]

Most of the men—all of the eight Canadians—were put up at the Bermuda Sailor's Home on Front Street in Hamilton. The home was run by Dickie Tucker, Superintendent, ably assisted by the Matron, Mrs. Darby. Demand was so high during the war that additional dormitories were added at the Bermudiana Hotel in conjunction with the Ladies Hospitality Organization 'to house torpedoed mariners who waited new shipping orders.' In fact, the *James E. Newsom* survivors' first concern was how to ship out again: 'Their first thought, given expression by all of them was "When can we get another ship?"'

The only crew not in the Sailors Home was a man from Monserrat:

It was discovered that the West Indian had relatives here, and for his own convenience Mr. Tucker made arrangements for him to be taken to the Canadian Hotel, where contact could be established. He was accompanied to the Reid Street Hostelry by a member of the previous survivor groups who before leaving the Sailor's Home asked the new arrival to share a soft drink with him.

This survivor might have been from any number of Allied ships whose survivors landed in Bermuda before 7 May 1942. From that spring alone, these included the *Lady Drake* (256 men and women, 6 May), the *Modesta* (twenty-three men, 26 April), the *Robin Hood* (twenty-four men, 25 April), the *Derryheen* or the *Agra* (eight and thirty-three men respectively, 22 April), the *Oakmar* (thirty men 24 March), or the *British Resource* (five men, 16 March). Certainly, the men from the *Newsom* would have found companionship—and perhaps even networked for their next berth—while in Bermuda. It is not recorded when they left for the mainland, but it would have been either by air to New York or possibly ships going to Halifax for convoy work (earlier in the war there were a number of such convoys from Bermuda).[14]

U-69's next victim was not until nearly two weeks later, on 12 May (the *Lise*), followed by three others on the same patrol: the *Norlantic*, the *Torondoc*, and the abandoned tug the *Letitia Porter*. *U-69* returned to St. Nazaire unscathed on 25 June 1942. *U-69*, Ulrich Gräf, and all forty-six men on the sub were lost less than a year later on 17 February 1943 when HMS *Fame*, a British destroyer, successfully attacked it east of Newfoundland. Gräf was twenty-seven years of age.[15]

21

1–4 May 1942: Six U-boats

Kapitänleutnant Günther Krech brought *U-558* on a complex thirteen-day patrol around Bermuda commencing 1 May and ending on 3 June 1942. Starting to the east-north-east of Bermuda, Krech motored west for three days, then exited the area on the 5th, heading for Hatteras. On the 13th, he returned, headed south-east from a point north-west of the island, then turned south to exit the region on 17 May south-west of Bermuda. Finally, his third incursion began on 1 June and lasted until the third, all well south-east of the island on the sub's return leg. During that part of his mission, Krech managed to sink the Dutch ship *Triton* on 2 June. Having left Brest on 12 April, *U-558* refueled from *U-459* on the 29th, north-east of Bermuda.[1] On the return trip, *U-558* again refueled from *U-459*, this time in mid-June west of the Azores. It returned to Brest on 21 June 1942.

Krech began his first patrol into the Bermuda area aboard the *U-558* on 15 May, a mere day after Bigalk and Von Mannstein. Like Bigalk, he opted for a straight line from Hatteras to the Windward Passage, and like his colleague, he sank a steamer— the Dutch *Fauna*—*en route* among the islands. The submarine also attacked and sank the HMS *Bedfordshire* (FY 141) on 12 May, off Cape Hatteras, then damaged the Canadian *Troisdoc*, the *William Boyce Thompson*, the *Beatrice*, and the *Jack* in the Caribbean and the *Triton* on the way home—north-east of the Caribbean on 2 June. Total tonnage for the patrol was 19,301 from seven ships.[2]

Günther Krech, aged twenty-seven at the time, became one of the better-known U-boat skippers of the war, made famous in part by his over twenty ships and over 100,000 tons sunk and his activity off the American coast. He is also remarkable for his youth and early recognition; he earned the Knight's Cross shortly after this patrol four days before his twenty-eighth birthday on 17 September 1942. On 20 July 1943, *U-558* was sunk by Allied aircraft in the Bay of Biscay, with Krech and four others surviving and being kept in captivity by the Allies during the balance of the war and sometime thereafter. Krech survived and lived until the age of eighty-five, passing in June 2000. A member of the crew of 1933, he had served in the Luftwaffe for four years before returning to the U-boat arm in November 1939 and serving under Schepke in *U-100*. He was the officer who commissioned *U-558*.[3]

Oberleutnant zur See Ulrich Gräf took *U-69* on a virtually straight line south-west from the day he sank the Canadian schooner the *James E. Newsom* north-east of the island on 1 May to when he exited a week later to the south of Bermuda on the 7th. It appears that east of the island, Gräf patrolled in a dog-leg or zigzag, looking for prey, starting on 3 May southbound, then northbound till the 5th and south again during the 6th and 7th. Later, *U-69* rendezvoused with *U-459* in order to refuel, like several of its predecessors, 500 miles north-east of Bermuda. Born on 15 December 1915 in Dresden, Gräf was killed in the North Atlantic on 17 February 1943 east of Newfoundland.

Dietrich Hoffmann, later *Korvettenkapitän*, spent nine days transiting around Bermuda without having sunk any ships. He entered the region on 2 May 1942 to the north-east of Bermuda and headed south-west towards the Bahamas until exiting on the 6th. Then a month later, on 6 June, he came back empty handed from a patrol to the Caribbean. Until 9 June, *U-594* headed from a position due south-west of Bermuda, exiting the area to the east of the island on the 9th. *U-594* sailed for the 7th U-boat Flotilla in St. Nazaire on 11 April 1942 and returned to the same base on 25 June.

On the way to the Bermuda area, Hoffmann refueled at the end of April from *U-459* to the north-east of Bermuda.[4] On 25 May, *U-594* engaged a tanker and lost one its crew over the side during the action. They were not recovered. On the way back to Europe, the sub was again refueled by *U-459*, this time west of the Azores. Dietrich Hoffmann was born in 1912. He began his naval career in the Crew of 1932 and served as watch officer on the cruiser the *Emden* and the light cruiser the *Leipzig*. He moved to staff positions (advisor to the OKM) from 1940 to 1941, and joined U-boats in March 1940. Hoffmann commanded *U-594* from October 1941 to July 1942, when he was replaced by Friedrich Mumm. After U-boats, he served as first officer of the destroyer Z 30 and later her caretaker commander until the end of hostilities. Over two patrols of ninety-three days, he neither damaged nor sank any Allied ships. He was promoted to *Korvettenkapitän* in July 1944 and received no decorations.

The patrol of *U-103* under *Kapitänleutnant* Werner Winter lasted for six days in the area, all of it inbound. Winter headed south-east from a position north of the island. On 5 May, on entering the area, he sank the *Stanbank* with a rich cargo of military supplies destined to fight Rommel in North Africa. Then, the sub turned south-west for a day, then west across the north of Bermuda until turning south-west on the 8th and exiting the area for the Bahamas area. Having left St. Nazaire on 15 April, the boat was refueled by *U-459* 500 miles north-east of Bermuda in early May. *U-103*'s victims included the *Ruth Lykes* on the 17th; the *Ogontz* two days later; both the *Clare* and the *Elizabeth* two days after that; and on the 23rd and a day later the *Samuel Q. Brown* and the *Hector*. On the 26th, he sank the *Alcoa Carrier* and on the 28th the *New Jersey*, for total tonnage of 42,169 tons sunk. All but the British *Stanbank* and the Dutch *Hector* were American ships.

On the return voyage, Winter again transited the Windward Passage—this time on 31 May. For the next four days, he steamed north-east, exiting the area south of

Bermuda on 5 June and heading for Biscay, which he had left on 15 April. On the day that he passed south of Bermuda, Winter was awarded the Knight's Cross via radio for an exceptionally successful patrol. Before that, his highest award was the Iron Cross First Class. Winter's career tally amounted to fifteen ships sunk for 79,302 tons; he appears to have been a thorough skipper, as none of his victims escaped merely damaged—all were finished off. Winter was promoted to *Korvettenkapitän* in March 1943. His total of five war patrols amounted to 209 sea days. A member of the crew of 1930, Winter had served on the light cruiser the *Emden* before joining U-boats in 1935. The previous skipper of *U-103* was the ace Viktor Schutze. Winter had been in a staff position between command of *U-22* and *U-103* and returned to that role in July 1942, in command of the 1st U-boat Flotilla in Brest. In that capacity, he would have sent out and welcomed home many of the patrols of his flotilla, been intimately involved in both instructing and debriefing the skippers, and reported to Admiral Dönitz. Captured in Brest in 1944, he was released in 1947. After a few years in the *Bundesmarine*, he retired as a *Kapitän zur See*, and lived a further two years until 1972 when he passed away in Kiel.[5]

Kapitänleutnant Gerhard Bigalk brought *U-751* to the north of Bermuda for five days inbound starting 3 May 1942. From the north-east of the island, the sub turned south-west for two days, then west until the 7th, when it exited the area. Having set off for the 7th U-boat Flotilla in St. Nazaire on 15 April and been refueled by *U-459* north-east of Bermuda in early May, *U-751* returned on 15 June. The large type VIIC boat *U-751* (commissioned in October 1939) sent the US fruit carrier the *Nicarao* to the bottom just east of the Bahamas. On 19 May, Bigalk sank the 3,110-ton American freighter the *Isabela* off Point Gravois, Haiti, for a total patrol of 4,555 tons. After ten days in the Caribbean, *U-751* exited via the Anegada Passage on the night of 28th and 29th May and began the transatlantic voyage back to France. Born in 1908, Gerhard Bigalk was a member of the crew of 1933 who joined the navy from the merchant marines. He then joined the naval air force, fighting over Spain in its civil war before joining U-boats in November 1939, commissioning *U-751* in January 1941. He was awarded the Knight's Cross in December 1941 after sinking the British escort carrier HMS *Audacity* of 11,000 tons. Bigalk was killed at age thirty-three on 17 July 1942 by British aircraft, which sank *U-751* off the north-west coast of Spain's Cape Ortegal—there were no survivors. His total over seven patrols of 218 days was five ships destroyed for 21,412 GRT, the *Audacity*, and a ship damaged for 8,096 tons.

Kapitänleutnant Hermann Rasch brought his command (*U-106*) on its second patrol to the Bermuda area for nine days starting 4 May 1942 and ending on 12 June. The day after he arrived, Rasch sank a 7,985-ton *Lady Boat*; the Canadian passenger ship the *Lady Drake* north-east of Bermuda, with a complement of 141 passengers and 115 crew, all of who survived and were taken to Bermuda by the USS *Owl* (AM 2). Steaming west for two more days, *U-106* left the theater for the Hatteras region. On 7 June, *U-106* returned, this time south-west of Bermuda and heading homeward on an east-north-easterly course. On the 10th, the sub jogged north for a day, then resumed a course north-eastwards, exiting the circle around Bermuda on 12 June. On the way to the patrol area, having left Lorient on 15 April, *U-106* was attacked by the destroyer USS *Broome* on 2 May.[6]

Rasch's next victim was as controversial as Suhren's sinking of the *Potrero del Lano* at roughly the same time—he kicked a hornets' nest and brought Mexico into the war against Germany by sinking the 6,067-ton Mexican tanker *Faja de Oro* between Key West and Havana on 21 May, killing ten of her crew of thirty-seven. His other victims on this patrol were the *Carrabulle*, the *Atenas* (of 4,639 GRT, damaged and managed to escape off New Orleans after a valiant counter attack by her naval armed guard), the *Mentor,* and the *Hampton Roads* (on 1 June), for a total tonnage sunk and damaged of 33,793 on one patrol. Three weeks later, he rounded Key West eastbound.

Rasch was twenty-seven at the time; his boat was the IXB type sailing from and to Lorient for the 2nd U-boat Flotilla. He would spend a total of sixteen days in the area on the sixth of ten war patrols for this battle-hardened submarine. Rasch had left Lorient on the same day as Winter in *U-103*, but arrived in the area by a less direct route and subsequently returned a week or so later. The return voyage home was eventful—*U-106* was refueled by *U-459* west of the Azores.[7] On 24 June, less than a week from home base, the U-boat stopped to pick up a survivor from the sunken steamer the *Etrib* which had been sunk by *U-552* on 15 June east-north-east of the Azores. The boat returned to Lorient with its grateful prisoner on 29 June 1942. Rasch was a member of the crew of 1934 and joined U-boats in 1940. His staff positions after leaving *U-106* in April 1943 concluded with command of midget U-boats, which lasted up to his captivity until 1946. He practiced journalism in Germany until his death in 1974 at age fifty-nine. Rasch's total over six patrols was twelve ships for 78,553 tons, one damaged, and an auxiliary warship of 8,246 tons damaged. He earned the Spanish Cross in Bronze with Swords in 1939 and the Knight's Cross in 1942.[8]

A German U-boat motoring in calm conditions. Judging from the wake showing ahead and to the left, as well as the relaxed stances and clean appearance of the men, the submarine is probably being escorted out of a French port. Note the cramped conditions in the conning tower. (*Deutsches U-Boot-Museum*)

5 May 1942:
SS *Lady Drake* and SS *Stanbank*

SS *Lady Drake*

The dual cargo and passenger steamship the *Lady Drake* was built by Cammell Laird of Birkinhead, England in 1928. The vessel weighed 7,985 gross tons and was 437 feet long, 59.1 feet wide, and 28.2 feet deep. Four steam turbines also built by Cammell Laird (she was yard number 940) turned two screws, propelling the ship at 14 knots. The *Lady Drake* was owned by the Canadian National Steamships Limited of Montreal and began its final round-trip voyage from Canada to the West Indies in mid-April 1942.[1] Her master was Captain Percy Ambrose Kelly, who earned an M. B. E. for his part in the torpedoing of sister ship the *Lady Hawkins* off Hatteras by *U-66* under Richard Zapp on 19 January that year.[2] The *Lady Drake* called at Boston for passengers, British Guyana for sugar, Trinidad, St. Lucia, St. Kitts, and Guantanamo before sailing to Bermuda. While in St. Lucia, they picked up extra crew from the *Lady Nelson*, which had been torpedoed and sunk in Castries Harbour by *U-161* under Achilles the previous month.[3] In Trinidad, the ship picked up British Royal Navy ratings on their way to the UK via Canada. Then, the *Lady Drake* sailed for Bermuda, where she picked up additional passengers for Halifax. The headquarters of the Royal Canadian Navy in Ottawa provided instructions for the vessel to sail for Boston (or possibly St. John, New Brunswick, just north) on Sunday, 3 May 1942. Though air cover was meant to be provided for the first day, it had been the ship's experience during the voyage that air and surface cover which was promised never materialized, and so it proved to be the case in this instance.[4]

The ship was twenty minutes late un-berthing in Hamilton and had to lay at anchor because the markers were unlit at night. They set off from Bermuda early on Monday, 4 May, fully aware that 'there was vigorous submarine activity almost amounting to a blockade 90 miles north of the island.' The conditions when the ship got underway were calm and clear—the seas were flat, the breeze gentle and the skies clear. The actual number of people on board varied according to who reported it. The survivors' statements by the US Navy state that 272 were on board: 141 passengers, 121 crew, and ten distressed seamen. USS *Owl* later reported 256 rescued (145 passengers and 111 crew) and twelve killed, for a total of 268; this author counted the USS *Owl*'s list of passengers and survivors and agrees that 268 were on board. These included forty-eight British Naval Ratings and ten men from the *Lady Nelson*. There was also said to be a Greek sailor kept prisoner in the brig, or holding cell of the ship; he survived.

In order to try to hasten the passage, a variety of engine oil which had been taken on in Trinidad was used, however it was found to produce a thick black smoke visible for 25 miles around when extra speed was asked for. Captain Percy was faced with going slower and imperiling the 268 people on board, or going faster and giving the ship's position away to prowling submarines. That afternoon, the ship's radio operator was able to detect chatter between U-boats in the vicinity right before the attack. US Naval intelligence reported that 'Prior to torpedoing, radio operator reported a suspicious radio message consisting of the call letters DB 7V followed by eight dashes, very close on the 704-meter wave length.' It was surmised these were U-boats communicating with each other. Indeed, on 5 May 1942, there were seven U-boats within 300 to 400 nautical miles of Bermuda: *U-106, U-69, U-103, U-201, U-558, U-751,* and *U-594*. Any of these submarines may have been utilizing their radios to communicate with each other, a U-tanker, or home base in France.

Kelly was correct inasmuch as the *Lady Drake* was easy prey. Not twenty-four hours into its passage, when just 186 miles north of the island and 430 nautical miles southeast of Nantucket, *U-106* under *Kapitänleutnant* Hermann Rasch struck with two torpedoes. In order to avoid submarine attack, Captain Kelly had deviated 45 degrees off course the, swung back hours later, and was zigzagging, so that the first torpedo was seen by the naval gunners to pass 50 feet from the stern. There were ten lookouts posted: one on the monkey island above the bridge, two on the lower bridge, one on the forecastle head, and two on the games deck aft, and four gunners on duty.

The second torpedo, however, was deadly to a dozen of the people on the ship: it struck between the cargo bulkhead and engine room, shutting out all power and lights on the ship before the lookouts could convey their intelligence to the bridge. Since the main radio was out of commission, the radio operators tried to send out on the emergency set; however, there is no indication that they succeeded, and it appears that due to a high level of static the messages never got out. NOB Bermuda's Commandant noted on 7 May that 'It seems strange that neither the *Lady Hawkins* nor the *Lady Drake* made a distress call.'

In the ten minutes from 9 p.m. to 9.10 p.m., the *Lady Drake* was evacuated of 256 survivors, with six passengers and six crew who perished unaccounted for. Among the dead were Ship's Boy Emanuel Cozier, aged twenty-four, Second Steward Harold Stanley, aged thirty-nine, two firemen in their twenties: Anthony Yearwood and Hewley Edward White, and General Servant Graham Carter. Among the passengers lost were Oscar Greenidge, aged twenty-three, Eric Seymour Hamblin, aged twenty-six, Cuthbert Alleyne Reid, aged twenty-nine, and Thomas W. Reid, aged twenty-one (it is not known if they were brothers), and Andrew R. Bradshaw. While being lowered, Number Four lifeboat was smashed against the side of the vessel;

however, it is not known whether this is the only one out of the six boats, which was not successfully manned. The only female known to be on the ship was a tall charismatic former showgirl of fifty-seven years' age named Miss Gwen Canfield. Originally from Long Beach California, she was residing in Simcoe, Ontario, to which place she was presumably returning. She told Bermuda's *The Royal Gazette and Colonist Daily*, in a story that was carried by *The Joplin Globe*, that the boat she was in was nearly crushed by another one above it coming down.

> One boat containing a Canadian lady, a youth and five others shipped a large quantity of water as it struck the sea and started sinking. Another lifeboat was noticed being lowered directly overhead. When it was only a few feet above, the youth grabbed the lady passenger and flung her from the sinking lifeboat into No. 6 boat before the latter reached the water. He then plunged into the overhanging lifeboat less than half a minute before it crashed on top of the boat in the water, smashing the boat to pieces.

It would appear from this that both boats—Number Four and Number Six—were operable. The destroyed boat is not named. Miss Canfield added that 'We picked up other survivors who were on two or three life-rafts.'

Given the complete darkness of night, coupled with absence of lighting from the disabled ship, it is remarkable that so many survived, and a tribute to the calm leadership and drilling of Captain Kelly and his officers. Some reports state that 'nobody even got feet wet'; however, reading Miss Canfield's report it is clear that the disembarkation was at least a bit chaotic and some had to swim for rafts or be transferred from damaged to better lifeboats. Soon, however, the survivors all managed to be allocated into five boats which she said were 'well navigated and there was enough food.'

The *Lady Drake* sank by 9.25 p.m., between twenty and twenty-five minutes after it was struck. 'We looked back,' said Miss Canfield, 'and saw the good old ship roll over on her side and sink.' At no time did they see or hear the German submarine. Thus, 256 souls found themselves alone on an unruffled sea, undulated by a gentle swell with nothing but the canopy of stars overhead. Presumably, the proximity to warm Gulf Steam waters kept temperatures reasonably warm. On the morning of Tuesday, 5 May, the survivors searched the area of the sinking for any sign of survivors. Finding none, they agreed to keep together—and did so. Then, they set sail southwards for Bermuda. Captain Kelly later ruminated that 'The immensity of the empty ocean seemed to be more real when seen from a small lifeboat, and the blue vaulted dome of sky curiously peaceful, as they made their way back to Bermuda under sail.'

The following day, Wednesday, 6 May, at 7.00 a.m., the survivors were excited when a familiar, elegant profile approached them at high speed—it was the Cunard Line's flagship, the *Queen Mary*, acting as a troop transport and bound from the UK to New York. It was a policy for troop ships not to stop and aid anyone, with their superior speed being their greatest asset in avoiding U-boats. The survivors in the boats

realized this and took comfort in the Aldis lamp message which read 'I will report…
I will report.' Indeed, on Thursday, 7 May (the next day), the British Routing Office in
New York received a message from the British Admiralty Delegation, which read:

> The R.M.S. *Queen Mary* arrived in New York at 0830 EWT today and Captain
> Bissett immediately sent a message ashore to me that at 1000 A. on the 6th of May,
> he had sighted in position 35.27N, 64.22W five boats loaded of survivors under
> sail, and had further passed an overturned lifeboat in the same vicinity. The boats
> when last seen were steering to the southward.

The overturned lifeboat may have come from the *Lady Drake*, or it might have been
some of the wreckage which Captain Kelly sighted on the ship's first day out of
Bermuda. Captain Kelly saw either the wreckage of the *Harpagon*, sunk 164 miles
north-north-west of Bermuda on 20 April 1942, or the *Modesta*, also British, sunk
on 25 April 1942, only 21 nautical miles north-north-east of Bermuda. There were
dozens of ships sunk in the theater that dreadful spring, and lifeboats making for
Bermuda were scattered across the sea—many of them setting sail for the island and
the men never making it, with their boats foundering *en route* from myriad dots in
the ocean where their ships had been attacked.

Back on the boats, Miss Canfield stated that 'during the ordeal… one man became
crazed and jumped into the water. He was pulled out—too late.' However, in no other
account does it state that any but the dozen victims killed on the ship perished, or
that there was a fatality on board the boats. There were up three passengers and
five crew members who suffered from 'bone fractures of various kinds—injuries
suffered when a lifeboat crashed down on top of a loaded boat being lowered away
from the sinking ship.'

Word appears to have reached the US Naval authorities in Bermuda before even
the British delegation in Bermuda. Captain Bissett of the *Queen Mary* must have,
at peril to his vessel, relayed word to the naval authorities before his arrival in New
York on 7 May because on Wednesday, 6 May, at 6.19 p.m., Lieutenant Frederick
George Coffin, US Naval Reserve, in command of USS *Owl* (AM 2) logged that
his vessel was 'Underway [from Bermuda] in accordance with N. O. B. dispatch
#061735 of 6 May 5.35 p.m. to pick up survivors of torpedoed ship said to be heading
south in five life boats.' He worked his ship up to 11 knots (115 rpm), manning the
machine guns and darkened ship. Coffin had taken over command of his charge less
than two weeks earlier, on 24 April 1942.[5]

USS *Owl*'s keel was laid in Todd Shipbuilding Company of Brooklyn New York
on 25 October 1917. It was a Bird Class minesweeper delivered to the US Navy on 11
July 1918. Its first assignment was coastal towing out of Norfolk. Originally known
as the *Minesweeper No. 2*, it became simply AM 2 on 17 July 1920; it would go on to
be re-classified an ocean tug, and renamed AT 137 on 1 June 1942. The tug weighed
1,350 tons and displaced 950 tons; it was 187.9 feet long, 35.5 feet wide, and 10.25 feet

deep. Her speed was originally 14 knots, then 11.2 knots by 1944. USS *Owl's* original complement was sixty-two men; by 1944, this was increased to seventy-eight—in any event, it would be difficult for a tug even 187 feet long to fit over 250 additional personnel, even if they were (mostly) mariners. The *Owl's* armament was two 3-inch guns and at least two machine guns.[6] Already, this war horse had done escort duty for ships like the *Freden*, the *Agra* and the *Anna*, Swedish vessels that, like the *City of Birmingham*, kept a lifeline of supplies and people trickling into beleaguered Bermuda.

The *Owl* also helped salvage the abandoned Argentine freighter *Victoria*, damaged by *U-201* under Adalbert Shnee on 18 April 1942, when under the command of Lieutenant Commander Charles Guequierre Rucker. The *Owl* took up its duties with NOB Bermuda in May 1941 and remained there until June 1943, when, after a refit in Norfolk, it crossed the Atlantic to support D-Day in 1944. The 256 survivors in the *Lady Drake* boats greeted Thursday, 7 April, with elation when the familiar drone of an airplane engine materialized into an aircraft bearing down on them from the direction of Bermuda. It was 6.30 a.m. and to their considerable relief the plane dipped its wings, encouraging them to think that a ship would be sent to rescue them. As the *Owl* was shortly behind the aircraft and just over the horizon, they were not disappointed.

At 9.10 a.m., Lieutenant Coffin logged that his men 'Sighted boat under sail bearing 355 degrees true, distance 8 miles—Between 0942 and 1116 sighted and picked up survivors from 5 life boats of the *Lady Drake*, Canadian merchant ship.' The position where the lifeboats were picked up was, according to the Admiralty, 70 nautical miles south of where the *Lady Drake* had been sunk, and 115 miles north of Bermuda. Ten minutes after the last survivors were aboard, while 'the ships company were at General Quarters and a plane covered the operations from the air', the USS *Owl* got underway again with the five life boats under tow, in an effort to salvage the equipment—something probably ingrained in any tug operator. The operation was not a success, as Coffin noted that 'During the late afternoon and evening all five life boats made water and swamped and had to be cut adrift.'

Like Captain Kelly, Coffin 'sheared off to the right 45 degrees for one half hour and then zigzagged through the night in accordance with zigzag Plan #12'; he was taking no chances with his precious cargo of people, and the guns were manned at all times. At 6.50 a.m. on Friday, 8 May, the men on the *Owl* sighted Bermuda. By 8.15 a.m., the sea buoy was abeam and they began transiting the Narrows. There was a grand reception for the *Owl* and her survivors when they arrived at Shed #6 in Hamilton at around 10.30 a.m. The Mayor of Hamilton, S. P. Eve was on hand, along with the Governor of the colony and the Commandant of the US Naval Operating Base. According to *The Royal Gazette and Colonist Daily*, 'On the dock as the rescue ship warped in were officers of the various British and American Services in Bermuda. Along Front Street were lined ambulances from the U.S. Mobile Base Hospital. The Director of Health, Dr. Henry Wilkinson, and civilian, army and navy doctors were there.'[7]

The article continued: 'The grim event was not without its light touch. Among the survivors was a Greek prisoner who was in the brig of the torpedoed ship. He is now comfortable in Hamilton Gaol.' The reporter also picked up on the exchange between Miss Canfield and her rescuers: 'As she came ashore, her lifebelt still in her hands, Miss Canfield turned towards the rescue ship where crewmen of the torpedoed vessel were lined up on deck. "Keep your chins up boys," she called out. "Are you alright?" "You bet," came the response from the grinning seamen, "You've got what it takes, lady!"' Since Miss Canfield had earlier been a guest of Police Constable and Mrs. Gooch of Pembroke Parish, she returned to stay with them.[8]

By 10.45 a.m., all the survivors were disembarked, and at 11.30 a.m., Admiral Jules James, the Commandant of NOB Bermuda was aboard, followed three minutes later by His Excellency Viscount Knollys, Governor of Bermuda, who 'came aboard and thanked the ship for the assistance rendered. A "Well Done" was received from the Admiral.' This ended the USS *Owl*'s log entry for the *Lady Drake* rescue. For the survivors, their recuperation and repatriation was just beginning; for an island already bulging at the seams with shipwreck survivors, there was the issue of where to put—and how to support—so many men. The British Admiralty noted with relief that day that 'All Naval personnel including F. A. A. from Trinidad safe'; this communication referred to the 48 Royal Navy Ratings boarded in Trinidad earlier in April, for whose safety the Admiralty had a vested interest.

While it is possible to list most of the several places the men were put up in Bermuda, it is only partially possible to list the many individuals who helped them. Fortunately for the eight hospital cases, 'No one of these is believed to be seriously injured. There were also a few exposure and shock cases of a minor nature.' There was a single US citizen aboard and he was met by Mr. Alonzo B. Cornell, Field Director of the US Red Cross, which used the United Services Organization's Club in The Flatts. Others of the men were accommodated at the United Services Club at the Hamilton Hotel. Dickie Tucker made what room he could at the Bermuda Sailor's Home, 'cramming his premises with survivors.' The Naval Recreation Rooms were made available as were local hotels. Other hostelries made available were the A. M. E. Lyceum on Court Street, at the A. M. E. Church (Rev. D. M. Owens, D. D. providing the welcome). There, the men were provided with sandwiches, soup and coffee, clothing and cigarettes.

Lady Knollys, wife of the Governor, visited the men at the Lyceum to provide 'ditty bags' and chat with the survivors. This was a distribution point for gifts from citizens and merchants. Gift boxes included soap, handkerchiefs, shaving kits, and cigarettes. A subscription began to raise funds for the survivors; by the first afternoon, it had reached £30. Survivors also went to the Canadian Hotel and the Church of God on Angle Street, Hamilton. The proprietor of the Canadian Hotel, James Richards, 'spent a considerable sum for clothing for the survivors.'[9] For the officers, Mrs. A. B. Smith provided the use of her home, Inverness, in Warwick Parish. The officers who stayed there reported on 20 May 1942:

[They] have expressed their keen joy of the place. It is like home to them. The cottage has been supplied with a cook and inhabitants of the district are doing all they can to make the stay of the survivors a pleasant one. Each day vegetables are brought to the cottage by neighbors and the environment for the officers is a particularly satisfactory one. Moreover, the cottage is conveniently located near the ferry.

On Wednesday, 13 May, the *Royal Gazette and Colonist Daily* ran a column entitled 'U. S. O. club News,' in which they attempt to thank some of the families and individuals 'who contributed so much to the comfort of the survivors.'[10] The list reads like a 'who's who' of Bermudian society; Outerbridge, Gibbons, Rutherford, Pearman, Penniston, Gardner, Haskell, MacDougall, Tucker, Zuill, Conyers, Hollis, Rubick, West, and Fleming are all cited. Some thanks are specific, like to Mrs. Power Crichton for 'six dozen sheets and pillow cases', and the B. W. A. F. 'who gave pajamas and slippers for all the men.' There is even a letter cited as being from survivors 'on the point of departure' likely from survivors of the *Lady Drake*. It reads:

> It was not only what you did for us, the innumerable kindnesses which we shall all remember, but the spirit of friendly anticipation of our wants which made our visit to Bermuda so delightful … If this is an example of Allied co-operation such a team is bound to win.

While Miss Canfield flew back to the New York on a Clipper aircraft, not wanting to risk another sea passage, the majority of the torpedoed crews of the *Lady Drake* and the *Lady Nelson* were fortunate to find passage on another vessel from the same Canadian fleet, the *Lady Rodney*. The Canadian authorities who had ordered the *Lady Drake* to sail unescorted had a change of heart when it came to the *Lady Rodney's* imminent departure from Bermuda; they decided to send a corvette down from Halifax to escort the passenger ship. 'It had taken the loss of a fine ship to win protection for another.'

The *Lady Rodney* sailed on or about Sunday, 24 May 1942, for Canada. Officers and crew from the *Lady Drake* were given one month's leave and two month's pay from the date of the ship's loss. The cost for the Britannia Steamship Insurance Association Limited to reimburse passengers and crew came to $36,009.31. The West Indians among the crew were repatriated not to Canada, but back to the Caribbean. Alcoa Steamship's vessel, the *City of Birmingham*, was chosen to take them. However, Assistant Purser J. M. Arsenault had a difficult time finding all but thirty-one of the men when it came time for sailing. With the help of local constables combing through various watering holes and haunts, they finally succeeded in corralling these men aboard the ship taking them to their homes.

Captain Kelly was awarded the Order of Merit of the British Empire (MBE) on 22 December 1942 for his exertions towards the saving of lives as Chief Officer of the *Lady Hawkins* before the *Lady Drake* sank. One of his recommendations to naval staff was that ships in danger of being torpedoed keep their life boats swung in, in other words not pre-deployed for emergency launch. He felt that there was less opportunity for the boats to be damaged by torpedo explosions that way, and the experience of the *Lady*

Drake survivors bore it out, so long as they could still be easily lowered, which for the most part (five out of six instances) they were. SS *City of Birmingham* was subsequently sunk by *U-202* under Hans-Heinz Linder on 1 July 1942, *en route* to Bermuda.[11]

SS *Stanbank*

The British steamship the *Stanbank* was built in 1942 by William Pickersgill and Sons Limited of Sunderland, England. Her owners were J. A. Billmeir and Company Limited of London, also known as the Stanhope Steamship Company Limited—their ships began with the prefix 'Stan.' The ship was 5,966 gross registered tons, and she was 415 feet long, 54.1 feet wide, and 33.1 feet deep. As the ship was sunk on what must have been its maiden cargo voyage (having sailed in ballast from the UK to New York following being launched), there are no images of the vessel or much history to refer to, as it was only afloat for a few months. A single triple-expansion Clark George engine developed 415 net horsepower and propelled the steel hull at 10 knots. The ship was armed with a 4-inch gun aft, two Oerlikorn cannons, two Twin-Marlin machine guns, a weapon called a 'pig trough', four parachute rockets, and kites.

The forty-nine men on board were led by Captain George Albert Niddrie. Second Radio Officer Frederick Clarke Smith was twenty-one years of age, as was DEMS (defensively equipped merchant ships) Gunner George Laidler Bell. Able Seaman John Barker Round was two years older than them. Overall, there were six naval or army gunners on board to man the defenses, and forty-three merchant sailors and officers. The cargo manifest of the *Stanbank* is a highly-detailed document spanning four single-spaced pages. The total tonnage loaded was 6,484 tons. Her estimated arrival at Port Sudan was given as 25 June. The cargo was consigned for Suez, Ankara, Turkey (medicines), El Kebir, Aden, the Department of Munitions of Supplies, Canada, the British Purchasing Commission, Navy Army Air Force Institute (491 tons of beer), and British Food Commission, among others. There were airplane fuselages on deck, manuals, spare parts for Curtiss Wright Kitthawks (six), 2 million 30-caliber links of ammunition, 1,611 tons of bituminous coal, nearly 2,000 loose tires with tubes, boxes for Massawa, Ethiopia, twelve Bofors cannons, 302 tons of Lend-Lease pork sausages, 207 tons of evaporated milk, and tens of thousands of drums of lubricating oils from Radbill Oil Company as well as Valvoline, Standard Oil, and Keystone Oil. Most of the airplane fuselages were stowed on the hatches on deck. The *Stanbank* departed New York Harbor on Friday, 1 May 1942 at 8 a.m.[12]

The patrol of the German submarine *U-103* under *Kapitänleutnant* Werner Winter lasted for six days in the area, all of it inbound. On 5 May, his route intersected quite by chance with the outbound *Stanbank*, with predictable results. The attack took place 210 nautical miles north-east of Bermuda and 540 nautical miles south-east of Nantucket. The weather at the time of *U-103*'s attack was fine with good visibility; the sea was described as smooth and the breeze light. Captain

Niddrie had been following the routing instructions given to him in New York and was steering south-east at 9.5 knots. At 2 a.m. on Tuesday, 5 May, the captain 'heard a muffled explosion which appeared to be deep down.' The torpedo had burrowed its way into the starboard side into the Number Two hold and beneath the bridge. There were four cases of airplane fuselages on the Number Two hatch cover.

Captain Niddrie observed that 'A large column of water was thrown up mast-high, but I did not see any smoke nor did the explosion leave any smell. I could hear the cargo running out from No. 2 Hold and gathered that there was a large hole in the ship's side.' His cabin was crushed and he could not retrieve any ship's papers from it. Fortunately, the chief engineer stopped the engines on his own initiative. However, the confidential codes were thrown overboard in a weighted perforated box and, as ordered, the radio operator tried to send an SOS; however, it was never received.

Niddrie then focused on the lifeboat and life raft situation. The large starboard lifeboat was destroyed by the torpedo explosion; however, the captain tried to free and lower the other starboard lifeboat. He was unsuccessful in doing this because he could not convince the men to come over to the side of the damage. By now, the ship was listing five degrees to starboard and sinking slowly by the head. The men focused their attention on releasing the two port lifeboats, one of them a small jolly boat and the other larger. They also managed to cut away three life rafts. The jolly boat with eleven men in it pulled away from the doomed *Stanbank* and the men rowed away, where they were approached by *U-103*. The second mate in charge of the boat, William Christie Stark, aged twenty-six, was asked by *Korvettenkapitän* Winter or his subordinate the name and destination of the ship, to which he replied 'That's one up on Roosevelt!' Winter then provided the survivors with a packet of twenty-five cigarettes and a box of French matches; he then said the war would soon be over. At 2.50 a.m., *U-103* then submerged and the merchant mariners did not see it again.

Survivors told US Navy interrogators later that 'On port side of conning tower appeared letters 'H' and 'N' between which was a pink or reddish shield with No. 26 beneath. Across the center of the shield was a silver-grey figure resembling a thin fluttering banner. The sub commander was a slim and active German, accent but good English.' This description is interesting to read, particularly as it is so divergent from the actual emblem of the U-boat. Captain Niddrie remained on his ship for ten minutes after the torpedo struck; then, after a wistful look around, he boarded the larger port lifeboat and pushed away from his ship. For the next few hours until daylight, the two boats bobbed around in the vicinity of the wreck. At dawn, Captain Niddrie ordered eight men each on the three rafts, nine men under the second officer on the jolly boat, and 16 men including Niddrie in the larger boat. Since there was no wind they began rowing west, in the general direction of Bermuda. Starting on the first day, the young Second Officer William Stark agitated to take his smaller boat and set off for Bermuda on its own. At first, Niddrie demurred, saying that as they had sent out an SOS they should remain in the vicinity of the sinking. However, by Thursday, 7 May, there was no sign of rescue ships or planes; therefore, at 1.30 p.m., Niddrie let the second officer choose the eight ablest men (Bell, Derry, Foreman, Jameson, McPhee, Round, Skinner, and Smith) and the nine of them set off without any rafts, heading for Bermuda. They were over the horizon in three hours. None of the nine men were ever seen again.

For that day and the following (the 8th), the forty remaining men rowed west. Niddrie rationed the water to 4 ounces per man three times a day. At breakfast, they had three spoonfuls of condensed milk; at lunch, two biscuits with pemmican spread on them as well as six milk tablets; and in the evening, six bars of chocolate. During this time, all three rafts were being towed by the large lifeboat and progress was understandably slow. Then, on Saturday, 9 May, two of the rafts were stripped of supplies and men and cast adrift, leaving just one raft trailing behind the boat. This contained thirteen men—the dozen 'Arab' sailors and the chief engineer. During the night, the tether connecting both vessels severed, and it took Niddrie and his men two hours to find the raft and reconnect the painter. That afternoon, a fresh breeze from the south-west sprung up; therefore, they abandoned the third and final raft to better enable them to sail, and all occupied the lifeboat.

The following day, Sunday, 10 May, at 2 p.m., a very heavy rain hit them, making the men wet and miserable. Nothing noteworthy appears to have happened on Monday the 11th; however, Niddrie must have noticed morale flagging, because on the 12th, he organized an impromptu music concert by initiating a solo performance of his own. In his words, 'I don't think [this] was very much appreciated. Anyway, the concert was a great success and the next day the men were quite happy planning another concert for the evening. I found these concerts helped considerably in keeping up the morale of the men.' There would be no third night of concerts. By Thursday, 14 May, a stronger breeze had developed from the east, and with it, a heavy ocean swell. At 1 p.m., Niddrie caught sight of a steamer heading south off in the distance. Not wanting to miss an opportunity to attract its attention, he personally climbed up the frail lifeboat's mast to wave a yellow quarantine flag. His unusual actions resulted in the *Rhexenor* spotting their little flotilla and diverting to the rescue, having been 'attracted by the lifeboat's red sails and a large yellow flag.'

Apparently, the men on the rescuing ship were still suspicious that the craft might be a decoy or a submarine, as they approached with all their weapons aimed at the survivors. 'With his guns bearing on us... he asked who we were and how long ago since being torpedoed, and on hearing ten days he came over and picked us up.' It was 2.30 p.m. The rescue took place exactly as Captain Niddrie estimated—96 miles south-west along the track to Bermuda from the wreck. They were 125 nautical miles north-east of Bermuda. Although all of the *Stanbank* sailors and four gunners managed to make it to the deck of the *Rhexenor* unaided, once there several of them 'had to be assisted,' wrote Niddrie, and even he 'found it very difficult to walk.' The *Rhexenor* was completed in March 1923 by the Taikoo Dockyard and Engineering Company of Hong Kong and owned by Alfred Holt and Company of Liverpool. The ship was 7,957 GRT and could carry 9,860 tons of cargo. She was 477.5 feet long, 58.4 feet wide, and 28.5 feet deep, and could make an impressive 14.5 knots.

The ship's master at the time of the *Stanbank* rescue was Captain Blair; Captain Niddrie of the *Stanbank* had nothing but praise for him.[12] Niddrie was effusive in his thanks 'for the very good job he made of picking us up, there was a heavy sea and swell running and he handled his ship magnificently. When on board we received every consideration and attention possible.'

Captain Niddrie added that 'On arrival [in Bermuda] I reported the missing boat and six 'planes were sent out to look for the 2nd Officer's boat but as far as I know without success.' Indeed, the Admiralty War Diary for foreign stations dated 15 May stated that 'Chief Officer and eight crew still missing, last seen in position of torpedoing steering S. W.' He also cited AB Blake Bremer, 'a trawler man and very handy on small boats, and it was due to his help and valuable assistance and devotion to duty that every thing went so well in the boats during the 9 ½ days.' He also recommended putting more water and condensed milk in the boats over the pemmican, which the men found 'very unpalatable.'

The *Rhexenor* covered the 125 miles in about twelve hours, arriving off St. George's at 10 a.m. There was a welcoming committee of volunteers to greet them, consisting of Mrs. Meyer, Mrs. Barnes, Mr. and Mrs. Pierce, Mrs. Snape, Mr. Morris, and Mrs. Schwab. They represented the St. George's branch of the Bermuda Sailor's Home— other representatives such as Dickie Tucker and Arthur Harriott had to come up from Hamilton by special train, which left the capital at 9 a.m. The forty survivors arrived at Richmond Road Railway Station and were taken to the Naval Recreation Rooms at the Bermudiana Hotel dormitories. There, the Ladies Hospitality Organization served a lunch for them.[13] The ship's officers were accommodated in private homes whilst the men—including the dozen Arab sailors—remained in the dormitories. The L. H. O. provided meals for the men in co-ordination with the Bermuda Sailors Home. The article in *The Royal Gazette and Colonist Daily* ends on an upbeat note, saying 'There were no hospital cases among the group and all seemed to have weathered their ten days in the lifeboats very well.'[14]

The *Rhexenor*'s captain was Leonard Eccles when she was sunk in mid-Atlantic by *U-217* under Reichenback-Klinke on 3 February 1943.[15] He was taken prisoner and served the balance of the war in the POW camp Milag Nord. On 5 January 1943, both Captain Niddrie and Able Seaman Blake Bremer received the King's Commendation in London. After the *Stanbank* attack *U-103* turned south-west for a day, then west across the north of Bermuda until turning south-west on the 8th and exiting the area for the Bahamas. Winter would return two weeks later after devastating attacks on eight other ships, mostly in the Yucatan Channel. On the return voyage, Winter again transited the Windward Passage—this time on 31 May—and opted to steam east of Inagua and through the Caicos Channel on 1 June. For the next four days, he steamed north-east, exiting the area south of Bermuda on 5 June and heading for Biscay, which he had left on 15 April.[16]

8–30 May 1942: Thirteen U-boats

Korvettenkapitän Ernst Kals spent sixteen days in the Bermuda area in May 1942, fruitlessly seeking targets. Starting on 8 May and homeward bound, *U-130* entered south of Bermuda, heading north-east for four days. Then, it jogged south for a day, then north-west, then south-west and west, until 16 May, which found it south-west of and within 200 miles of Bermuda. After that, Kals headed due north till the 19th, and finally north-east until the 23rd, when *U-130* exited the area north-east of the island, heading for France. Born in 1905 and a member of the Crew of 1924, Kals obtained the rank of *Kapitän zur See* in 1944, following which he was awarded the Knight's Cross. Kals began his career as a Sea Cadet; he ended it with a tally of seventeen ships sunk for 11,249 GRT, three auxiliary warships sunk for roughly 35,000 tons, and another ship sunk for just shy of 7,000 GRT. Kals went on to command the 2nd U-boat Flotilla in Lorient from January 1943 to the end of the war; in retribution, the French detained him for three years. He lived until age seventy-four, dying in Emden, Germany, in 1979.[1]

Korvettenkapitän Alfred Manhardt von Mannstein conned the Type VIIC *U-753* into the region for eight days both inbound and outbound between 10 May and 9 June. To start with, from the north-east, *U-753* headed south-west, passing quite close to the island on the 13th. The sub exited the region west of Bermuda on 15 May, the day after Bigalk entered just west of him on *U-751*. After an active patrol in the Bahamas and the Caribbean, *U-753* returned to the region around Bermuda when it skimmed the south-east corner of the box between 8 and 9 June, homeward bound. Having left La Pallice on 22 April, the boat refueled from *U-459* 500 miles north-east of Bermuda in early May.[2] In the US Gulf, *U-753* sank two Allied ships and damaged another two for a total of 20,677 GRT. Attacking every two days from 20 May, it struck the *George Calvert* (sunk), damaged the British schooner the *E. P. Theriault* of 326 tons with gunfire and charges (requiring the sub crew to board the ship), damaged the *Haakon Hauan*, and sank the *Hamlet* on the 27th. This was the first boat to sail to and from La Pallice for the 3rd U-boat Flotilla. *U-753* was caught by a Whitley bomber in the Bay of Biscay, which damaged the boat on 23 June.

A member of the crew of 1928 and aged thirty-three at the time, Von Mannstein was promoted to *Fregattenkapitän* in May of 1943 just prior to his death on the 13th of that month at the hands of the HMCS *Drumheller* and HMS *Lagan* and a Canadian Sunderland aircraft in the North Atlantic. The entire crew of forty-seven were killed during the 'Black May' of 1943—a period during which the Allies counterattacked the U-boats so decisively as to turn the tide of the Battle of the Atlantic in their favor. Von Mannstein had commissioned the *U-753* in June 1941. Over a career of seven patrols and 252 days, he was responsible for sinking or damaging five ships for over 30,000 tons (three sunk for 23,117 and two others damaged for 6,908 tons). He was not decorated during his career or posthumously.

Kapitänleutnant Gerhard Feiler initiated an intense patrol of nearly three weeks in the Bermuda area on 16 May 1942 and did not exit the area eastbound until 17 June, including a foray off Hatteras. During that time of crisscrossing the region to the north-west of Bermuda, *U-653* sank the merchant ship *Peisander* on 17 May (the day after arriving) and then the USS *Gannet* on 6 June. The submarine left the Bermuda region westwards between 19 May and 6 June. *U-653* was one of seven U-boats in the *Padfinder* group operating 3,400 miles off the US coast, looking for offshore prey. The *Peisander*, which Feiler sank, was a British motor ship of 6,225 tons, and was sunk between Bermuda and Nantucket. The USS *Gannet* was a converted aircraft tender engaged in escorting a British warship, which subsequently abandoned its escort and fled for the safety of Bermuda.

Feiler's efforts off the US coast returned no results, and so, he moved the sub further east towards Bermuda, where he sank the *Gannet*. Moving north-east, he was able to refuel from *U-459* about 500 miles north-east of Bermuda before returning to Brest, where it was based with the 1st U-boat Flotilla. The patrol had begun on 25 April, and ended on 6 July 1942. Feiler was thirty-two at the time, having been born in Breslau in 1909. A member of the Crew of 1934, he served on the destroyer *Karl Galster* between 1938 and 1940, before joining U-boats in July of that year. He commanded *U-653* between 1941 and 1943. Over seven patrols in the same sub for 412 patrol days, he managed to attack five ships worth 9,382 tons. He was awarded the German Cross in Gold in 1944. Gerhard Feiler lived until 1990.

Korvettenkapitän and U-boat ace Fritz Poske returned to the area for six days inbound, taking a course from east of Bermuda on 19 May 1942 to the south-west and exiting on the 24th. The patrol in the region basically looks like a straight line with a short trip to the west on the 21st. Thereafter, Poske took *U-504* from a point midway between Bermuda and Anegada and motored straight for the Windward Passage. He then sank six ships of 19,418 tons, all off the south-west coast of Cuba and in the Yucatan Channel: the *Allister* on 29 May, the *Rosenborg*, the Dutch passenger ship *Crijnssen*, the freighter *American*, and the Latvian *Regent* between 8 and 14 June. Thereafter, he proceeded to the Anegada Passage, leaving the area via that route between 20 and 21 May after a highly effective patrol lasting from 2 May to 7 July 1942.

Poske went on to become a *Kapitän zur See* and was awarded the U-boat War Badge 1939, the Iron Cross First Class immediately after this patrol, and the Knight's Cross in November 1942. Born in October 1904, he was thirty-seven and one of the older skippers. Poske began his naval career in the class of 1923 before serving on cruisers and a torpedo boat, joining U-boats in 1940. At the time of his first command, he (atypically) did not have command experience. He became chief of staff for Marine Infantry towards the end of the war, was imprisoned by the British for nearly a year, rejoined the German Navy in 1951, and lived until 1984, dying near Bonn at seventy-nine years of age.

Korvettenkapitän Harro Schacht utilized the area around Bermuda to head back to base for four days between 21 and 24 May 1942. The patrol took a straight line from north-west of Bermuda to north-east over four days and was uncomplicated. *U-507* sank the *Federal*, the *Norlindo*, the *Munger T. Ball*, the *Joseph T. Cudahy*, the *Alcoa Puritan*, the *Ontario* (Honduran), the *Torny* (Norwegian), the *Virginia*, the *Gulfprince*, and the *Amapala* (damaged and salvaged after an Allied plane surprised the Germans preparing to scuttle the ship) for a total score of nine ships sunk for 44,782 tons and one ship damaged (the *Gulfprince*) for 6,561 tons. The *Norlindo* was sunk north-west of Key West, whereas the other vessels met their fate deeper inside the Gulf. The boat headed back to Lorient, opting to exit the area on 22 May, not far from the west coast of Bermuda. The patrol began on 4 April and ended on 4 June.

Kapitänleutnant Otto von Bülow brought *U-404* for two incursions into the Bermuda area in May and June 1942 as part of a highly successful patrol in which he sank seven ships of 31,061 tons. Initially, *U-404* just dipped into the north-east corner of the Bermuda area between 22 and 25 May. Then, the sub returned on the 30th, this time from the north-north-west, during which it sank the US ship *Alcoa Shipper* of 5,491 tons. *U-404* then motored south-west until 1 June, when it intercepted and sank the US steamship the *West Notus* of 5,492 tons west north-west of Bermuda. For nearly a week, *U-404* zigzagged north-west of Bermuda, sinking the Swedish steamship the *Anna* of 1,345 tons on 3 June. Von Bülow then took is command east till the 7th, south till the 8th, and west towards Hatteras on 9 June. Off the US coast, *U-404* sank the 3,289-ton Yugoslavian steamship the *Ljubica Matkovic* off Cape Lookout on 24 June, then the steamship the *Manuala* (US flagged and 4,772 tons), and the *Nordal*, a Panamanian ship of 3,485 tons. On the 27th, *U-404* sank the *Moldanger*, 6,827 tons of Norway, but was counterattacked by aircraft. They obliged von Bülow to head back to France, and reached St. Nazaire on 14 July 1942.

U-404 sailed for the 6th U-boat Flotilla of St. Nazaire on 6 May as part of the *Padfinder* group, of which seven submarines were active from 23 to 27 May, before they split off to hunt independently. On the way out to the US coast, *U-404* also participated in the *Hecht* group from 8 to 11 May. Otto von Bülow was born in 1911 and a member of the Crew of 1930. Early in his naval career, he served on the *Duetschland* and the *Schleswig-Holstein* and with naval flak units. He joined U-boats in April 1940 and commanded *U-3*, a training boat. He commissioned *U-404* in August 1941 and went on to accrue 280 patrol days in six missions. His total tally of ships sunk and damaged was seventeen vessels of 89,259 tons, though he had to retract a claim of sinking the USS *Ranger* as it was a misunderstanding (he had hit HMS *Biter* instead).

In 1945, von Bülow commanded *U-2545*, and then a Naval Assault Battalion. Joining the *Bundesmarine* in 1956, he took over a former US Navy destroyer and re-commissioned it Z 6 in Charleston in 1960. His later responsibilities were as base commander in the Hamburg area. Among his many accolades, von Bülow received the Knight's Cross in October 1942 following this patrol, supplemented by the Oak Leaves in April 1943. To this, the U-boat War Badge with Diamonds was added a month later, and the War Merit Cross 2nd Class with Sword in April 1944. Von Bülow lived until January 2006 and the age of ninety-four.[3]

Kapitänleutnant Hans-Heinrich Giessler brought *U-455* on a zigzag course to the north and west of Bermuda for eight days, starting 23 May 1942 and ending on the 30th. At first, the sub headed south-east, then it dog-legged to the west, back towards Hatteras until the 27th, at which point it headed north-east of France, exiting north of Bermuda on the 30th. *U-455* left St. Nazaire on 22 August to lay mines at Charleston. After investigating the waters of Newfoundland, it moved south and completed its mine-laying mission on 18 September. No ships were reported to have hit any of the mines laid by Giessler. After its incursion south of the Carolinas, the boat called at the Gulf of St. Lawrence and Cape Race, Canada—again without encountering Allied shipping. She arrived in St. Nazaire on 28 October 1942.[4]

Giessler was born in January 1911. His career total was two ships sunk for 13,908 tons. Promoted to *Korvettenkapitän* in October 1943, he earned the Iron Cross First Class. Over four patrols, he served 185 days at sea, following which he was moved to the Torpedo Inspectorate. This was a crucially important role at the outset of the war, when many of the German torpedoes malfunctioned to the great frustration of accomplished U-boat skippers, with concomitant erosion of morale amongst entire crews. After a stint at the Ministry of Armaments and War Production, Giessler ended the war as first watch officer of the destroyer Z20, the *Karl Galster*.

Kapitänleutnant Victor Vogel brought *U-588* for a brief incursion into the area north north-west of Bermuda between 23 and 25 May 1942. The submarine sailed for the 6th U-boat Flotilla in St. Nazaire on 19 April and returned on 7 June. While *en route* to its primary patrol area off Canada, *U-588* operated briefly in conjunction with *U-455*, *U-553*, and *U-593*; however, they were not successful in tracking a convoy.[5] While off Halifax on 9 May, Vogel damaged the *Greylock*, a US ship of 7,460 tons, which was later sunk by *U-255*. The following day, *U-588* sank the *Kitty's Brook*, a British ship of 4,031 tons and, on the 17th, sent the steamer the *Skottland* (a Norwegian ship of 2,117 tons) to the bottom of Cape Sable. Off Yarmouth, the next day, she attacked the *Fort Bringer* but the torpedoes did not explode. Further south, Vogel sank the US steamer the *Plow City* of 3,282 tons off Rhode Island. At the time, the ship was engaged in retrieving survivors of the *Peisander* (sunk by *U-653* on the 17th) from their lifeboat. Vogel then sank the British steamer the *Margot* on 23 May off Nantucket before heading back to Europe, which it reached on 7 June. Victor Vogel was born in 1912 and was twenty-nine at the time. His four patrols of 130 days were all aboard *U-588*, which was sunk with all hands, on 31 July 1942 off Canada. Originally, he had served in anti-submarine and mine-sweeping roles before joining U-boats in March 1941. His career total of ships sunk or damaged was nine ships for 44,623 tons. He received no decorations during his career.

Korvettenkapitän Ernst-August Rehwinkel entered the region around Bermuda on 25 May 1942 and would spend an aggregate of fourteen days there. Two days after his entry, Rehwinkel sank the Dutch motor vessel the *Polyphemus* of 6,269 tons north of Bermuda on the 27th. The *Polyphemus* survivors would have a series of eventful voyages in lifeboats after two of the ships that rescued them were attacked by U-boats. The following day, he exited the area northbound towards New York. Off Nantucket, he was able to sink the Norwegian motor ship the *Berganger* of 6,826 tons, after *U-213* failed to sink her the same day. *U-578* returned to the Bermuda region on 10 June for an intense patrol north of the island, which lasted from 11 June for a week until the 18th, when it peeled away for the north-east, leaving the area on 19 June 1942. During the second incursion, no ships were attacked or sunk.

The sub sailed for the 7th U-boat Flotilla of St. Nazaire, and left that port on 7 May, returning to it on 3 July. Originally, it was part of the seven-boat *Padfinder* group some 400 miles east of New York. After trying the north-east, the U-boat dipped down towards Hatteras before retracing its route north of Bermuda and then east. This was *U-578*'s second patrol to the north-east US coast; however, on the previous patrol in which he sank the tanker the *R. P. Resor* and the USS *Jacob Jones* off Atlantic City, the sub did not come within 400 miles of Bermuda.

Ernst-August Rehwinkel was born in 1901, making him one of the oldest commanders to patrol the Bermuda area. He was a member of the Crew of 1923. From 1937 to when he joined U-boats in the fall of 1940, he was an instructor in the Naval Gunnery School. He commissioned *U-584* in July of 1941 and led her on five patrols for 133 patrol days. Overall, he managed to sink five ships of 24,725 tons. Promoted to *Fregattenkapitän* on 1 August, 1942, his submarine was lost in the Bay of Biscay to unknown causes four days later. Rehwinkel, aged forty at the time, and his entire crew perished.[6]

Oberleutnant zur See Amelung von Varendorff patrolled intensely north and north-west of Bermuda between 26 May and 6 June 1942 without sinking any ships. Earlier in the patrol, von Varendorff had managed to insert a German espionage agent into the Bay of Fundy, on 15 May near St. John (the spy spent the money given him and surrendered when it was gone). *U-213* was one of the seven *Padfinder* boats operating east of New York.[7] Von Varendorff attempted to sink the Norwegian motor ship the *Berganger* of 6,826 tons on 27 May, between Bermuda and Nantucket, but the ship was sunk later that day by Rehwinkel in *U-584*. The track of *U-213*'s patrol led from north of Bermuda to a box to the north-west of the island as the sub circled around looking for prey, then a leg east as the boat returned towards France.

U-213 sailed for the 7th U-boat Flotilla of Brest, which it originally left on 23 April, only to return two days later to retrieve its secret agent. The patrol ended in Brest on 21 May 1942. Von Varendorff was born in Kiel in 1913 and was a member of the Crew of 1935. He was a second watch officer on *U-47* during Prein's famous raid on Scapa Flow. He was an instructor until taking command of *U-213* in August 1941. On 31 July 1942, *U-213* was caught and depth-charged by HMS *Erne*, HMS *Sandwich*, and HMS *Rochester*; and sank with all hands west of Punta Delgada, Azores. Overall, von Varendorff accrued 120 patrol days on three missions. He did not manage to sink any ships of his own and was awarded the U-boat War Badge of 1939.

Kapitänleutnant Gerd Kelbling took his command *U-593* across the northern sector of Bermuda from west to east between 27 May and 2 June 1942. He sank no ships in the region; however, he was returning from moderate success off the US coast, where he had sunk the 8,426-ton Panamanian motor ship the *Persephone* on 25 May, two days before arriving off Bermuda. The boat experienced a counterattack from the navy ships escorting the *Persephone*'s convoy, but was undamaged. This had followed a partially successful attack on the Greek steamer the *Stavros*, 4,853 tons, on 14 May off Atlantic City; the ship was on charter to Swiss interests and made it to New York, where it was repaired. *U-593* sailed for the 7th U-boat Flotilla of St. Nazaire on 20 April and initially participated in an attempted wolf pack action against a convoy off Cape Sable, Canada on 1 May. The convoy hugged the coast, contact was lost, and the pack dispersed. *U-593* patrolled southwards. The patrol ended on 18 June in St. Nazaire.

Gerd Kelbling had a very active naval career, which he was fortunate to survive; he lived until 2005 and the age of eighty-nine. Born in 1915, he was a member of the Crew of 1934, following which he joined minesweepers. Early in 1941, he joined U-boats and sailed on *U-557* as commander-in-training. He commissioned *U-593* in March 1942 in Kiel, and sailed for St. Nazaire, where front-line boats were based, that same month. Overall, Kelbling accrued seventeen patrols and 338 days at sea. In that time, he sank or damaged sixteen ships of 57,721 tons, up to December 1943. On the 12th of that month, having been patrolling in the Mediterranean since October 1942, his boat was attacked by two Allied destroyers—USS *Wainwright* and HMS *Calpe*. All of the men on board, including Kelbling, were captured and imprisoned when the boat was scuttled. Kelbling was sent to Canada (fortunate not to be torpedoed *en route*) until September 1947.[8]

Kapitänleutnant Erich Würdemann spent only five days in the southern Bermuda area, but in that time, he sank two ships: the *Fred W. Green* and the *Yorkmoor*. His patrol began south-west of Bermuda on 28 May (the day he sank the *Yorkmoor*) and proceeded in a line straight east. Then, on the 31st, Würdemann encountered and sank the *Fred W. Green* and took a course change to the north-east until it exited the region to the east-south-east of Bermuda the following day. Aside from the *Sama*, the seven other victims of Würdemann's patrol were all American and accounted for a highly impressive 63,264 tons damaged or lost—the *William C. McTarnahan*, the *Sun*, and the *Aurora* were all damaged, and the *David McKelvy* was declared a constructive total loss. The ships sunk following the *Sama* were the *Gulfpenn*, the *Gulfoil*, the *Heredia*, and the *Halo*, most of them lost near the mouth of the Mississippi River.[9]

The British-flagged *Yorkmoor* (4,457 GRT) was the only other ship attacked in the Bermuda region on this patrol; she met her end south-west of Bermuda on 28 May 1942 while *U-506* was homeward bound. The submarine left the area on 30 May two days later. A member of the 10th U-boat Flotilla of Lorient, it returned to that port on 15 June 1942, having set out on 6 April. Würdemann was a member of the crew of 1933 and racked up a significant portion of his career totals of 69,893 tons sunk in fourteen ships, and three ships damaged for 23,358 tons on this patrol. He made nearly a dozen war patrols on destroyers before transferring to the U-boats in 1940. His early training included a patrol under Wolfgang Lüth on *U-43*. *U-506* was involved in both Hartenstein's *Laconia* incident and a long-range patrol into the Indian Ocean with *Monsun* boats in the Far East.[10] The boat was sunk with all but six hands while on the first week of its fifth patrol west of Spain by a US Air Force aircraft. Würdemann was not among the survivors—he was twenty-nine.

Kapitänleutnant Dietrich Borchert brought *U-566* briefly into the area north of Bermuda on 30 May 1942. Two days later, on 1 June, he sank the British 8,967-ton steamer *Westmoreland* north-north-east of Bermuda. On the way back to Brest, *U-566* was refueled by *U-459* west of the Azores in mid-June and made it back to base on 30 June 1942.[11] Sailing for the 1st U-boat Flotilla, *U-566* joined six other boats as part of the *Padfinder* line east of the US coast, looking for offshore prey. The patrol began in Brest on 8 April.

After unsuccessfully probing New York, Borchert tried the Gulf of Maine north of Boston with similar results—none—until it dipped south of the Gulf Stream towards Bermuda. Dietrich Borchert was born in 1909. Early in his naval career, he was involved with naval aircraft weaponry up to November 1939, when he joined the U-boat arm. He began as an instruction commander and, from August 1940, he led *U-24*. He commissioned *U-566* in April 1941 and led her on this patrol a year later. After July, he moved to various shore roles and received the Iron Cross First Class. Over five patrols Borchert accrued 196 patrol days and accounted for two ships sunk of 13,148 tons.[12]

31 May 1942: SS *Fred W. Green*

The small steamer the *Fred W. Green* was built for the US Shipping Board in 1918 and had the unique distinction of being the only derrick ship sunk in the Bermuda region during the war. Her main value was the fact that she had two highly maneuverable cranes embedded in her deck—the ship's cargo holds were filled with four feet of concrete, which of course would prove difficult for *U-506* under Eric Würdemann's gunners to penetrate. The *Fred W. Green* was 2,292 tons and built by the Great Lakes Engineering Works of Ecorse, Michigan. Her original name was the *Craycroft*. Nine years later, in 1927, she was converted to a derrick ship with the 1,000 tons of concrete added along with two cranes capable of lifting 30 tons at a time each. She was renamed by the new owner, John J. Roen of Cherlevoix in Grand Haven, Michigan.[1]

Five years later, in 1935, she was sold to the North-western Company of Wilmington, North Carolina. In 1941, ownership transferred again to the British Ministry of War Transport from the US Maritime Commission. Her operators were Furness, Withy of Liverpool. The charterers on her final voyage were the Elder Dempster Lines of the UK. Her dimensions were 255 feet long, 45 feet wide, and 21.5 feet deep.[2] On her final voyage, the *Fred W. Green* sailed from New York on 15 May 1942, bound for Freetown, Sierra Leone. *En route*, she called at Bermuda, sailing from that port in a south-easterly direction on 29 May. Her British crew of forty-one persons included naval gunners and was led by Captain Arthur Gould Sampson.[3] Late the next day, the ship was on course 131 degrees true and steaming at 7.5 knots, without zigzagging. The two lookouts were on the upper bridge and the aft gun respectively. The weather was settled, with a strong moon, a gentle wind from the south, and only a moderate swell.[4]

The *Fred W. Green* had only made it 200 miles south-east of Bermuda when she was found and followed by Würdemann in *U-506*. However, the sub had expended the last of its torpedoes and was down to only thirty-four shells to fire on the patrol—each one had to count. They were not counting on finding set concrete in the hold, as of course shells bounced right off the hull. Perhaps for that reason, Würdemann held off attacking the slow-moving ship for seven hours, trailing it through the afternoon until 7.45 p.m.[5] The first shells hit from the starboard side and took down the aerials, meaning no SOS could be sent. The gun was manned and Leslie Lumsden, a gunner aged twenty-five, managed to fire off some shots of the 20-milimeter Oerlikon gun before he and the entire gun platform were blown away by the submarine's guns. Fortune favored the submariners, as their very last incendiary shell set fire to the forecastle of the ship, and Captain Sampson and his crew abandoned ship in two lifeboats. The master was last seen ensuring that there was no one left on board before leaping off the bow; however, the boats were unable to find him afterwards.

The submarine approached the boats while the ship burned and slowly sank in the background. They were told that the ship was heading for Cape Town, not Freetown. The survivors refused assistance. After apologizing for sinking the ship, the Germans used their anti-aircraft gun to puncture the hull below the waterline and expedite the sinking. This proved ineffectual, even dangerous, as the projectiles bounced back. Ultimately, the ship sank on its own, two hours and fifty minutes after the initial salvo and some ten hours after the ship was initially sighted. *U-506* was seen motoring off to the south-east at 11.30 p.m. that night. Having abandoned ship at 9 p.m., thirty-two men manned one lifeboat, and four men took the other. Five men (including the master, the gunner and three crew) were lost and presumed killed.[6] Two days later (on their second full day in boats—1 June), the men managed to attract the attention of a US Navy aircraft using red flares. This plane alerted a nearby convoy, AS 3, which was led by the cruiser USS *Texas*.

The destroyer USS *Ludlow* under the command of Lieutenant Commander C. H. Bennett was dispatched to rescue the thirty-two survivors in the first boat, which it found. The occupants of the second life boat were rescued by the USS *Barnadou*, another destroyer escorting the same convoy, five miles to the south.[7] Twenty-four of the survivors were transferred to the *Texas* and landed in Bermuda at mid-day on 17 June 1942, no doubt having been well fed in the two-week interim. Three out of the four naval gunners were saved. It is not known when the eight other survivors were landed, but they were also put ashore in Bermuda.[8]

1 June 1942: SS *West Notus*

The US-flagged steamship the *West Notus* was built in 1920 by the South Western Shipbuilding Company of San Pedro, California as yard number seventeen. Her 2,800 ihp, triple-expansion engine powered by three boilers was built by Llewellyn Iron Works of Los Angeles and turned a single propeller to give the ship 10.5 knots of speed. The ship was 5,492 gross tons in weight, 412.8 feet long, 54.5 feet wide, and 30 feet deep. The *West Notus'* original owners were the United States Shipping Board of Washington DC up until 1926, when she was sold to the Pacific Argentine Brazil Line of San Francisco. That firm owned the steamer until 1941, when Moore and McCormack bought her through subsidiaries Mooremack Lines and American Scantic Lines of New York. In 1921, the ship was advertised sailing from Buenos Aires for San Pedro, San Francisco, Seattle, and Portland via Brazil and the Panama Canal.[1]

In 1926, the Oakland *Tribune* ran an article entitled 'West Notus Has Rich Cargo for South America; Freighter Is First Craft to Sail in New Service for Mooremack Lines.'[2] The ship was reported on 4 April to have been loaded with 4,000,000 feet of lumber in holds and on deck. In Oakland, it topped up on 1,000 tons of canned salmon and 1,500 tons of general cargo. Apparently, the McCormick Line took over the Pacific-Argentine-Brazil service that year. On 18 August, the same paper touted a shipment of 1,500 bags of Brazil nuts—the first importation of them in California—that the *West Notus* brought to Oakland from Para, Brazil.[3]

Captain Loren McIntyre (who in 1971 discovered the source of the Amazon River while on assignment with *National Geographic*), wrote that in 1935 'I signed on the *West Notus*. It sailed up and down the coasts of South America, stopping everywhere. In Belem, we loaded Brazil nuts and mahogany, swinging to and fro on the world's highest freshwater tides.'[4] He went on to become a leader in South American exploration. In August 1940, FBI Director J. Edgar Hoover's men captured a *West Notus* crew member, Keawe Kamakela, aged thirty-five, from Hawaii, on suspicion that he had sabotaged the ship's engines by pouring sand into the bearings on 27 September 1939.[5] Fortunately, Kamakela's deeds were discovered, and the sand under his fingernails matched with that in the engine, before the motors were engaged. On 25 March 1938, the *West Notus* was in radio contact with Kingston,

Jamaica's Cable and Wireless station 'VQI.'[6] In September 1940, she was tied up in Seattle due to action by the Marine Fireman's Union.[7] She sailed from New York three times in 1941—in February, May, and October—and on 26 February 1942.[8]

On her final voyage, beginning in May 1942, the *West Notus'* master was Captain Hans Gerner, from Los Angeles. There was a total of forty men on board the ship, five of them military gunners, the other thirty-five merchant marine officers and crew. After loading a full cargo of 7,400 tons of flax seed in Bahia Blanca, Argentina early in May 1942, the ship stopped in Trinidad for bunkers *en route* to discharge in New York. In the book *Time Tide and Timber: A Century of Pope and Talbot*, her departure from Trinidad is conveyed poetically: 'just as the tropical sunrise was gilding the tree-lined shore of Trinidad, the *West Notus* cast off her hawsers and slipped out to sea, bound for New York. The day was Sunday, May 24, 1942.'[9] The voyage went uneventfully for just over a week. On Sunday, 31 May, the US Navy radioed a change of routing instructions to Captain Gerner, which he complied with.

Then, at dawn on Monday, 1 June, the German submarine *U-404* under Otto von Bülow decided to mount a surface attack on the ship from the port quarter. They were 300 nautical miles north-west of Bermuda, and 312 nautical miles east-north-east of Cape Hatteras. There were two lookouts, on the bridge and the forecastle up forward. The conditions were described as clear, with a moderate easterly wind, good visibility and moderate seas. The ship was heading 295 degrees north-north-west at 10 knots.

At 5.15 a.m., von Bülow recorded in his war diary:

Steamer in sight bearing 160°. Target angle bow right 45°, range = 4000 meters, coming out of the morning mist. It is too bright for a surface attack, in addition the clear horizon is behind us. At this range the target angle is already too great for a submerged attack. Diving unseen to maneuver ahead later at the limit of vision for a submerged attack already appears questionable and not promising given the strong zig zagging expected from the experience of sinking Alcoa Shipper.[10]

Two minutes later, von Bülow wrote that his artillery was ready and the U-boat was running to meet the ship. As to why he attacked with deck artillery instead of torpedoes, the commander later recalled that 'She was attacked by our deck gun, as I had not enough fuel on left on board to overtake her and find a position from which to fire the torpedoes.' He noted the large cannon on the *West Notus'* stern as well as machine guns. At 5.21 a.m., the submarine opened fire from 2,200 meters away. The following minute, the German commander recorded:

After 2 far and 2 short hits on the bridge observed. Steamer turns away 50° and opens fire with his cannon. The first impacts lie far behind the boat. [Machine gun] C 30 broke down after a few shots, the cocking lever is broken again. The range is too great for effective suppression with the [machine gun] C 34. There were continual hits on it, the steamer and already good fire effects observed. On 2 well placed impacts ahead of the boat turned away with …hard rudder.

When the attack began, 'Gerner ran into his cabin to recover his documents and secret papers. No sooner had he disappeared inside than a shell struck the Captain's quarters. He emerged from the flaming wreckage, staggered to the rail, and ordered all hands to abandon ship. A few minutes later he collapsed and died.' Witnesses say that Captain Gerner lasted three minutes from the abandon ship order to his death. There was no opportunity to send a distress message by radio, presumably because one of the radio operators had been killed and the equipment must have been damaged or destroyed at the same time.

Able-bodied seaman Charles K. Toguchi, from Hawaii, related:

I was at the wheel when the fight began and although we had some machine guns, they were no match for the sub's 20-mm cannons. Shells began hitting the wheelhouse and the captain's cabin, but I was not hit. Soon the captain blew the whistle and gave the order to abandon ship and the crew got into two lifeboats. Chief Engineer [W. C.] Edwards hurried below to shut off the engines while the men made for the lifeboats. As one was being lowered, it was struck and burst into flames. Two of the starboard lifeboats were launched, and the chief engineer and seventeen crewmen manned one boat, while Chief Mate [Lambert] Kat, twelve members of the crew, and five of the gun crew occupied the other. The gunfire had killed Third Mate [Harry S.] Morris [Scottish], Radio Operator [Wilfred] Clarkson [British] and Assistant Engineer [Victor P.] Williams.

The survivors later reported that by 5.30 a.m., thirty-five of the remaining men left the *West Notus* in two lifeboats. One of the survivors was unaccounted for.

At 5.25 a.m., *U-404* ceased fire and prepared to dive, but ultimately remained in the surface. Von Bülow observed that the *West Notus* was on fire, had blown off engine steam, and that the men aboard were taking to the lifeboats. At 5.33 a.m., *U-404* again approached the ship, and must have never dived since artillery was at the ready. Von Bülow noted that the ship continued making headway and turned to starboard, though by this time no one was on board. The Germans opened fire from 1,800 meters and hit the defenseless ship each time. By 5.40 a.m., nineteen minutes after the initial attack, the *West Notus* was ablaze from stem to stern. At that point, von Bülow records:

'Cease fire! Drove around the steamer, no more people aboard. On the stern and bow badly painted over name: *West Notus* could be read, U.S.A. steamer 5492 GRT. Pacific Argentine Line.'[11] He would have obtained the latter information from the *Groner* guide to Allied merchant shipping which every U-boat carried to identify their victims with.

At 6.15 a.m., von Bülow brought *U-404* to within 3,000 meters. At that time, he found that the Allied gunners had damaged his submarine in two places—the port exhaust piping and the stern covering the deck torpedo canister. This necessitated repairs, particularly to the exhaust manifold, though it was found the torpedo was undamaged. At 7.10 a.m., the Axis commander noted 'A drifting leaky boat with the first officer and five men is towed to two boats sailing fully occupied.' He interacted with the American chief officer to learn the ship's cargo, recent ports and destination. He also noted that his shelling of the bridge had killed Captain Gerner. Then, for the next two hours, *U-404* motored 'Back and forth in the vicinity of the steamer wreck to effect repairs.' The Allied narrative picks up:

> The boats stayed together, and the submarine soon headed in their direction. The Germans delivered to the chief engineer's boat an injured oiler... ...who had been picked up after several hours in the water. The Germans had already given him medical attention. The German officer on deck advised them in fluent English that they were 350 miles from land, and went on to give them their position. He also handed over a supply of fresh water.

Survivors state that they were given Perrier water and a piece of paper giving them a course to Hatteras of 275 degrees 320 nautical miles distant. Some survivors said the Germans handed them a tin of soup marked 'Linsen, Santos, Brazil'; however, it is possible this floated up from their own ship's supplies and was merely given back to them.

The statements of the survivors record the interactions between the foes in considerable detail:

> The officer spoke to survivors in good English but with German accent ... Crew dressed in shorts, tanned, apparently in southern waters, 20 to 30 age, some bearded, were solicitous regarding casualties, congratulated gun crew describing situation a 50-50 battle. In reply, the commander, about 25, medium build, big uniform, fair complexion, was told the *West Notus*' port of departure, destination, cargo, etc.

The survivors' proximity to their adversary for such a prolonged time enabled them to observe that the paint '...was clean without barnacles and the Diesel oil used was believed to be high grade as it emitted no odor and only a faint blue exhaust.'

Von Bülow logged that 'During the repairs a lightly wounded American seaman was fished out and brought to sailing lifeboats.' Fifteen minutes later, the Germans observed the American ship's ammunition detonate, throwing a high column of flame. Von Bülow noted at 2 p.m. that 'Steamer has a slight list. Flaxseed flows from many shell holes just above the waterline. Ten further shots of explosive munitions are fired from the immediate vicinity into the water line.'

Some fifty years later, von Bülow described this attack to a friend of his from the Allied merchant marine, John Lawton:

She was, it turned out, loaded with linseed oil which kept flooding out of the ship through the shell holes, the more holes we made, the more oil came out, the higher the ship sat in the water and would not sink. Eventually lifeboats put off from the ship. I noticed that a boat was stuck in the 'falls' of the ship, so I drew alongside and told the men to jump. I then picked them up and took them to the other boats, where I asked if any were injured; I gave them First Aid kits, bandages, blankets, brandy and a chart.

U-404's gunners pumped six more shots of explosive shells into the ship at the waterline, yet still she did not sink. By 6.30 p.m., on 2 June, the attack had been going on for over thirteen hours; von Bülow decided to change tactics and blow the ship up with satchels of explosives fixed to the sides. He records that: 'By driving up and throwing a grapnel, an explosive cartridge was affixed to the side of the steamer's hull and initiated. However, there was no detonation, probably the rope holding the charge was burned on the hot side of the hull.' Nothing seemed to be going the German's way.

In the evening twilight, the sub dove to test the repairs. Fort-five minutes later, it stopped in sight of the *West Notus*, which had still not yet sunk. By 6 a.m., the attack had been going on for over twenty-four hours. The commander noted that 'A new demolition charge is fastened in the same manner to the side of the hull and initiated.' Seven minutes later, 'Detonation. Steamer wreck sinks slowly deeper.' Exasperated, *U-404*'s men remained in the vicinity, repairing their submarine and trying to sink the *West Notus*. At about 1 p.m., some thirty-two hours into the attack, von Bülow wrote 'Wreck still smokes strongly. Is observed to sink deeper, submerging more of the shell holes.'[12]

An hour later, there was finally a break in the siege; the lookouts in the German submarine sighted the neutral Swedish ship *Anna* and motored off to attack, leaving the *West Notus* to slowly sink.[13] The stubborn American vessel had cost the Germans two instances of damage, the expenditure of a high number of shells, and a day and a half of their precious time. The American witnesses in the distance were unaware that the submarine approached the side of their ship. According to them, a shell managed to find the engine room fuel tanks; the ship exploded and buckled in two amidships and sank.

Each of the two lifeboats had eighteen occupants. The boat led by Second Officer Pieter J. Sas (a naturalized American) included injured sailor Francis J. Sherlock, who suffered from a shrapnel wound, as well as Filipino Democrito D. Hortelano, and two Puerto Rican messmen—Julius Morales and Manuel A. Perez. Chief Engineer Edwards found that the water was stale and should have been refreshed every fifteen days. He felt that 20 gallons of water should have been allocated to each boat and that the sails should be light rather than dark red, which resembled a submarine conning tower. This is probably because the men in his boat reported sighting an Allied ship, which 'immediately altered course and ran away from the lifeboat.'[14]

The men in Second Officer Sas's lifeboat sighted an airplane on Tuesday, 2 June, which they took to be a Clipper amphibious plane, which did not appear to have sighted them. Then at 8.40 a.m. on Thursday, 4 June, the eighteen men were discovered by the Swiss merchant ship SS *Saentis*. The position given by the *Saentis* for the rescue was 132 nautical miles south-south-west of the sinking location, so the lifeboat achieved roughly 1.5 knots. The *Saentis* delivered the crew to New York the following day, at 6.43 p.m. on Friday, 5 June.

The motor ship *Saentis* was built by Harland and Wolff in Belfast in 1912 as the MV *Falstria* and only joined the Swiss merchant marine in New York on 12 December 1941—the day after Hitler declared war on the United States. In the intervening years, she had been named the *Olymp*, the *Matros*, and the *Norseland*. She was named by the Swiss for a mountain in the east of Switzerland. Her first voyage for KTA, Bern was a limited success and was characterized by engine troubles, and occurred in April 1942, mere weeks before her rescue of the *West Notus* survivors.[15] The *Saentis* continued on its course to New York, carrying twenty survivors from the Swedish ship *Anna*, which had also been sunk by von Bülow. *Saentis* arrived in New York on Friday, 5 June. On arrival, F. J. Sherlock was admitted to the Marine Hospital in New York.

The US Eastern Sea Frontier Enemy Action and Distress Diary of 5 June records the arrival of both *West Notus* and *Anna* survivors at 6.43 p.m. on 5 June 1942:

> M. V. *Saentis* (Swiss) arrived at quarantine with following survivors: 17 survivors from SS *West Notus* (U.S. cargo, 5492 tons) rescued from lifeboat at 0840 June 4. *West Notus* was attacked by shellfire (350 miles east of Cape Henry) at 0630 June 1 and finally sunk at 1515 June 1. Another boat with 18 men still missing, reported as probably south of position of boat rescued.

Since the survivors or the *Saentis'* captain got word to US Naval authorities that a lifeboat from the *West Notus* was still unaccounted for, the war diary of the Naval Operating Base Norfolk on 6 June records that 'Two PBO's [aircraft] searching for survivors (SS *West Notus*). *Owl* [USS *Owl*, a US Navy ship based in Bermuda at the time] on scene today.'[16] Following their rescue, Chief Engineer Edwards gave his opinions as to occupancy numbers (fewer men so more could ride out storms in the bottom of the boat), rudder pintles (reinforced), food cans (riveted lids, not soldered), and cigarettes (one pack per man). Being the head of the engine department, he felt that extra sun block or lotion should be provided for the engine room men, as they were more vulnerable to the extreme sun conditions of a lifeboats than their counterparts who worked on the deck.

The men in the other boat were even more fortunate in their rescue in that they spent less time in an open boat. This boat was under the command of the First Officer Lambert Kat held included Ordinary Seaman Marshall Howard, who suffered injuries around the neck and head. On Wednesday, 3 June, after roughly three days in an open boat, the eighteen men were discovered and rescued by the Greek merchant ship the *Constantinos H.*[17] This vessel's generous master took the men to Bermuda, where they arrived on Friday, 5 June.

The *Constantinos H.* was built by AG Neptun in Rostock, Germany in 1905. She was 2,527 gross registered tons and could carry 4,530 deadweight tons of cargo. In 1919, the ship was ceded to France as war reparations, sold to *Companie des Bateaux a Vapeur du Nord* in Dunkirk and renamed the *Nanceen.* The ship appears to have traded with Algeria during the next twelve years until it was sold in 1921 to a Greek firm named D. C. Tillellos and Company of Piraeus. For three years until 1933, the vessel sailed as the SS *Anthemis,* so named after a flower. In 1933, she was sold to Iliopoulos, Ilias and Athanassios of Athens and provided with her final name.[18]

It is not known who the master of the *Constantinos H.* was at the time of the rescue, perhaps because the owners were a single-ship firm and their routes were 'general tramping.' She left New York Harbor on 4 March and 26 May 1942. On 24 November 1942, she was in a small convoy (Prep King Convoy 121) in the US Gulf along with the SS *Domino* (itself later attacked by a U-boat in the Old Bahama Channel), and escorted by CG 83351. She also appeared in Convoy TAG 77 from Aruba and Trinidad to Guantanamo in early August 1943.[19] The *West Notus* men were repatriated to New York and reunited with their shipmates on Sunday, 14 June. The *Constantinos H.* sailed until she was scrapped in 1958 at the age of fifty-four.[20]

From the *West Notus,* able-bodied seaman Charles Toguchi went on to survive another sinking by an Axis submarine; SS *Kaimoku* sunk south-east of Greenland by *U-379* under Paul-Hugo Kettner on 8 August 1942. He is said to have survived three wars.[21] There is a story, perhaps apocryphal, that *West Notus* survivors met with von Bülow on an American television program in the 1970s.

5–6 June 1942: Three U-boats

Next into the region was Wolf Henne in command of *U-157*. He entered the area in a line going west-south-west on 5 June 1942, and exited the region four days later on the 13th. *U-157* was on a death-march without knowing it. The sub rounded the Turks and Caicos on the 10th and transited the Caicos Passage just east of Inagua that day for the Old Bahama Channel. *U-157* proceeded up the coast of Cuba for three days, its progress being tracked by US and Cuban forces via radio and from volunteer Pan American and a US Navy aircraft on 10 June. On the 11th, it sank the 6,401 US molasses tanker *Hagan* five miles north of Cuba. It was to be the only tanker sunk by either the skipper or the boat. Later on the same day, a US B 18 bomber spotted the boat and dropped four depth charges. As a result of the sinking and other tracking inputs, by the time the U-boat reached the new US anti-submarine base off Key West on the 13th, it was attacked and sunk by seven depth charges from the USS *Thetis*, a destroyer under Lt. N. C. McCormick, and a pack of other Allied vessels in a determined and systematic attack. It was the second U-boat sunk on a patrol to the region after Rostin in *U-158* met its demise off Bermuda some weeks before.[1]

Wolf Henne sailed to the Bahamas and Bermuda as an officer in the German merchant marine before the war. Born in Futschau, China, in 1905, he was thirty-six years of age when killed by the Allied hunter-killer group hastily organized for the task. A member of the Crew of 1924, Henne had been given the rank *Korvettenkapitän* in 1939—he received no promotions or decorations in the intervening three years of his life. The sinking of *U-157* underscores the stark fact that most U-boats or their commanders were lost on first or early patrols. Unlike the vast majority of U-boats which attacked the region that were on their third, fourth, or fifth war patrols, *U-157* and her commander were relatively untested in combat, having experienced a short eleven-day patrol before its final one. Normally, a submarine would go on several forays into convoys in the North Atlantic or the region west of Biscay before setting off on transatlantic missions of long duration.[2]

Oberleutnant zur See Paul-Karl Loeser brought *U-373* westward north of Bermuda in a straight line from 6 June 1942 to the 9th. Returning from the US eastern seaboard, he proceeded in another straight line, this one west to east between 16 and 19 June. One of the reasons that the courses were so straight and the sinkings so few is that the submarine was on a mission to lay 15 TMB-type mines off the Delaware Bay, which it accomplished on 11 June. Loeser claimed hits on the 14th off the US coast, but the torpedo did not explode. The following day, he claimed to have hit a steamer, but it apparently caused no damage. The submarine's only confirmed victim was the tug the *John R. Williams*, of 396 tons, which struck one of *U-373*'s mines and sank, taking fourteen of her crew with it.[3]

U-373 was a member of the 3rd U-boat Flotilla out of La Pallice, from which it sailed on 18 May 1942 and to which it returned on 8 July. Born in Berlin in 1915, Loeser was a member of the Crew of 1935. In 1938, he was second watch officer of *U-33* and then *U-40*, followed by first watch officer of *U-43* in 1939. He commissioned *U-373* in May 1941 and went on nine patrols of 367 days aboard her until August 1943. In 1943, Loeser became a training officer in the 20th U-boat Flotilla, followed by an anti-aircraft officer, and finally a member of the Dönitz Guard Battalion until the capitulation. He was captured in the spring of 1945 and released in August of that year. Loeser's total tally was three ships sunk for 10,263 tons. He received no decorations and lived until 1987 and the age of seventy-one.[4]

Kapitänleutnant Friedrich-Hermann Praetorius brought *U-135* to the region west-north-west of Bermuda on 6 June 1942. Motoring east, he managed to sink the Norwegian motor ship the *Pleasantville* of 4,549 tons north-west of Bermuda. From there, he proceeded north-east and patrolled in zigzag pattern for roughly a week north-north-west of Bermuda between 11 and 17 June. After that, he headed due east, exiting the region on 18 June for France.

U-135 sailed from Brest on 26 April 1942 for the 7th U-boat Flotilla. The U-boat was part of the sixth wave of boats to attack the US coast in Operation Drumbeat.[5] There were thirteen boats in that particular wave. After sinking the British steamship the *Fort Qu'Appelle* east of New York, *U-135* contributed to forming the line of seven boats in the *Padfinder* group, looking for offshore prey.[6]

U-135 then proceeded to the area off Cape Hatteras, where it sank no victims until finding the *Pleaseantville en route* home. She was refueled by *U-459* west of the Azores around 18 June. On 5 July, *U-135* arrived back in St. Nazaire, a different base from that which she had departed (Brest). Friedrich-Hermann Praetorius was born in Kolberg in 1904, making him one of the older skippers to patrol the Bermuda region. He was a member of the Crew of 1934 and joined U-boats in April 1940. After serving as first watch officer on *U-98* until May 1941, he commissioned *U-135*, in which he led four patrols of 208 days up until November 1942. He then became a training officer in the 27th U-boat Flotilla and then the 25th U-boat Flotilla until the surrender. He was a master in the merchant marine following the war. He lived until 1956 and the age of fifty-two. Aside from the Iron Cross First Class and the 1940 Destroyer War Badge (suggesting that he served in destroyers before joining U-boats), Praetorius was awarded the U-boat War Badge of 1939. His total tally was three ships of 21,302 tons, most of them sunk during this patrol.[7]

7 June 1942: USS *Gannet*

USS *Gannet* was laid down at *Minesweeper Number 41* at the Todd Shipyard Corporation of New York on 1 October 1918. Launched on 19 March 1919, she was commissioned at the New York Navy Yard on 10 July that year. On 17 February 1920, the ship received the designation AM 41. The minesweeper displaced 840 tons and had a length of 187 feet 10 inches, beam 35 feet 5 inches, and draft 8 feet 10 inches. Manned by seventy-eight officers and men, the vessel achieved 14 knots. A single 1,400 shp engine built by Hollingsworth Corporation drove one shaft. Her weaponry consisted of twin 3-inch guns on dual-purpose mounts.

The *Gannet* had a career that covered a variety of weather zones. Leaving New York, it performed shakedown maneuvers in Cuba before joining the Pacific Fleet in San Diego. Among many duties, she tended aircraft squadrons, towed and transported ships and passengers. In 1926, 1929, and then 1932–1935, the *Gannet* supported aerial surveys of Alaska and the Aleutian Islands. On 30 April 1931, she was reclassified a minesweeper for duties with aircraft. In January 1936, the ship was reclassified as a Small Seaplane Tender and given the numerals AVP 8.

In August 1937, the *Gannet* was sent to Coco Solo, Panama to tender aircraft there. Then, in June 1939, the vessel went to Norfolk, tending US Navy airplanes in Key West, Bermuda, St. Lucia, and Trinidad. In September 1941, she was sent to Kungnait Bay, Greenland, setting up an advanced seaplane base. In November, she returned to Norfolk. When Pearl Harbor was attacked, the *Gannet* was in Hamilton. After a short voyage back to Norfolk, she returned to Bermuda for the balance of her war. From 15 June 1941 until the ship's demise on 7 June 1942, her commander was Lieutenant Francis Edward Nuessle. On 1 June, the British steamship the *Westmoreland* was sunk by *U-566* under Dietrich Borchert roughly 220 nautical miles north of Bermuda. The ship sent out an SSS, which was received by shore stations.[1]

Rear Admiral Jules James, officer in charge of the Naval Operating Base, Bermuda, ordered the *Gannet* and HMS *Sumar* to rescue the sixty-five survivors; however, unbeknown to authorities in Bermuda, the survivors were in fact picked up by two merchant ships, the *Cathcart* and the *Henry R. Mallory* shortly after the sinking.[2,3] Several aircraft were sent to the site of the sinking from Bermuda as well.

The yacht *Sumar* was commissioned by David C. Whitney (1865–1942) of Grosse Point, Detroit Michigan and named for his wife Susan Marshall. It was built of steel by the Todd Shipyards Corporation in Brooklyn—the same yard as the *Gannet* was built—except it was built by their Tebo Yacht Basin subsidiary.

The vessel was 160 feet long; propulsion was by twin diesel engines which turned two propellers she produced 13 knots. The naval architect was Henry J. Gielow. Her beam was 26 feet and weighed 319 tons. The engines were built by Cooper-Bessemer and developed 420 horsepower. The vessel was manned by a crew of twenty-one. In 1927, her captain was B. Madsen; in May, she was in transit from Manila to Colombo via Singapore. Built in 1926, the *Sumar* had logged 85,000 nautical miles of cruising by April 1931, including a circumnavigation. She ranged from the east and west coasts of the Americas, the Mediterranean and Black Seas, the British Isles, Scandinavia, and the Caribbean. The first part of her route took her to Port of Spain, Rio, Montevideo, then to Hammerfest Norway. Her captain in 1930 was named Barney; he had skippered the British war prize *Germania* and been responsible for 104 idle Hog Island-built ships for two years.

Sometime before June 1942, the *Sumar* was sold to the British and commissioned as HMS *Sumar*. In Bermuda, she was listed as an anti-submarine vessel and was at one point under the command of Lieutenant Commander C. A. King, DSC, RNR. In July 1941, she was simply fitting out in Bermuda. The *Sumar* was based at Her Majesty's Dockyard in Bermuda.

HMS *Sumar*'s commander was a Canadian named Lieutenant Gordon Emerson Kernohan of the Royal Canadian Naval Voluntary Reserve.[4] A 1926 graduate of Upper Canada College, Lt. Kernohan hailed from Winnipeg and Toronto. He was one of the survivors when the armed merchant cruiser (AMC) HMS *Forfar* (F 30) was sunk on 2 December 1940 by Otto Kretschmer in *U-99* west of Ireland. 172 of her complement of 193 perished; twenty-one survived.

Nuessle on the *Gannet* was expecting a corvette to rendezvous with him five nautical miles east of Gibbs Hill Light. Instead, he and his men were unpleasantly surprised to find the converted yacht *Sumar*. It got worse; they had no common communications signals, the *Gannet* did not have a working sonar and neither did the *Sumar*, and both the radio and compass on the *Sumar* were defective. The resultant erratic changes in course made the *Sumar* yaw so much that Nuessle wryly observed she might has well have been zigzagging.[5]

The converted yacht could only make 10 knots, and so the *Gannet* took up station, laboriously trying to stay within 500 yards of its companion during the voyage northwards. In order to stay in contact with each other, both ships rigged lights for the other to see, making them easier prey to lurking submarines. Since the airplanes found no survivors from the *Westmoreland* (they had already been rescued), at 1 p.m. on 6 June, both navy ships were ordered back to Bermuda. By then, they had sailed into the sights of a German U-boat, *U-653* under *Kapitänleutnant* Gerhard Feiler. Feiler was a determined adversary; however, he underestimated the draft of the two ships he was aiming for. He described his targets as a 'navy tender' and a 'large escort', and also describes seeing a 'white-painted destroyer.' They were first sighted at about 6.22 a.m. He finally lined up his torpedo shots at 10.20 p.m. on 7 June. Remarkably, all four shots—all of them with the modern G7e homing torpedo—missed the mark. Feiler was exasperated, logging 'So much for our first attack in all this time—four misses! A bitter disappointment.' By 1.42 a.m. local time, he fired another pair of torpedoes, these ones set for just about 7 feet depth. After thirty-eight seconds, he wrote that 'tender blows up immediately, presumably the magazine. Once the explosion cloud has cleared we can see only small pieces of sinking wreckage, debris from the blast is spread far and wide.' He noted that the *Sumar* turned and headed towards the U-boat, and observed seeing 'emergency signals for about ten min.'[6]

Apparently, HMS *Sumar*'s men didn't see the emergency signals, or mistook them for more mundane communications from her escort, as the ship motored on for Bermuda, arriving there without the *Gannet* the following day and causing a damaging rift between the US and British navies. The explosion was indeed devastating to the *Gannet*: fourteen men of her company were killed in the blast. The vessel only stayed afloat for four minutes before rolling over and sinking, taking with it two lifeboats and leaving the sixty-two survivors to cling to flotsam and a pair of rafts. Nuessle was sucked underwater by the sinking ship and barely managed to escape with his life.[7] Once on the surface, he ordered the injured to be placed on the rafts and the other men to tread water nearby, holding on. The majority of them were doomed to spend seventeen hours in that state.

Due to the *Westmoreland* sinking and numerous sightings of life rafts reported to the air arm in Bermuda, and by a good measure of luck, a US Navy Mariner airplane whose specific call sign was 74 (for the squadron) P 2 piloted by Lieutenant W. L. Pettingill came upon the survivors.[8] Having no idea that the *Gannet* had been sunk, he presumed the men to be merchant mariners and radioed base in Bermuda to receive permission to land, which was against standing orders.

In Pettingill, the men of the *Gannet* were blessed with the right man at the right time. When he flew low over the survivors, he determined (correctly) that they were in need of immediate medical attention and were desperate. Disregarding his orders and protocol, he landed his flying boat on the rough seas and was shocked to learn that they were his compatriots from the *Gannet*. He immediately raised the alarm via radio and, although his plane had been slightly damaged on the struts by his landing, managed to gather eleven of the worst cases into the plane and take off for Bermuda.[9] The condition of some of the men was so bad that one of them died *en route*. On learning of the fate of the *Gannet* men, and not knowing of the activities of the *Sumar*, Rear Admiral James immediately dispatched more aircraft as well as USS *Hamilton*, USS *Trippe*, and USS *Owl*.[10]

The USS *Hamilton* was a flush-decked four-stacker destroyer built in 1918–1919 at Mares Island Naval Shipyard near San Francisco. She was commissioned as a destroyer (DD 141) on 7 November 1919 and decommissioned on 20 July 1922. The vessel was recommissioned on 20 January 1930. On 17 October 1941, the ship was reclassified as a fast minesweeper and given the designation DMS 18. The *Hamilton* was 1,090 tons, 314 feet 5 inches long, 31 feet 9 inches wide, and 8 feet 8 inches deep. She was capable of 35 knots' speed when built, and manned by 113 officers and men. Her main weapons were four 4-inch guns, three .30-caliber machine guns, and twelve torpedo tubes. Between 1939 and 1941, the *Hamilton* patrolled the Grand Banks out to Iceland and Greenland. When the US joined the war, she escorted convoys as far south as Panama.

On 7 June, Admiral James ordered the *Hamilton* to rescue survivors of the *Gannet* north of Bermuda, in coordination with the naval aircraft also assigned to the task. These aircraft succeeded in attracting the *Hamilton* commander, Lieutenant Commander Harold Oscar 'Swede' Larson's attention and vectored the former destroyer to the location of the forty remaining men.[11]

Specifically, Lieutenant Commander J. W. Gannon in the Mariner of P 7 from Squadron VP 74 guided the *Hamilton* to the scene, and he too, bravely landed on the open sea and retrieved eleven of the most ill men, including Lt. Cdr. Nuessle. Both the plane and the *Hamilton* then returned to Bermuda, where the survivors were landed and some placed in the Naval Infirmary there.

The War Diary dated 8 June records laconically that 'Enroute to Base Mike [Bermuda] escorting the *Joseph T. Dickman*, *Hamilton* left convoy to do some sub elimination duty and picked up some survivors of USS *Gannet*. Convoy arrived Base Mike with *Stansbury* escorting.'[12] Due to the military nature of the loss and rescue, the events did not make the local press.

After supporting Operation Torch in North Africa, then supporting the US Marines' invasion of Kwajalein Atoll, USS *Hamilton* was re-classified as a miscellaneous auxiliary (AG 111) on 6 May 1945 and struck from the Navy Register on 1 November 1945. She was sold for scrapping just over a year later. HMS *Sumar* was used as a training ship in 1944 and sold out of the service in 1946. One of the conditions of the US Navy regarding the *Sumar* incident was that Lt. Kernohan no longer command any Allied ships. Not being interested in participating in courts-martial of an ally, however, they sent most of the witnesses, including Lt. Nuessle, to the US mainland quickly following the incident.

There were heated exchanges of letters between Rear Admiral James and his British counterpart, Admiral Sir Charles Kennedy-Purvis. The gist of these were that the Americans didn't want to be given substandard ships and inferior commanders who passed up an opportunity for bravery and glory in counterattacking a U-boat and rescuing their Allies. The British retorted by questioning why it was sent on a mission for which it was grossly ill-suited by the American admiral.[13] Lt. Kernohan went on to command, by September 1943, the Naval Reserve Unit named HMCS *Cataraqui* (also spelt *Cararagin*) in Kingston, Ontario. By June 1945, he was in command of HMCS *Chippawa*, a naval base in Winnipeg, Manitoba, where 28,000 Canadian naval personnel had to be processed for civilian life after demobilization. It was the wartime naval establishment's equivalent of being sent to Siberia.[14]

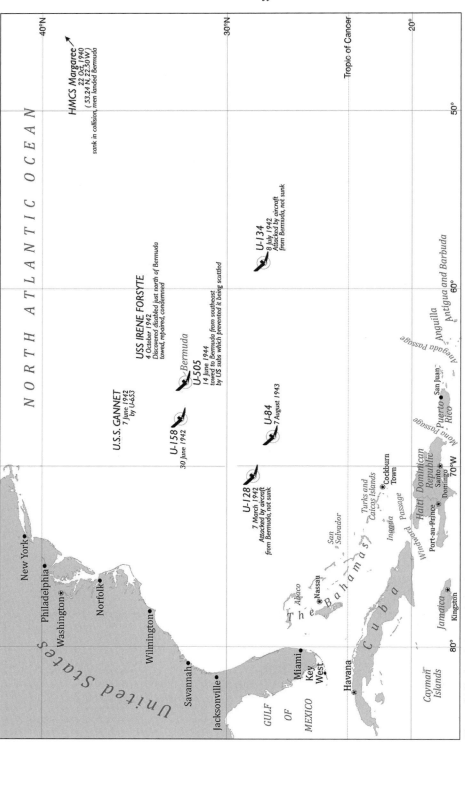

Chart of Allied and Axis military losses or near-losses affecting Bermuda between October, 1940 and June, 1944., including a sampling of some of the many Allied aircraft attacks on U-boats. Most important are the losses of *U-158* and *U-84* due to Bermuda-based aircraft, as well as the sinking of the USS *Gannet* by *U-653*—the only Allied warship loss in the region directly attributed to German or Italian submarines in World War Two. (*Robert Pratt, for the author*)

8 June 1942: One U-boat

Kapitänleutnant Hans-Ludwig Witt in *U-129* transited the region for eleven days south of Bermuda starting on 8 June 1942 and ending on 1 August. Entering east-south-east of the island, Witt patrolled west-south-west until the 10th, when he sank the Norwegian ship the *L. A. Christensen*. Then two days later, on the same south-west course, it found and sank the British *Hardwicke Grange* over 400 miles south of the island. Witt exited the area southbound on 13 June.[1]

On 28 July, *U-129* returned; however, this time it was homeward bound. It motored generally east until 1 August, again well south of Bermuda and out of the area to the south-south-east. Overall, Witt's *U-129* patrol lasted over three months (ninety-four days) with refueling *en route*.[2] During the patrol, he achieved a tonnage cache of 41,570 by sinking eleven ships, four of them in the Bermuda sphere. On his way back from the US Gulf (where he sank the *Tuxpam* and the *Las Choapas* of Mexico, the *Cadmus* and the *Gundersen* of Norway, the Soviet tanker the *Tuapse*, the *Tachira* of the US, and the *Port Antonio* of Norway), then he sank the *Onondaga* of 2,309 tons in the Old Bahama Channel. On *U-129*'s return trip across the Atlantic, she was refueled by *U-463* west of the Azores.[3] She returned to Lorient on 21 August 1942.

A member of the Class of 1929, Witt was awarded the Knight's Cross after this patrol, amassing over his career 100,773 GRT of confirmed tonnage sunk in nineteen ships. Like others before him, he served in the school ship the *Gorch Foch* and entered U-boat school in October 1940. Like Ali Cremer, Witt returned to the new electric U-boats towards the end of the war. Overall, he experienced three patrols of 275 sea days before moving ashore to join the *BdU* (headquarters) staff under Dönitz. He lived until 1980 and age seventy.[4]

10 June 1942: MV *L. A. Christensen*

The Norwegian motor ship the *L. A. Christiansen* was built in 1925 by *Deutsche Werft A. G., Betrieb Finkenwärder* in Hamburg. Her owners were Roed and Co. (also known by the names Roed, McNair & Co., whose principals were Sigurd and Hjalmar Roed of Tønsberg Norway).[1] The ship was under the control of the Norwegian Shipping and Trade Mission (Nortraship) who had chartered her to the British Ministry of War Transport. She was 4,362 gross tons and her dimensions were 385 feet long by 52.5 feet wide; a single diesel engine pushed her at 10 knots. Her master was Captain Arne Host Olsen, and he was responsible for thirty other sailors, one of whom was a gunner.[2] On its final voyage, the *L. A. Christensen* left Karachi for New York, with a call at Bombay. *En route*, she rescued the survivors of the British steamship the *Clan Ross*, which had been sunk by the Japanese submarine I-6 on 2 April 1942, 300 miles south-west of Bombay. The Norwegian crew was to see the favor returned in just over two months.[3]

After leaving Durban on 9 May, its final port was changed to Philadelphia. On 10 June, the ship was about 250 miles south its destination. At 1.50 p.m., the *Christensen* was steering 70 degrees west at 10 knots. She was zigzagging evasively by as much as 90 degrees. The sea was settled, the weather clear and calm, with just a light and variable breeze. There was a single lookout, Ordinary Seaman Reidar Vistung, on the monkey island atop the bridge. Ordinary Seaman Finn Nossum was at the wheel and Second Mate Fridjof Nilsen was on the bridge along with Captain Olsen.

Suddenly a torpedo fired by Hand-Ludwig Witt in *U-129* struck the ship between the Number One and Number Two cargo holds forward on the starboard side. As a result of the explosion, hatches were blown into the air, the radio aerials were damaged, and hatch Number One was badly twisted. Captain Olsen ordered the engines stopped and the ship abandoned.

Seven minutes later, all thirty-one men were aboard two standard lifeboats and one motorized boat, which made away from the ship. The radio operator had been unable to send a distress message, and the gunner unable to bring his 4-inch or the other Marlin and Hotchkiss machine guns to bear. Two officers from *U-129* asked in English about the ship's ports of departure and destination. After confirming the ship's name on the rafts and debris, and giving the men in the boats the course and distance to Bermuda, the submarine then headed off in a southerly direction on the surface.[4]

By 2.05 p.m., the *L. A. Christensen* had sunk beneath the waves in 18,000 feet of water. The survivors kept the three boats together, and were fortuitously discovered the next morning at 8.25 a.m. the following morning by the fellow Norwegian steamship, the *Bill*. They were landed in Bermuda the following day, 12 June 1942; all thirty-one men made it ashore safely.[5] The *Bill*, of 2,445 tons, was sunk just six weeks later by *U-155* under Adolf Cornelius Peining east of Barbados.[6] Out of a crew of twenty-four—mostly Norwegian sailors—all but one, Brazilian helper Aurelino Alves de Quieroz, survived.

11–24 June 1942: Three U-boats

Oberleutnant zur See Joachim Deeke spent a week in the Bermuda area in aggregate, transiting east and west bound from dropping off saboteurs in Florida. *U-584* entered the area on 11 June 1942 and motored west for three days before exiting north-west of Bermuda on the 13th. Then, on 4 July, it returned from the same area, this time heading eastbound, which it did for three days, exiting the region north-east of the island on 7 July. *U-584*'s unique short mission into the region was for the purpose of landing enemy saboteurs at Punta Vedra, Florida, an achievement the submarine pulled off on 17 June 1942, as part of Operation Pastorius (in conjunction with *U-202* landing saboteurs on Amagansett beach, New York on 13 June).[1] As with *U-98*, which mined nearby Jacksonville earlier, this was a one-off type of raid, but the patrol did not result in sinkings.[2]

On a patrol of eighty-nine days out of Brest, in which the submarine made its way safely back there, *U-584* spent four days devoted to the Bermuda region. The boat was refueled by *U-460* west of the Azores in early July, and returned to Brest on 22 July. *Kapitänleutnant* Joachim Deecke turned thirty years of age ten days later, on 29 June. This would have made the rendezvous with fellow U-boat *U-460* more celebratory. A member of the crew of 1933, he was promoted from *Oberleutnant zur See* in April 1941, and a year later, he earned the Iron Cross First Class; an award of the German Cross in Gold was given posthumously. Deecke accrued 328 days at sea on nine patrols, all of the in *U-584*, which he commissioned at the end of 1941 (U-9, on which he served, did not go on war patrols). His career total was 18,684 tons for four ships sunk, including a Soviet ship of 206 tons and the American *West Madaket* in convoy ONS 5. *U-584* was lost in the North Atlantic during an attack from US Avenger aircraft armed with homing torpedoes, which launched from the USS *Card* on 31 October 1943. All hands—including Deecke, by then thirty-one years old—were lost.[3]

Kapitänleutnant Heinz-Otto Schultze brought *U-432* on its second patrol to the Bermuda region, starting on 13 June 1942. Entering the area to the north-north-west of the island, Schultze headed south-east until the 14th, then turned eastwards. For the next four days, *U-432* patrolled in an east-north-east direction, leaving the region on 17 June without having struck any Allied ships on the sphere. The patrol began with the 3rd U-boat Flotilla on 30 April in La Pallice, and ended there on 2 July. South of Nova Scotia, she destroyed the US fishing vessel the *Foam* of 324 tons on 17 May. *U-432* then participated in the *Padfinder* group east of New York on 21 May, disbanding several days later.[4]

On 23 May, Schultze encountered and sank the British steamship the *Zurichmoor* of 4,455 tons east of New York. While many of the *Padfinder* group moved to the New York and Hatteras areas, Schultze went north to the Gulf of Maine, where she sank the British steamship the *Liverpool Packet* of 1,180 tons on the 31st. On 3 June, *U-432* destroyed the fishing vessels the *Ben* and the *Josephine* of 102 tons and US-flag, and the *Aeolus*, of 41 tons, also American, off Yarmouth. By 9 June, *U-432* overtook and sank the Norwegian motor ship the *Kronprinsen* of 7,073 tons off Cape Sable; it is possible Schultze damaged another ship at the same time. The submarine then moved south, where it dipped into the area north of Bermuda before laying course east for Europe. Late in June, *U-432* received extra fuel from *U-459* between Bermuda and the Azores.

Schultze was born in Kiel in 1915 and was part of the Crew of 1934. He joined U-boats early, in 1937 and commanded four of them: *U-4*, *U-141*, *U-432*, and *U-849*, for a total of 325 patrol days. His father, Otto Schultze, had sunk fifty-two ships of 129,540 tons with *U-63* during World War One. Overall, the younger Schultze sank or damaged twenty-two ships of 83,657 tons, for which he was awarded the Knight's Cross in July of 1942. He was killed when *U-849* was sunk west of the Congo River estuary on 25 November, 1943; he was twenty-eight at the time.[5]

Kapitänleutnant Johannes Liebe brought *U-332* on a circumnavigation of Bermuda of thirteen days, starting on 24 June 1942 and ending on 16 July. Liebe began to the north-west of Bermuda and headed south-east until 26 June. Then, he turned south-west while he was due east of Bermuda and headed south. On the 28th, he attacked and sank the US freighter the *Raphael Semmes* before turning west to keep his boat in a circular pattern. The *Semmes* was bound from Bombay to New York via Trinidad with manganese ore, licorice, wool, rugs and tobacco. Nineteen were lost, the balance being picked up the *Explorer* on 16 July, which landed in New Jersey. Liebe assisted ten of the survivors, dressing their wounds and giving them water and food. By 2 July, *U-332* was west-south-west of Bermuda and exited the area towards Hatteras. Coming back to the region from the same spot on 12 July, Liebe opted to motor north-east in a straight line, intersecting his earlier course north-north-east of Bermuda and exiting the region on the 16th, when north-east of the island. *U-332* was a Type VIIC boat out of the 3rd U-boat Flotilla, sailing to and from La Pallice on 24 May.

On this seventy-day patrol, Liebe would sink two ships, including the Greek steamer the *Leonidas M.* that he sank on 19 July on his way home from a patrol along the coasts of Cape Hatteras and Long Island, New York. Two officers from the *Leonidas M.* were taken prisoner and taken to France—a fate marginally better than being cast adrift in an open boat. *U-332* was refueled by *U-461* in late-July, when west of the Azores.[6] She returned to La Pallice on 1 August 1942. Liebe's total tonnage for the patrol was 10,600. A member of the crew of 1933, Liebe began U-boat training after a stint at the Naval Airfield Headquarters. His first boat was *U-48* under Schultze, sinking four ships on their first patrol. On his first patrol off Hatteras, he sank four ships of 25,000 tons despite being low on fuel. Liebe moved ashore in January 1943 and, after a brief detention following the war, was released in July 1945. His decorations included Iron Cross First Class based on total tonnage 46,729 tons from eight ships sunk. Liebe lived until the age of sixty-nine, dying in late 1982.[7]

26 June 1942: MV *Jagersfontein*

The Diesel ship the *Jagersfontein* was built by the Netherlands Shipbuilding, or *Nederlandsche Scheepsbouw Mij. N. V.*, in Amsterdam in December 1934. She was designed to carry both cargo and passengers, with dimensions of 10,083 gross registered tons, 489 feet long, 63.1 feet wide, and 34.1 feet deep. With a hull built of steel; her double six-cylinder Stork diesel engines developed 2,334 net horsepower and propelled the ship at an impressive 16 knots.[1] At the beginning of World War Two, the *Jagersfontein* was sent to the Far East in October 1939, along with the *Klipfontein* and the *Boschfontein*.[2] That year, the Singapore *Free Press and Mercantile Advertiser* recorded that 'The three ships, which are owned by the United Netherlands Line, have been chartered by the Java Pacific Line for the passenger and cargo service between Java and the United States Pacific Coast, calling at Singapore and Manila.'[3]

The *Jagersfontein* was sent from South Africa, where it was serving the Holland-Africa Line, and was due to sail from Singapore on 16 December 1939. She departed from the Golden Gate on 3 February 1939.[4] According to the 'Port Director's Report' for Honolulu, by an amazing coincidence, the *Jagersfontein* arrived in that port at 9.30 a.m. on 7 December 1941—right in the middle of the attack on Pearl Harbor nearby.[5] During World War Two, the ship was armed with a 105-millimeter gun mounted on the stern. The ship's owners were *Vereenigde Nederlandsche Scheepvaart Mij.* (VNS), based in The Hague. On her final voyage, there were 220 people under the command of Captain Machiel A. van der Est. There were fourteen men to man the gun, 108 crew, and ninety-eight passengers, among them women and children. Of the ninety-eight passengers, there were eighty-six United States Army officer as well as a dozen civilians.

Among 9,000 tons of general cargo, the vessel carried resins, copper, cotton, timber, and lead. On Thursday, 18 June 1942, the ship left Galveston bound across the Atlantic to Liverpool, heading across the Gulf of Mexico, around the southern tip of Florida. After passing through the Bahamas, she sailed independently to pass south and east of Bermuda. By Thursday the 25th, the ship was 500 nautical miles east-north-east of Bermuda. Captain van der Est zigzagged his ship during his voyage in order to throw off enemy submarines known to be lurking nearby.[6] At 9.45 p.m. on 25 June, Gelhaus—in command of *U-107*—sighted the *Jagersfontein*. He observed the ship heading 70 degrees east-north-east and making 16.5 knots. He noted in the submarine's log that 'Because the night is nearly as bright as day, and the sea is quite flat with heavy marine phosphorescence, I decide to wait to attack after moonset.'

At 3.13 a.m. on the 26th, Gelhaus fired two torpedoes from tube one and tube two from about 5,000 feet. It took the missiles four and a half minutes to strike the ship forward of the after mast and behind the main superstructure.[7] Though the *Jagersfontein* started settling by the stern, she maintained headway at between 13 and 14 knots. Gelhaus decided he would attack from ahead. As dawn spread across the sky, the passenger ship maneuvered closer to its attacker until at 4 a.m., it fired on the sub with its stern cannon. This caused Gelhaus to sound the alarm and dive. The men on *U-107* were able to hear the *Jagersfontein* transmit an SSS signal via the radio, providing its name, position, and tonnage. Captain van der Est kept his ship zigzagging, sometimes even ascribing circles across the ocean's surface to throw off its attacker. Gelhaus continues in his war diary:

> At one moment, I am positioned favorably ahead of him to shoot however, with this duck pond the periscope is discovered by the numerous people standing on deck. The steamer again turns away. I am only surprised that he has not departed, but continues to drive in this area. Perhaps he wants to have calm water to take to the boats. Therefore, I go back to the attack location. The steamer is approximately 15,000 meters away, when I reach the location. I surface. A lot of cotton bales float there but no boats. He has loaded cotton. Shortly after surfacing, the steamer reports that he taking to the boats, and abandoning the steamer. He has also stopped and has settled astern a little bit deeper. I go back to him and see that to port two lifeboats have gotten away.

At 8.59 a.m., *U-107* submerged and approached the damaged ship. Then, Gelhaus sent a third torpedo, this one from tube five, at his prey. This *coup de grâce* struck the ship beneath the bridge, causing a large steam cloud to rise from the single stack. Gelhaus observed as the *Jagersfontein* settled deeper and ultimately sank by the stern. The submarine surfaced and observed:

> Four lifeboats and a raft float about. The lifeboats are heavily occupied, also a number of women. Approached close to the lifeboats. Ran off. Lifeboat 3 is equipped with a radio and transmits SOS. According to the radio message there are 220 men in the boats. SOS was heard by a Swiss and even by 2 Portuguese. The Swiss takes them aboard during the night.

U-107 went on to rendezvous with the *milchkuh* or milk cow U-tanker *U-459* under the command of Georg von Wilamowitz-Möllendorff.

The *St. Cergue* was registered to Basel, after being flagged to Panama earlier in the war. It was one of several Swiss ships that had a Swiss national as a captain:

Fritz Gerber began his career in 1898, at the age of 18, on a sailboat assigned to Bremen. The captain continued on German ships, sent to Siberia and the Far East. At the beginning of World War Two, Gerber was first appointed captain St. Cergue, and then led the team on the other Swiss ships.

Gerber was skipper of the *St. Cergue* at the time of her rescue of the *Jagersfontein* survivors.[8]

In early June 1941 Dutch resistance fighter Peter Tazelaar 'mustered as a stoker on the Panamanian-flagged, Swiss freighter *St. Cergue*. The ship was in the port of Schiedam and was voyaging to New York to pick up a supply of corn for the Germans.' The ship, formerly known as the British *Felldene* until 1939, was 4,332 gross tons and flagged to Panama, then Basel.[9] She arrived in New York on 29 March 1940, and in 1941, sailed from that port on 13 August, 8 October, and 6 December. In 1942, she sailed from New York on 19 February, 25 April, and 20 June—right before her voyage to Galveston.

The following is an entry about the *St. Cergue's* war career and rescue of the *Jagersfontein*:

The first voyage under Swiss flag was with a full load of grain for Switzerland from New York to Genoa, returning back to the USA with Swiss machines and other quality products. Note during the entire war the Swiss ships were working under orders from the KTA, Bern. The *St. Cergue* was, what the sailors call a lucky ship. During a crossing towards New York, on 15 April 1942, she saved 10 survivors of the Norwegian motor tanker *Koll*, who had been torpedoed by the German submarine *U-571* on 6 April 1942. The exhausted survivors were landed in New York on 17 April, and the injured hospitalized. On 27 June, the *St. Cergue* was steaming between New York and the Bermudas, bound for Genoa, when some weak distress calls were received. Ten hours later the ship arrived on the indicated position. Several crowded lifeboats from the Dutch combo-cargo liner *Jagersfontein* were found drifting in the sea. Fortunately, one of the life boats had a small emergency transmitter and could launch the alarm. The Dutch freighter had escaped the Japanese invasion in Indonesia across the Pacific to the USA. In Houston 100 US-soldiers joined to go to Europe. Now she was underway to a British port, when a German submarine stopped her, forced the crew and the passengers to abandon the ship and then sank her with torpedoes.

A total of 209 survivors, including some women and children were taken aboard the *St. Cergue*. When finishing the rescue operation, the crew and passengers were frightened for a moment, when a German submarine surfaced and circled the ship, but finally signaled "bon voyage" and submerged again. The US-soldiers were transferred to an American war ship the next day and the remaining people were taken to Gibraltar where they disembarked on 9 July 1942 (the ship had always sufficient provisions after sailing from New York).[10]

At 9.38 a.m. on Saturday, 27 June, the US Navy destroyer USS *Bernadou* came upon the *St. Cergue* on the open ocean. Launched in 1918 at the William Cramp yard in Philadelphia, the ship was commissioned into the navy on 19 May 1919. Displacing 1,154 tons, she was 314.5 feet long, 31.8 feet wide, and 9 feet deep. Capable of 35 knots, she was manned by 122 officers and enlisted men. By June 1942, the destroyer was assigned to a route between Iceland and Newfoundland. It so happened that the *Bernadou* was in Bermuda, training in conjunction with the submarine R 1, at the time.[11] At 12.47 p.m. on Friday, 26 June, it broke off exercises to head on course 93 degrees east at 23 knots in order to rescue survivors of the *Jagersfontein*. The commander since October 1941 was Robert Edgar Braddy, Jr., USN.[12]

The Swiss ship was ten miles distant and was identified to the Americans by 10.12 a.m. At 10.15 a.m., Commander Braddy decided to circle the Swiss merchant ship. By 11 a.m., the Americans had already begun transferring survivors of the *Jagersfontein* from the *St. Cergue*. By 12.30 p.m., they had 'completed taking the following: eighty-six U.S. Army officers and twelve British and Dutch gunners from the *St. Cergue*.' There were five Defensively Equipped Merchant Ship ratings, six British anti-aircraft gunners, and two Dutch Army soldiers listed as other ranks. The total number rescued was ninety-eight, of whom eighty-five were US Army officers, including members of the Medical Corps.[13]

At 12.44 p.m., the destroyer set a course for Bermuda and ramped up speed to 20 knots. USS *Bernadou* anchored in Port Royal Bay, Bermuda at 4.03 p.m. on Sunday, 28 June 1942, after steaming 493 nautical miles since noon the previous day, at 22 knots. The sea was calm and wind was very light. Her men first sighted Bermuda at noon, sighting Mount Hill Lighthouse 10 miles out at 12.26 p.m. The same report went on to say that 'Rescued crew 100 including 2 women and also 12 passengers continuing voyage in *St. Cergue*.' Clearly, this intelligence is based on interviewing survivors in Bermuda and can be deemed accurate.

At 1.15 p.m., Lieutenant Colonel Hastings from the US Army 'came on board to interview survivors.' At 2.20 p.m., the destroyer entered Two Rocks Passage Channel. At 2.37 p.m., she moored at Shed Six Dock in Hamilton. Thirteen minutes later, at 2.50 p.m., Hastings led the survivors of the *Jagersfontein* off of the vessel. At 3.16 p.m., the *Bernadou* left Hamilton, passed Pearl Island Light abeam to port, and anchored in Port Royal Bay.

U-boat researcher Guðmundur Helgason adds this unusual vignette:

An interesting story exists about this rescue: It is said that some days after, a German U-boat surfaced near the Swiss ship and passed before the bow. When passing, the Germans shouted from the conning tower: Hallo *Jagersfontein*, Hallo *Jagersfontein*! and the U-boat disappeared.

26–30 June 1942: Seven U-boats

Korvettenkapitän Werner Hartenstein merely dipped into the area east-south-east of Bermuda between 26 and 28 June 1942 on its way back to base. Two days before, the submarine had sunk the British steamship the *Willimantic* of 4,558 tons by gunfire well south-east of Bermuda (the captain was taken prisoner on *U-156*). Hartenstein was at the center of two major episodes of World War Two naval warfare—the shelling of Aruba refineries and the sinking of the *Laconia*—and was one of the most recognized U-boat skippers of the era. The patrol began on 22 April, from where *U-156* sailed for the 2nd U-boat Flotilla. On 13 May, the sub sank the Dutch motor ship the *Koenjit* and later the same day the *City of Melbourne*, a British ship of 6,630 tons. Off the Windward Islands and at times very close to Vichy-France-held Martinique *U-156* sank a succession of ships in the following weeks: the Norwegian *Siljestad*, the Yugoslavian *Kupa*, the British *Barrdale*, the US *Quaker City*, and the British *San Eliseo* (damaged).[1]

Off Martinique, Hartenstein sank the steamship the *Presidente Trujillo* and then the US destroyer USS *Blakely* on 25 May. The sub was counterattacked for a week, then managed to sink the British steamer the *Norman Prince*. On the way back, *U-156* sank the Brazilian steamer the *Allegrete* and the 80-ton British sailing schooner the *Lilian*. Hartenstein was thirty-three years of age at the time of his patrol, and a member of the class of 1928. Two days before he entered the region, he was awarded the German Cross in Gold and was to earn the Knight's Cross by the end of the year. He was killed at age thirty-five on 8 March 1943 in an attack on his submarine east of Barbados, following five patrols of 294 days.[2] Before joining the U-boat arm in March 1942, he completed sixty-five patrols in torpedo boats. His total career total was twenty ships for 97,504 GRT, three more damaged for 18,811 tons, plus a 1,190-ton warship damaged.

Kapitänleutnant Helmut Möhlmann arrived on 26 June 1942 north-east of Bermuda in the Type VIIC boat *U-571* and spent eight days transiting to the south-west, exiting on 3 July. By the 29th, the boat was only 100 or so miles south-east of Bermuda, then it jogged closer to the west on the 30th, before heading south-east for a day. Between the 1st and 3rd of the month, *U-571* headed due west and out of the area, to the south-west of the island. Thereafter, *U-571* proceeded west-south-west. *U-571* exited the area mid-way between Bermuda and Anegada on 23 July, making for La Pallice again where it was based with the 3rd U-boat Flotilla. The other victim of this patrol was the 11,394-ton tanker *Pennsylvania Sun* (damaged), bringing total tonnage lost or damaged (the *J. A. Moffett* was a constructive total loss) to 30,374 GRT. On the way to the patrol area, *U-571* took part in a patrol line, called the *Endrass*, initially against convoy HG 84 along with five other boats. When the patrol line was disbanded, *U-571* was refueled west of the Azores by *U-459*. The patrol began in La Pallice on 11 June and ended there on 7 August 1942. A member of the Class of 1933, Möhlmann was promoted to *Korvettenkapitän* in the last weeks of the war. He joined U-boats in April 1940 and sailed in eight patrols of 344 days before joining the *BdU* staff headquarters, eventually commanding the 14th U-boat Flotilla in Narvik, Norway. In April 1943, he received the Knight's Cross and, a year later, the U-boat Front Clasp. His awards began in June 1939 with the Spanish Cross in Bronze without swords. Over his career, Möhlmann sank five ships for 33,511 tons, including the *Margaret* off the US coast, plus the *Pennsylvania Sun* damaged, the *Moffet* a loss, and an auxiliary warship for 3,870 tons. Möhlmann lived until 1977, passing away at age sixty-three.[3]

On the same day, and in roughly the same position as Loewe in *U-505*, *U-575* under *Kapitänleutnant* Günther Heydemann in the Type VIIC boat *U-575* entered the region on a similar course—from east and south of Bermuda south-south-west to the Mona Passage, which he entered and cleared into the Caribbean on 5 July. Overall, Hedyemann spent just four days on an inbound transit heading south-west from a point east of Bermuda starting 28 June 1942. By 1 July, the boat was out of the region and heading for the Caribbean.

While off the north-east tip of the Dominican Republic, the submarine encountered and sank the *Norlandia* on 4 July. The other ships hit by *U-575* on this patrol included the *Empire Explorer*, the *Comrade* and the *Glacier* (both schooners), and *San Gaspar* (damaged)—all in the southern Caribbean in the vicinity of Trinidad and Tobago. The total tonnage his during this patrol was 21,088, all victims aside from the *Norlandia* being of British registry. Like the *U-571* before it, on the way to the patrol area, *U-575* took part in a patrol line called *Endrass*, initially against convoy HG 84. *U-575* was then refueled west of the Azores by *U-459*. The patrol began in St. Nazaire on 10 June and ended there on 7 August 1942. A member of the Class of 1933, Heydemann achieved that rank in April 1941 while serving in the 7th U-boat Flotilla out of St. Nazaire, from which the boat sailed on this patrol. He joined U-boats in April 1940 after serving in line-of-battle ships before commissioning *U-575* in the spring of 1941. Altogether, Heydemann spent eight patrols and 395 sea days on this boat before becoming an instructor based on shore. His total career tally of eight ships sunk for 36,010 and one ship damaged for 12,910 earned him the Knight's Cross in July 1943. He lived until 1986 and the age of seventy-one, passing away in Hamburg.

U-437 under *Kapitänleutnant* Werner-Karl Schulz entered the region between Bermuda and Anegada on 28 June inbound, and spent eight days in total transiting the south-east corner of the box both inbound and outbound. From 28 June to 1 July, they patrolled south-west and then out of the area. It returned three weeks later, on 25 July for four days, heading north-east. Ultimately, Schulz took the boat out of the area on 27 July and homeward for France. After his inbound transit past Bermuda, Schulz headed for the Windward Passage. Like *U-571, U-575, U-134,* and *U-84* before it, on the way to the patrol area *U-437* took part in a patrol line called *Endrass*, initially against convoy HG 84. The boat was then refueled west of the Azores by *U-459* late in June. The patrol began in St. Nazaire on 6 June and ended there on 12 August 1942. A member of the crew of 1934, Werner-Karl Schulz was only made *Korvettenkapitän* in March 1945. Born in October 1910, he was thirty-one during this patrol and lived until 1960 and the age of fifty. He received no decorations during his naval career and neither sank nor damaged any Allied vessels over four patrols in command of *U-437*, lasting 161 days in aggregate.[4]

Kapitänleutnant Irwin Rostin only spent two fateful—and final—days in the Bermuda region before being sunk by Bermuda-based aircraft on 30 July west-north-west of the island. Though he entered on the 29th, it was a busy patrol leading up to the boat's demise. Since the events of the patrol are linked directly to the Allies tracking and destroying the boat they bear recounting. Having entered the area on 24 May, *U-158* proceeded due west as far as the US Gulf on the 31st. After nearly a month and a record number of attacks in the waters off Cuba, Yucatan and the Gulf of Mexico, *U-158* returned via a similar route to Grand Bahama between 26 and 29 June. At that point, Rostin did four fateful things—he stopped the Latvian ship *Everalda*, took her commander aboard as a neutral captive, managed to secure vitally important Allied signals, codes and routing instructions, and then he repeatedly transmitted to Germany about his exploits. This would be fatal, as the US sent an aircraft over the submarine's projected position and, on 30 June, that airplane (a USN Mariner piloted by Lt. R. E. Schreder) succeeded in surprising it on the surface and sinking it with an extremely accurate depth charge that lodged in the submarine's deck plating.[5]

The list of the dozen ships worth 62,536 GRT sunk by U-158 on this patrol is as diverse as it is long: the *Darina* of Britain, the Canadian *Frank B. Baird* (sunk north and east of Bermuda on the way in during May), the *Knoxville City* (US), the *Nidarnes* (Norway), the *Velma Lykes*, the *Hermis* and the *Scheherazade* (both Panamanian), the *Cities Service Toledo*, the *San Blas* (Panamanian), the *Moira* (Norway), and the American *Major General Henry Gibbins*—all sunk in the Gulf of Mexico and adjacent waters. The *Scheherazade* alone was an impressive 13,467 tons and the *Darina* a further 8,113 GRT. One of the crew of 1933, Rostin joined U-boats from minesweepers in March 1941. On his first war patrol, without battle experience, he sank five ships of over 38,000 tons.

Rostin was awarded the Knight's Cross two days before the air attack. The extensive radio communication between the boat and base is what enabled the Allies to track the U-boat and accurately predict its position, precipitating its doom; the Allied expression 'loose lips sink ships' was turned on the enemy. Rostin was given the U-boat War Badge posthumously on 1 July. He had sailed in the 10th U-boat Flotilla out of Lorient. Had the submarine managed to reach German-occupied France with the Allied convoy signals and the *Everalda*'s confidential papers (which the Allies were aware, from survivors, had been taken), the results could have been highly disruptive to the Allies—another of history's many 'what if' scenarios.[6]

U-84 under *Oberleutnant zur See* Horst Uphoff spent eleven days patrolling in the Bermuda box, first west-bound for the Straits of Florida and then eastbound homeward, beginning 29 June 1942 and ending on 31 July. Starting on 29 June 1942, *U-84* steamed west, south of Bermuda on its way toward the Straits of Florida. It left the region on 3 July. Then, on 26 July, the boat returned, this time heading east-north-east and passing quite close to Bermuda on the 28th. Proceeding eastbound, it exited the area east of the island on 31 July.

After its initial incursion, on 6 July, while poised to enter the Straits of Florida, the boat effected a nearly 180 degree turn and Uphoff opted instead to head east until the 8th. At that point, just north-east of Abaco, the boat turned right nearly 90 degrees and steamed towards the Crooked Island Passage, which it transited between 10 and 11 July. *U-84* then headed north-west up the Old Bahama Channel between 11 and 13 July, when it encountered the *Andrew Jackson*, an American steamer of 5,990 tons, which it sank west of the Cay Sal Bank. On 21 July, the boat headed north until the 24th, at which point it passed West End Grand Bahama and turned 90 degrees eastward for Bermuda. On the 29th, it passed just south of St. David's Light, Bermuda and headed back to Brest, where it was based with the 1st U-boat Flotilla.

Like *U-571* and *U-575* before it, on the way to the patrol area, *U-84* took part in a patrol line called *Endrass*, initially against convoy HG 84.[7] The boat was then refueled west of the Azores by *U-459*. The patrol ended in Brest on 13 August 1942; it had begun on 10 June. On the return voyage, *U-84* was again refueled, this time by *U-463* west of the Azores for its return trip across Biscay. The submarine was to leave its bones and those of its crew south of Bermuda within a year. Uphoff was only twenty-five at the time of this patrol. A member of the crew of 1935, his rank at the time was *Kapitänleutnant*. Joining U-boats in October 1939, he served under Endrass in *U-46* for four patrols, sinking seventeen ships of 90,000 tons plus two others for 15,000 GRT. Uphoff commissioned the new VIIB boat *U-84* in April 1941, leaving on its first patrol from Bergen. Over a year and half, Uphoff would lead *U-84* on eight patrols for 461 sea days. His total tally was six ships sunk for 29,905 and one damaged for 7,176 GRT, which earned him the Iron Cross First Class while alive, and the German Cross in Gold posthumously, in January 1944.

Commander Rudolf Schendel contributed four patrol days to the southern area of the box around Bermuda, between 30 June and 3 July. During that time, the boat's progress was due west and Schendel exited the region for a long and fruitless patrol of the Bahamas. Like *U-571*, *U-575*, and *U-84* before it, on the way to the patrol area *U-134* took part in a patrol line called *Endrass*. The boat was then refueled west of the Azores by *U-459* late in June. The patrol began on 11 June in La Pallice and ended there on 1 September 1942. On the return voyage, *U-134* was again refueled for its return trip across Biscay, this time by *U-463* west of the Azores.[8]

Though he was promoted to *Korvettenkapitän* in late 1944, it is perhaps not surprising given the results of this patrol that Rudolf Schendel was not a decorated officer, though clearly from the track of his voyage, this was not for lack of effort, but rather the lack of opportunity. *U-134* would be taken over by Hans-Günther Brosin, whose patrols in the region were only marginally more successful and included the downing of US Navy airship K 74. A member of the crew of 1932, Schendel and his boat survived their patrols and he lived until age fifty-six in 1970. His total tonnage sank over seven patrols and 271 days at sea was 12,147 GRT.[9]

1 July 1942: SS *City of Birmingham*

The US-flagged passenger transport ship the *City of Birmingham* was built by the Newport News Shipbuilding and Drydock Company in 1923. Her owners were the Ocean Steamship Company, known as the Savannah Line of New York, and her final charterers were the Alcoa Steamship Company. The vessel was comparatively large at 5,861 tons and was capable of carrying cargo and over 400 people, including over 100 crew. She was 382 feet long, 52.2 feet wide, and 26.9 feet deep. A three-cycle triple-expansion steam engine developed 398 net horsepower and drove the ship at 13.5 knots.

The *City of Birmingham* was registered to Savannah. One of its jobs was to keep Bermuda supplied with goods and passengers. In 1942, with a massive military base construction program under way, there was a need for labor on the island.[1] Ships like the *City of Birmingham* helped meet the need for people and materiel. Bermudian historian Jonathan Land Evans pointed out that 'the freighter SS *City of Birmingham* (noted by the island's early wartime chronicler as 'our last regular visitor') [was] carrying a large cargo destined for the island. Bermuda had not received a significant shipment of food and other essential supplies for five weeks at the time'—June 1942.[2]

Among the young Americans traveling on the *City of Birmingham* to Bermuda that summer were two men from Titusville, Florida—Stanley Matuszewski, aged forty-two, and Maynard Hipwell. Hipwell worked for a boiler making firm named Struthers Wells, and Matuszewski was taking up a year-long assignment at the Naval Operating Base being built by the Americans on the island.[3] There were '262 other civilian employees of the base contract, bound for the job in Bermuda. The vessel, a medium sized ship, also carried tons of food for Bermuda.'

The master of the *City of Birmingham* on her final voyage had, like the ship he commanded, a long and varied career. During World War One, Captain Lewis Preston Borum commanded the SS *City of Memphis* between Cardiff and New York when the ship was torpedoed and sunk by UC-66 south-west of Ireland on 17 May 1917. Born on 4 July 1883, he was destined to spend his foty-ninth birthday in 1942 on Bermuda. Though born in Matthews, Virginia, his home base was Savannah, where he served in the US Naval Reserve. He was a thin, erect-standing man of medium height. He had also worked for the Alcoa Steamship Company, to whom the *City of Birmingham* was on charter in June 1942. The ship had earlier rescued survivors of the ship the *Empire Dryden*, which had been sunk in the area, by *U-572* under Hirsaker on 20 April 1942, some 240 nautical miles north west of Bermuda.

On Monday, 29 June 1942, the *City of Birmingham* left Norfolk bound for Bermuda. On board, she carried 2,400 tons of general cargo as well as 381 persons—263 passengers, 103 crew, and five armed guards whose job it was to man one 4-inch and two 30-calibre machine guns.[4] There were at least four women on board—a stewardess and three female passengers. The stewardess was Mary Cullum Kimbro, fifty-three, of Nashville, Tennessee.[5] The passengers included Miss H. Cline, Miss Evelyn Parker, and Miss E. Johnson; they were all civil service employees going to work in Bermuda.[6]

A World War One-era destroyer, the USS *Stansbury* (DD 180) was assigned to escort her all of the way.[7] By late June, some seventy Allied ships, mostly merchant but including two naval (USS *Gannet* and USS *Atik*), had been sunk in the waters around Bermuda—not including those coastwise in the US. The *Stansbury* was built at the Union Iron Works in San Francisco and launched on 16 May 1919. By the time of her commissioning in January 1920, her *raison-de-être*, World War One, was over. By 27 May 1922, she was decommissioned and laid up for the next eighteen years. The *Stansbury* was recommissioned on 29 August 1940. The ship had four smoke stacks, which spewed exhaust. She was 314 feet 6 inches long, 3 feet 8 inches wide, and 9 feet 10 inches deep. Crewed by 103 persons, the destroyer could achieve 35 knots. The *Stansbury*'s commander at the time was Lieutenant Commander Joseph Benedict Maher, who took over from Lt. Cdr. Robert N. McFarlane earlier that year.[8]

Late that June, *Kapitänleutnant* Hans-Heinz Linder was returning to France from landing saboteurs in New York when *U-202* came across the small convoy. He was bringing his sub in a straight line north of Bermuda *en route* back to base in Brest. All three vessels—a US destroyer, its lone charge, and the German U-boat—were to meet on the night of 30 June–1 July at a point halfway between Bermuda and Norfolk, 325 miles west-north-west of Bermuda.[9]

That evening, there was a flurry of signals being exchanged by the *Stansbury* with the recalcitrant *City of Birmingham*.[10] The merchant ship simply was not comprehending or carrying out the destroyer's orders to zigzag. Though the navy-issued voyage orders were clear that zigzagging would be maintained at night, the slower ship was having trouble understanding the coded messages being sent by the navy ship. As a result, an order to change from 133 degrees to 99 degrees was not understood and effected until between minutes and hours afterwards. The naval ship tried *mersig* or merchant signals (blinking lights), and, when that failed, maneuvered to signal by flag, or semaphore. In any event, there was a breakdown in communication, which led to considerable frustration on the *Stansbury* and befuddlement on the *City of Birmingham*. In the affidavits and accusations that followed, it was argued that the convoy should have been at least eight miles away at the time and out of the scopes of the prowling submarine— all hypothetical of course, as the German sub was highly maneuverable, had not been detected, and could make over 20 knots speed on the surface.

The *City of Birmingham* had five lookouts on duty; four on the bridge (preoccupied no doubt with signals) and one in a crow's nest high above. Her speed was 10.5 knots on a base course of 99 degrees, north-east. There was a light swell from the direction they were heading, and the weather was clear and visibility good. Though survivors place the attack at during or after dinner time, the US Navy Intelligence report states that it occurred at 11.30 p.m., and the *Stansbury* men said it was 6.50 p.m. In any event, *U-202* managed to fire three torpedoes at the *City of Birmingham* and get two of them around the escort, which was ahead of the passenger ship on the port side. One of the torpedoes was seen to pass ahead of the merchant ship, but two of them struck, the first about 30 feet back from the bow 'in No. 1 hatch close to the surface; the second under the bridge and at a greater depth.'

According to the witnesses on the *Stansbury* roughly a mile away, the merchant ship 'listed an estimated 20 degrees to port, slightly down by the head and commenced to sink rapidly.' She also managed to get out an SOS message in plain language, which was picked up by Radio Norfolk. The *Stansbury* dashed to the side of the stricken ship and ensured that the majority of the survivors, who were scrambling down the side on nets could find life rafts or life boats to board and stay afloat while the navy ship went on the offensive. Forty minutes later, at 7.30 p.m., the *Stansbury* began dropping depth charges on a sound contact, which was presumed to be the location of *U-202*. Meanwhile, back on the merchant ship, over 300 individual dramas were unfolding.

Evelyn Parker was one of the female passengers on board the *City of Birmingham*. She later spoke with journalist David Ballingrud about her experience. He wrote:

Parker and two of the three other women aboard had just begun dinner with the ship's officers when Capt. Lewis P. Borum was called away [from the table] to respond to an urgent message from the *Stansbury*. Moments later, Parker heard a muffled bang and felt a shock run through the ship. The first of two torpedoes struck the ship about 100 feet from the bow. Moments later the second torpedo struck just beneath the bridge, slightly nearer the stern. 'We were heading for the lifeboats when the second one hit,' Parker recalled. 'It knocked the pocketbook out of my hand, and I remember asking one of the seaman if I should go back for it. He said, "Suit yourself, but I wouldn't." So, I didn't. My clothes were going to the bottom of the sea anyway.'

Parker said she climbed down a rope net thrown over the side of the vessel, then jumped into the water from about 20 feet above the surface. She then swam to an overloaded, almost swamped raft, where she waited for rescue with about 40 other people. The two quick explosions broke the bow section away from the rest of the ship, and the *City of Birmingham* went down in about five frantic minutes. The *Stansbury* took aboard some survivors and lingered at the scene until the remainder were in life rafts. Then it disappeared into the darkness, in pursuit of the *U-202*. 'We sat in water up to our waists for four hours,' Parker said. 'We sang songs and pretended it was a party. There was no time to be frightened.'[11]

Stanley Matuszewski told another reporter that he was reading after having had supper. The second sitting (Parker and Borum's) was still in session. After a violent explosion, Stanley 'found himself in the passageway. He started to reach for a lifebelt, and then came another explosion.' When he came to from the second concussion, there was water at his feet and the ship was listing. Then, 'the ship came back on an even keel and Stanley slipped into the water, still holding the lifebelt which he had not had time to put on… The entire port side had been torn away, Stanley later heard.' Matuszewski related that from his perspective:

> The passengers and crew managed to launch three of the twelve lifeboats, but [he] did not enjoy the comfort of a seat in one. Later in the evening he got in a small rubber life craft, but this was overturned in the darkness by a gasoline-powered lifeboat. … As the night grew darker, the warship began to pick up small groups and Stanley was hauled aboard [*Stansbury*] about midnight. … The destroyer, with about 370 extra persons on board, was jammed, to say the least. … Stanley said the torpedoing happened so fast that there was no time for fire on the ship, and there was very little panic.[12]

In fact, according to an amalgam of survivor's statements, the crew and passenger's 'conduct was exemplary, abandoning ship in orderly fashion in 5 lifeboats, five rafts, and seven floats.'

At 7.56 p.m., the *Stansbury* regained contact on an underwater object, having lost it. At 7.38 p.m., the ship had made a contact on which it had dropped seven charges at 7.40 p.m. Just before 8 p.m., they dropped two more charges. According to the *Stansbury* officers, the *City of Birmingham* stayed afloat for forty-four minutes, from 6.50 p.m. until 7.34 p.m.; however, most survivors say the ship plunged below the waves within five minutes, or by 7 p.m. At 8.21 p.m., the *Stansbury* abandoned its chase of *U-202* and dropped a life raft close to the overcrowded lifeboats.[13] This must have been one of the rubber boats which Stanley Matuszewski climbed aboard. By 8.32 p.m., given that darkness was fast approaching, the *Stansbury* performed a very daring rescue in the face of the obvious danger from being torpedoed—it lowered the ship's motor whale boat and the small gig boat. For two hours, Lieutenant J. C. Morgan directed the rescue of 373 survivors, pulling them one by one up the steep, lurching sides of the destroyer. One of them was in such bad shape from roughly four hours in the tossing seas that he died aboard the naval ship.

During the operation, the gig's rudder was damaged by the debris littering the waters. The wind continued to build throughout the rescue operation, and with it the swell. The gig's motor also failed, leaving Lieutenant A. F. Alexander in the whale boat to rescue over 100 people and bring them to the ship. Captain Borum, on being rescued, went back out in the whale boat to pull in more survivors. Despite all these efforts, eight people perished in the waters including the stewardess Mary Kimbro, oiler William E. Cannon, butcher William H. Greene, cook Marion W. Hurd, fire watcher Charles Jones, pantryman Theodore N. Morgan, and cook James Stanley, as well as two passengers.

By 10.45 p.m., the retrieval of survivors was considered complete. It took a quarter of an hour for the destroyer to hook and hoist the whale boat, on the basis of which it was decided to abandon the damaged gig to the elements. For the next fifty-five minutes, the *Stansbury* performed widening circles looking for any remaining survivors. Finding none but making a sound contact, it dropped seven more depth charges at 11.40 p.m. Following this, the destroyer went back to the area of the sinking for a final time before departing at 1.45 a.m. for Bermuda, making 27 knots. At 6.59 p.m. that evening, USS *Stansbury* and its 475 souls (103 navy sailors, 372 survivors, and one cadaver) arrived at Port Royal Bay anchorage in Southampton. They were met by Rear Admiral James. A naval doctor also came on board to do what they could for those who had been traumatized. Within an hour and forty minutes, all of the *City of Birmingham* people had been disembarked.[14]

In the NOB diary, Commandant James notes 'Went aboard the STANSBURY on her arrival with the *City of Birmingham* survivors. A check indicates that only about 12 of those who were on board were lost. The first report from the *Stansbury* said 40.' In fact, nine souls were lost. Lieutenant Commander Maher, in his official report filed 11 July 1942, had glowing words to say about the conduct not only of the men under his command, but the men and women aboard the *City of Birmingham*; this was reciprocated. Ensign E. D. Henderson ends his summation of survivor's statement, dated 15 July 1942 by observing 'The survivors emphasized the value of embarkation nets in getting safely away from the ship, and were warm in their praise of the manner in which rescue was effected by the escorting destroyer, USS *Stansbury*.'

Maher's report is detailed in its praise, some of which would bear repeating, as it also describes events:

> The discipline and composure of the crew and passengers of the SS *City of Birmingham* were excellent. People that were rescued early in the operation turned with a will and assisted the *Stansbury*'s crew in taking others on board and in caring for the injured. Captain Borum and Chief Officer Hart, the latter an ex-Navy Quartermaster, were extremely helpful in distributing survivors about the ship and in maintaining passageways on the crowded deck.

Maher continues: 'Mr. Tom Davis, a surviving passenger, who had an excellent knowledge of First Aid work, assisted Lieut. (jg) H. J. Truax (MC) U. S. N. R., throughout the night. Mr. Davis's effort and the cheerful manner in which he applied himself was particularly noteworthy.' Maher goes on the single out the three women passengers who were rescued, naming them. He explained:

> [They] were rescued quite early in the evening. They immediately took station in the wardroom and were of great assistance to the Doctor in attending badly injured personnel. Miss Johnson was rescued with a large group from a life raft. As this raft was towed alongside I noted that it was one of the most orderly. The

passengers on this raft boarded ship very quietly. This young lady seemed to be in charge and had the situation well under control.[15]

Unfortunately, not all of Maher's praise was reciprocated, as a later report on the 'Birmingham Incident—comments on sinking of' ends with the observation that 'convoy discipline was poor.' The surviving crew and passengers were well looked after in Bermuda. On the very day after their arrival in Bermuda—Thursday 2 June—a special meeting of the US military base personnel was held on St. David's Island. The purpose was to praise the base workers of all branches of the military as well as recognize the survivors of the *City of Birmingham* and present them with $1,500—a considerable sum at the time—which was raised from individual donations by base personnel.

The Royal Gazette and Colonist Daily of Monday, 6 July, reported:

> The United States Army Band from Castle Harbour played several selections during the evening…. [and] was warmly welcomed by an audience of approximately 900 persons. Several of the survivors arose during the latter part of the programme and recounted some of their experiences. A collection was taken among the base workers during the day, a sum of approximately $1,500 being raised for the sole benefit of the survivors.[16]

U-202 escaped the *Stansbury*'s many bombardments largely unscathed. On the return voyage to Europe, the sub refueled from *U-460* and then prowled behind Convoy OS 34 near the Azores, vectoring other boats in on the attack. Linder

Captain Lewis Preston Borum and crew of the passenger ship SS *City of Birmingham* awaiting further transport from Bermuda, July 1942. (*Acme News Pictures, author's collection*)

and *U-202*'s most notorious act of this patrol was the landing of four saboteurs at Amagansett, Long Island, was successfully effectuated on 13 June. This was no small task considering the submarine touched bottom on a sand bank and its engine maneuvers were so loud that they were heard from shore, imperiling the ultra-secret mission. Much has been written about his landing and another off Punta Vedra beach near Jacksonville by *U-584*, as part of Operation Pastorius.[17]

The Aviators

During World War Two, there were thousands of reconnaissance and other flights flown out of Naval Operating Base and Naval Air Station Bermuda—mostly from Kindley Field. Many of them were amphibious flying boats and almost all were flown by the US Navy. The war diary for Patrol Bombing Squadron VP 105 notes that 'Operating conditions in the area were extremely favorable and permitted all crews excellent opportunity for training in their new type of aircraft. The morale of all personnel was high and living conditions were good.'

'Manifold recreational facilities were available to all, including golf, tennis, sailing, swimming, and fishing, plus the additional luxury of an ideal climate. Operations during the squadrons' stay at Bermuda consisted of offensive anti-submarine sweeps and long-range patrols covering up to 2,400 miles per trip.' Certain individuals can be highlighted for their attacks on U-boats and rescue of Allied survivors from the seas.

On 7 March 1942, 150 miles south of Bermuda, *U-128* under Ulrich Heyse dived when two PBM Mariner flying boats of Squardon VP 74 appeared from low cloud.[18] The first aircraft released two depth charges set for 50 feet just as the U-boat's stern disappeared, but they were duds. A second pair of depth charges was then dropped, followed by two more from the other aircraft. *U-128* escaped undamaged and remained submerged until dusk.[19]

On 7 April 1942, *U-571* under Helmut Möhlmann had just sunk the Norwegian motor tanker MT *Koll* when it was surprised on the surface and attacked unsuccessfully over a period of hours by three US Navy aircraft. One was piloted by Lt. Cdr. John W. Gannon, another by Lt. William W. Soverell, and a third by Lt. A. E. Carlson.

On 28 January 1942, Lt. Commander William A. Thorn of VP 74 was thanked by the master of the *British Corporal* for helping to ward off an attack by *U-66* under Richard Zapp, which was foiled by the appearance of aircraft. On 3 June, in the middle of an effort to rescue men from the sunken merchant ship the *Westmoreland*, Ensign John H. Cushman's aircraft crashed at sea, most likely due to a sudden downdraft causing the aircraft to 'catch a wing tip' on a wave. The entire crew of P6, Squadron VP 74 perished, and an exhaustive but futile search was instituted. The following day, Lt. Winslow Lockwood Pettingell, a recent Harvard graduate and track star there, daringly landed on the water to rescue nine of the most gravely injured survivors of USS *Gannet*, a navy ship that had been sunk the day before by Gerhard Feiler in *U-653*. He was followed by Lt. Cdr. Gannon who rescued another batch of survivors despite the rough seas.[20]

While this painting by Floyd Davis shows a submarine off the coast of Bermuda during World War Two, it is misleading. The submarine is in fact controlled by the Allies and is being used by US Navy airplanes and ships as a decoy on which to practice anti-submarine warfare. It is little known that between February 1943 and October 1944 six French, eight Italian and one German submarines were captured and brought to Bermuda for intelligence and training purposes. Davis flew with the US Navy and did witness anti-submarine training, however is it unlikely that submarines motored this close to the reef-strewn coast of Bermuda. (*Life Magazine*)

Among other aviators who landed at sea to rescue survivors off Bermuda were 1st Lt. Rex Knorr and his co-pilot Lt. M. Kaufman, who landed on the waves 9 May to rescue survivors of the *Melbourne Star*, which had been sunk five weeks before by Hans-Ludwig Witt in *U-129*. There were only four survivors of a total complement of 119 persons. On 23 April 1942, an unknown pilot from Bermuda rescued eight survivors of the *Derryheen* south-west of Bermuda and took them back to the island. In order to land on the water, the pilot had to jettison two depth charges. On return to the boat, it was too rough to land. The ship had been sunk on 22 April by *U-201* under Adalbert Schnee. Over a week later, sixteen other survivors of the same ship were identified by Ensign K. R. Peachee out of Banana River NAS in Florida. On 27 June 1942, Lt. (jg) D. D. Durant landed on the water to rescue an injured sailor from a convoy passing north of Bermuda.

There were numerous attacks on submarines, two of them successful. Lt. George Koch attacked an unknown submarine on 15 April. On 8 July 1942, Lt. John Hitchcock attacked *U-134* under Hans-Günther Brosin, and though neither aircraft nor sub was mortally damaged, the airplane limped back to Bermuda with bullet holes in its propeller and fuselage. When the *Halcyon* was sunk by *U-109* under Heinrich Bleichrodt north of Bermuda on 6 February 1942, the PBM Mariner P 12 of Squadron VP 74 flew to the rescue and vectored the merchant ship *British Prestige* to pick up survivors.

On 3 July 1942 Lt. Junior Grade George W. Brown attacked a U-boat twice unsuccessfully—possibly *U-134* under Brosin. Two days later, Lt. (jg) John R. Steetle of the US Naval Reserve sighted what may have been *U-159* under Helmut Freidrich Witte south of Bermuda and north of Puerto Rico and attacked. On his way back to base, Steetle encountered *U-527* under Herbert Uhlig but, since he had spent his bombs on the first attack, had nothing with which to attack the submarine.

The two successful attacks on submarines resulted in the sinking of *U-158* under Erwin Rostin and *U-84* under Horst Uphoff. Lt. Richard E. Schreder was led to the location of *U-158* on 30 June 1942 by signals intelligence, which was impressively accurate.[21] Rostin on *U-158* was in the habit of punctually informing headquarters of his impressive tally of ships sunk. Right on schedule he began transmitting north-west of Bermuda and Schreder dove in from behind the clouds for a kill. At first it seemed the depth charges did no damage, however one of them lodged in the casing, or deck of the U-boat, so that when the boat crash-dived, the pressure ignited the bomb at the designated depth and the detonation destroyed it. Schreder's sketch, however, shows the officers 'sunbathing' on the conning tower—this might have included the neutral Spanish skipper of the *Everalda* that Rostin had sunk days before.[22]

On 11 February 1943, a Martin PBM Mariner seaplane (74-P-7 flying in the 74th Squadron, based in Bermuda) landed on the rough sea to rescue nine survivors of the Allied ship SS *San Arcadio*, sunk 31 January by *U-107* under Harald Gelhaus, and take them back to base.[23] The pilot was US Navy Lieutenant Joseph Abraham Jaap.[24] This feat of airmanship was memorialized by a painting commissioned by *Life Magazine* artist Floyd Davis, who was based in Bermuda for a year.[25]

While Schreder was awarded the Naval Air Medal and his fellow officers ensign Jack 'Jocko' Gierisch and radioman Wrencie Vickers were also so honored, the next pilot to sink a sub in the region received no accolades for it. He was Lt. Thomas Rudolph Evert, and on 7 August 1943, he and his crewmates attacked a German submarine south of Bermuda; however, they were denied credit as squalls prevented the crew from witnessing or filming the sub's demis. Evert and most of his crew perished in a training exercise in the Bay of Biscay eleven weeks later. U-boat historian Dr. Axel Niestlé summarizes the attack thus:

A Liberator B-4 of VB-105 USN, operating from Bermuda, sighted a surfaced U-boat steering a course of 90° true, identified as a probable 500 tons Type VII boat, at 1045. The aircraft attacked it in the face of heavy anti-aircraft fire with a stick of four Mk47 depth charges, reporting a straddle with at least two charges exploding on the starboard side and one on the port side. The U-boat attacked continued in a tight turn to the left for the next 16 minutes, exchanging gun-fire with the circling aircraft. Then the boat started to dive, whereupon the aircraft dropped a Mk 24 Mine 100 feet forward of the swirl just as the top of the conning tower went under.

Due to reduced visibility owing to a rain squall no direct results were observed but about twenty minutes later a narrow oil slick extending crosswind for about ¾ of a mile was observed close to the diving position. Several other similar streaks appeared within the next three hours while the aircraft circled the location of attack. The attack was later classified as 'U-boat present and probably damaged.'[26]

Evert's squadron commander also bemoaned the absence of automatic cameras that would have enabled the plane to confirm a sinking—instead, the final attack went unrecorded and was rendered invisible by rain squalls for ten minutes. No signals were ever received or detected from *U-84* again. The victim was led by Horst Uphoff, responsible for sinking or damaging seven Allied ships of over 37,000 tons.

5 July–1 August 1942: Sixteen U-boats

Kapitänleutnant Hans-Heinz Linder brought *U-202* in a straight line north of Bermuda from west to east on between 5 and 7 July 1942. He was *en route* back to base in Brest, which the sub reached on 25 July 1942, having set off on 27 May. On 1 July, four days before entering the Bermuda region, Linder cut the island off from an essential supply mission when it sank the US *City of Birmingham*. Ultimately, 372 passengers were landed in Bermuda, but not of course the cargo. On 22 June, off New York Linder also sank the Argentinian steamer the *Rio Tercero* of 4,864 tons. The neutral ship's captain was taken aboard the submarine, but released to lifeboats when US aircraft and a blimp counter-attacked. Linder was born in 1913 and turned twenty-nine during this patrol. Part of the Crew of 1933, he served on *U-18* and *U-96* under Lehmann-Willenbrock. In March 1941, he took command of *U-202*, on which he served for six patrols and 236 patrol days up to September 1942. His total tally was seven ships sunk, for 33,693 tons in aggregate. In late fall 1942, he moved ashore to naval staff duties, and died on 10 September 1944 at age thirty-one.[1]

Kapitänleutnant Hans-Dieter Heinicke began his second and final incursion into the waters of Bermuda by entering to the north-east on 6 July 1942, proceeding west. He exited the area to the north-west of the island on the 9th, and was sunk by US forces off Hatteras on 15 July 1942. *U-576* sailed for the 7th U-boat Flotilla out of St. Nazaire on 16 June. She was refueled by *U-460* north of the Azores later that month before proceeding westwards.[2] After transiting Bermuda, on the 14th, the submarine was detected while surfaced by two US Navy OS2U-3 airplanes and quickly submerged; however, several depth charges forced the boat to re-emerge.[3] It was again depth-charged and sank in a swirl of oil. Under most circumstances, that would have been the end of the U-boat.

Apparently, Heinicke was cut from different cloth. Effecting repairs on the sea bottom, he determined that one of his main ballast tanks was irreparably damaged, and a great deal of fuel had been lost. He opted to head back to base. However, the sight of an Allied convoy the following day proved too much for him, and Heinicke moved in to attack. He successfully sank the Panamanian motor ship the *J. A. Mowinckel* of 1,114 tons, the Nicaraguan steamer the *Bluefields* of 2,063 tons, and the

US-flagged *Chilore* of 8,301 tons. However, it was to be the last stand of *U-576*. Two other US Navy aircraft, of the Kingfisher type, were escorting the convoy and dove in to attack the submarine. It is also possible that the steamship the *Unico* rammed it. In any event, Heinicke's sub was now mortally damaged and forced to the surface, where her men fell victim to Naval Armed Guard gunners. Overwhelmed, the boat submerged, taking all forty-five German sailors with it, including Heinicke, who was twenty-nine. Heinicke was born in 1913 and a member of the Crew of 1933. He served as watch officer of the U-boat tender the *Wiechsel* in 1939 and 1940, at which point he began U-boat training. He served on *U-73* and helped commission *U-576*, on which he accrued 163 patrol days over five missions. His career tally was six ships sunk or damaged for 34,907 tons, for which he received no decorations.

Oberleutnant zur See Hans-Gunther Kühlmann committed only four days of his final patrol to the region in *U-166*. It began south-east of Bermuda on 6 June and, by the 8th, the sub was only a few hundred miles south-west of the island. Then, Kühlmann changed course for the south and destiny, leaving the area on the 9th to be sunk in the US Gulf on 30 July 1942.[4]

The next patrol into the region, beginning south of Bermuda on 6 July 1942 was remarkable both for its success (three Allied sinkings) and its failure south of New Orleans. *U-166* left a trail of destruction for the Allies to follow, and on 30 July, after the boat had left the area on the 16th, it caught up with *U-166*. In a pitched battle with the 5,184-passenger ship the *Robert E. Lee* (which carried survivors of earlier U-boat sinkings) and her escorts off New Orleans, *U-166* was sunk on 30 July by a US Coast Guard plane under H. C. White. The *Robert E. Lee* went down as well. The only U-boat to leave its hull in the US Gulf, it was discovered by an oil drilling survey team. Kühlmann was twenty-eight when he was lost, far from his birthplace of Cologne-Sulz. In two patrols of fifty-four days at sea, he sank a total of 7,593 tons, including the small coastwise ships the *Carmen* and the *Gertrude*. He won no decorations. The patrol had begun in Lorient on 17 June 1942.[5]

Kapitänleutnant Hans Oestermann began his second and final patrol to the Bermuda area on 9 July 1942 to the north-east, and departed heading north-west two days later. *U-754* sailed for the 1st U-boat Flotilla in Brest on 19 June. It was refueled by *U-459* west of the Azores early in July. On 29 June, it managed to intercept and sink the British motor ship the *Waiwera* north-north-west of the Azores. After refueling, *U-754* headed to off Hatteras, where it was one of the last seven U-boats to do so. It found few targets and headed north to Canadian waters. On 19 July, the submarine and three others (*U-89*, *U-132*, and *U-458*) were moved near Nova Scotia. On the 28th, *U-754* sank the trawler the *Ebb* off Halifax. Then, on the 31st, the boat was caught on the surface a Royal Canadian Air Force Hudson aircraft and inexplicably failed to submerge. It was a fatal mistake, and the boat was bombed into submission and sank with all forty-three hands.

Born in 1913, Oestermann was a member of the Crew of 1933 and turned twenty-nine during this patrol. Early in his career, he served aboard the destroyer the

Hermann Shoemann before joining U-boats in July 1940. His only boat before commissioning *U-754* was *U-151*. Overall, he accrued 135 patrol days in three war-going patrols and sank or damaged fourteen ships of 56,149 tons. He received no decorations.

Kapitän zur See Heinz-Ehler Beucke brought *U-173* on a six-day patrol of the area around Bermuda inbound starting on 9 July 1942, and ending on the 14th. From a position east-north-east of Bermuda the boat proceeded south-west in a straight line and exited on the 14th. Beucke, aged thirty-eight at the time, sailed from Kiel on the Type IXC boat *U-173*. Sailing on a ninety-eight-day patrol, the boat left Lorient for the 2nd U-boat Flotilla, it proceeded rapidly south-west for the Windward Passage. No tonnage was struck or sunk during this patrol. On 16 August, *U-173* was sighted by an American Hudson aircraft under Pilot Officer Kennard, who dropped four depth charges. These damaged the boat, but it managed to escape. Twelve days later, on the 28th, another Hudson under Sillcock dropped four more depth charges on her, damaging the boat heavily.[6] The same day, a USAF B 18 attacked *U-173*, and she was ordered to return to base. Before she could do so, a Hudson under Badger attacked her on the 29th. Having left Kiel on 15 June to reposition to Lorient following the patrol, the submarine was refueled by *U-460* in the central North Atlantic in mid-July. Over his career, since joining the navy in the Crew of 1922, Beucke was not able to achieve any ships sunk or damaged. This was his only patrol in command of a submarine, and he received no decorations, living until the age of seventy-five in 1979.

In contrast, *U-173*'s skipper after Beucke, *Oberleutnant zur See* Hans-Adolf Schweichel, managed to sink or damage four US destroyers of 29,274 tons—USS *Joseph Hewes*, USS *Winooski*, USS *Hambleton*, and USS *Electra*—in the first sixteen days of its next patrol, starting on 1 November. The boat was sunk off Casablanca on 16 November 1942 by depth charges from the US destroyers USS *Woolsey*, USS *Swanson*, and USS *Quick*. All fifty-seven men on board were killed.[7]

Kapitänleutnant Freiherr Sigfried von Forstner entered the region in the Type VIIC boat *U-402* on 9 July for what would be a ten-day incursion in three portions. First, he entered north-east of Bermuda and motored east until the 12th, when he exited for Hatteras. Then, on 16 July, he returned briefly west of the island, headed north and then exited again on the 18th. Finally, while homebound, *U-402* reappeared north-west of the island and motored east for three days, from 22 to 24 July 1942 back to France. On the way to the Bermuda region, *U-402* received fuel from *U-460* in the central Atlantic. The boat had no success against more organized Allied defenses, including convoys. In fact, on 14 July, *U-402* escaped destruction by a US Coast Guard aircraft, which damaged the U-boat. *U-402* was the last wave of seven U-boats ordered to patrol the Hatteras area—thereafter, they were pulled back to other more profitable zones such as South America and the Caribbean.

Sailing from St. Nazaire with the 3rd U-boat Flotilla, *U-402*'s only commander was von Forstner, who took her on eight patrol of 349 days, right up to her demise on

13 October 1943. She was destroyed with all hands by aircraft from the escort carrier USS *Card* in the Central Atlantic. Von Forstner was promoted to *Korvettenkapitän* a year after his incursion into Bermuda, and earned the Knight's Cross in February of that year. He was a member of the Crew of 1930 before serving on the *Nürnberg* during the first year of the war. He joined U-boats in April 1940, and served under the ace Kretschmer on *U-99* before commissioning his own boat, *U-402*. Thirty-one years of age when he patrolled the area, he was thirty-three when killed, having been born in Hannover on 19 September 1910.

Kapitänleutnant Günther Pfeffer, aged twenty-seven, led the next mission into the area, arriving on the Type IXC boat *U-171* south of Bermuda on 11 July 1942. It was to be the boat's first and final patrol, as it was sunk on the return voyage after fifteen days in the Bermuda area. After heading south-west for five days, the boat exited the zone south-east of Bermuda on 15 July 1942. Then, it took the conventional track for the Windward Passage. The boat proceeded to the Yucatan Channel and US Gulf where it was able to sink the Mexican tankers the *Oaxaca* and the *Amatlan* on 26 July and 4 September respectively. On 13 August, it sank the US freighter *R. M. Parker* in the US Gulf for a patrol tonnage of 17,641. On the way from Kiel, *U-171* was refueled by *U-460* in the central North Atlantic in mid-July. On the return voyage she was also refueled, this time by *U-462* on around 20 September north-west of the Azores. It would meet its end on 9 October in the Bay of Biscay near Lorient. *U-171* was sunk by mines with thirty surviving and twenty-two perishing—Allies at that point were able to sow mines from the air. Pfeffer would return to the region in command of a different submarine, *U-170*, in March 1944.

Kapitänleutnant Günther Pfeffer survived the mining of his boat. A member of the Crew of 1934, he went on to sink only one more ship aside from this patrol, for a career total of 22,304. He was the commissioning officer of *U-171* at Bremen in October 1941. He also commissioned *U-170*. Pfeffer was awarded the U-boat War Badge in 1939. In 1944, he moved the *U-548* from France to Norway to Germany. Pfeffer lived until the age of fifty-one, passing in Bonn in 1966 after attaining the rank of *Fregattenkapitän* in the *Bundesmarine*.[8]

Kapitänleutnant Kurt Diggins brought his submarine *U-458* patrolling north and north-west of Bermuda for eleven days in July 1942. The incursion began to the north-east of the island on 13 July, with *U-458* on a south-west course. Then, Diggins turned west for three days and exited the area on 17 July to the now fruitless and well-protected coast off Hatteras. On 22 July, *U-458* returned north-west of Bermuda, this time heading east, until the 24th. By the 25th, the sub was heading north, which it continued to do until it left the area north of Bermuda on 27 July. This was the first of *U-458*'s seven war patrols. It began for the 3rd U-boat Flotilla on 21 June in Kiel and ended in St. Nazaire on 27 August 1942.

Just over a week into the patrol, Diggins sank the Norwegian motor ship the *Mosfruit* of 2,714 tons in the Central North Atlantic. *U-460* refueled U-458 shortly thereafter. While Diggins was off Hatteras as one of the last seven U-boats to patrol that area, the submarine was ordered by headquarters to be withdrawn from the region. This order resulted in part from the recent losses of *U-214* and *U-576* in the area. *U-458* headed north instead to the waters off Nova Scotia. After chasing a convoy in conjunction with *U-754*, that submarine was sunk and *U-458* was attacked and damaged by Canadian Hudsons on 31 July. Despite these countermeasures, Diggins managed to sink the British tanker the *Arletta* of 4,870 tons off Newfoundland. She set off back to France in the middle of August, returning on the 27th of the month.

Diggins was born in 1913 and was a member of the Crew of 1934. Originally, he served as an *aide-de-camp* aboard the *Admiral Graf Spee*, and was subsequently interned when the ship was scuttled in a famous naval action off Uruguay. He made it back to Germany by stowing away on a steamer and pretending to be Romanian, and enrolled with a minesweeping flotilla until joining U-boats in April 1941. He commissioned *U-458* in December 1941 and led her on seven patrols of 170 days, many of them in the Mediterranean. *U-458* was sunk by HMS *Easton* and the Greek escort destroyer the *Pindos* on 22 August 1943, off Pantelleria, Italy. Though eight men were killed, thirty-nine survived—Diggins was among them. He was taken as a Prisoner of War until September 1947. Over his career, all of Diggins' sinkings—two ships of 7,584 tons—were achieved on this patrol. He was awarded the Iron Cross First Class as well as the Italian Bronze Medal for Valor. Kurt Diggins lived until March 2007 and the age of ninety-four.

On 11 July, *Kapitänleutnant* Albrecht Achilles brought the Type IXC *U-161* back into the region for his second patrol around Bermuda. Coming from the Caribbean, *U-161* headed steadily north-east from a position south of Bermuda, then it sank the US steamer the *Fairport* on 16 July. The *Fairport*, part of convoy AS 4, was loaded with supplies for the North Africa campaign against Rommel. The following day, *U-161* exited the region south of Bermuda and homeward bound for Lorient, where it returned to the 2nd U-boat Flotilla. It was the boat's third of six patrols and was extraordinary for its length: 102 days. At the outset, having left Lorient on 28 April, *U-161* shadowed the SL 109 convoy off the Cape Verde Islands, then went to patrol the coast of Brazil, followed by Trinidad. Later in the patrol, *U-161* performed one of its characteristically daring probes into Porto Limon, Costa Rica, where it sank the *San Pablo*.

The return on this patrol was about 100 GRT a day, or a total of 9,500 tons. On the return voyage, *U-161* refueled from *U-461* west of the Azores and made Lorient on 7 August 1942. Albrecht Achilles was born in 1914 and a member of the Crew of 1934. After serving aboard the school ship the *Schleswig-Holstein*, he became signals officer on board the *Gneisenau*, a battleship. He joined U-boats from the Mürwik academy in April 1940. Then, he made three patrols under Zapp in *U-66* until November 1941. He assumed command of *U-161* in January 1942 and was very active in the Caribbean. Achilles was promoted posthumously in April 1945 to *Korvettenkapitän*. Over six patrols in *U-161*, he accrued 435 days and daringly penetrated the defenses of Port-of-Spain Trinidad and Castries Saint Lucia. His career total was an impressive twenty ships sunk or damaged (six damaged) for 105,664 tons. For this, he was awarded the Knight's Cross in January 1943. On 27 September 1943, *U-161* was caught by a US Navy Mariner aircraft off Bahia, Brazil and sunk with all hands, Achilles among them. He was twenty-nine years of age.[9]

Fregattenkapitän Karl-Heinz Wolff only dipped off the south-east corner of the Bermuda box for a day, on 20 July 1942. Overall, on this patrol, no ships were sighted or sunk by Type IXC *U-509*. Like Beucke, was replaced on arrival, in his case by Werner Witte. It was the boat's first patrol of four—in the other patrols, she would accumulate 56,234 tons of Allied shipping before her demise after 276 patrol days in July 1943. Wolff's patrol to the area began roughly halfway between Bermuda and Anegada and was a straight course to the Mona Passage lasting only five days, from 21 to 25 July. Once inside the Caribbean, the boat made for the Yucatan, patrolled north of Havana, and then swung east to patrol off the north-eastern Caribbean near Guadeloupe before returning to Lorient for the 10th U-boat Flotilla after a patrol of eighty days. Leaving Kiel on 25 June, *U-509* refueled from *U-460* north of the Azores in early July. On 2 August, the boat was attacked by a Catalina from Guantanamo and damaged by depth charges. She returned to base on 12 September, having not struck any ships. Wolff led only one patrol in U-boats. A member of the Crew of 1928, he received no decorations. He lived until the age of sixty, passing away in June 1970.

Kapitänleutnant Georg Staats brought *U-508* to the Bermuda region for two days between 26 and 28 July 1942, gradually making his way south-west from north-east. For the first four days, the sub back-tracked roughly 300 miles north-east of the island, going west, east and back again. Then, it headed south-west to exit the region south-south-west of the island on 28 July. Two ships were sunk on the patrol. *U-508*, a Type IXC out of the 10th U-boat Flotilla in Lorient arrived in the region south of Bermuda on 26 July and took the familiar route to the Crooked Island Passage by heading south-west. Between the 24th and 27th, the sub headed north-east out of the area and back to Lorient. Like *U-509* on a maiden voyage before it, the patrol had originated in Kiel which they left on 25 June, the same day as *U-509*. *U-508* received fuel from *U-460* north of the Azores in early July. She attacked a ship without damaging it north of Cuba on 6 August. She returned to her new base in Lorient on 15 September. Staats would go on to command *U-508* for six patrols of 294 days, sinking fourteen ships for 74,087 GRT. In July 1943, he was awarded the Knight's Cross. *U-508* was sent to the bottom of the Bay of Biscay on 12 November 1943 with all crew, victim of bombs from an American Liberator aircraft north of Cape Ortegal Spain.[10]

Kapitänleutnant Hans Senkel of *U-658* spent ten days south-south-east of Bermuda waiting to refuel from *U-463* between 28 July and 7 August. Its refueling complete, *U-658* headed for a successful patrol off the Windward Passage, exiting the Bermuda area. Near Guantanamo Senkel and his men sank four ships in quick succession: the *Medea* on 13 August, and the *Fort la Reine*, the *Laguna* (damaged, from which as sailor was buried in Bermuda) and the Egyptian *Samir*, all on 17 August. Having left Kiel on 7 July, the boat was refueled by *U-463* west of the Azores later the same month. On the return leg, *U-658* refueled, supposedly by *U-462*, west of the Azores. She arrived in her new base at St. Nazaire on 12 September 1942. A member of the Crew of 33, Senkel's only successes against the enemy were during this patrol; he received no decorations. He and his entire crew were killed by a Canadian Hudson aircraft east of Newfoundland on 30 October 1942.

Korvettenkapitän Gottfried Holtorff led the next incursion into the area aboard the Type VIIC *U-598*. There were two legs to Holtorff's patrol around Bermuda. The first portion lasted from 29 July to 5 August and involved refueling from *U-463* south-east of the island. *U-598*'s course was generally south-west during this time, though there were jogs to the south in order to keep the rendezvous. Having attacked ships in the Windward Passage and Old Bahama Channel, the sub then returned on 25 August on its homeward bound leg, heading north-east from a position south-west of Bermuda, and exiting on 28 August 1942 for France. Like most boats, he entered the area midway between Bermuda and Anegada; like other recent submarines, he had sailed directly from Kiel. Two days before entering the area, it met with *U-463*, a *milchkuh*, or floating fuel station, in the mid-Atlantic. During the fueling operations, machinist Will Bredereck was diving on the hydroplanes and propellers when he was drowned. *U-598* motored north-east back towards St. Nazaire, exiting the area south of Bermuda on 28 August. This was the boat's first patrol, having left Kiel on 7 July. *U-598* was again refueled, this time by *U-462*, west of the Azores. She arrived on 13 December 1942. A member of the Crew of 1936, Holtorff was promoted to *Kapitänleutnant* during this patrol at age thirty. Over his naval career, the three ships he sank or damaged off Ragged Island Bahamas accounted for his career total. He led four patrols of 211 days before being caught by two Allied Liberator aircraft off Natal Brazil and sunk on 23 July 1943. There were two survivors—Holtorff was not one of them.

Fregattenkapitän Karl Neitzel led the next patrol to the south-eastern fringe of the area between 29 July and 6 August 1942. During this time, the sub managed, during complex maneuvers over nine days, to sink the Argentinian *Maldonado* on 2 August. From 29 July to 1 August, the boat proceeded south-west roughly 400 miles south-east of Bermuda. Then, it turned north to intercept the *Maldonado*, then east till the 3rd, then west, and finally south on 6 August, on which day it left the area to enter the Bahamas and Caribbean theaters. Like the sinking of the *Montevideo* by the Italian sub the *Enrico Tazzoli* earlier, this incident inflamed Uruguayan sentiment against the Germans and pried that country and others further away from neutrality. Neitzel opted to take the master of the *Maldonado* captive as a witness.

After that, *U-510* steamed east until 4 August, then back west to just east of the line between Bermuda and Anegada; finally, on the 5th, Neitzel set a straight course south-south-east to a point just east of Anegada. His other victims on this patrol (out of the area) were the *Alexia*, damaged on 10 August (and towed to Puerto Rico) and *Cressington Court* nine days later—both British-flagged, and 8,016 and 4,971 tons respectively. This was *U-510*'s first patrol, originating in Kiel on 7 July. She was refueled later that month by *U-463* west of the Azores. On 18 August, Nietzel claimed to have attacked a steamer east of the Caribbean. On the 20th, *U-510* made a rendezvous with *U-155*, which had been damaged in an attack and could not dive. The two boats moved eastwards together. Despite another rendezvous with *U-460*, *U-155* still could not submerge and so *U-510* escorted the boat most of the way home, arriving in Lorient on 13 September 1942 with no further attacks.

Of the boat's following seven patrols before her surrender in France, Neitzel would command three of them and Alfred Eick the balance. The boat would go on to become a *Monsun Boat* and be taken to Penang, Malaysia, Singapore, Kobe, Japan, and Batavia before returning to France in 1945. She would accrue 574 patrol days and 148,976 tons of Allied shipping attacked. Nietzel began in the King's Navy in 1917 on torpedo boats. Born on 30 January 1901, he was forty-one. He gave up command of the First Minesweeper Flotilla to join U-boats in February 1941 and commissioned *U-510* in November of that year. On one attack on a convoy he sank three ships and damaged five for over 54,000 tons in just three hours. Neitzel's total tonnage including damaged ships would reach over 75,000 tons. He was awarded the Knight's Cross in March of 1943. He moved back to shore command in May and was in command of a Marine-Grenadier regiment at the end of the war, at which point he spent seven months in captivity. He lived until the age of sixty-five, dying in 1966.[11]

Korvettenkapitän Leo Wolfbauer commanded one of Germany's innovations—the refueling tanker submarine *U-463* which was also known as a *milchkuh* or milk cow, as it provided liquid sustenance to other U-boats in faraway battle zones. On this particular patrol—Wolfbauer's first one in command of this vessel—the submarine refueled a number of compatriots south-east of Bermuda. As the rendezvous were essential to so many U-boats that patrolled around Bermuda, the tanker is included here although it was not actively pursuing Allied ships—much as other subs that deposited saboteurs and mined US ports are included. The patrol began in Kiel for the 10th U-boat Flotilla on 11 July 1942. *U-463* entered the Bermuda area on 31 July east of the island and made steady progress south-west. It reached an area between 400 and 500 miles south-south-east of Bermuda and remained there for over a week, between 3 and 13 August, refueling U-boats.

In the course of this patrol, *U-463* provided fuel, medical treatment, fresh food, and other equipment to the following dozen U-boats: *U-164*, *U-217*, *U-510*, *U-564*, *U-598*, *U-600*, *U-654*, *U-658* (all to continue their patrols) and, for their returns to Europe, *U-84*, *U-129*, *U-134*, and *U-154*. Her job complete and the tanks most likely empty, *U-463* commenced her return voyage about 16 August, leaving the Bermuda region to the south-east of the island on 29 August. She made it back to her new base in St. Nazaire on 3 September 1942. Wolfbauer was born in the 1800s, making him the oldest skipper out of 143 patrols. At the time, he took *U-463* on this patrol he turned forty-seven on 21 July, ten days before his tanker entered the region on 31 July. Starting in 1913, Wolfbauer served in the Austro-Hungarian Navy as a *Korvettenkapitän* during the First World War. He was third officer of *U-29* in 1917, then second officer until the Armistice. He joined German U-boats in March 1940 and commissioned *U-463* in February 1942. He and the entire crew of fifty-seven men were lost when surprised by a British Handley Page airplane in the Bay of Biscay south of the Scilly Islands in western England on 16 May 1943. Since his submarine was a supply tanker, there were no ships hit by Wolfbauer in his career which covered five patrols and 204 days from July 1942 to May 1943.

U-98 under *Korvettenkapitän* Wilhelm Schulze returned to the region for a unique mine-laying operation on 5 August. The sub transited the north of Bermuda twice—both inbound and outbound—for a total of nine days. First, *U-98* headed west from 1 to 5 August 1942 and exited in the direction of Hatteras on that day. Then, on the 27th of the same month, Schulze returned, reaching a point north of the island on the 28th before heading north-east until the 30th, when it again exited, this time north-east of Bermuda. After transiting north of Bermuda, *U-98* set a course south-west for the Jacksonville, Florida area. *U-98* laid twelve mines off Jacksonville on 9 August. The delicate mine-laying operation might explain the dearth of other targets the submarine attacked, as the safety of the mines from depth charging would have been paramount in the captain's mind. On 10 August—just one day after the mine field was laid—it claimed its first and only victim: the US armed merchant cruiser USS *Bold* (AMC 97) which necessitated a shutdown of the river until the mines could be cleared some time later. *U-98* began its patrol in St. Nazaire on 14 July. On her return from her second patrol to Florida, the boat was refueled by *U-462* late in August, west of the Azores.[12] She returned to France on 16 September 1942. Born in 1909, Wilhelm Schulze received no decorations during his career. He was a member of the Crew of 1928 and accrued 133 patrol days on *U-177* and *U-98*. The USS *Bold* is his only confirmed enemy damage inflicted.

2 August 1942: SS *Maldonado*

The steamship the *Maldonado* of 5,285 tons was the second Uruguayan ship sunk by the Axis in the region in the space of a few months, the *Montevideo* having been sunk by the Italian submarine *Enrico Tazzoli* in March. The ship had a colorful history, starting when it was built by Ropner and Sons, Limited of Stockton-on-Tees, UK. It was launched on 21 October 1918 and managed by Stamp Mann and Company, and not completed until January 1919. The ship's original name was *War Mallow* and she was operated by The Shipping Controller of London and put to work winding down the logistics of World War One. She was sold the same year to Constantine and Pickering Steam Ship Company of Middlesburgh, UK. At that time, she was renamed the *Briarwood*.[1]

The following year, Woods, Tylor and Brown—Tower Steamship and Woodfield Steamship of London bought her, but again for only a year. In 1921, the same firm renamed her the *Heathfield*, a title which was to stick until 1933. Between 1933 and 1938, Anastase Dennis Callinicos of A. D. Callinicos of Ithaca and Athens owned her and renamed the ship the *Nedon*. In 1938, Italian interests led by Hugo Trumpy purchased her and named her the *Fausto*. September 1941 found the Italians on the side of the Axis and the *Fausto* interned in port in Montevideo. She was seized by the Uruguayan government (National Admiralty of Ports) and renamed the *Maldonado* in 1942.[2]

The *Maldonado*'s dimensions were 402 feet 5 inches long by 52 feet 6 inches wide. Her 517-net-horsepower triple expansion engine drove a single propeller which pushed the ship at 11 knots. On her final voyage the master was Captain Mario Giambruno and her officers and crew totaled forty-nine Uruguayans. The cargo loaded in Montevideo and destined for New York included 5,800 tons of tinned corned beef, 1,000 tons of general cargo and fats, and 1,000 tons of leather and wool, for about 7,800 tons. The ship left Montevideo on 8 July and steamed up the South Atlantic, across the Equator, and almost to New York without refueling.[3]

On the evening of 1 August 1942, the *Maldonado* was roughly 260 miles south-south-west of Bermuda and steaming north-west at 312 degrees true at 10 knots in 16,800 feet of water. Her sides were fully lit with two reflector lights illuminating the national flag of Uruguay on the stern. At 7 p.m., a submarine had been sighted trailing the ship and so the crew were on high alert for the next five hours. Captain Giambruno maintained course and asked the radio operator not to send any messages to convince the skipper of the submarine that it was a genuine neutral and meant no harm. The ship was unarmed. It was a calm night with a gentle wind from the east, a full and bright moon, and clear visibility. There were two lookouts on the bridge, and two on the monkey island above it.

Meanwhile, on the submarine, *U-510* under the command of Karl Nietzel, there were frantic radio signals being exchanged with Berlin.[4] Assuming the flag was Greek not Uruguayan, and that the cargo was contraband, he requested permission to sink the ship. The reply which finally came back instructed him that so long as the ship was not Argentine, Portuguese, Swiss or obviously chartered by the Red Cross, then the ship was fair game. On that basis, at 11.45 p.m., Neitzel fired three warning shots across the bow of the ship and signaled by Morse lamp that the crew were to abandon ship immediately. The *Maldonado*'s crew complied so promptly that within three minutes, all the men were away in two boats. The sub stood by 1,000 meters off the port beam.

At 11.55 p.m., Neitzel fired a torpedo into the port side amidships of the *Maldonado*. The engines were destroyed and the lights on the ship went out. At roughly five minutes after midnight local time on 2 August, the German commander fired another salvo of either one or two torpedoes, which broke the vessels' back. The *Maldonado* sank immediately on impact. The men had abandoned ship in four lifeboats. Neitzel nudged the submarine among the boats and demanded that both the master and chief engineer board his submarine. By the time that Captain Giambruno was aboard, he apparently no longer required the engineer. The captain was taken aboard as prisoner, most likely to help verify the neutrality or at least the status of the ship and clear up any misunderstanding. *U-510* then submerged and headed off in a north-westerly direction, leaving forty-eight men hundreds of miles from land.

Thirteen men in one boat were spotted by the USS *Owl*, rescued, and landed in Hamilton on 6 August.[5] Another boat with thirteen survivors were retrieved by USCG 491.[6] They were landed in Cape May, New Jersey on 16 August.[7, 8] The last batch of survivors of the *Maldonado* were sighted by a US Navy Catalina patrol plane on 5 August.[9] The plane vectored the British troop transport the *Capetown Castle* under Captain E. H. Thorton to the two boats with twenty-two men in them.[10] They were landed in Halifax on 8 August.[11] Embarrassed at having captured the officer of a non-belligerent neutral ship, the Germans released Captain Giambruno, who escaped through Switzerland and managed to return to Uruguay by November 1942.[12] There were riots in the streets of Montevideo over the treatment of the Uruguayan ship and the men who manned it.[13] One can only imagine that the tenor would have been angrier had anyone been killed.

2 August–3 September 1942:
Fourteen U-boats

Teddy Suhren was next to return to the region, again on *U-564* for its second patrol. Like Neitzel's, it would be a brief incursion that occurred largely to the far eastern perimeter of the region and would involve only one incident of note. On 3 August, Suhren brought *U-564* just within the boundaries of the area between Bermuda and Anegada, and on the 4th, he turned south towards Anegada. The following day, he stopped the Swedish neutral steamer the *Scania* on the high seas and carried out one of the rarely detailed stop and frisks of the Second World War by firing a shot across the clearly marked neutral ship, requested that an officer bring the ships' cargo manifest papers over, and then, convinced by the First Watch Officer Lund that the cargo was genuinely neutral (the *Scania* was destined for neutral Brazil), he let the ship sail.[1] Suhren continued southwards and exited the area east of Anegada on 8 August. This patrol began in Brest on 9 July. On the 18th, *U-564* was called to pursue convoy OS 34 north of the Azores. This resulted in Suhren sinking the *Empire Hawksbill* of 5,724 tons and the *Lavington Court* of 5,372 tons—both British.[2] The next day, the boat resumed its patrol and, in late July, was refueled by *U-463* west of the Azores. On 19 August, Suhren came across convoy TAW (S) south of Grenada and sank the *British Consul* (6,940 tons) and the *Empire Cloud* (5,969 tons)—again, both British flagged. On the 30th, she sank the Norwegian tanker *Vardaas* of 8,176 tons north of Tobago. The submarine returned to Brest on 18 September 1942.[3]

U-654 under *Oberleutnant zur See* Ludwig Forster led a patrol of six days into the Bermuda region between 4 and 10 August, following which the boat was lost off Panama. This is one of the few patrols where the boat came right up against Saint David's Light, Bermuda—probably to obtain a navigational fix—on 8 August 1942. Originally, Forster entered south-east of the island, headed west, then south-west, then north. After a fly-by of south-east Bermuda, the boat exited towards the Caribbean on 10 August. The sub took the conventional route from Lorient to Panama via the Windward Passage. *U-654* was refueled west of the Azores by *U-463* in late July.[4] There would be no return voyage as the sub was sunk off Panama north of Colon on 22 August by depth charges from a US Digby B 18 bomber piloted by Lt. P. A. Koenig. All forty-four hands were lost. Forster was a member of the Crew of 1936 who earned the Iron Cross Second Class in September 1939. His total tally was three ships sunk for 17,755 GRT and one warship sunk for 900 tons. He effected four war patrols in command of *U-654* over 162 days in the 1st U-boat Flotilla out of Brest. He was twenty-six years of age when killed of Panama.

Kapitänleutnant Bernhard Zurmühlen in the Type VIIC boat *U-600* led the next attack on the region, spending a total of nine days transiting the box around Bermuda both inbound and outbound. He entered the area on the 5th, staying until 8 August 1942 south-east of Bermuda, then headed south-west for the Windward Passage. After circumnavigating the island of Cuba Zurmühlen returned on the sub's homeward leg on 1 September for five days, heading north-east. By the 5th, *U-600* was clear of the region, south-east of the island, and bound back to France. The patrol had begun on 14 July and ended on 22 September 1942. *En route* to the Caribbean *U-600* was refueled by *U-463* west of the Azores in early August. By way of punishment, on 23 August, the submarine was sighted in the Windward Passage by an American Catalina and depth-charged and damaged. *U-600* was refueled again on the way home by *U-462* west of the Azores in early September. Zurmühlen was a member of the Class of 1933 and worked with radios on a battleship and in signals on shore before joining U-boats in March 1941. He was serving under von Tiesenhausen on *U-331* when the boat sank the British battleship HMS *Barham* in the Mediterranean in November 1941. He commissioned *U-600* as its first (and only) commander in December 1941. This patrol was its first. Zurmühlen's total tonnage sunk amounted to five ships of 28,600 tons and a further three ships damaged for 19,230 tons. He was thirty-two years of age at the time of this patrol. His highest decoration, the following year was the German Cross in Gold. *U-600* was sunk near Ponta Delgada, Azores by the British destroyers HMS *Bazley* and HMS *Blackwood* on 25 November 1943. The boat took all fifty-four hands with it to the bottom of the sea.[5]

Korvettenkapitän Axel-Olaf Löwe utilized the area south-east of Bermuda to refuel *U-505* from *U-463* between 7 and 9 August 1942. During these three days, the boat simply nipped the south-east corner of the box around the island before proceeding homeward to France. *U-505* was later to become famous for its capture by the US Navy, and for spending years in Bermuda as a highly-prized secret during the war. It is now on display in the Museum of Science in Chicago. *U-505* under Löwe (also spelt Loewe), a Type IXC boat, entered the region between Bermuda and Anegada on 30 June 1942 and proceeded on a south-westerly course for three days, as though headed for the Windward Passage. However, on 2 July, *U-505* took a sharp turn and steamed instead for the Mona Passage between Puerto Rico and Hispaniola, which it reached and transited inward for the Caribbean on the 3rd.

Later, Löwe requested permission to return to base due to acute pain. On his return on 25 August, the commander had his appendix removed. On the way to Biscay *U-505* met with *U-214* under Günther Reeder and gave the outgoing boat her surplus fuel and supplies. In the Caribbean, the sub was forced to dive thirty times due to aircraft, though these aircraft actually attacked only once. Only 498 hours were spent under water, the overwhelming balance of 12,842 hours were spent motoring on the surface, indicating a general lack of fear of Allied attack. A member of the Crew of 1928, Löwe joined the *Reichsmarine* in 1928 and after staff positions joined the U-boat arm in November 1940, starting with a patrol under Kentrat on *U-74*. He commissioned *U-505* in August 1941 and during over one year of command sank seven ships of nearly 38,000 tons for the 2nd U-boat Flotilla. Löwe's successor Harald Lange was in command when she was captured by the Allies in the Central Atlantic and towed to Bermuda in mid-1944. From 1944 to April 1945, Löwe served under Albert Speer in the ministry for armament and production before being detained and released by the Allies. Löwe survived the war to live until 1984 and the age of seventy-five. He received no decorations or promotions.

U-164 under *Korvettenkapitän* Otto Fechner took a customary course from south of Bermuda to the Mona Passage in just four days, starting on 8 August 1942, and exiting on the 13th. The entire time, the sub took a south-westerly course. Around 12 August, *U-164* refuelled from *U-653* before continuing its patrol. Shortly after exiting the Bermuda area for the Caribbean, two ships were encountered: the *John A. Holloway*, Canadian of 1,745 tons, and *Stad Amsterdam*, Dutch of 3,780 tons. The third victim, the Swedish *Brageland* of 2,608 tons, sank later on New Year's Day 1943, which was to be the week of his and the boat's demise.

The patrol began in Kiel on 18 July 1942. On the way out, U-164 stumbled upon convoy ON 115 off Greenland. Along with *U-210*, *U-217*, *U-511*, and *U-553*, *U-164* took part in the *Pirat* patrol line.[6] Then she broke off to be refueled by *U-463* west of the Azores. On 19 August, *U-164* made contact with convoy TAW (S) north of Trinidad but to no effect. Ten days later, it was attacked by a Hudson and escaped with minor bruising. A depth-charge attack by a USAF bomber on 13 September resulted in ruptured fuel tanks. As a result, the boat was refueled again by *U-461* north-west of the Azores, and arrived in its new base of Lorient on 7 October 1942. A member of the Crew of 1924, Fechner completed two patrols of 121 days before being sunk. The boat was assigned the 10th U-boat Flotilla of Lorient, where this patrol ended. It was an extended positioning patrol from Kiel in the Baltic to the Atlantic. Thirty-seven-year-old Fechner's decorations culminated with the U-boat War Badge of 1939. His total sinkings were three ships of 8,133 tons. Thirty-nine days into his next and final patrol, *U-164* was surprised by a US Catalina airplane off the coast of South America and sunk on 6 January 1943. Only two out of a crew of fifty-four survived; Fechner was not one of them.

U-217 under *Oberleutnant zur See* Kurt Reichenbach-Klinke was the next to enter the region on 8 August 1942. His track was basically identical to that of U-164 before him. On 8 August, the sub passed east-north-east of Bermuda heading south-west for six days until the 13th, when it exited towards the Caribbean. The submarine also refueled from *U-463* to the south-south-east of Bermuda. *U-217* took the most-traveled route, from south of Bermuda and north of Anegada south-west. Instead

2 August–3 September 1942: Fourteen U-boats

of opting for the Windward Passage, Reichenbach-Klinke entered the Caribbean through the Mona Passage three days later, on 16 August. This long patrol began in Kiel on 14 July and would include not one but two refuelings. In order to chase convoy ON 115 south of Greenland *U-217* formed a patrol line with other boats called the *Pirat*.[7] The submarine entered the Caribbean region in league with *U-164*, *U-511*, and *U-553*, and obtained fuel from *U-463* west of the Azores in early August. Reichenbach-Klinke was a member of the Crew of 1935 and was aged twenty-five at the time of this patrol. His total tally of enemy ships was three sunk for 10,651 tons over 235 patrol days. He received no decorations. *U-217* was sunk in the mid-Atlantic on 5 June 1943 after being depth-charged by an American Avenger aircraft from the USS *Card*. All fifty hands including Reichenbach-Klinke were killed.

Kapitänleutnant Friedrich Steinhoff of *U-511* was a talented former merchant marine officer, in command of *U-511*. Entering the area south of Bermuda on 9 August, he motored west for four days until the 12th. Then, the sub jogged east until the 13th in order to rendezvous with *U-463* for fuel. By 14 August 1942, *U-511* was on its way for a busy patrol in the Caribbean. Though he made no kills while in the immediate area, in the Windward Passage, Steinhoff sank the *San Fabian*, the *Esso,* the *Aruba,* and the *Rotterdam* in Convoy TAW 15 near Point Gravois south-west of Haiti. This patrol was the first for *U-511* and began on 16 July. On the way out, U-511 was vectored towards convoy ON 115 south of Greenland. Then, the boat took part in the *Pirat* patrol line on 1 August. On 16 August, while north of Puerto Rico, U-511 was sighted by a Hudson aircraft under Flight Sargeant Henderson. Even though the aft end of the submarine stuck out of the ocean, making a seemingly easy target, the boat managed to escape. The sub refueled from *U-460* south-west of the Azores in mid-September and arrived at her new base in Lorient on 29 September 1942.[8] Steinhoff would end the war by surrendering his U-boat, as he was ordered to, in Portsmouth, New Hampshire. As a result of his unorthodox treatment by the Americans, he killed himself in the common goal at Charles Street jail in Boston on 19 May 1945, depriving his captors of intelligence on sub-launched missiles which his brother later perfected for the US military.[9] His brother researched the latest rocket technology at Peenemünde and therefore *U-511* and both Steinhoffs were involved in highly secretive tests involving launching rockets from submarines.[10] He is buried in Fort Devens, Massachusetts with a number of other German and Italian POWs.[11] A member of the Crew of 1934 he was thirty-three years of age at the time of this patrol. In March 1944 Steinhoff commissioned *U-873*. Over his career, he sank two ships of 21,999 tons and another damaged for 8,773 tons. He was awarded the U-boat War Badge of 1939.

U-86 under *Kapitänleutnant* Walther Schug was next into the region, to and from Brest on its fourth of eight patrols for the 1st U-boat Flotilla based there. It would be a roughly fifteen-day incursion into the region, with two weeks of intense back-and-forth patrols to the north-west of the island. The patrol to the Bermuda area began on 10 August, then quickly morphed into a zigzag course between the island

and Hatteras, as Schug no doubt hoped to catch ships heading offshore and avoid being sunk off Hatteras. His strategy does not appear to have succeeded as he found no ships there. Then, on the 26th, the sub headed south for two days, then, while south-west of Bermuda, headed east and finally south on 31 August, exited the area. On 6 August, Schug chanced upon and sank the 342-ton Barbadian schooner the *Wawaloam* under the indefatigable Captain Luis Kenedy. This patrol began on 2 July and took the sub past Newfoundland outward bound. Following its transit of Bermuda, the boat entered the Bahamas area, emerging nearly a week later midway between Bermuda and Anegada. The dates were 27 August to 1 September 1942, and no ships were struck. The boat participated in two patrol lines, both named *Wolf*, and went after convoy ON 113. *U-86* was provided fuel from *U-461* on 29 and 30 July. On her way back to Brest, the boat may have been attacked and damaged by an Allied aircraft.

Korvettenkapitän Karl Thurmann, a veteran on the boat's eighth patrol, arrived next, transiting inwards for four days between 10 and 13 August, simply clipping the south-east corner while inbound heading south-west. It appears the sub passed the area of subs refueling from *U-463* without joining the fray; however, the duration of the patrol—from 19 July to 17 September—as well as the distance—from Newfoundland to the Caribbean—suggests that it was refueled at some point. The submarine was attacked by HMS *Pimpernel* and kept on the defensive. On a patrol to and from St. Nazaire for the 3rd U-boat Flotilla, *U-552* spent a total of nine patrol days in the area, and re-entered on 26 August via the Mona Passage. From there, the boat headed due east over the north coast of Puerto Rico and east of Anegada on the 28th.

Interestingly, on the way to the patrol area via the northern route off Newfoundland, *U-553* damaged the *Belgian Soldier*, of 7,167 tons. This patrol began on 19 July in St. Nazaire and ended there on 17 September. *U-553* participated in the *Pirat* patrol line. This resulted in the sinking of the British *Lochkatrine* east of Newfoundland on 3 August. A member of the Crew of 1928, Thurmann worked his way up from *Seekadett* (cadet) serving on light cruisers the *Emden* and the *Köln* to *Korvettenkapitän* in August 1942, during this patrol. There would have been a ceremony on board to celebrate this high honor—when conditions permitted of course. Thurmann joined U-boats in April 1940 and commissioned *U-553* three days before Christmas the same year. Aged thirty at the time, Thurmann would live until 20 January 1943. His total tonnage was 61,390 tons sunk plus a warship of 925 tons destroyed and two ships damaged for 15,273 tons. His final patrol began on 16 January 1943 from La Pallice. A week later, his enigmatic final radio message was 'periscope not clear' from the mid-Atlantic. The submarine and its forty-seven crew were never heard from again.

Korvettenkapitän Kurt-Eduard Engelmann took *U-163*, through the Windward Passage and back in the next incursion into the area. The submarine entered south of Bermuda for three short days, between 12 and 14 August. It does not appear to have refueled from *U-463* like so many of its sister ships; however, it utilized

U-462 for fuel on the way home in late August. The patrol began in Norway. After skimming Bermuda, *U-163* motored south-south-west towards Mona between 13 and 16 August 1942. Then, Engelmann swung west and south of the Turks and Caicos, along the north coast of the Dominican Republic. On 18 August, the boat was through the Windward Passage and exited the region, only to return in four days' time.

On 22 August, *U-163* re-entered the area via a different route. Entering via the Windward Passage, Engelmann emerged into the North Atlantic from the Crooked Island Passage, the U-boat headed east-north-east and back to Lorient. It exited the region for the final time on 27 August. *U-163*'s patrol began in Kristiansand Norway on 23 July 1942 and ended in Lorient on 16 September. Originally, the voyage had begun in Kiel on the 21st. On 17 August, while north of the Dominican Republic, she came across the westbound convoys PG 6 and TAW 13, but was unable to attack. Overall, the submarine achieved no sinkings or even attacks during this patrol. Born in 1903, Engelmann was twenty-nine at the time of this patrol. *U-163* was attacked and sunk north-west of Spain's Cape Finisterre by the Canadian corvette HMCS *Prescott* on 13 March 1943. There were no survivors of the crew of fifty-seven men. A member of the Crew of 1923, Engelmann was awarded the U-boat War Badge of 1939. His next patrol was more successful inasmuch as he sank four ships of 17,011 east of the Caribbean in November of the same year, thus exonerating himself somewhat from earlier and later patrols.

Günther Krech returned to the region on 15 August 1942. From just south-east of Bermuda, he and U-558 headed straight for the Caicos Passage, which it transited on the 24th. The five-day patrol line is steady and straight until 19 August when the sub left the Bermuda zone. Krech exited the area on the 25th via the Windward Passage, having not sunk ships during his week in the area. However, soon after entering the Windward Passage, Krech encountered and sank the 1,987-ton British ship *Amakura* from convoy TAW 15 in the Windward Passage. During the same patrol and roughly two weeks later, Krech put himself in the thick of a convoy action on 13 September. He sank the 7,915-ton *Surinam* of Holland, the British *Empire Lugard* of similar tonnage, and damaged the Norwegian *Vilja* so that it would never sail again. All were sailing with the TAG 5 convoy from Trinidad to Aruba and Guantanamo. Three days later, *U-558* also came across the American 2,606-ton *Commercial Trader* and sank her. All attacks occurred north-west of Trinidad and of the north-east coast of Venezuela. Sailing for the 1st U-boat Flotilla, *U-558* sailed both to and from Brest on its eighth patrol. This highly successful mission lasted eighty days. The patrol began on 29 July in Brest. In mid-August, *U-558* received fuel from *U-462* west of the Azores. On the return leg, the boat was also refueled, this time by *U-461* north-west of the Azores in late September. The boat returned to Brest on 16 October 1942.

Kapitänleutnant Bruno Vowe brought *U-462* into the Bermuda area for six days starting on 15 August 1942. Arriving from the east-north-east, the boat motored south-west for a day, headed due east from Bermuda on the 17th, then returned westwards before heading south then south-east out of the area on the 20th. *U-462* was a refueling sub, operating as part of the 10th U-boat Flotilla out of St. Nazaire. The sub left Kiel on its first war patrol on 23 July. Between mid-August and early September, the boat zigzagged west of the Azores as far as the eastern fringe of Bermuda. During that time, *U-462* supplied fourteen U-boats, nine of them for outward operations and five for the return to base. The outbound boats were *U-94, U-135, U-176, U-373, U-512, U-516, U-558, U-569,* and *U-755*; the inbound ones were *U-66, U-98, U-163, U-173,* and *U-600*. Not all of these submarines were resupplied in the Bermuda area. *U-462* repositioned itself to St. Nazaire on 21 September 1942.

Vowe was born in 1904—like Wolfbauer, he was one of the older commanders. Vowe was a member of the Crew of 1923; by May 1940, he was involved in the U-boat arm. By December of that year, he was watch officer of *U-107* until March 1941. He commissioned *U-462* in March 1942 after a year of work-up. Overall, Vowe was to invest 180 patrol days over eight patrols in the boat before they were captured on 30 July 1943. On that day in the Bay of Biscay, the boat was attacked from many angles: a Halifax bomber aircraft and HMS *Wren*, HMS *Kite*, HMS *Woodpecker*, HMS *Wild Goose*, and HMS *Woodcock*. He received no decorations and sank no ships. Vowe was held prisoner until July 1943 and lived until 1978 and the age of seventy-four.

Uberleutnant zur See Otto Ites brought *U-94* on its first patrol into the area which would also prove to be the boat and commander's tenth and last. Beginning south-east of Bermuda on 20 August, the boat spent five days in the area, first heading south-west, then deviating to the north and a position to the east-north-east of the island on the 22nd, about 250 miles away. Ites then resumed a south-westerly course, exiting the area on 24 August 1942. *U-94* had left St. Nazaire as part of the 7th U-boat Flotilla on 3 August and refueled on the 21st from *U-462* west of the Azores. After transiting Bermuda, the boat went around the south end of Turks and Caicos on the 25th and 26th, and entered the Windward Passage late on the 26th. Two days later it was caught on the surface and sunk by a coordinated Allied attack (an American Catalina aircraft and the HMCS *Oakville* which went rammed the U-boat) off Point Gravois, Haiti.[12] Nineteen crew were killed in the sinking but 26 survived, including Ites, who would go on to live until 1982. Ites had already earned the prestigious Knight's Cross on the back of 15 sinkings for 76,882 GRT and another Allied vessel of 8,022 tons damaged.[13] The boat's officers and men were credited with twenty-seven ships over ten war patrols. A member of the Crew of 1936—called the Olympia Crew because the Olympic Games were held in Germany that year—Ites began his naval career in torpedo boats. Joining U-boats in October 1938, he served aboard *U-51* and *U-41* before commanding *U-146*. He took over command of U-94 from Herbert Kuppisch in August 1941. During and after the war, Ites was held captive until May 1946, going on to first become a dentist, then rejoin the *Bundesmarine* in 1956, where he commanded a destroyer for two years. On his retirement in 1977, Ites was a *konter*, or vice, admiral. Over seven patrols, he underwent 235 sea days.[14]

Kapitänleutnant Hans-Jürgen Auffermann brought *U-514* into the area north-east of Bermuda on 3 September 1942 on a north-south patrol leg which would last five days. The boat headed south-south-west until the 5th, when it turned due south, east of Bermuda, and motored in that direction until 7 September, when it left the area. On the 6th, Auffermann sank the British 167-ton schooner the *Helen Forsey* using gunfire alone. Later, during the patrol off Barbados on 11 September, he damaged the British steamer the *Cornwallis* of 5,458 tons. On the 15th, Auffermann sank the British ship the *Kioto* of 3,297 tons off Tobago Island and was counterattacked by a US Mariner aircraft. A US destroyer then damaged the submarine, necessitating four days of repairs. *U-514* then motored south to the delta of the Amazon River. During that tour, it penetrated the defenses of USS *Roe* to sink the steamers the *Ozorio* (2,730 tons) and the *Lages* (also Brazilian, 5,472 tons) on 28 September. On 11 October, Auffermann sank the US steamer the *Steel Scientist* of 5,688 tons off South America. Two days later, she was attacked without damage by a US B-18 bomber. She arrived in her new base at Lorient on 9 November 1942.

Auffermann was born in 1914 and turned twenty-eight during this patrol on 1 October. He was a member of the Crew of 1934 and joined U-boat training in January 1941. This led to a role as first watch officer of *U-69* in April of that year, from which he was given command when the skipper, Metzler, was incapacitated by illness. Then, Auffermann commissioned *U-514* in January 1942 and served four patrols aboard *U-514*, accruing 199 sea days. Overall, he sank or damaged eight ships of 13,551 tons. On 8 July 1943, *U-514* was attacked by rockets fired from the air by a British Liberator near Cape Finisterre, Spain. The boat and its full complement were killed. In 1942, Auffermann was awarded the Iron Cross First Class, and in 1944, he was posthumously awarded the German Cross in Gold.[15]

6 September 1942: SV *Helen Forsey*

The 167-ton Canadian sailing schooner the *Helen Forsey* was built as the *J. Smith* at Smith and Rhuland Shipbuilding Limited in Lunenburg, Nova Scotia. She was thus part of the same naming convention as the *Vivian P. Smith* and her sister ship the *Francis W. Smith*—all were built on spec by Smith and Rhuland and successfully sold.[1] In the case of the *Helen Forsey*, she was bought and renamed by William Forsey Limited, also of Lunenburg. Registered to Lunenburg, like the *Wawaloam*, the schooner traded between the West Indies and eastern Canada's Maritime Provinces, on the traditional runs carrying rum, molasses, salt from the islands and dried fish, lumber and other products south to the islands. This was a continuation of one leg of what had been known as the Triangle Trade.

On its final voyage, the *Helen Forsey* departed Martinique in the French West Indies loaded with 180 tons of molasses and rum. It then sailed for Bridgetown, Barbados prior to setting off for Saint John's, Newfoundland. It left Barbados on 28 August 1942 under the command of Captain John Ralph with a crew of five other merchant mariners.[2] By midday on 6 September, the schooner was roughly 500 miles east-south-east of Bermuda when it was shelled at 6 a.m. without warning by the gunners on *U-514* under Hans-Jürgen Auffermann. As they both missed from a distance of two and a half miles fired off the port bow, the first two shell shots were like a warning, and Captain Ralph and his small crew of British subjects rapidly launched the lifeboat in an effort to clear the ship. Auffermann did not let up, however, and the submarine continued with more accurate fire up until it was firing at point blank range at the wooden waterline. Right after the boat was launched, two crew members—seventeen-year-old Leslie Rogers and Arthur Bond—were killed by an errant shell. The remaining four officers and crew—Tom Bold, Bill Keating, Jacob Penwell, and Captain Ralph—made off in the boat.[3]

The *Helen Forsey* caught fire and was sunk by 7.16 a.m. The men on the *U-514* approached the lifeboat and asked if they had enough food and, oddly, a razor. Auffermann promised to transmit their position to Bermuda. Eleven days later, Captain Ralph and his men arrived off Bermuda and tried to signal airplanes and naval craft there without success. On the afternoon of 18 September, they were discovered by a local fisherman named Gilbert Lamb of Cassia City, St. David's and towed into the narrow Town Cut which leads to Saint George's Harbour.[4, 5] Lamb had been tending to his nets when he rescued the *Helen Forsey* survivors off East End.[6] He was given a certificate from the Admiralty, and bought the lifeboat for a token amount. He renamed the boat the *John Ralph* after the schooner's skipper and used it for fishing until he was forced to retire due to his health.[7]

12–21 September 1942: Two U-boats

Kapitänleutnant Hans-Heinrich Giessler brought *U-455* both east and westbound across northern Bermuda *en route* to and from laying mines off Charleston. The first leg began on 12 September 1942, heading westbound, and exited the area on the 15th at a point north-west of the island. On the return voyage, *U-455* entered the area at the same point on 26 September 1942, then headed north-east, altering course to the north and east. This lasted four days until the 29th, when Giessler and his men exited the region homeward bound. *U-455* left St. Nazaire on 22 August to lay mines of Charleston. After investigating the waters of Newfoundland, it moved south and completed its mine laying mission on 18 September.[1] No ships were reported to have hit any of the mines laid by Giessler. After its incursion south of the Carolinas, the boat called at the Gulf of St. Lawrence and Cape Race, Canada—again without encountering Allied shipping. She arrived in St. Nazaire on 28 October.[2]

Oberleutnant zur See Ulrich Gräf brought *U-69* on its second incursion into Bermuda waters on 21 September 1942. He was heading back to base and simply headed north-east for four days, exiting the area north of the island on the 24th. The patrol began in St. Nazaire on 15 August as a mine-laying operation for the 7th U-boat Flotilla. *U-69* successfully laid its mines off the Chesapeake Bay on 9 and 10 August then motored to Hatteras on patrol. Gräf then opted to head for Canada, where he entered the St. Lawrence River and sank the British steamship the *Carolus* of 2,375 tons. Constantly under threat of Canadian aircraft, the submarine retreated.[3] Despite damage, *U-69* was able to sink the railway ferry the *Caribou*, and survive depth charge counterattacks by its escort, the *Grandmere*. In the disorder that ensued, 136 passengers and crew—including many women and children—drowned or died of hypothermia.[4] *U-69* managed to escape and even attacked the steamer the *Rose Castle*; however, the torpedo did not detonate. The submarine arrived in Lorient on 1 November, having been refueled by *U-463* on 28 October west of the Azores.[5]

27 February 1943: SS *St. Margaret*

The steamship the *St. Margaret* was built by the yard of Joseph L. Thompson, of Sunderland, England. Originally named the *Hellenic* for a year, she then briefly became the *Nailsea Belle* until 1937. Thereafter, the ship was named the *St. Margaret* and owned and operated by the South American Saint Line Limited, a division of B&S Shipping, of Cardiff. The firm was also known simply as the Saint Line. The *St. Margaret* was 4,312 gross tons and capable of carrying 7,910 tons of cargo. Her length overall was 414.3 feet, the beam was 56 feet, and her depth 23.4 feet. Her steam engine propelled the ship at 10 knots.

The *St. Margaret* had visited Bermuda at least once during World War Two, starting on 3 September 1940. At the end of August that year, the Canadian warship HMCS *Prince David* (F 89) came upon the *St. Margaret* between Bermuda and the Caribbean. The steamship was beset with engine trouble and a potential sitting target for U-boats.

> When *Prince David* closed, the vessel's master asked for the Canadian's engineer officer to come over to have a look, which he did, and reported he did not believe the *St. Margaret* could make it. Bermuda was nearest land, 800 miles west. Expecting that either U-boat or surface raider would sink her, if she did not founder first, Captain Adams decided to intervene, and took the merchantman in tow. The *St. Margaret* was brought into Bermuda safely on 3 September.[1]

It is not known how long the *St. Margaret* stayed in Bermuda, but some of her officers and crew were destined to return to that lovely isle under similar circumstances.

Chief Officer George Hamilton's account in the company magazine relates how the *St. Margaret* loaded 6,000 tons of general cargo in Liverpool. The cargo was consigned to Lamport and Holt Lines in ports which included Montevideo, Uruguay and Buenos Aires. Captain Davies elaborates that the cargo consisted of machinery, whisky, stout, textiles, military stores for the Falklands Islands and Yardley's products. There were also ninety bags of mail stowed between decks in the Number Five hold, aft. A single bag of special mail was kept in the confidential book box in the bridge for emergency disposal in the event of Axis attack. The voyage would require a stop for more coal for bunkers, which was planned for Pernambuco, Brazil.

Among the passengers aboard the *St. Margaret* were three women. These included 'a German mother and daughter who had escaped from Germany just before the war and now [were] on their way to join the father in Buenos Aires.' From the passenger list, this must have been Octave Osten and her daughter Ruch Schaeffear and son-in-law Tony Schaeffear. Matron Francis Gowans was matron-in-charge of Port Stanley, Falkands Islands' hospital when HMS *Exeter* arrived from the Battle of the River Plate in September 1939. Gowans was returning from purchasing a trousseau in England and planned to be married after the voyage.

The four other passengers consisted, in the words of Captain Davies, of 'an estate manager from the Falklands, two Belgians and a Hungarian Jew.' Overall, there were fifty persons on board the *St. Margaret*, including the seven passengers, five naval gunners, and thirty-eight merchant marine officers and crew. The five gunners operated a single four-inch gun, a 12-pound gun, two Oerlikons, two twin Marlin machine guns, and four PAC rocket and kite apparatus.

The *St. Margaret* left Liverpool in Convoy ON 165 at 8 a.m. on Tuesday, 2 February 1943, in position number eighty-three. There were thirty-nine merchant ships in this convoy, escorted by sixteen naval vessels. It was bound for New York, where it arrived Monday, 1 March; however, the *St. Margaret* and other ships dispersed from the convoy on Friday, 19 February.[2] On Friday, 5 February, the weather worsened considerably; for the next two weeks, the *St. Margaret* and the other ships in the convoy endured hellacious weather for which the winter in the North Atlantic is infamous. Despite a succession of severe gales, the ships struggled to remain in formation. Ships on either side of the *St. Margaret*, particularly those sailing light or in ballast, signaled 'not under command'—essentially out of control. The ships with cargos labored under decks awash with ocean swells. According to Captain Davies, 'The crew's quarters and passenger accommodation were flooded for days. The more delicate sex had been granted the use of part of the master's accommodation, the others slept in the lounge.'[3]

According to Chief Officer Hamilton, two of the four emergency rafts were washed away during the storms. Captain Davies opted to keep the four lifeboats swung inwards, close to the superstructure, rather than outboard, closer to the ocean, where they might be damaged by the seas. At 9 a.m. on Friday the 19th, the ship was ordered to proceed independently of the convoy and set off due southwards. Each day the weather improved. On Thursday, 25 February, the British Admiralty warned the ship via radio that there was an enemy submarine operating about 345 miles to their south-east. At 9 p.m. on the following day, another message was received; however, it was not deciphered using the merchant signals book until some hours later. It advised that if the ship was north of a certain point, it was to proceed directly for St. Thomas British Virgin Islands, some 1,300 nautical miles to the south-west. If they were south of the given position, the captain was to ignore the message.

The message was deciphered at 4.20 a.m. on Saturday, 27 February. Oddly, although the *St. Margaret* was 2,250 nautical miles from Pernambuco, Hamilton writes that '...we were making for Pernambuco to refuel, and we had insufficient fuel to reach St. Thomas. The Captain therefore decided to carry on the course to make Pernambuco,' on the north-eastern shoulder of Brazil, in the South Atlantic. Five hours later, at 9.42 a.m. on Saturday the 27th, the ship was 1,145 nautical miles south-east of Bermuda and 1,175 miles north-east of Antigua, essentially in the middle of the Sargasso Sea. The *St. Margaret* was making nine and a half knots, heading 180 degrees south. The wind was from the east at about 12 knots, and the sea was moderate with heavy swell from the south-east. Visibility was good, and the atmosphere was described as 'fine and clear' despite the occasional clouds.

Captain Davies noted that the passengers were very cheerful, given the improving conditions. He notes that 'At breakfast, passengers discussed how they were going to take their trunks out on deck to dry the contents, how they would be sunbathing, etc. There was quite an atmosphere of cheerfulness and some relief on faces.'[4] The five naval gunners were cleaning their equipment. Chief Engineer John Bradford Meadley, aged thirty-four, who was also a close friend of Captain Davies, went down to the engine room. While waiting for the chief engineer to return for an inspection of damage caused by the storm, Captain Davies sought out Chief Officer Hamilton, who he found on the after deck on the port side. At 9.42 a.m., a torpedo slammed into the engine room on the port side amidships. It caused a 'terrific explosion' in the words of Captain Davies, 'followed by huge columns of black smoke, steam, water and oil combined, several hundred feet high.' According to Hamilton, an apprentice had seen the torpedo streaking towards them six points off the bow; however, he thought it was a porpoise and did not raise an alarm. Hamilton explained that immediately the engine room was flooded to the engine tops and, as a result, they were stopped. The wireless system was wrecked and two of the port lifeboats were damaged. Since the ship started to settle, Captain Davies ordered abandon ship and the two lifeboats on the starboard side—Number One and Number Three—were lowered. The first (Number Three) had twenty-five people including all passengers except one of the Belgian men, the gunners, and the three women.

The other starboard boat (Number One) was lowered with seven to eight crewmembers. Captain Davies opted to remain on board with officers and crew to get off the remaining boats and rafts. Davies made a head count and found that three of his men were missing: George Brady, a twenty-one-year-old fireman, Chief Engineer Meadley and Patrick Edward Loughran, a twenty-four-year-old donkeyman. Davies struggled through 18 inches of incoming water to make the ship's wheelhouse to destroy codes and special mail, and was dismayed to find they had not been thrown overboard. They were sunk by the third officer after some colorful language from the captain. When Davies went to his cabin for a life jacket, he found one of the Belgian passengers there, who was crying. For whatever reason, this made Davies laugh. The Belgian was looking for a life jacket, so Davies sent him on deck with his own jacket, grabbed a Welsh bible, and went to look for the three missing engine room staff.

By now, several minutes had elapsed and it was between 9.45 a.m. and 9.50 a.m. Though the *St. Margaret* was on an even keel and 'there appeared no immediate danger of her sinking', Davies correctly surmised that his hidden adversary would strike with another torpedo before long. There were fewer than a dozen men now left on the ship, including the master, mate, second cook, third officer, four sailors and two firemen. They remained calm and cooperative. Chief Officer Hamilton was 'not very well' and one of the lifeboats came under the stern to retrieve him after he slid down a rope to it. The men on board launched the smaller port-side lifeboat, but it capsized and was no use. Davies ordered the third officer to free the larger port-side boat and went to the engine space to try to find his friend Meadley and the two others. He found the engine room flooded to the height of the surrounding sea. Through the debris, he was unable to espy any injured survivors. He could not find any signs of life—or bodies—in the accommodation spaces either. While going forward, he found the British nautical ensign lying on deck and hoisted it two thirds of the way, where it jammed. He rationalized that 'It struck me that the *St. Margaret* should go down with her flag flying.'

By the time Davies made it aft, the larger port-side lifeboat was hanging halfway to the water. He looked one last time for his 'very good friend' Meadley and then followed the calls of his shipmates into the boat by sliding down a lifeline. He writes that 'it was with a very deep feeling of regret and almost guilt that I left the *St. Margaret*. The impression came over me that I was deserting her in her time of trial … [she] appeared very proud and defiant, although mortally injured.' As this lifeboat pulled away from the ship, Davies had the men take off their hats and he 'committed our unfortunate shipmates, whom we were leaving behind, to God's care and mercy.'

Chief Mate Hamilton was meanwhile juggling men and provisions between the other three lifeboats and two rafts. The planks on Number One boat, in which seven or eight crew had gotten away initially, were split at the bilge and the boat had to be cast adrift. The Number Four lifeboat became waterlogged and so provisions were moved from it to a raft and it, also was set adrift.

An hour and three minutes after the first torpedo struck, Markworth sent a second torpedo into the side of the *St. Margaret* at 10.45 a.m. At the time, the boats were roughly 1,200 feet away.[4] In the words of Hamilton, the torpedo struck near the Number Three hold on the port side; 'This was a very violent explosion, which caused cascades of water to pour through the ventilators, the ventilator covers being blown off. We did not see a flash or flame.' The *St. Margaret* ultimately sank bow first with a port list at 10.55 a.m.—ten minutes after the second torpedo. The stern was the last to submerge.

Meanwhile, the boat that Captain Davies was in was filled so much that the men in it were sitting in water. They were still 600 feet from the better lifeboat when the second torpedo struck. As the ship sank Davies had all the people in both boats bare their heads and Davies gave a talk commending the dead to the deep and asking for guidance to those in the boats. Davies and the men in his boat went aboard the large starboard lifeboat, which had twenty-five in it originally, and now had roughly thirty-four. Shortly after the *St. Margaret* sank, and with it any threat of counter-attack, Markworth took *U-66* to the surface and approached the people in the boats. Davies saw the periscope before the sub emerged. Apparently, Markworth was upset, as Davies relates 'When a short distance away, the Commander started howling at us to come alongside. I say "howling" as that is the only way to describe it. He was exactly as if mad.' The men on the U-boat covered the survivors with 'many guns of different caliber' the whole time they interacted.

Markworth first called the third officer aboard *U-66*, as he was wearing a badged cap. Then Captain Davies was asked for and went aboard the submarine. He relates that 'The Commander spoke reasonably good English and had by now calmed down a little. He apologized for having to leave the ladies in the boats, and said that I would be going with him to Germany.' Hamilton said that the second and not third officer was taken on board the sub. The submarine then approached Hamilton's boat and took him aboard for questioning. After being asked the destination and cargo and photographed extensively, he was released. He observed the image of German Swastika with a wolf through it on the conning tower (in fact, it was a 'growling lion's head inside a circle' or black diamond). Ultimately, everyone was released back to the boats except Davies, who was taken as a prisoner of war. That left forty-six survivors on the boats: fifty minus the three killed and the captured captain. The nearest land, Bermuda, was over 1,000 miles away.

Since interactions between German submariners and Allied survivors were brief (on the rare occasions when they occurred at all), it is worthwhile to recount Hamilton's impressions of *U-66* and its crew, and how the Allies were treated:

> The commander was tall, lean, dressed in a rather shabby khaki uniform, and wore a red beard. He seemed very fit. I noticed that he spoke poor English. The crew all wore long khaki trousers, in an equally shabby state of repair. The Commander took our boat's wireless transmitting set from the lifeboat, together with a few tins of provisions from my raft. Whilst I was in the conning tower, a Lieutenant asked survivors on the raft for some cigarettes, for which he gave them in exchange for some cigarettes of a very inferior quality, of German manufacture. The submarine then steamed away on the surface.[5]

At 2 p.m. local time, roughly three hours after the *St. Margaret* sank, Hamilton organized the single seaworthy lifeboat and took two of the life rafts under tow. They set course for St. Thomas, roughly 1,300 nautical miles to the south-west. For fresh water, they had 35 gallons as well as another 30-gallon tank salvaged from the damaged lifeboat. Additionally, each raft had a ten-gallon tank of water. As well as smoke floats, rockets, and flares, the lifeboat had a red sail and yellow protective suits. Given that Hamilton estimated it would take them a month and a half to reach land, each person was rationed to 1.5 ounces of water, three tablets of Horlicks, and two spoons of pemmican (meat paste). At first, there were twenty-seven men and women in the lifeboat, ten in one raft, and nine in the other raft. At 3 a.m. on Sunday the 28th, both rafts were separated from the boat when the rope connecting them parted. Hamilton waited a few hours until daybreak to reconnect them, given his concern for damaging the craft in a heavy swell (a raft had already collided with the boat's rudder). At 5.30 a.m., the craft were reconnected and the lifeboat set sail. The prospect of the boat continuing without the nineteen people in the raft was mooted; the majority did not favor it and it was 'shelved.'

That same day, one of the rafts began to break up. The men were transferred to the lifeboat, making it very crowded. Ten men remained on the other raft. At 5 a.m. the following day (Monday, 1 March), some of the men informed Hamilton that they had seen an airplane. Though the chief officer did not see the plane himself, they fired three smoke flares, three rockets, and some red flares. Hamilton reckoned that the men were seeing things; however, at 7 a.m. on Tuesday, 2 March, they spotted another plane, this time far to the south-east. Ten minutes later, a second plane was visible. Hamilton let off distress signals, but by 7.25 a.m., both planes were out of sight without apparently seeing the boat and raft. Soon after sighting their third plane in two days, a fourth aircraft appeared in the north-easterly quarter. As it seemed to be getting closer, Hamilton took a chance and fired off the remaining rockets, and thus the boats successfully attracted the attention of the plane from ten miles away. By 7.45 a.m., the airplane buzzed the boat and gave recognition signals. The survivors settled in to wait for hopeful rescue; they did not have to wait long.

At 8.15 a.m. Commander Kenneth Loveland of USS *Hobson* (DD 464), a destroyer built in the Charleston Navy Yard in September 1941 and commissioned only weeks before (22 January 1942), logged that '*Corry* left formation to investigate lifeboat reported by *Ranger* aircraft.' A few minutes before USS *Ellison* (DD 454, another US destroyer), logged at 8.11 a.m. that 'Plane reported sighting two rafts with survivors bearing 300 [degrees] true distance twenty miles. *Corry* left screen to investigate.'[6] Judging from the position provided, the *St. Margaret* lifeboat convoy had made it 93 nautical miles to the south-west in less than four days, an impressive distance, averaging over one knot. At 8.38 a.m., the USS *Ellyson* reports that the '*Hobson* left screen to investigate rafts.' Loveland on the *Hobson* reported that at 8.30 a.m. local time:

Sighted red sail on horizon bearing 330(T). 0[8]35 went to general quarters, set material condition Able; left formation to investigate sail. 0[8]45 Identified one boat towing life raft with survivors aboard. 0[8]50 Made all preparations to rescue survivors. 0[9]00 Gave boat first line, commenced taking survivors aboard.[7]

Loveland then went on to name all forty-six survivors taken aboard; for some reason, Hamilton says forty-five were in the rafts and boat, but he may not have been counting himself. By 9.10 a.m., the ship had resumed 'steaming on various courses, at various speeds resuming station in formation.' The rescue was complete. The lifeboat and raft were destroyed by gunfire, as was customary when naval vessels rescued civilians. Careful to manage expectations aboard the life boat and raft, Hamilton noted:

> [He] thought it would take some considerable time for a rescue craft to reach us, but at 0900 several funnels and masts were sighted to the NE. I now ordered the motor to be started, and lowered sails on the raft and the lifeboat. I had deliberately reserved the petrol for such a purpose. When the ships came into full view we recognized them as United States warships. I maneuvered the lifeboat and raft to the lee side of the American Destroyer *Hobson*, and at 10:03 everyone was taken on board.

Hamilton credits himself with navigating 65 nautical miles, 30 miles less than actually covered.

The three women and forty-three men plucked from likely death on the open sea were landed in Bermuda on Friday, 5 March. Commander Loveland of the *Hobson* recorded that, at 8 a.m. that morning, they sighted Fort Saint Catherine behind Saint George's. By 9.35 a.m., they had cleared The Narrows and at 10.04 a.m. entered DunDonald Channel. By 10.30 a.m., they were moored to a navy buoy (PR 1) at Port Royal Bay, NOB. At 10.35 a.m., when the engines were stopped, 'Lieut. Horner, USNR and two officers came aboard to take charge of survivors.' By 11.11 a.m., 'All survivors left ship for disposition by NOB, Bermuda... B.W.I. for disposition by the British Command.' NOB Bermuda base commander Jules reported in the base's war diary:

> The escorting destroyer, *Hobson*, had on board 46 British and Allied refugees who were turned over to the British. Our agreement is that all but U.S. survivors and those from Latin American nations will be turned over to them. The U.S.O. often looks after survivors of any nation.[8]

The Admiralty meanwhile reported on the same day their satisfaction that 'Masters and W/T Operators books thrown overboard in weighted and eyeleted bags in 2,000 fathoms. No apparent possibility of compromise. Survivors will be fully interviewed tomorrow. Master, D.M.S. Davies, taken prisoner.' The Bermuda newspaper *The Royal Gazette and Colonist Daily* dutifully recorded the reception shown the *St. Margaret* survivors on that island.[9] On Saturday, 6 March, on the front page they ran an article entitled 'Group of Survivors Landed Yesterday: Adrift Five Days Before a Rescue Ship Found Them.' Hamilton wrote that two of the men were injured in the explosion, and it turns out that one of them was blinded. They corroborated that

Captain Davies was the last to leave the ship. The reporter gleaned that during the interrogation of the *St. Margaret*'s officers, 'The survivors in the boats and on the rafts had the uncomfortable feeling during all this that the enemy submarine might at any moment decide to pump a few bullets at them, but this did not happen.'

The account continues: 'The survivors were well provisioned with water and food, and the weather was very favorable, not too hot, not too cold, and the sea was not very rough.' The reporter notes that 'There were two ladies and a small girl on the stricken ship, and they were all well cared for in the open boat and by the ship which saved them.' The *St. Margaret*'s men were looked after by members of the Ladies Hospitality Organization and put up in the staff dormitories of the Bermudiana Hotel. On Friday night, 5 March, 'they appeared to be enjoying themselves. Each of them hopes that their stay will be brief. Whether this was their first or fourth torpedoing, as in several cases, the men want to go back to sea. Every assistance is being given the men by the Bermuda Sailor's Home and several other organizations.'

There is a story published in the Fitchburg, Massachusetts *Sentinel* of 4 May 1944, in which Chief Steward James Mathieson claims to have been given a sweater hand-knitted by Fitchburg volunteer Ellen C. Dinardo. He says that in March 1943, 'After six days in a lifeboat we were picked up and landed in Bermuda at a port named St. George.' The facts of his survival closely align with those of *St. Margaret*'s survivors, but they do not match—for instance, he writes in a letter to Ms. DiNardo (who lived until 28 May 2013) that 'we were bound for the Mexican gulf, and were torpedoed nine days out from home', whereas the *St. Margaret* was bound for South America and was over two weeks out of port, having left in February not March.[10]

From Bermuda, the men were placed aboard 'an H.M. ship' on Monday, 15 March 1943. They were repatriated to Portsmouth, UK, a week later, on 22 March. Captain Davies had an eventful and frustrating war. On about 1 March 1943, he was transferred from *U-66* under Markworth to *U-460* commanded by *Kapitänleutnant* Ebe Schnoor. *U-460* returned to base in St. Nazaire four days later, on 5 March. Davies was sent to a merchant navy POW camp. This camp was liberated by the Welsh and Scots Guards at 10.30 p.m. on 27 April 1945—they were a highly welcome sight to Davies, who was Welsh and spoke that language. The HMCS *Prince David*, which towed the *St. Margaret* earlier in the war, was renamed the *Charlton Monarch* as an immigrant ship to Australia in 1947. A year later, she had to be towed to Pernambuco by the SS *John Biscoe*. By 1951, the ship was sold for scrap and went under the welder's torch in Swansea, Wales, in 1951.

The USS *Hobson* experienced a horrific ending during training exercises for the Korean War. On 26 April 1952, the *Hobson* was escorting the aircraft carrier USS *Wasp* roughly 600 miles west of the Azores when the *Wasp* had to make a sudden course change to retrieve aircraft.

The carrier's escort vessels had two options, slow down and let the *Wasp* turn, or cross in front of the carrier. The *Hobson*'s Commanding Officer, Lieutenant Commander

W. J. Tierney and the ship's Officer of the Deck, Lieutenant William Hoefer, argued over which option was to be carried out. The Commanding Officer won, and decided to cross the bow. Lt. Hoefer announced on the deck 'Prepare for collision! Prepare for collision!' The *Hobson* crossed the carrier's bow and was promptly struck amidships. The force of the collision rolled the destroyer-minesweeper over, breaking her in two. The *Rodman* (DD 456) and the *Wasp* rescued many survivors, but the ship and 176 of her crew were lost, including Tierney.[11]

It was one of the US Navy's worst post-war accidents.

U-66 was sunk west of the Cape Verde Island by depth-charges, ramming and gunfire from aircraft flying off the USS *Block Island* and destroyer USS *Buckley* on 6 May 1944—thirty-six of her crew survived. Markworth lived until age seventy-eight, passing away in 1994.

28 February 1943: One U-boat

The next boat into the area was the Type IXC4 boat *U-185* under *Kapitänleutnant* August Maus, sailing to and from Lorient in the 10th U-boat Flotilla. This patrol is remarkable for how close Maus steered to Bermuda on 3 March 1943. The incursion began on 28 February north-east of the island and proceeded south-west until the 3rd, when *U-185* passed along the north coast of Bermuda. Rounding the north-west tip of the reefs, the sub then headed due south for two days until the 5th. Then, it proceeded west and out of the region on the following day. This patrol began on 8 February 1943 in Lorient and ended in Bordeaux on 3 May. During the passage home, *U-185* was refueled by *U-117* south of the Azores in mid-April.[1] In a period of less than a month, in a region where the defenders were highly organized and arguably dominant in such chokepoints as the Windward Passage, *U-185* and Maus extracted the sinking of three Allied vessels of 20,504 tons. Overall, Maus accrued 229 days at sea on three patrols before being captured.

Twenty-eight years old at the time, Maus achieved a total of nine ships of 62,761 tons, plus one ship damaged for 6,840 tons. In September, he was awarded the Knight's Cross.[2] Instead of returning to Lorient, he must have been ordered to Bordeaux. Maus was a member of the Crew of 1934 and joined U-boats from cruisers and school ships in April 1940. He served under Merten in *U-68*. Maus commissioned *U-185* in June of 1942 and served on her until his capture. On 24 August 1943, *U-185* was caught and sunk in the Central Atlantic by three aircraft from the escort carrier USS *Core*. During the next three years, he moved from Tennessee to Arizona then the British Zone in Germany, after he succeeded in escaping in February 1944, only to be captured along with Friedrich Guggenberger in Tuscon, Arizona. Becoming a successful businessman in Hamburg, he lived until the age of eighty-one.

2 April 1943: SS *Melbourne Star*

The large, 12,806-ton *Melbourne Star* was a twin-engined armed merchant ship capable of carrying passengers. Some of her cargo holds were also refrigerated. Built in Cammell, Laird and Company in Birkenhead, near Liverpool, in 1936, her two propellers were powered by Sulzer diesel engines instead of steam. Her dimensions were 542 feet long by 70 feet wide, and 32 feet deep. The owners were the Union Cold Storage Company and her managers were the famous Blue Star Line Limited of London.[1] On her final voyage from Liverpool to Sydney via Greenock and the Panama Canal, the *Melbourne Star* was under the command of Captain James Bennett Hall.[2] On board were seventy-six crew plus eleven Royal Navy Gunners and thirty-one passengers, for a total of 119 souls. The passengers included four French naval officers, several Australian military officers, twelve women, and two children. Sadly, none of them—or the naval gunners—were slated to survive.[3]

The *Star* left Liverpool on 22 March 1943 and Greenock, on the River Clyde, on the 24th. The ship was no stranger to wartime dangers, having been bombed by German aircraft off Ireland in 1940 and survived two resupply missions to the besieged Allied fortress of Malta. On their way across the Atlantic, the *Melbourne Star* came across an abandoned lifeboat that, on closer inspection, proved to be empty; it was a harbinger of things to come. By 2 April, the *Melbourne Star* was already north-east of Antigua and roughly half way between Bermuda and the Caribbean.[4] She was 480 miles to the south-east of Bermuda and steering 220 degrees south-west at an impressive 17 knots. *U-129* under Hans-Ludwig Witt was ecstatic to have found such a large target unescorted and in the wide expanses of the Atlantic, where counterattack from Allied aircraft would be rare and from Allied naval vessels nearly non-existent.

On this voyage, the ship was deeply laden with torpedoes, ammunition, silk, and general cargo, including twelve airplanes in crates on deck. Captain Hall kept his men busy—the ship zigzagged constantly, day and night.[5] Also, there were two lookouts on the forecastle, three on the bridge, and two on the aft gun. During the day, one lookout supplemented the other seven aft of the bridge. These men had observed a ship hull-down on the horizon on 30 March and saw a Portuguese ship roughly three miles off on 1 April. The weather was fine when, suddenly at 3.23 a.m., two torpedoes slammed into the ship just behind the bridge. A few seconds later, another penetrated forward of the bridge and amidships. The latter torpedo must have set off the ammunition, because three fourths of the ship were destroyed in a matter of seconds. The forward portion of the *Melbourne Star* sank in about one and a half minutes, and the stern remained floating for between two to four minutes before it also sank.[6]

Out of 119 persons, only eleven managed to float free of the ship and clamber on board two floating rafts. Though they heard other voices calling for help in the dark, at daylight, these eleven divided up the space on the two life rafts. Four of them— greaser William Best, greaser William Burns, Ordinary Seaman Ronald Nunn, and Able Seaman Leonard White—remained on the smaller raft, with seven on the other.[7] Soon, these small vessels, if one could call them that, were separated. The raft with seven men was never seen again.

Witt and his U-boat crew lingered in the area until sunrise, then approached the raft. The German officer seemed perturbed to learn that no officers survived the wreck to speak to him. He asked the tonnage, departure and destination ports, and nature of the cargo. When Witt learned that she was 12,000 tons, he was elated, cheered, and yelled the good news up to his men on the conning tower. They in turn celebrated their substantial kill with loud yells of '*Heil* Hitler'.

After getting what they wanted from the survivors—without asking after their wellbeing—the submarine motored among the wreckage for some time, without picking anything up. Then, it steamed eastwards a few hours after sunrise. Witt was described as being roughly thirty-four years of age, slim, and in good health. The crew were said to be tanned and wearing khaki shorts. An emblem on the conning tower appeared to be a crest with the word 'Hamburg' written in ornate script below it. Onboard the only raft to survive the ordeal, the men found eight tins of biscuits, other tins of chocolate, pemmican, malted milk tablets, and 22 gallons of water as well as two gallons of oil for massaging their skin, to protect them from sunburn and water immersion. The biscuits, stamped 1942, were moldy and inedible, and the water tasted oily.

Though there was no fishing equipment provided, two weeks into the saga, the men, who had been constipated until then, fashioned a hook out of one of the can openers. They made a spinner from part of a can and fishing line from some rope that they unraveled. As a result, the men were able to catch over fifty fish, which cured them of their constipation, no doubt saved their lives, and boosted their morale, not to mention gave then a positive activity on which to focus. They even saved and stored five or so fish on the raft at any given time.

Altogether, the four men survived for thirty-eight days, until early on the afternoon of 9 May 1943, when a US Catalina aircraft flying out of Bermuda spotted them and circled overhead for half an hour. The navy PBY aircraft was piloted by Lieutenant M. Kaufman and 1st Lieutenant Rex Knorr of the VP 63 Squadron, who saw the smoke and the men holding some sixteen hand flares.[8] The men had lit a Roman Candle-style light to attract attention as the smoke bombs were wet. They were roughly 250 miles south-east of Bermuda.

After surveying the situation, Kaufman decided to land and rescue the men. Once the plane was on the sea surface, a small boat was launched, and an officer rowed over to the survivors. Once the men were satisfactorily identified, the airplane joined the raft and the small boat. The four men who, aside from skin ulcers, were in surprisingly good shape, then boarded the plane and it took off, arriving in Bermuda early in the evening of the same day. The survivors were so grateful that they offered to share some of their prized dried fish with their rescuers, who demurred.

2 April 1943–24 August 1944:
Twenty-four U-boats

The type IXC *U-129* under recently promoted *Korvettenkapitän* Hans-Ludwig Witt began its seventh of nine patrols in Lorient with the 2nd U-boat Flotilla. It was a complicated twenty-four-day mission around Bermuda, making it the longest such patrol to the area. It can be broken into three legs. From 2 to 11 April, the boat passed from south-east of Bermuda to north-west, spending five days close to the eastern shore of the island. In transit north-west from the 2nd to the 5th, the boat then slowed down and patrolled off St. Davids until the 8th, then sped up again, changed course from north to north-west, and exited the area on the 11th north-west of Bermuda. During this nine-day mission from east of Hatteras, the sub managed to sink the American liner *Santa Catalina* on 24 April 1943. On 21 and 22 April, *U-129* was chased away from a New York to Guantanamo convoy by the destroyer USS *Swanson* off Hatteras. On the 25th the boat turned east until the 27th, then north-north-west until 1 May, when it returned to the Hatteras region. Witt also sank the Panama-flagged *Panam*, 7,277 tons, on 4 May. The final leg was a straight trajectory homeward bound of five days between 8 and 12 May, when it exited the area.

This was the boat's third patrol to the area (starting with Nico Clausen) and Witt's second. Aside from sinking the *Santa Catalina*, *U-129* experienced a busy patrol. On 26 April, in the western Atlantic, it encountered what Witt described as an enemy submarine and fired three torpedoes, all of which missed; it is not known which submarine this was. On the voyage back to France on 21 May, while refueling from *U-459*, two members of *U-129*'s crew were washed overboard by a large wave; only one of them was recovered. This patrol began in Lorient on 11 March 1943 and ended there on 29 May. Witt's total tally for this patrol was 26,590 tons.

Under the command of recently promoted *Korvettenkapitän* Adolf Cornelius Piening, *U-155* merely dipped into the south-west corner of the 400-mile-radius around Bermuda on 11 and 12 April 1943. This two-day incursion was part of a larger patrol spent largely in the Bahamas. Piening both entered and exited the area midway between Bermuda and Anegada. In eighty-two days of patrolling, the boat had accounted for a respectable (for the time) 7,973 tons. *U-155* also fended off an attack during its return voyage when on 27 April, inbound to France, it was attacked by an unknown Allied aircraft. It was the boat's fifth of ten patrols, but its only trip into the region.

Piening had already earned the Knight's Cross for sinking twenty-five ships for 126,664 tons, as well as a warship (HMS *Avenger*) of 13,785 tons sunk and an auxiliary warship of 6,736 tons damaged. He was thirty-two at the time of this patrol and lived until 1984 and the age of seventy-three. During the closing weeks of World War Two, while in command of *U-255*, he mined the approaches to St. Nazaire against an Allied attack and spent until 1947 in captivity. He rejoined the *Bundesmarine* in 1956 for thirteen years and achieved the rank of *Kapitän zur See*. A special route to avoid Allied aircraft in the Bay of Biscay became known as the *Piening* route, as he perfected it. He achieved 459 days at sea on eight patrols over his career, after initially serving on the cruiser the *Deutschland* and *U-48*.

The *U-176*, a Type IXC under Rainer Dierksen, entered the area on 28 April 1943 on the by-now familiar trajectory from south of Bermuda; this patrol aimed for the Mona Passage instead of the Windward Passage. It was an unusual incursion inasmuch as the sub changed directions twice. On 28 April, Dierksen headed west-south-west from a point south-east of Bermuda. Then, on the 30th, it turned sharply south-east, exiting the area on 1 May, heading east. Aged thirty-five, Dierksen and the boat were on their third and final patrol together—fate awaited them at the hands of the Cubans a fortnight into the future. For one week, *U-176* headed almost due south, ending off the mouth of the Mona Pass on 8 May. On that day, instead of entering the Mona Passage, Dierksen opted to head due west along the coast of Hispaniola, also bypassing the Windward Passage on the 11th in favor of a patrol up the Old Bahama Channel.

When the submarine sank the *Mambi* and the ammonia tanker the *Nickeliner* (one of the only ships of its kind) on 13 May south of Andros Island, the activity did not go unnoticed. In fact, both US and Cuban naval forces picked up on the Mayday messages, and began tracking the course of the sub up the channel. By the time *U-176* reached the St. Nicholas Channel on 15 May, a convoy with Cuban escorts was awaiting to attack and destroy the boat. A small Cuban patrol boat named CS 13 depth-charged the submarine into submission and, having sunk its prey, proceeded in an almost cavalier way to have lunch in a nearby port.[1] Dierksen was a *Korvettenkapitän* with eleven sinkings of 45,870 tons and one ship damaged for 7,457 tons in 216 sea days during three patrols.

Known for his dogged pursuit (he once spent forty-eight hours and eight torpedoes sinking the Dutch freighter the *Polydorus*), Dierksen was no greenhorn, sailing with the 10th U-boat Flotilla out of Lorient. The recipient of the U-boat War Badge of 1939 in February 1943, he was awarded the German Cross in Gold in January 1944—posthumously. He joined the *Reichsmarine* in 1933 and started off in minesweeping flotillas, taking command of the 32nd U-boat Flotilla until March 1941, when he joined the U-boat arm.

U-161 under the daring *Kapitänleutnant* Albrecht Achilles dipped southwards towards Bermuda for only three days from 8 to 10 April 1943. Aside from sinking the British 255-foot schooner *Angelus* 700 miles east of New York on 19 May, little was achieved offensively on this patrol, primarily because *U-161* was ordered mostly to resupply blockade running ships, several of them captured by German raiders. These included the *Regensberg* of Germany on 23 March, the Italian *Pietro Orseolo* the following day and then the *Irene* (ex-Norwegian *Silvaplana*). After these operations, both *U-161* and *U-174* moved west towards New York; however, *U-161* was attacked off Nantucket two days after leaving the Bermuda area by a US Navy Kingfisher based in Quonsett Rhode Island. On 25 May, *U-161* was fruitlessly chasing a convoy off Cape Sable, Canada and its compatriot *U-174* was sunk by Allied aircraft two days later. On the return voyage to Lorient, *U-161* was refueled, probably by another patrolling U-boat, and arrived in Lorient on 7 June 1943.

U-190 under *Kapitänleutnant* Max Wintermeyer spent nine days patrolling the region mostly north of Bermuda, starting on 27 May and ending two months later on 26 July 1943. The boat transited Bermuda both inbound and outbound. On 23 May, *U-190* entered the area north-east of Bermuda and headed west. Then, it dipped south to the north of Bermuda and finally due west, to exit the region on the 27th. Wintermeyer returned on 23 July and passed quite close to the western tip of Bermuda the following day, evading detection from the Allied aircraft, submarines, and surface ships based there. On the 25th, the sub turned east-north-east and exited the region north-east of Bermuda the following day. The submarine entered the region east of Savannah and headed south-east for three days until 21 July. Then, for two days, it motored east before turning north-east towards Bermuda on 23 July. On the 24th, *U-190* passed just to the west of Bermuda and out of the area. *U-190* left Lorient on 1 May 1942, and aside from being attacked by a USAF Liberator off Cape Henry, Delaware, she did not encounter other Allies. This patrol was typical because 'a marked increase in American air activity made U-boat operations extremely difficult and ship-sinkings were few.'[2] Wintermeyer brought his charge back to Lorient on 19 August 1943.

A member of the Crew of 1934, Wintermeyer was promoted to *Kapitänleutnant* in April 1942. Born in February 1914, he was twenty-nine during this patrol. He was awarded the U-boat War Badge 1939 on the back of four patrols of 348 total sea days. Having begun his naval career on *U-105* and *U-62*, he commissioned *U-190* and survived several patrols on her to move ashore in July 1944, after which he held staff positions on land.

Kapitänleutnant Klaus Bargsten nipped the area north-west of Bermuda between 27 and 29 May 1943 en route to being caught and sunk on 2 June. The *U-521* sailed from Lorient for the 2nd U-boat Flotilla on 5 May. After transiting off Bermuda having not sunk any ships, it was detected on 31 May off Hatteras by a US Navy aircraft based in Norfolk. On 1 June, Bargsten trailed a convoy bound from New York to Guantanamo. The next day, an escort patrol craft, *PC 565*, managed to attack the submarine undetected until it was too late. The sub was badly damaged by five depth charges. The only survivor was Bargsten when he ordered abandon ship and raced up the conning tower. The boat sank too quickly for the rest of the fifty-one men, and was further pounded into submission by other depth charges. Klaus Bargsten was born in 1911 and began his nautical career in the German merchant marine. A member of the Crew of 1936, he joined U-boats in April 1939 and initially served on both *U-6* and then *U-99* under Otto Kretschmer. He commissioned U-563 in March of 1941 until February 1942. Then he joined *U-521* in October 1942, accruing 262 patrol days over seven missions. Bargsten's total tally was five ships sunk for 22,171 tons, including HMS *Cossack* in October 1941 and HMS *Bredon* in February 1943. He received the Knight's Cross in April 1943 less than a week before the commencement of his final patrol.[3] He was held captive by the Allies until the end of November 1946 and went on to live until August 2000 and the age of eighty-eight.

Kapitänleutnant Freidrich Markworth in U-66 spent three days in the Bermuda area and two months in the Bahamas region starting in May 1943. The Bermuda incursion consisted of an entry to the south-east of the island on 28 May 1943, followed by one day of travelling west on the 29th, then a north-west course, providing for an exit of the area the following day on the 30th. The boat, on its eighth of nine patrols, with a Knight's Cross holder at the periscope, patrolled north-west for five days until it arrived off the Savannah–Jacksonville cruising ground, where it was to remain for the better part of six weeks.

U-66 turned east and made its way back to Lorient, crossing its inbound track and exiting the area south of Bermuda on 25 July. To have attacked three large American tankers and sunk two of them in highly contested waters and with the Banana River Florida Naval Air Station so close was an accomplishment. U-66 was sunk west of the Cape Verde Island in 6 May 1944 under a different commander. Markworth live until 1994 and the age of seventy-eight.

Kapitänleutnant Herbert Uhlig on the Type IXC boat *U-527* spent three days south of Bermuda heading east back to Lorient; however, the boat was intercepted two weeks later in mid-Atlantic and sunk on 23 July 1943. The Bermuda portion of the patrol consisted of an entry point south of the island on 5 July, a trip to the north, putting the boat about 350 miles south of Bermuda, then a south-easterly course out of the area the following day. Off the Azores, *U-527* was sunk by combined Allied efforts when surprised by an aircraft which bombed the sub twice and damaged its fuel tanks. This was a near-fatal blow since the oil leaking from the tanks gave the boat's position away to the Allies. This damage resulted in a nineteen-hour attack by destroyers; however, Uhlig managed to escape.

U-648 was ordered to assist the damaged U-boat and they met on 23 July. While they were sharing equipment and fuel, an Allied Avenger aircraft captained by Lt. R. L. Stearns from the USS *Bogue* attacked. Uhlig dashed to a nearby fog bank and determined to fight it out on the surface, while U-648 managed to escape. The Avenger dropped six depth-charges on the boat, whose anti-aircraft gun had jammed. *U-527* began to sink, with the spot marked by smoke floats. Only thirteen men, Uhlig among them, managed to escape and were picked up by the USS *Clemson* and later landed in Casablanca by the *Bogue*. Forty men drowned. Accountable for sinking one ship of 5,242 tons, plus a warship of 291 tons and another ship damaged for 5,848 tons, Uhlig was twenty-seven years of age at the time of this patrol which he undertook in the 10th U-boat Flotilla. Uhlig underwent 138 patrol days on just two patrols and received no decorations and went on to live eighty-one years, having served the balance of the war as a captive of the Americans.

Kapitänleutnant Hans-Günther Brosin in *U-134* spent four days transiting Bermuda inbound. Starting to the south-east of the island on 9 July 1943, the boat proceeded westerly until the 12th, then exited heading west. The boat was attacked no fewer than four times by Allied forces, the final attack being fatal to the boat. Fortunes had indeed changed for the U-boats by mid-1943. *U-134* steamed eastwards and exited the region on 1 August at a point south of Bermuda. Three weeks later, the U-boat escaped a fourth close call when Wildcat and Avenger aircraft from the USS *Croatan* (engaged in escorting a convoy off Europe) attacked the submarine—however Brosin was able to escape once again. Ultimately, *U-134* was sunk four days later, on 24 August off Vigo, Cape Finisterre. A Gibraltar-based Leigh Light Wellington bomber led by D. F. McRae attacked during the night. All forty-eight crew were killed. Brosin began his final patrol as an *Oberleutnant zur See* and ended it—and his life—as a *Kapitänleutnant*, having been promoted on 1 July 1943; he was twenty-six years of age. Aside from the U-boat War Badge of 1939, this member of the Crew of 1936 achieved no ships sunk. The fact that he was on war patrol for an impressive 134 days speaks to the challenges facing U-boat commanders in the later years of the war in the Caribbean area. Whereas a study of a typical patrol in mid-1942 would include roughly four attacks on Allied shipping, by mid-to-late 1943 the patrols like Brosin's were a catalogue of nearly half a dozen Allied attacks on submarines, with no effective retribution achieved.

Kapitänleutnant Hans Hornkohl brought *U-566* on its second patrol into the Bermuda region on 23 July 1943. This patrol was a mission to the US coast to lay mines and sink shipping. For that reason, the track is a more or less straight line from north-east of Bermuda going west and south-west to a point north of Bermuda on the 25th. On the 27th, Hornkohl left Bermuda for the US. Two days later, U-566 deposited a dozen MTB mines off Norfolk, however they claimed no victims. On 2 August, a US Mariner spotted the U-boat off Cape Henry, but it escaped. From then on, the Allies were on *U-566*'s trail, and she was tracked by USS *Plymouth*. However, *U-566* was able to turn the tables and attacked and sank the US navy boat off Cape Hatteras on 5 August.

Two days later, a US Ventura aircraft attacked the boat off Cape Charles, but U-566 fought it off and it crashed after bombs that it dropped failed to detonate— Lieutenant F. C. Cross and his crew were killed. Another Ventura attacked and was also shot down with the loss of its crew. A third aircraft, a Mariner, appeared and forced *U-566* to the surface with bombs. The sub fought off this aircraft as well as two others and two blimps until it escaped in the dark. A Mariner found her in the moonlight but she again escaped, proving to be a charmed boat. On 8 August, a Catalina from Halifax found *U-566* off Nantucket Shoals and vectored in three US Navy destroyer escorts that the submarine managed to evade with the assistance of an innovative radar decoy device named Aphrodite. *U-566* sailed for the 1st U-boat Flotilla on 5 July, returnbing to Brest on 1 September 1943.

Hans Hornkohl was born in 1917. He served in the Crew of 1936. Between 1939 and August 1941, he was assigned to the Luftwaffe's long-range naval reconnaissance unit. Then, he joined U-boat training and served aboard *U-753*. He took over command of *U-566* in January, serving there until October 1943. Hornkohl's later commands included *U-3509*, which was bombed and mined during trials in Danzig, in the Baltic. He transferred to *U-3512*. In the waning days of the war, he commanded *U-2502* and *U-3041* on no war patrols in April 1945 until the capitulation. He was imprisoned but freed in August 1945. The only Allied vessel he sank in his career was USS *Plymouth* of 2,265 tons on this patrol.

Kapitänleutnant Paul Siegmann brought his submarine *U-230* to the north of Bermuda both westbound and eastbound starting on 24 July 1943. The first leg cut due west from north-east of the island to the north-west, exiting on the 26th. The return leg led from north-west of Bermuda starting on 2 August and lasted just three days, until the fourth. *U-230* sailed for the 9th U-boat Flotilla from Brest on 5 July 1943. Its primary mission was to lay TMC mine off the US. Siegmann did so on 31 July, off Norfolk. He then patrolled off the coast near Hatteras until early August, when he backtracked north of Bermuda. On the 13th, he was east of Bermuda and supposed to rendezvous with *U-117*; however, *U-117* did not keep the meeting. On the 17th, *U-230* was able to rendezvous instead with *U-634* and then both boats were told to proceed to *U-847* some 800 miles south-west of the Azores for more fuel. They arrived on the 27th to find three other submarines there. After refueling them, *U-847* radioed to headquarters in France that her job had been completed, in reward for which she was tracked, discovered, and destroyed by the Allies within three hours. *U-230* meanwhile managed to return to Brest on 8 September 1943.

Siegmann was born in Munich in 1913 and was a member of the Crew of 1935. He first served as the first watch officer of the torpedo boat the *Greif* from 1940 to 1941. He commissioned *U-612* from March to August 1942, when it was sunk in a collision with *U-444* in August. In October 1942, he commissioned *U-230* and stayed with her until August 1944, for seven war patrols of 253 days. Overall, Siegmann tallied four ships sunk for 6,453 tons, including two Royal Navy LSTs and one US Navy Patrol Craft, all in 1944. That year, he was awarded the German Cross in Gold.

Like Rostin in *U-158*, *Kapitänleutnant* Horst Uphoff and his men in *U-84* entered the Bermuda region only to be caught by Allied air patrols from that island and destroyed a day later. To leave Biscay, *U-84* had sailed in company with *U-306* and *U-732*. The boat was refueled by *U-536* late in June west of the Azores. Then, the submarine entered the region south-west of Bermuda on 6 August 1943 and was sunk the following day, on the 7th. Close analysis by expert Dr. Axel Niestlé confirms that *U-84* and her men actually perished south of Bermuda on this date.[4] Aged twenty-six at the time of his death, Uphoff was awarded the German Cross in Gold in January 1944 once it was clear that he and his crew were on eternal patrol.

U-732 under *Oberleutnant zur See* Claus-Peter Carlsen began its four-day patrol into the area on 9 July 1943. The boat entered south-west of Bermuda homeward bound and proceeded east-north-east until the 12th, when it exited towards France. It was not a successful patrol. To get there, it had crossed Biscay with *U-84* and *U-306*. Following that, the boat was refueled by *U-488* west of the Azores. On entering the Bermuda area, *U-732* motored south-west towards Cape Mole Haiti, utilizing the north coast of Hispaniola rather than attempting either the Caicos or Crooked Island passages. Carlsen had good reason to avoid fortified Allied channels—he would be attacked twice in or near the Windward Passage. Rounding the north-west tip of Haiti on 11 July, two US OS2U Kingfisher scout aircraft surprised the Type VIIC boat on the surface the following day, damaging it slightly but not injuring any of the crew.

Having exited the area, Carlsen took the boat on a short box-grid search south-east of Jamaica before returning to the Windward Passage on 27 July. Then, while between Inagua and Cape Maysi Cuba the following day, Carlsen initiated an attack on a convoy of repair ships and destroyers, only to be depth-charged into retreat after being forced beneath the surface. The convoy was ON 376 southbound, only 30 miles west of Great Inagua Island, Bahamas. The corvette USS *Brisk* depth-charged the sub.[5] Carlsen made the unsubstantiated claim that he had hit two of the ships in this convoy and sank one of them. The patrol began on 10 June and ended in Brest on 31 August 1943. No ships were sunk or even damaged. According to the war diary, *U-732* spent a week between 28 July and 6 August patrolling off the west coast of Inagua in the entrance to the Crooked Island Passage. On 7 August, the boat bent a course for home, transiting out of the region south of Bermuda and bound for the 1st U-boat Flotilla in Brest. It departed the region on 11 August, five weeks after its arrival. Carlsen, a member of the B Crew of 1937, was twenty-three at the time of this patrol and achieved no sinkings during his three patrols of 136 days; the next patrol was to be the boat's final one. In 1942, he was awarded the Iron Cross First Class. *U-732* was sunk off Tangier, North Africa, on 31 October 1943 by HMS *Imperialist* and the British destroyer HMS *Douglas*. Though thirty-one crewmen were killed, eighteen survived, including Carlsen.

U-518 next patrolled the region under *Kapitänleutnant* Friedrich-Wilhelm Wissman for ten days, starting 22 September 1943. *U-518* was leaving the Savannah-Hatteras area and headed south-east for several days, until 25 September. Then, the sub headed east, to a point south of Bermuda before jogging north to about 200 miles south-east of Bermuda on the 28th. Finally, on the 29th, the boat resumed heading north-east, leaving the region on the last day of September, bound back to France. U-518 entered the region midway Bermuda-Anegada on 16 September 1943 and proceeding due west and after a patrol in the US Gulf returned via Key West on 14 October, roughly two weeks later. Motoring up the Gulf Stream for the next few days, it rounded West End Grand Bahama on the 16th, and was in the open North Atlantic by the following day. Continuing north-east until the 19th to a point roughly a third of the way between

Savannah and Bermuda, the boat then turned south-east and motored until 24 October. At that point, it turned due east and exited the area at the same position it had arrived, on 26 October. On this 106-day patrol out of Lorient and into Bordeaux for the 2nd U-boat Flotilla, *U-518* neither attacked nor sank any ships from 18 August to 1 December 1943. Wissman was a member of the Crew of 1935. After serving in minesweepers, he was first watch officer on *U-109* under Heinrich Bleichrodt. Over four patrols of 304 days, he sank eight ships for 52,346 tons and damaged two others for 15,440 GRT. Wissman was selected for the secret mission to land a special agent on the North American mainland in 1942. Not only did *U-518* succeed in the mission, landing a saboteur in Chaleur Bay Canada on 9 November 1942, but he managed to sink four ships and damage two in the vicinity. Not decorated during the war, he lived until the age of forty-seven, passing in 1963.

Oberleutnant zur See Rupprecht Stock brought *U-214* for a brief two-day incursion of the area far south-east of Bermuda in order to refuel from *U-488*. The sub simply skimmed the imaginary box around Bermuda on 23 and 24 October 1943, heading north-east for its rendezvous with its comrades on the refueling tanker near the Azores early in November. The boat returned to Brest on 30 November 1943. A Type VIID with the 9th U-boat Flotilla, its patrol in the region was limited. *U-214* sewed a field of mines of the Panamanian port of Colon which may have claimed the US submarine *Dorado* (SS 248) on 14 October, though this is not confirmed. The patrol began on 22 August and the sub was attacked by an Avenger aircraft from the USS *Croatan* when 90 miles south-west of the Azores. *U-214* badly damaged the aircraft and would probably have been sunk by the nine aircraft sent to destroy it, had darkness not intervened. On 22 November, Stock claimed to have struck a ship north-east of the Caribbean; however, that claim has not been verified. On the way home, the sub was refueled by *U-488* near the Azores in end-November. The patrol ended in Brest on 30 November 1943. A member of the Crew of 37A, Stock became *Kapitänleutnant* in mid-1944. Awarded the German Cross in Gold a month later, he sank one ship of 200 GRT, is credited with sinking the USS *Dorado*, and damaged another for 6,507 tons. Over his career, he embarked on six patrols and accumulated 333 days of war patrols. He was to live until December 2002 and the age of eighty-six. *U-124* was sunk by HMS *Cooke* with all forty-eight crew in the English Channel on 26 July 1944.

Kapitänleutnant Kurt Lange brought his sub, *U-530*, to the south-east of Bermuda for five days in order to refuel from *U-488*, starting on 9 November 1943. Entering the region to the east south-east of Bermuda, the sub headed south-west until 11 November, where it rendezvoused with the U-tanker *U-488*. On the 12th, the boat headed south, leaving the region on 13 November. *U-530* sailed for the 10th U-boat Flotilla out of Lorient on 17 October, for the Caribbean. *U-488* then entered the Caribbean Sea near Martinique and made it as far as Panama. Off that coast on the day after Christmas, she damaged the tanker the *Chapultepec* of 10,195 tons. On 29 December, another tanker, the *Esso Buffalo*, rammed the U-boat; however, *U-530* made good its escape. The submarine returned to Lorient on 22 February

1944. Lange was born in August 1903 and was a member of the Crew of 1922. In his early naval career, he served in a VP-boat flotilla before joining U-boats starting in September 1941. Over six patrols in U-530 starting in February 1943, Lange accrued 369 days on patrol. During that time, he sank or attacked three ships of 22,258 tons. He was awarded the German Cross in gold and lived until 1995.

Oberleutnant zur See Erwin Bartke brought his submarine tanker to the region far south-east of the Bermuda zone for five days in November 1943, with the primary task of providing fuel to *U-530* and other subs including *U-129*, *U-193*, and *U-214*.[6] U-488 arrived in the area on 11 November 1943, lingered in the same spot to the far south-east of Bermuda on the 12th and 13th, and then tracked off eastwards and out of the zone on the 14th. *U-488* sailed for the 12th U-boat Flotilla in Bordeaux on 7 September 1943. Between 28 September and 4 October, she supplied *U-68*, *U-103*, and *U-155*, all of them outbound west of the Azores Islands. On or near the 11th, she met with *U-402*, *U-584*, and *U-731* in the same region. The group was under surveillance by a hunter-killer group lead by USS *Card* the following day. This was a defensive patrol, and the group had to find a new area to replenish fuel. Under the protection of flak boats *U-256* and *U-271*, *U-488* was able to refuel *U-402* north of the Azores; however, that boat was sunk the following day, with *U-488* possibly damaged.[7, 8]

U-488 then moved further south-west and into the region south-east of Bermuda. There, it managed to supply *U-129*, *U-193*, and *U-530* to continue their patrols plus *U-214* for the homeward voyage in late October and early November. Then, the boat returned to base, arriving in Bordeaux on 12 December 1943. On this patrol, Lange lost two of his crew, one from sickness, another from cardiac arrest. Erwin Bartke was born in 1909 and only joined the U-boat arm at the age of thirty-three. In 1941, he served as second watch officer of *U-403* and he commissioned *U-488* in January 1943. After leaving *U-488*, he took command of *U-1106* and was lost when that boat was destroyed less than a year later, on 29 March 1945 in the North Atlantic. Overall, Lange accrued 160 days aboard both subs in three patrols. He was awarded the U-boat Front Clasp in October 1944.

Fregattenkapitän Hans Pauckstadt brought *U-193* for a ten-day patrol south of Bermuda, starting on 15 November 1943 and ending on 11 January 1944. First, U-193 entered south-east of the island and motored to the north-west, in a generally straight line. The sub exited the area on the 20th in the direction of Savannah and Hatteras. While returning to Europe over a month later, the boat headed on a north-easterly heading, starting on 8 January. This leg lasted only four days and ended on the 11th, when Pauckstadt and his crew headed north-east out of the region, to the south-east of the island. Rather than return to La Pallice, where it was based with the 2nd U-boat Flotilla, the boat was forced to duck into El Ferrol, Spain due to urgent repairs after it was attacked by Allied aircraft on 9 February.

The re-positioning patrol from El Ferrol in neutral Spain (which required permission from the Spanish government to undertake) took five days for the submarine to arrive in Lorient. This patrol began on 12 October and *U-193* refueled from *U-488* east of Bermuda in late October. *U-193* was attacked twice while in the Caribbean by US Navy aircraft. The *Touchet* was the only ship sunk by Pauckstadt. A member of the Crew of 1926, he survived the collision and sinking of *U-18* ten years later. At the time of outbreak of war in 1939, he was an officer on the training ship the *Gorch Foch*. After that, he led the 5th U-boat Flotilla, then commissioned *U-193* in Bremen at the end of 1942. At the time of the German surrender, Pauckstadt was in command of the 8th U-boat Flotilla (training) and another training flotilla. In total, he acquired 185 patrol days at sea in two war patrols. Pauckstadt lived until 1984 and the age of seventy-seven. *U-193* was posted as missing from the Bay of Biscay on 23 April 1944 without him—no precise explanation is given for its loss.

U-129 began its next patrol the region under *Oberleutnant zur See* Richard von Harpe on 16 November 1943. There were three components to this long nineteen-day incursion. Between 16 and 21 November 1943, *U-129* entered south-east of Bermuda inbound and motored west for three days, until the 18th. Then, it turned north-west until the 21st, exiting the area for the Savannah–Hatteras area on that date. Then, roughly three weeks later, *U-129* returned, this time west of Bermuda and heading south-east from the 6 to 11 December. At that point, von Harpe turned west and out of the region on the 13th, again towards Hatteras and Savannah. Finally, on the last day of 1943, von Harpe utilized the waters north of Bermuda for the submarine's homeward patrol. Entering north-west of Bermuda on 31 December, the sub headed east until 3 January 1944. Then, it jogged to the north-east, heading out of the region and back to Europe on 4 January. *U-129* refueled from *U-488* east of Bermuda. During this patrol, *U-129* sank the 5,441-ton Cuban freighter the *Libertad*, off Hatteras. On the way back to France, *U-129* and *U-516* were to obtain fuel from *U-544* on 16 January 1944 north-west of the Azores. When the mothership did not appear, *U-516* sought fuel elsewhere and *U-129* made Lorient on 31 January without it. On the way, the boat lost a crewman overboard on 21 January.[10] Von Harpe's career total was three ships sunk for a total of 17,362 tons. These successes earned him the German Cross in Gold in 1944. Over his career, von Harpe embarked on three patrols of 276 days. The boat sailed for the 2nd U-boat Flotilla. Von Harpe was twenty-six at the time of this patrol and would be promoted to *Kapitänleutnant* in January 1945 before taking *U-3519* on its only mission—it was sunk with its commander in the Baltic on 2 March 1945, six weeks before the end of the war. Born in Estonia, von Harpe was an *Auslander Deutsche*, or overseas German.

Kapitänleutnant Günther Pfeffer returned to his second patrol to the region, having survived the sinking of his previous command, *U-171*, by a mine at the entrance to the port of Lorient. This patrol began on 9 February 1944. On 16 March, *U-170* entered the region midway between Bermuda and Anegada and motored west for a week, passing out of the region on 20 March at a point south-west of the island. Leg two of this patrol to the Bermuda area began on 26 March 1944 and lasted for just four days, until the 29th. The boat arrived south-west of Bermuda, headed north-east for a day, then north, and finally north-west on the 29th, at a point west of the island. The submarine was heading back to patrol the Hatteras and Savannah region. On 23 April, *U-170* exited the region, again midway between Bermuda and Anegada. The boat returned to Lorient on 27 May 1944. Pfeffer was twenty-nine at the time and lived until 1966. The photographs of him during the war show a young man with a rakish tilt to his cap, a jagged front right tooth, and an infectious smile framed by large ears.[11]

Kapitänleutnant Kurt Petersen spent fourteen fruitless days in *U-541* crisscrossing the waters south of Bermuda between 4 April and 23 May 1944. The first leg was inbound and began well south-east of Bermuda. Going south-west until 5 April, the boat then assumed a straight westerly heading until the 9th. Then, *U-541* turned north-west and out of the area, in the south-west corner of the 400-mile radius around the island. On his return voyage, Petersen arrived south-west of Bermuda on 15 May 1944 and first motored south-east for a day. Then, the boat turned east towards Europe until the 20th, with a jog to the south on the 18th. From the 20th to when it exited the region south-east of Bermuda on 23 May, *U-541* headed north-east in a trajectory back to base.

His return home was more interesting but no less frustrating. On 26 May, less than a week after exiting the area, U-541 stopped and searched two neutral ships: the Portuguese *Serpa Pinto* and the Greek *Thetis*, which was carrying 200 passengers including Jewish refugees. As the *Thetis* was chartered to a neutral Swiss party, and Portugal was not a neutral that Germany wished to incite (thereby making the transit to and from Biscay by U-boats even more dangerous, should that country side with the Allies), both ships were allowed to proceed after consultation with Berlin. Petersen did, however, imprison two US citizens aboard his submarine for the return voyage to Lorient, which was reached on 22 June 1942. Twenty-seven at the time of this patrol, Petersen was awarded the German Cross in Gold in 1944 six weeks before setting off from Lorient on 29 February. Petersen was a member of the Crew of 1936 whose second rank, in 1938, was a sea cadet. Over his career of 316 days on four patrols, he sank one ship of 2,140 tons. He took command at a time when Allied ships were harder to find and glory immeasurably more difficult to obtain. Petersen survived the war.

U-505's voyage to Bermuda was unique in that it was not a patrol at all, rather the submarine had been captured off West Africa and was towed by US Navy vessels to the island. US Rear Admiral Daniel Gallery led the overall carrier task force responsible for the capture of the boat intact. Though *U-505* does not fall under the category of enemy patrols around Bermuda, it remained on the island until after the war, and its contribution to the Allies' understanding of German U-boats, their machinery, manning, torpedoes, codes, and other technologies was inestimable. Harald Lange was in command when she was captured by the Allies in the Central Atlantic and towed to Bermuda in mid-1944.[12]

Kapitänleutnant Hans-Jürgen Lauterbach-Emden in *U-539* spent only three days in the Bermuda area between 26 and 28 July 1944, before proceeding to Puerto Rico for one of the last successes of the German campaign against the Caribbean area, the sinking of the escorted US tanker the *Pillory* off Puerto Rico. The boat was homebound in late July, when it skimmed the south-east area around Bermuda and exited on the 28th, heading north-east for Europe. *U-539* was a large Type IXC/40 boat based out of Lorient with the 10th U-boat Flotilla. On 22 July, *U-539* turned more northerly and eventually exited the region south of Bermuda on the 26th. The route home was uncertain and circuitous, given that the Allies were blockading the Bay of Biscay. As a result, *U-539* had to obtain its precious fuel for the return leg from *U-858* roughly 400 miles south-west of Iceland. Though bound for Flensburg after a patrol of extraordinary length—nearly five months—*U-539* was forced to call first at Bergen on 17 September. This makes it the only submarine to attack the Bermuda area which began or ended its patrol in Bergen. It made Flensburg on 22 September 1944. The boat was surrendered in Bergen at the end of the war and destroyed by scuttling in Operation Deadlight by the British. Its commander, aged twenty-four at the time, joined the navy as a member of the Crew 'B' of 1937 and made *Kapitänleutnant* in March of 1944.[13]

Oberleutnant zur See Hans-Werner Offermann brought U-518 into the Bermuda area for six days inward bound between 24 and 29 August 1944. It was the last boat patrolling the Bermuda and Hatteras areas of the war, though some still probed the New York—New England and Canadian waters and the bauxite route from Trinidad southwards in waves, up to 1945. *U-518*'s patrol around Bermuda began to the north-east on 24 August and took it south, then west to an area roughly 200 miles north-north-west of the island on the 27th. Then Offermann turned due west and exited the area towards the US coast on 29 August. Thus ended two years and eight months of enemy incursions into the area, which had been begun by Hardegen in *U-123* in January 1942.

The final patrol by a German submarine into the Bermuda area was initiated by *U-518*, this time under a new commander. It was a brief dip into the area from Hatteras made notable not only because the boat rode out a hurricane (easier to do under water than on the surface) but also because it was in the vicinity of the USS *Warrington*, a destroyer which was sunk by hurricane with heavy loss of life north-east of the Bahamas on 14 September. This patrol was the second to the region undertaken by a submarine with the new snorkel equipment which enabled the boat to remain underwater, ventilate the boat, and charge the batteries all from beneath the ways—a game-changing modification which arrived too late in the game. The boat left on 15 July and returned to Norway on 24 October. Taking up the duties that *U-858* had been engaged in off Iceland when it refueled *U-539* weeks before, *U-518* was assigned weather-reporting duties for roughly a month from mid-September through mid-October. A member of the Crew 'X' of 1939, Offermann was twenty-three at the time, and would only live for less than a year, going down as one of the youngest commanders during World War Two. He was killed on 22 April 1945 north-west of the Azores, sunk with all hands by the destroyer escorts USS *Carter* and the USS *Neal A. Scott*. He was forty-two days into his third patrol at the time. Offermann received the German Cross in Gold at the end of 1943.[14]

Conclusion:
Summary of Allied Activities

As with any battlefield, the human toll is the saddest element. Steel on steel is one form of warfare—the young men who cling to life on a barren life raft for weeks in the Atlantic tell another type of tale, one of tenacity and of perseverance. The men from ships like the *Muskogee*, abandoned by their antagonists to die a slow death on the windswept crests of North Atlantic waves, would of course never live to tell their tale. They leave it to others to piece together.

Were it not for Bermuda sticking its stubborn, reef-strewn hide out of the northern seas astride the Gulf Stream, over a thousand Allies would likely have perished, two U-boats escaped, and the carnage in the nearly half-million-mile-wide region been vastly more devastating. Thanks to the kindness and generosity of strangers, the men and women from disparate backgrounds who landed on the island were treated humanely, welcomed by kindred souls whether in the African Methodist Church, the Anglican graveyard, a sailor's canteen, the hospital or the Sailor's Home, not to mention private homes. The fact they were not treated like commodities (shipwrecked Allied sailors in Archangel Russia were forced to work in factories), speaks volumes to the spirit of hospitality of the tight-knit island community.

These exemplary characteristics can still be found today, and tenets of which are still practiced by members of the Guild of Holy Compassion, as they patiently tend the graves of those lost nearly three generations ago, with no thought to the recognition they are unlikely to receive in any event. No offspring having been borne of the survivors' short sojourns in the Somer's Isles, these white-washed grave sites stand silent sentinel for the hundreds more who made it off the island's war-ravaged coast and back into the fray. There are not likely to ever be U-boats waging war off Bermuda again, and the hulks of most of the victims lie still tantalizingly beyond our grasp.

The Allied ships came from all over—mostly British, US and Norwegian flagged, they also hailed from Latvia, Canada, the Netherlands, neutral Sweden, Uruguay, and Argentina. They steamed ploddingly from Portuguese East Africa or raced from New York, from the Caribbean to Canada, the Pacific to the US, from up South

American rivers to US ports like Baytown and Weehawken. Most of them were on their way between Europe and the Americas, ports like Liverpool and Halifax or New York, or the islands and US Gulf to Halifax to convoy east.

During World War Two, there were 1,224 survivors landed in Bermuda from 24 ships (one US Navy, one Canadian Navy), between 17 October 1940 and 27 February 1943. Most of them were passengers on liner ships, followed by merchant sailors and then naval officers and men. The largest number of survivors was from the *City of Birmingham* (372 landed 1 July 1942, nine fatalities), and the *Lady Drake* (256 landed 6 May 1942, twelve deaths). The fewest were the schooner the *Helen Forsey* and the *Melbourne Star* with four each. Some men from the following ships were landed by air: the *Derryheen*, USS *Gannet*, the *San Arcadio*, and the *Melbourne Star*. Only the following succeeded in rowing and sailing their way to Bermuda on their own: the *Helen Forsey* (four Canadians) and the *James E. Newsom* (nine Canadians).

While other merchant ships picked up most survivors, a number were rescued by naval vessels: the *Jagersfontein*, the *City of Birmingham*, the *Lady Drake*, HMCS *Margaree*, the *British Resource*, and USS *Gannet*. Of those landed in Bermuda, most (twelve ships with 243 men) came from British ships, five ships from the USA accounted for 506 survivors and three Canadian vessels for 299 persons. Other ships whose men landed in Bermuda had been flagged to Uruguay, Sweden, Norway, and Netherlands (one ship each). Six ships experienced the longest survival voyages on open boats or rafts: the *Melbourne Star* for thirty-eight days; the *Empire Dryden* for nineteen days; the *Fred W. Green* for eighteen days; the *San Arcadio* for fifteen days; the *Helen Forsey* for twelve days; and the *Stanbank* for ten days. All the other eighteen ships experienced voyages of nine days or less, with five ships' crews on the water for one day or less. There were several weeks of particularly intense activity on shore when several ships' survivors arrived in Bermuda:

Late October 1940: the *Uskbridge* on 28 October and HMCS *Margaree* on 1 November 1940.
Mid-March 1942: the *British Resource* on 16 March and the *Oakmar* on 24 March 1942.
Late April 1942: the *Agra* and the *Derryheen* on 22 April, the *Robin Hood* on 25 April, and the *Modesta* on 26 April
Early May 1942: the *Lady Drake* on 6 May, the *Empire Dryden* on 8 May, the *James E. Newsom* on 10 May, and the *Stanbank* on 15 May.
Mid-June 1942: the *West Notus* on 5 June, USS *Gannet* on 7 June, the *Melbourne Star* on 10 June, the *L. A. Christiansen* on 12 June, and the *Fred W. Green* on 17 June 1942.
Early July 1942: the *Jagersfontein* on 28 June, and the *City of Birmingham* on 3 July 1942.

Some, like the *Derryheen*, *Maldonado*, *Uskbridge*, and *West Notus*, only had a portion of their crew landed in Bermuda. The others were rescued by ship or air and taken to different ports. Excluding the passenger ships, the average number of men per ship with survivors landed in Bermuda was 27. Including all ships attacked around Bermuda, but excluding the *Uskbridge* and HMCS *Margeree*, which happened before Operation Drumbeat, the attacks began on 24 January with *U-106* under Rasch's attack on the *Empire Wildebeeste* and ended on 27 February 1943 with the attack by *U-66* under Markworth on the *St. Margaret* some 1,140 nautical miles from Bermuda.

Attacks inside the central cirrcle lasted eighteen months, though the U-boat patrols lasted longer—into 1944. The busiest month of attacks was April 1942 with twenty, followed by May 1942 with fifteen and March 1942 with fourteen. The only months during which there were more than one attacks were January to July 1942, generalizing that the sustained attacks lasted for the first seven months of 1942, though many patrols transited the area and random attacks were made after that period.

Four attacks took place on 20 April 1942: the *Agra*, the *Empire Dryden*, the *Steel Maker*, and the *Harpagon*; another four happened on 5 May 1942: the *Lady Drake*, the *Stanbank*, the *Santa Catalina*, and the *Freden*.

There were 3,942 people aboard eighty ships attacked by U-boats between 24 January 1942 and 27 February 1943 (thirteen months—excluding the *Uskbridge*, sunk off Iceland). A total of 957 men were killed, or a mortality rate of roughly twenty-five percent. Luckily, 2,985 men survived. Of the survivors, approximately forty-one percent of the survivors and thirty-one percent of the overall number of people attacked landed in Bermuda. The majority, or forty-four, of Allied ships were steamships laid out to carry general, or dry bulk cargo, as opposed to tankers or other types. There were eight motor ships that carried dry or general cargo, meaning fifty-two out of eighty (sixty-five percent) were dry cargo ships. There were twenty-one tankers, of which eighteen were the more modern motor tankers, and three were steam tankers. Thus, twenty-six percent of the ships carried liquid cargoes, and most of them were motorized, whereas steam-driven machinery propelled most of the dry ships.

Additionally, there was a US Navy minesweeper, two schooners, and four passenger ships, of which three (the *Lady Drake*, the *San Jacinto*, and the *City of Birmingham*) were steam and one (the *Jagersfontein*) was motorized. Some other ships, including the *Fairport* and the *Santa Catalina*, carried passengers as well as freight. There were only five ships (the *Frank B. Baird*, the *Leif*, the *Astrea*, the *Anna*, and the *Freden*) between 1,191 and 1,748 tons, and two—both schooners—less than 1,000 tons: the *James E. Newsom* at 671 tons and the *Helen Forsey* at 167 tons. The total gross registered tonnage of all eighty ships was 473,420 tons, so the GRT of the average ship would be 5,918 tons. The largest ships were the *San Gerardo* (12,915), *Victolite* (11,410), and *Montrolite* (11,309). There were four ships between 10,000 and 10,389 tons: the *Narragansett*, the *Opawa*, the *Jagersfontein*, and the *Koll*.

Generally, the tankers were larger than their dry-bulk cousins; of the top twenty-five ships by tonnage, all except the *Lady Drake*, the *Westmoreland* and the *Hardwicke Grange* were either tankers or motor ships. Out of eighty ships, twelve of them, or fifteen percent were proceeding in ballast—in other words, their cargo holds or tanks were empty except for water or sand, carried to keep them at a safe trim for ocean passages. The *Halcyon*, for example, was 3,531 tons and carried 1,500 tons of ballast to keep the ship steady in rough seas.

On the dry cargo side, the cargoes were the most varied. They included coal, motor boats, military stores, beer, nitrates, motor trucks, chrome ore, cement, bauxite ore, phosphate, aircraft, locomotives, timber, manganese ore, mahogany, anthracite coal, refrigerated cargo (i.e. meats, butter), gas storage tanks, metal piping, flour, automobiles, wine, cereal, canned meat, wool, eggs, leather, fertilizer, explosives, and bags of mail. The variation continues, with ships carrying wheat, tungsten, nitrate, fuel in drums, steel, tires, small arms, fats, flax seed, tobacco, licorice, rugs, 'war supplies,' construction equipment, cigarettes, tanks, lead, asbestos, chrome ore, copper, resins, cotton, zinc concentrates, asphalt, burlap, rubber, linseed, and tea.

On the tanker side, cargoes varied from petrol and paraffin to linseed oil, crude oil, fuel oil, aviation spirit, high-grade diesel oil, gas oil, lubricating oil, gasoline, heavy crude oil, benzene and white spirit, kerosene, furnace oil, and petroleum products. The *Helen Forsey* was not a tanker, but rather a schooner; nevertheless, she carried molasses and rum—presumably in barrels, not in bulk.

Ships attacked in the Bermuda area flew the flags of eleven countries: Great Britain (thirty-four ships), USA (fifteen), Norway (twelve), Canada (five), Sweden (four), Netherlands (three), Panama (two), Uruguay (two), Argentina (one), Latvia (one), and Yugoslavia (one). Great Britain accounted for forty-three percent of ships lost in the region, the US eighteen percent, and Norway fifteen percent, with the others trailing significantly. Nine out of the thirty-four British ships, or twenty-five percent of them, were tankers. In contrast, only two out of fifteen US-flagged ships (thirteen percent) were tankers. On the Norwegian side, five out of twelve (forty-two percent) were tankers.

Eleven ships left from New York, followed by ten from various ports in the UK and ten from Trinidad—the three lead destination ports. Eight left Bermuda, and seven left Curacao in the Dutch West Indies (invariably tankers loaded with petroleum or distillates), five from the US Gulf, and two from British Guyana. Five ships had made stops in Cape Town on their way from Middle Eastern and Indian ports. Four ships sailed from Halifax. Ten ships had last called at Port-of-Spain, Trinidad, to receive bunkers, or fuel, on long voyages from South America or South Africa. One sailed from Buenos Aires, with another four from Norfolk or Hampton Roads. Three sailed from Panama (having left New Zealand or Australia), and four left Philadelphia. One left from Savannah, another three from St. Thomas, US Virgin Islands. One ship left Portuguese East Africa (Mozambique), and another from Recife, Brazil. Yet another sailed from Montevideo, Uruguay. Small ports like Turks and Caicos and Barbados were hailed by the schooners. Ship destinations are somewhat clouded by the reality that, if the ship is included in this study, it was attacked by an Axis submarine and most likely never made it to port.

Twelve were going to Halifax, but sixteen were going to Canada; two to St. John, as well as Sydney Nova Scotia and Montreal.

Sixteen were going to New York. Six were destined for Bermuda, one for Aruba, one for Baltimore, one for Iran, eleven to Cape Town and thence the Middle East or India. Two were destined for Venezuela, one for Cuidad Trujillo, Dominican Republic, three for Curacao Dutch West Indies to load petroleum products, one to Freetown Sierra Leone, one for Georgetown, British Guyana. One was bound for Iceland, two for Norfolk, two for Philadelphia, one for Pernambuco, another for San Juan and yet another for Rio de Janeiro. One ship was bound for Texas City and another for Trinidad, and yet another for Pointe-a-Pitre, Guadeloupe.

The overall goal of this study was to include ships attacked within a roughly 450-mile circle around Bermuda, and the majority of the attacks (sixty-eight out of eighty) occurred within that circle. There is a fine line between attacks which occurred off the US coasts of, say New England and Cape Hatteras, and Bermuda, and some ships were included whereas others, like USS *Atik*, were not. For the most part, exceptions to the 450-mile-radius rule were made because the attacks occurred to the east and south of Bermuda, where they might not receive book-length treatment otherwise, and because Bermuda was the nearest land to the site where the ships were attacked, and was thus naturally an island to which the men may have set out to find salvation.

The average distance of victim vessels from Bermuda (excluding the *Uskbridge*), was 350 nautical miles. The *Modesta*, sunk on 25 April 1942, was the closest to Bermuda at 121 miles, or ten hours' steaming at 12 knots. Next came the *Harpagon* the same week, at only 164 miles distant, followed by the *Raphael Semmes* and the *Westmoreland*, both 175 miles away. The *Tonsbergfjord* was sunk 176 miles from Bermuda by the Italian submarine the *Enrico Tazzoli* in March 1942. The *Astrea* was sunk the same week by the same sub 194 miles from the island, and the *Ramapo* and the *Fred W. Green* roughly 185 miles away. There were twenty-two ships struck between 200 and 300 nautical miles from Bermuda, and thirty-three between 300 and 400 miles away. Eight Allied merchant ships were attacked between 400 and 500 miles from Bermuda, and four between 500 and 600 miles away; more if Cape Hatteras was included in this study. These ships would have been sunk to the east and south of Bermuda. Five ships were sunk more than 600 miles from the island, but were included in this study because their survivors were landed on Bermuda: the *Uskbridge* and the *St. Margaret*. The other three ships were the *Pan Norway* (sunk 743 miles away), the *Triglav* (919 miles), and the *Athelknight*, sunk 1,000 miles away. Since this study is about the men and women who landed in Bermuda during World War Two, their stories are included.

Ultimately, history is told not so much in statistics as through the eyes of the participants. Behind every number in this analysis are the tales of men and women caught unawares and pitched into the merciless North Atlantic. The fact that the majority of them survived and a good number made landfall in Bermuda is a testament not only to the tenacity of their rescuers, who came across the seas and from the clouds, but also to the survivor's good fortune. For many, the ordeal was not over, as they had to ship out on other vessels and brave the same seas again to reach North America or Europe.

As illustrated in these pages, the people of Bermuda—both civilian and those in uniform—did the very best they could under the circumstances to welcome, accommodate, and resuscitate the survivors so that they could sally forth and adjust back into their individual roles in an all-consuming, global war that continued for a further three years. These are the victors of the campaign; men and women who were given up on by both Germans and perhaps by their colleagues ashore, but who battled to survive—and did. By comparison, in the Bahamas only 257 sailors made it ashore from many more ships (130). And in New England 547 landed from thirty-five vessels.

Were it not for fortress Bermuda providing a welcome landing platform for these desperate souls, who would have faced some 650 more nautical miles to make the mainland, most of them would undoubtedly have perished. Bermudians managed the integration of over 1,000 people into a population of 30,000 with aplomb and grace, tending to survivors of all creeds and ages, ranks and genders—the living and the dead. Not only that, but even before the United States joined the fight, they had fortified the island colony with runways and air bases for land as well as sea planes, so that they could not only collect survivors from the air, but avenge the attackers as well. What more could Allied mariners, their passangers, and navy sailors ask of any small and isolated populace?

The small British steamship SS *Modesta*, which under Captain Murray was torpedoed by *U-108* off Bermuda. The fellow merchant ship the *Belgian Airman* rescued and ferried twenty-three survivors to Bermuda. Eighteen men, including Trinidadian Lewis Waldron, aged thirty-seven, who left behind an unborn child, perished. Note the timber stacked on deck, the 'J W' on the funnel, and the lifeboat in davits. (*Steamship Historical Society, sshsa.org*)

Details of Eighty Allied Merchant Ships Sunk Around Bermuda in World War Two

NAME	TONS	FLAG	TYPE	DEPART	DATE SUNK	BOUND	
Uskbridge	2,715	British	Steamship	Swansea, Wales	17/10/1940	Montreal	
Empire Wildebeeste	5,631	British	Steamship	UK, Halifax, NS	24/01/1942	Baltimore, MD	
Culebra	3,044	British	Steamship	London	25/01/1942	Bermuda & Kingston	
Pan Norway	9,231	Norwegian	Motor ship	Avonmouth & Belfast UK	27/01/1942	Aruba	
San Arcadio	7,419	British	Motor tanker	Houston, TX	31/01/1942	Halifax & Mersey, UK	
Tacoma Star	7,924	British	Steamship	Bunos Aires	01/02/1942	Hampton Roads, VA & Liverpool	
Montrolite	11,309	Canadian	Motor tanker	Port of Spain, Trinidad	05/02/1942	Halifax, NS	
Halcyon	3,531	Panama	Steamship	Halifax, NS	06/02/1942	Georgetown, British Guyana	
Opawa	10,354	British	Motor ship	Panama & Lyttelton, NZ	06/02/1942	Halifax, NS & UK	
Victolite	11,410	Canadian	Motor tanker	Halifax, NS	11/02/1942	Las Piedras, Venezuela	
Ramapo	2,968	Panama	Steamship	Bermuda & London	16/02/1942	Philadelphia	
Opalia	6,195	British	Motor tanker	Curacao, DWI	16/02/1942	Halifax & Iceland	
Somme	5,265	British	Steamship	Loch Ewe & London	18/02/1942	Bermuda & Curacao	

CARGO	BY	UNDER	DIST	PAX	KIA	SURV	BDA
4,000 tons of anthracite coal	*U-93*	Korth	2540	29	2	27	21
ballast	*U-106*	Rasch	505	43	9	34	34
general cargo, including aircraft parts	*U-123*	Hardegen	590	45	0	45	
ballast	*U-123*	Hardegen	743	41	0	41	
6,600 tons of gas oil and 3,300 tons of lubricating oil	*U-107*	Gelhaus	370	50	41	9	9
5,107 tons of refrigerated & general cargo	*U-109*	Bleichrodt	405	97	97	0	
crude oil	*U-109*	Bleichrodt	305	48	28	20	
1,500 tons of ballast	*U-109*	Bleichrodt	310	30	3	27	
8,575 tons of refrigerated foodstuffs, general cargo and 3,000 tons of lead	*U-106*	Rasch	398	71	56	15	
ballast	*U-564*	Suhren	270	47	47	0	
ballast	*U-108*	Scholtz	183	38	38	0	
petrol and paraffin	*U-564*	Suhren	335	40	0	40	
general cargo	*U-108*	Scholtz	245	52	52	0	

Leif	1,582	Norwegian	Motor ship	New York, NY	28/02/1942	Cuidad Trujillo, DR	
Finnanger	9,551	Norwegian	Motor tanker	Halifax, NS & UK	01/03/1942	Curacao, DWI	
Gunny	2,362	Norwegian	Steamship	Trinidad & West Africa	02/03/1942	New York, NY	
Rapana	8,017	British	Motor tanker	Liverpool, UK	03/03/1942	Curacao, DWI	
Tonsbergfjord	3,156	Norwegian	Steamship	Cape Town & Bombay	06/03/1942	New York, NY	
Astrea	1,406	Dutch	Steamship	Port of Spain, Trinidad	06/03/1942	New York, NY	
Montevideo	5,785	Uruguay	Steamship	St. Thomas USVI	09/03/1942	New York, NY	
British Resource	7,209	British	Motor tanker	Curacao, DWI	14/03/1942	UK	
Oakmar	5,766	US	Steamship	Trinidad & Calcutta	20/03/1942	Boston, MA	
Davila	8,053	British	Motor tanker	Curacao, DWI	20/03/1942	UK	
Muskogee	7,034	US	Steam tanker	Trinidad & Caripito	22/03/1942	Halifax NS	
Empire Steel	8,138	British	Motor tanker	Baton Rouge, LA	24/03/1942	Halifax, NS, UK	
Narragansett	10,389	British	Motor tanker	Port Arthur, TX	25/03/1942	Halifax & UK	
Svenor	7,616	Norwegian	Motor tanker	Curacao, DWI	27/03/1942	Halifax, NS	
San Gerardo	12,915	British	Steam tanker	Curacao, DWI	31/03/1942	Halifax, NS	
Loch Don	5,249	British	Steamship	New York, NY	01/04/1942	Cape Town	
Eastmoor	5,812	British	Steamship	Savannah, GA	01/04/1942	Halifax, NS, UK	
Ensis	6,207	British	Motor tanker	Curacao, DWI	04/04/1942	Iceland	
Koll	10,044	Norwegian	Motor tanker	Baytown & Galveston, TX	06/04/1942	Halifax & UK	
Kollskegg	9,858	Norwegian	Motor tanker	Curacao, DWI	06/04/1942	Halifax & UK	

2,300 tons of general cargo, mostly cement	U-653	Feiler	275	25	15	10	
ballast	U-158	Rostin	475	39	39	0	
3,100 tons of manganese ore & mahogany	U-126	Bauer	315	26	14	12	
ballast	*Tazzoli*	di Cossato	365	40	40	0	
rubber & tea	*Tazzoli*	di Cossato	176	33	0	33	
General cargo	*Tazzoli*	di Cossato	194	27	0	27	
5,998 tons of wine, cereal, canned meats, wool, eggs, leather, and fertilizer	*Tazzoli*	di Cossato	300	49	14	35	
10,000 tons of benzine & white spirit	U-124	Mohr	235	51	46	5	5
Manganese ore, burlap & rubber	U-71	Flachsenberg	325	36	6	30	30
petroleum	*Enrico Tazzoli*	di Cossato	363	40	0	40	
67,265 barrels of heavy crude oil	U-123	Hardegen	345	34	34	0	
11,000 tons of aviation spirit and kerosene	U-123	Hardegen	345	47	39	8	
14,000 tons of clean petroleum product	U-105	Schuch	208	49	49	0	
11,410 tons of furnace oil	U-105	Schuch	320	37	8	29	
17,000 tons of fuel oil	U-71	Flachsenberg	365	57	51	6	
6,000 tons of general cargo	U-202	Linder	338	47	3	44	
7,500 tons of general cargo	U-71	Flachsenberg	370	52	16	36	
9,000 tons of aviation spirit	U-572	Hirsacker	213	66	0	66	
96,067 barrels of high grade diesel oil	U-571	Möhlmann	234	36	3	33	
8,000 tons of crude oil & 6,300 tons of fuel oil	U-754	Oestermann	255	42	4	38	

Empire Prairie	7,010	British	Steamship	Halifax, NS	10/04/1942	Cape Town, Alexandria	
Robin Hood	6,887	US	Steamship	Trinidad & Cape Town	16/04/1942	Boston, MA	
Alcoa Guide	4,834	US	Steamship	Weehawken NJ	17/04/1942	Pointe-à-Pitre, Guadeloupe	
Victoria	7,417	Argentina	Motor tanker	Recife, Rio & Buenos Aires	18/04/1942	New York, NY	
Harpagon	5,719	British	Steamship	New York, NY	20/04/1942	Cape Town, Bombay	
Empire Dryden	7,164	British	Steamship	New York, NY	20/04/1942	Cape Town, Alexandria	
Agra	4,659	Swedish	Motor ship	Philadelphia	20/04/1942	Cape Town, Port Sudan, Suez, Alexandria	
Steel Maker	6,176	US	Steamship	New York, NY	20/04/1942	Cape Town & Abadan, Iran	
Bris	2,027	Norwegian	Steamship	Baltimore, MD	21/04/1942	Natal, Brazil	
Derryheen	7,217	British	Steamship	Philadelphia, Hampton Roads VA	22/04/1942	Cape Town, Middle East	
San Jacinto	6,069	US	Steam passenger ship	New York, NY	22/04/1942	San Juan, PR	
Empire Drum	7,244	British	Motor ship	New York, NY	24/04/1942	Cape Town, Alexandria	
Modesta	3,849	British	Steamship	St. Thomas USVI & Trinidad	25/04/1942	New York, NY	
Mobiloil	9,925	US	Steam tanker	Norfolk & New York	29/04/1942	Caripito, Venezuela	
Pipestone County	5,102	US	Steamship	Port of Spain, Trinidad	30/04/1942	Boston, MA	
James E. Newsom	671	Canadian	Sailing schooner	Turks & Caicos & Barbados	01/05/1942	St. Johns, NFLD	

9,022 tons of general cargo	U-654	Forster	397	49	49	0	
8,725 tons of chrome ore, asbestos, concentrates and general cargo	U-575	Heydemann	407	38	14	24	24
5,890 tons of general Army supplies, including 8 gas storage tanks, metal piping, flour, cement, lumber, beer, trucks and automobiles	U-123	Hardegen	335	34	6	28	
linseed oil	U-201	Schnee	338	39	0	39	
8,017 tons of general cargo, including explosives, aircraft and tanks	U-109	Bleichrodt	164	49	41	8	
7,000 tons of general cargo and military stores	U-572	Hirsacker	245	51	26	25	25
6,666 tons of general cargo, including nitrate, motor trucks and fuel in drums	U-654	Forster	282	39	6	33	33
7,660 tons of war supplies	U-654	Forster	315	48	1	47	
Asphalt, flour	U-201	Schnee	256	26	5	21	
11,036 tons of general cargo and military stores, including beer, nitrates and motor trucks	U-201	Schnee	300	51	0	51	8
3,200 tons of general cargo & 104 passengers	U-201	Schnee	312	183	14	169	
6,000 tons of military stores, including 1,270 tons of explosives	U-136	Zimmermann	363	41	0	41	
5,800 tons of bauxite ore	U-108	Scholtz	121	41	18	23	23
ballast (water)	U-108	Scholtz	360	52	0	52	
4,970 tons of bauxite ore	U-576	Heinicke	341	46	0	46	
molasses	U-69	Gräf	340	9	0	9	9

Lady Drake	7,985	Canadian	Steam passenger ship	Bermuda	05/05/1942	St. Johns, NFLD	
Stanbank	5,966	British	Steamship	New York, NY	05/05/1942	Cape Town & Alexandria	
Freden	1,191	Swedish	Steamship	Bermuda	05/05/1942	New York, NY	
Santa Catalina	6,507	US	Steamship	Philadelphia, PA	05/05/1942	Burreh, Iran	
Clan Skene	5,214	British	Steamship	Beira, Cape Town	10/05/1942	New York, NY	
Peisander	6,225	British	Motor ship	Panama & Newcastle, Australia	17/05/1942	Liverpool, UK	
Freden	1,191	Swedish	Steamship	Bermuda	19/05/1942	Norfolk, VA	
Norland	8,134	Norwegian	Motor tanker	Glasgow & Gourock UK	20/05/1942	Corpus Christi, TX	
Darina	8,113	British	Motor tanker	Stanlow, UK	20/05/1942	Texas City, TX	
Frank B. Baird	1,748	Canadian	Steamship	Demerara, British Guyana	22/05/1942	Sydney, NS	
Athelknight	8,940	British	Motor tanker	Barry, Wales	27/05/1942	Curacao, DWI	
Yorkmoor	4,457	British	Steamship	St. Thomas, USVI	28/05/1942	New York, NY	
Alcoa Shipper	5,491	US	Steamship	Port of Spain, Trinidad	30/05/1942	New York, NY	
Fred W. Green	2,292	British	Steamship	Bermuda & New York	31/05/1942	Freetown, Sierra Leone	
Westmoreland	8,967	British	Steamship	Panama & Wellington NZ	01/06/1942	Liverpool, UK	
West Notus	5,492	US	Steamship	Trinidad & Bahia Blanca, Argentina	01/06/1942	New York, NY	
Triton	2,078	Dutch	Steamship	Demerara & Trinidad	02/06/1942	New York, NY	

147 passengers	*U-106*	Rasch	211	268	12	256	256
6,488 tons of military stores	*U-103*	Winter	225	48	9	39	39
general cargo	*U-201*	Schnee	285	30	0	30	
6,700 tons of lend-lease cargo, including tanks, steel, tires, gasoline, small arms and a deck cargo	*U-129*	Witt	327	95	0	95	
2,006 tons of chrome ore	*U-333*	Cremer	303	82	9	73	
6,590 tons of wheat, 97 tons of tungsten and wool	*U-653*	Feiler	320	65	0	65	
general cargo	*U-98*	Schulze	250	30	0	30	
ballast	*U-108*	Scholtz	457	48	0	48	
ballast	*U-158*	Rostin	557	56	6	50	
2,457 tons of bauxite ore	*U-158*	Rostin	415	23	0	23	
ballast	*U-172*	Emmermann	1000	52	9	43	
6,700 tons of bauxite ore	*U-506*	Würdemann	420	45	0	45	
8,340 tons bauxuite ore	*U-404*	von Bülow	342	32	7	25	
725 tons of military stores and general cargo, including 48 motor trucks, construction equipment, beer, cigarettes and 48 bags of mail	*U-506*	Würdemann	185	41	5	36	36
6,480 tons of general cargo, refrigerated meat and foodstuffs, 9,554 bales of wool and 406 bags of mail	*U-566*	Borchert	175	68	3	65	
7,400 tons of flax seed	*U-404*	von Bülow	257	40	4	36	18
3,100 tons of bauxite and 60 tons of timber	*U-558*	Krech	464	36	6	30	

Anna	1,345	Swedish	Steamship	Norfolk, VA	03/06/1942	St. George's, Bermuda	
USS Gannet	840	US	Minesweeper	Bermuda	07/06/1942	Bermuda	
Pleasantville	4,549	Norwegian	Motor shipo	New York, NY	08/06/1942	Cape Town & Alexandria	
L. A. Christiansen	4,362	Norwegian	Motor ship	Durban & Karachi	10/06/1942	Philadelphia	
Hardwick Grange	9,005	British	Steamship	Newport News VA	12/06/1942	Trinidad, Buenos Aires	
Jagersfontein	10,083	Dutch	Motor passenger ship	Galveston, TX	26/06/1942	Liverpool, UK	
Harpagon	6,027	US	Steamship	Trinidad & Bombay	28/06/1942	New York, NY	
Everalda	3,950	Latvian	Steamship	Philadelphia, Cape Henry	29/06/1942	Riod de Janeiro	
City of Birmingham	5,861	US	Steam passenger	Norfolk, VA	01/07/1942	Hamilton, Bermuda	
Triglav	6,363	Yugoslavian	Steamship	Portuguese East Africa	09/07/1942	New York, NY	
Fairport	6,165	US	Steamship	New York, NY	16/07/1942	Cape Town, Suez	
Maldonado	5,285	Uruguay	Steamship	Montevideo	02/08/1942	New York, NY	
Helen Forsey	167	British	Sailing ship	Barbados & Martinique	06/09/1942	Bermuda & Newfoundland	
HMCS Margaree	1,375	Canadian	Destroyer	Liverpool	22/10/1942	Halifax	
Saint Margaret	4,312	British	Steamship	Liverpool, UK	27/02/1943	Pernambuco & Buenos Aires	
Melbourne Star	12,806	British	Motor ship	Liverpool, UK	02/04/1943	Sydney, NSW	

1,739 tons of coal and two motor boats as deck cargo	U-404	von Bülow	215	20	0	20	
armament & 62 US Navy personnel	U-653	Feiler	225	78	16	62	62
3,000 tons of phosphate and war material, including cars, trucks, aircraft and two locomotives as deck cargo	U-135	Praetorius	203	47	2	45	
ballast	U-129	Witt	274	31	0	31	
7,000 tons of refrigerated cargo	U-129	Witt	377	78	3	75	
9,000 tons of general cargo, including lead, copper, resins, cotton and timber, plus 98 passengers	U-107	Gelhaus	503	220	0	220	99
7,500 tons of manganese ore, tobacco, licorice, wool and rugs	U-332	Liebe	175	37	19	18	
General cargo	U-158	Rostin	275	36	0	36	
2,400 tons of general cargo, passengers	U-202	Linder	350	381	9	372	372
9,000 tons of manganese ore & zinc concentrates	U-66	Markworth	919	43	24	19	
8,000 tons of war material and a deck cargo of tanks	U-161	Achilles	300	123	0	123	
7,000 tons of tinned meat, wool and fats	U-510	Neitzel	258	49	0	49	
180 tons of molasses and rum	U-514	Auffermann	450	6	2	4	
Naval officer and ratings	Colission	Port Fairy	2,200	176	142	34	34
6,000 tons of general cargo & coal	U-66	Markworth	1140	50	3	47	47
8,285 tons government stores, general cargo, ammunition, and torpedoes	U-129	Witt	459	119	115	4	4

APPENDIX II

Details of Axis Submarine Commanders Who Led 143 Patrols around Bermuda

TYPE	#	DATE	DAYS	RANK	NAME	AGE	
IXB	123	20/01/1942	5	*Korvettenkapitän*	Reinhard Hardegen	28	
IXC	66	26/01/1942		*Korvettenkapitän*	Richard Zapp	28	
IXC	130	29/01/1942	9	*Korvettenkapitän*	Ernst Kals	36	
IXB	107	30/01/1942	7	*Kapitänleutnant*	Harald Gelhaus	26	
IXC	125	30/01/1942	4	*Kapitänleutnant*	Ulrich Folkers	26	
IXB	109	03/02/1942	6	*Korvettenkapitän*	Heinrich Bleichrodt	32	
IXB	106	04/02/1942	3	*Kapitänleutnant*	Hermann Rasch	27	
IXC	128	07/02/1942	19	*Kapitänleutnant*	Ulrich Heyse	35	
VIIC	98	08/02/1942	3	*Kapitänleutnant*	Robert Gysae	31	
VIIC	564	08/02/1942	8	*Kapitänleutnant*	Reinhard Suhren	26	

DIED	FLOTILLA	DEPARTED	RETURNED/ FATE	DECORATIONS	VSLS	TONNAGE
Alive	2nd	Lorient	Lorient	Knights Cross with Oak Leaves, U-boat War Badge with Diamonds	21	N/A
17/07/1964	2nd	Lorient	Lorient	Knights Cross	17	N/A
02/11/1979	2nd	Lorient	Lorient	Knights Cross	17	N/A
02/12/1997	2nd	Lorient	Lorient	Knights Cross U-boat Front Clasp	19	10,068
06/05/1943	2nd	Lorient	Lorient	Knights Cross	17	82,873
09/01/1977	2nd	Lorient	Lorient	War Merit Cross 2nd Class with Swords	24	N/A
10/06/1974	2nd	Lorient	Lorient	Knights Cross	14	91,438
19/11/1970	2nd	Lorient	Lorient	Knights Cross	12	83,639
26/4/1989	7th	St. Nazaire	St. Nazaire	Knights Cross with Oak Leaves, U-boat Front Clasp	26	N/A
25/08/1984	1st	Brest	Brest	Knights Cross with Oak Leaves and Crossed Swords, War Merit Cross 2nd Class with Swords	18	95,544

VIIC	432	08/02/1942	8	*Kapitänleutnant*	Schultze	26	
IXB	103	09/02/1942	5	*Korvettenkapitän*	Werner Winter	30	
IXC	504	13/02/1942	12	*Korvettenkapitän*	Hans-Georg Friedrich Poske	37	
IXB	108	15/02/1942	4	*Korvettenkapitän*	Klaus Scholtz	34	
VIIC	653	24/02/1942	9	*Korvettenkapitän*	Gerhard Feiler	32	
IXC	126	26/02/1942	10	*Kapitänleutnant*	Ernst Bauer	28	
IXC	502	01/03/1942	2	*Kapitänleutnant*	Jürgen von Rosenstiel	29	
VIIC	96	01/03/1942	3	*Fregattenkapitän*	Heinrich Lehmann-Willenbrock	31	
IXC	156	03/02/1942	1	*Korvettenkapitän*	Werner Hartenstein	33	
IXC	158	03/02/1942	8	*Kapitänleutnant*	Erwin Rostin	34	
VIIC	588	02/03/1942	4	*Korvettenkapitän*	Victor Vogel	29	
IXC	155	02/03/1942	8	*Korvettenkapitän*	Adolf Cornelius Piening	31	
Calvi	*Tazzoli*	05/03/1942	9	*Capitano di Corvetta*	Carlo Fecia di Cossato	33	
VIIC	332	08/03/1942	10	*Kapitänleutnant*	Johannes Liebe	28	
IXB	124	12/03/1942	8	*Kapitänleutnant*	Johann Mohr	25	

25/11/1943	3rd	La Pallice	La Pallice	Knights Cross	20	67,991
09/09/1972	2nd	Lorient	Lorient	Knights Cross	15	79,302
01/10/1944	2nd	Lorient	Lorient	Knights Cross	15	78,123
01/05/1987	2nd	Lorient	Lorient	Knights Cross with Oak Leaves	24	N/A
15/01/1990	1st	Brest	Brest	Greman Cross in Gold	3	14,983
12/03/1988	2nd	Lorient	Lorient	Knights Cross	24	N/A
05/07/1942	2nd	Lorient	Sunk: Biscay	U-boat War Badge 1939	14	78,843
18/4/1986	7th	St. Nazaire	St. Nazaire	Knights Cross with Oak Leaves	27	N/A
08/03/1943	2nd	Lorient	Lorient	Knight's Cross	20	97,504
30/06/1942	10th	Lorient	Sunk: Bermuda	Knights Cross and U-boat War Badge 1939	17	N/A
31/07/1942	6th	Lorient	St. Nazaire	0	7	31,492
15/05/1984	10th	Kiel	Lorient	Knights Cross	25	N/A
27/08/1944	Betasom	Bordeaux	Bordeaux	Iron Cross	16	86,535
18/10/1982	3rd	La Pallice	La Pallice	Iron Cross First Class	8	46,729
02/04/1943	2nd	Lorient	Lorient	Knights Cross with Oak Leaves	27	N/A

VIIC	94	16/03/1942	3	*Oberleutnant zur See*	Otto Ites	24	
IXB	105	21/03/1942	12	*Fregattenkapitän*	Heinrich Schuch	36	
IXB	123	21/03/1942	13	*Korvettenkapitän*	Reinhard Hardegen	29	
IXC	160	21/03/1942	10	*Korvettenkapitän*	Georg Lassen	26	
VIIC	202	01/04/1942	10	*Korvettenkapitän*	Hans-Heinz Linder	29	
VIIC	71	02/04/1942	6	*Kapitänleutnant*	Walter Flachsenberg	33	
VIIC	572	03/04/1942	15	*Kapitänleutnant*	Heinz Hirsacker	27	
VIIC	571	05/04/1942	7	*Korvettenkapitän*	Helmut Möhlmann	29	
VIIC	754	05/04/1942	4	*Kapitänleutnant*	Hans Oestermann	28	
VIIB	85	06/04/1942	4	*Oberleutnant zur See*	Eberhard Geger	27	
VIIC	575	11/04/1942	20	*Kapitänleutnant*	Günther Heydemann	28	
VIIC	654	11/04/1942	19	*Oberleutnant zur See*	Ludwig Forster	26	
VIIC	552	11/04/1942	4	*Fregattenkapitän*	Erich Topp	28	
VIIC	582	13/04/1942	20	*Korvettenkapitän*	Werner Schulte	29	

02/02/1982	7th	St. Nazaire	St. Nazaire	Knights Cross	15	76,882
21/01/1968	2nd	Lorient	Lorient	0	6	37,641
Alive	2nd	Lorient	Lorient	Knights Cross with Oak Leaves, U-boat War Badge with Diamonds	21	N/A
18/01/2012	10th	Helgoland	Lorient	Knights Cross with Oak Leaves, U-boat War Badge with Diamonds	26	N/A
10/09/1944	1st	Brest	Brest	0	7	24,811
11/03/1994	7th	St. Nazaire	La Pallice	0	5	38,894
24/04/1943	3rd	Brest	La Pallice	U-boat War Badge 1939	3	14,813
17/04/1977	3rd	La Pallice	La Pallice	Knights Cross U-boat Front Clasp	5	33,511
31/07/1942	1st	Brest	Brest	0	13	55,659
14/12/42	3rd	St. Nazaire	Sunk: Hatteras	0	3	15,060
02/01/1986	7th	St. Nazaire	St. Nazaire	Knights Cross	8	36,010
22/08/1942	1st	Lorient	Sunk: Panama	Iron Cross 2nd Class	3	17,755
26/12/2005	7th	St. Nazaire	St. Nazaire	Knights Cross with Oak Leaves and Crossed Swords	35	N/A
05/10/1942	1st	Brest	Brest	0	7	38,872

VIIC	203	15/04/1942	4	*Kapitänleutnant*	Rolf Mützelburg	29	
IXB	109	17/04/1942	10	*Korvettenkapitän*	Heinrich Bleichrodt	32	
VIIC	201	17/04/1942	18	*Kapitänleutnant*	Adalbert Schnee	28	
VIIC	402	17/04/1942	15	*Korvettenkapitän*	Siegfried von Forstner	31	
VIIC	576	19/04/1942	4	*Kapitänleutnant*	Hans-Dieter Heinicke	28	
VIIB	86	21/04/1942	5	*Kapitänleutnant*	Walter Schug	31	
VIIC	136	21/04/1942	3	*Kapitänleutnant*	Heinrich Zimmermann	34	
IXB	108	23/04/1942	12	*Korvettenkapitän*	Klaus Scholtz	34	
IXC	154	23/04/1942	4	*Fregattenkapitän*	Walther Kölle	34	
VIIC	564	24/04/1942	9	*Kapitänleutnant*	Reinhard Suhren	26	
VIIB	84	25/04/1942	5	*Kapitänleutnant*	Horst Uphoff	25	
VIIC	98	25/04/1942	9	*Korvettenkapitän*	Herbert Schulze	32	
VIIC	333	26/04/1942	7	*Kapitänleutnant*	Peter Erich Cremer	31	
VIIC	352	27/04/1942	4	*Korvettenkapitän*	Hellmut Rathke	31	

11/09/1942	1st	Brest	Lorient	Knights Cross with Oak Leaves	19	81,961
09/01/1977	2nd	Lorient	Lorient	War Merit Cross 2nd Class with Swords	24	N/A
04/11/1982	1st	Brest	Brest	Knights Cross with Oak Leaves	21	90,189
13/10/1943	3rd	St. Nazaire	St. Nazaire	Knights Cross	15	71,036
15/07/1942	7th	St. Nazaire	St. Nazaire	0	4	15,450
23/11/1943	1st	Brest	Brest	0	3	9,614
11/07/1942	6th	St. Nazaire	St. Nazaire	0	5	23,649
01/05/1987	2nd	Lorient	Lorient	Knights Cross with Oak Leaves	24	N/A
10/01/1992	2nd	Lorient	Lorient	0	7	31,352
25/08/1984	1st	Brest	Brest	Knights Cross with Oak Leaves and Crossed Swords, War Merit Cross 2nd Class with Swords	18	95,544
07/08/1943	1st	Brest	Brest	German Cross in Gold	6	29,905
Alive	7th	St. Nazaire	St. Nazaire	0	0	0
05/07/1992	3rd	La Pallice	La Pallice	Knights Cross with Wounded Badge in Silver and U-boat Front Clasp	6	26,873
07/10/2001	3rd	St. Nazaire	Sunk: Hatteras	Iron Cross 2nd Class	0	0

VIIC	564	30/04/1942	23	*Kapitänleutnant*	Reinhard Suhren	26	
VIIC	69	01/05/1942	7	*Kapitänleutnant*	Ulrich Gräf	26	
VIIC	558	01/05/1942	13	*Kapitänleutnant*	Günther Krech	27	
VIIC	594	02/05/1942	9	*Korvettenkapitän*	Dietrich Hoffmann	29	
IXB	103	03/05/1942	6	*Korvettenkapitän*	Werner Winter	30	
VIIC	751	03/05/1942	5	*Kapitänleutnant*	Gerhard Bigalk	33	
IXB	106	04/05/1942	9	*Kapitänleutnant*	Hermann Rasch	27	
IXC	130	08/05/1942	16	*Korvettenkapitän*	Ernst Kals	36	
VIIC	753	11/05/1942	8	*Korvettenkapitän*	Alfred Manhardt von Mannstein	34	
VIIC	653	16/05/1942	20	*Korvettenkapitän*	Gerhard Feiler	32	
IXC	504	19/05/1942	6	*Korvettenkapitän*	Hans-Georg Friedrich Poske	37	
IXC	507	21/05/1942	4	*Fregattenkapitän*	Harro Schacht	34	
VIIC	404	22/05/1942	13	*Korvettenkapitän*	Otto Von Bülow	30	

25/08/1984	1st	Brest	Brest	Knights Cross with Oak Leaves and Crossed Swords, War Merit Cross 2nd Class with Swords	18	95,544
17/02/1943	7th	St. Nazaire	St. Nazaire	0	6	16,627
03/06/2000	1st	Brest	Brest	Knights Cross	17	93,186
Alive	7th	St. Nazaire	St. Nazaire	0	0	0
09/09/1972	2nd	Lorient	Lorient	Knights Cross	15	79,302
17/07/1942	7th	St. Nazaire	St. Nazaire	Knights Cross	5	21,412
10/06/1974	2nd	Lorient	Lorient	Knights Cross	14	91,438
02/11/1979	2nd	Lorient	Lorient	Knights Cross	17	N/A
13/05/1943	3rd	La Pallice	La Pallice	0	3	23,117
15/01/1990	1st	Brest	Brest	German Cross in Gold	3	14,983
01/10/1944	2nd	Lorient	Lorient	Knights Cross	15	78,123
13/01/1943	2nd	Lorient	Lorient	Knights Cross	19	77,143
05/01/2006	6th	Brest	St. Nazaire	Knights Cross with Oak Leaves, U-boat War Badge with Diamonds, War Merit Cross 2nd Class with Swords	14	71,450

VIIC	455	23/05/1942	8	*Korvettenkapitän*	Hans-Heinrich Giessler	31	
VIIC	588	23/05/1942	3	*Korvettenkapitän*	Victor Vogel	29	
VIIC	578	25/05/1942	14	*Fregattenkapitän*	Ernst-August Rehwinkel	41	
VIID	213	26/05/1942	12	*Oberleutnant zur See*	Amelung von Varendorff	30	
VIIC	593	27/05/1942	7	*Kapitänleutnant*	Gerd Kelbling	26	
IXC	506	28/05/1942	5	*Kapitänleutnant*	Erich Würdemann	28	
VIIC	566	30/05/1942	4	*Korvettenkapitän*	Dietrich Borchert	33	
IXC	157	05/06/1942	4	*Korvettenkapitän*	Wolf Henne	36	
VIIC	135	06/06/1942	11	*Kapitänleutnant*	Praetorius	38	
VIIC	373	06/06/1942	8	*Kapitänleutnant*	Paul-Karl Loeser	27	
IXC	129	08/06/1942	11	*Kapitänleutnant*	Hans-Ludwig Witt	32	
VIIC	584	11/06/1942	7	*Kapitänleutnant*	Joachim Deecke	29	
VIIC	432	13/06/1942	5	*Kapitänleutnant*	Schultze	26	

Alive	7th	St. Nazaire	St. Nazaire	Iron Cross 1st Class	2	13,908
31/07/1942	6th	St. Nazaire	St. Nazaire	0	7	31,492
06/08/1942	7th	St. Nazaire	St. Nazaire	0	4	23,635
31/07/1942	9th	Lorient	Lorient	U-boat War Badge 1939	0	0
09/06/2005	7th	St. Nazaire	St. Nazaire	Knights Cross	9	38,290
12/07/1943	10th	Lorient	Lorient	Knights Cross	14	69,893
Alive	1st	Brest	Brest	Iron Cross 1st Class	2	13,148
13/06/1942	2nd	Lorient	Sunk: Key West	0	1	6,401
16/04/1956	7th	Brest	St. Nazaire	U-boat War Badge 1939	3	21,302
02/01/1987	3rd	La Pallice	La Pallice	0	3	10,263
13/02/1980	2nd	Lorient	Lorient	Knights Cross, U-boat Front Clasp	19	N/A
31/10/1943	1st	Brest	Brest	German Cross in Gold	4	18,684
25/11/1943	3rd	La Pallice	La Pallice	Knights Cross	20	67,991

VIIC	332	24/06/1942	13	*Kapitänleutnant*	Johannes Liebe	28	
VIIC	571	26/06/1942	8	*Korvettenkapitän*	Helmut Möhlmann	29	
IXC	156	26/06/1942	3	*Korvettenkapitän*	Werner Hartenstein	33	
VIIC	437	28/06/1942	8	*Korvettenkapitän*	Werner-Karl Schulz	31	
VIIC	575	28/06/1942	4	*Kapitänleutnant*	Günther Heydemann	28	
IXC	158	29/06/1942	2	*Kapitänleutnant*	Erwin Rostin	34	
VIIB	84	29/06/1942	11	*Kapitänleutnant*	Horst Uphoff	25	
VIIC	134	30/06/1942	4	*Korvettenkapitän*	Rudolf Schendel	28	
VIIC	202	05/07/1942	3	*Korvettenkapitän*	Hans-Heinz Linder	29	
IXC	166	06/07/1942	4	*Oberleutnant zur See*	Hans-Günther Kuhlmann	28	
VIIC	576	06/07/1942	4	*Kapitänleutnant*	Hans-Dieter Heinicke	29	
IXC	173	09/07/1942	6	*Kapitän zur See*	Heinz-Ehler Beucke	38	
VIIC	402	09/07/1942	10	*Korvettenkapitän*	Siegfried von Forstner	31	

18/10/1982	3rd	La Pallice	La Pallice	Iron Cross First Class	8	46,729
17/04/1977	3rd	La Pallice	La Pallice	Knights Cross U-boat Front Clasp	5	33,511
08/03/1943	2nd	Lorient	Lorient	Knights Cross	20	97,504
20/11/1960	6th	St. Nazaire	St. Nazaire	0	0	0
02/01/1986	7th	St. Nazaire	St. Nazaire	Knights Cross	8	36,010
30/06/1942	10th	Lorient	Sunk: Bermuda	Knights Cross and U-boat War Badge 1939	17	N/A
07/08/1943	1st	Brest	Brest	German Cross in Gold	6	29,905
12/04/1970	3rd	La Pallice	La Pallice	0	3	12,147
10/09/1944	1st	Brest	Brest	0	7	24,811
30/07/1942	10th	Lorient	Sunk: New Orleans	0	4	7,593
15/07/1942	7th	St. Nazaire	Sunk: Hatteras	0	4	15,450
23/05/1979	2nd	Lorient	Lorient	0	0	0
13/10/1943	3rd	St. Nazaire	St. Nazaire	Knights Cross	15	71,036

VIIC	754	09/07/1942	3	*Kapitänleutnant*	Hans Oestermann	29	
IXC	171	11/07/1942	5	*Kapitänleutnant*	Günther Pfeffer	27	
VIIC	458	13/07/1942	11	*Kapitänleutnant*	Kurt Diggins	29	
IXC	161	16/07/1942	5	*Kapitänleutnant*	Albrecht Achilles	28	
IXC	509	20/07/1942	1	*Fregattenkapitän*	Karl-Heinz Wolff	32	
IXC	508	21/07/1942	8	*Kapitänleutnant*	Georg Staats	26	
VIIC	658	28/07/1942	10	*Kapitänleutnant*	Hans Senkel	32	
IXC	510	29/07/1942	9	*Korvettenkapitän*	Karl Neitzel	39	
VIIC	598	29/07/1942	12	*Korvettenkapitän*	Gottfried Holtorf	30	
XIV	463	31/07/1942	20	*Korvettenkapitän*	Leo Wolfbauer	47	
VIIC	98	01/08/1942	9	*Korvettenkapitän*	Wilhelm Schutze	33	
VIIC	654	04/08/1942	6	*Oberleutnant zur See*	Ludwig Forster	26	
VIIC	600	05/08/1942	9	*Kapitänleutnant*	Bernard Zurmühlen	33	
IXC	505	07/08/1942	3	*Korvettenkapitän*	Axel-Olaf Loewe	33	
IXC	164	08/08/1942	6	*Korvettenkapitän*	Otto Fechner	36	
VIID	217	08/08/1942	6	*Kapitänleutnant*	Kurt Reichenbach-Klinke	25	

31/07/1942	1st	Brest	Sunk: Halifax	0	13	55,659
25/04/1966	10th	Kiel	Sunk: Biscay	U-boat War Badge 1939	2	22,304
01/03/2007	3rd	Kiel	St. Nazaire	Iron Cross 1st Class, Medaglia di Bronzo al Valore Militare	2	7,584
27/09/1943	2nd	Lorient	Lorient	Knights Cross	12	60,107
11/06/1970	10th	Lorient	Lorient	0	0	0
12/11/1943	10th	Kiel	Lorient	Knights Cross	14	74,087
30/10/1942	6th	Kiel	St. Nazaire	0	3	12,146
13/11/1966	10th	Lorient	Lorient	Knights Cross	3	14,128
23/07/1943	6th	St. Nazaire	St. Nazaire	0	2	9,295
16/05/1943	12th	Kiel	St. Nazaire	0	0	0
Alive	7th	St. Nazaire	St. Nazaire	0		
22/08/1942	1st	Lorient	Sunk: Panama	Iron Cross 2nd Class	3	17,755
25/11/1943		Kiel	La Pallice	0	5	28,600
18/12/1984	2nd	Lorient	Lorient	0	7	37,832
06/01/1943	10th	Kiel	Lorient	U-boat War Badge 1939	3	8,133
05/06/1943	9th	Kiel	Brest	0	3	10,651

IXC	511	09/08/1942	6	*Kapitänleutnant*	Freidrich Steinhoff	33	
IXC/40	732	09/08/1942	4	*Oberleutnant zur See*	Klaus-Peter Carlsen	23	
VIIB	86	10/08/1942	15	*Kapitänleutnant*	Walter Schug	31	
VIIC	553	10/08/1942	4	*Korvettenkapitän*	Karl Thurmann	32	
IXC	163	12/08/1942	3	*Fregattenkapitän*	Kurt-Eduard Engelmann	29	
VIIC	558	15/08/1942	5	*Kapitänleutnant*	Günther Krech	27	
XIV	462	15/08/1942	6	*Kapitänleutnant*	Bruno Vowe	38	
VIIC	94	21/08/1942	5	*Oberleutnant zur See*	Otto Ites	24	
IXC	514	03/09/1942	5	*Kapitänleutnant*	Hans-Jürgen Auffermann	27	
VIIC	455	12/09/1942	8	*Korvettenkapitän*	Hans-Heinrich Giessler	31	
VIIC	69	21/09/1942	4	*Kapitänleutnant*	Ulrich Gräf	26	
IXC/40	185	28/02/1943	6	*Kapitänleutnant*	August Maus	28	
IXC	129	02/04/1943	24	*Kapitänleutnant*	Hans-Ludwig Witt	33	
IXC	155	11/04/1943	2	*Korvettenkapitän*	Adolf Cornelius Piening	32	
IXC	176	28/04/1943	4	*Korvettenkapitän*	Rainer Dierksen	35	

19/05/1945	10th	Kiel	Lorient	U-boat War Badge 1939	2	21,999
Alive	1st	Brest	Brest	Iron Cross 1st Class	0	0
23/11/1943	1st	Brest	Brest	0	3	9,614
20/01/1943	3rd	St. Nazaire	St. Nazaire	Knights Cross	12	61,390
13/03/1943	10th	Kiel	Lorient	U-boat War Badge 1939	3	15,011
03/06/2000	1st	Brest	Brest	Knights Cross	17	93,186
26/12/1978	10th	Kiel	St. Nazaire	0	0	0
02/02/1982	7th	St. Nazaire	Sunk: Haiti	Knights Cross	15	76,882
08/07/1943	10th	Kristiansand	Lorient	German Cross in Gold	4	16,329
Alive	7th	St. Nazaire	St. Nazaire	Iron Cross 1st Class	2	13,908
17/02/1943	7th	St. Nazaire	Lorient	0	6	16,627
28/09/1996	10th	Lorient	Lorient	Knights Cross	9	62,761
13/02/1980	2nd	Lorient	Lorient	Knights Cross, U-boat Front Clasp	19	N/A
15/05/1984	10th	Lorient	Lorient	Knights Cross	25	N/A
14/05/1943	10th	Lorient	Sunk: Cuba	German Cross in Gold	11	53,307

IXC	161	08/05/1943	3	*Kapitänleutnant*	Albrecht Achilles	28	
IXC/40	190	24/05/1943	9	*Kapitänleutnant*	Max Wintermeyer	28	
IXC	521	27/05/1943	2	*Kapitänleutnant*	Klaus Bargsten	30	
IXC	66	28/05/1943	3	*Kapitänleutnant*	Friedrich Markworth	28	
IXC/40	527	05/07/1943	2	*Kapitänleutnant*	Herbert Uhlig	27	
VIIC	134	09/07/1943	4	*Kapitänleutnant*	Hans-Günther Brosin	26	
VIIC	566	23/07/1943	5	*Kapitänleutnant*	Hans Hornkohl	25	
VIIC	230	24/07/1943	6	*Kapitänleutnant*	Paul Siegmann	29	
VIIB	84	07/08/1943	1	*Kapitänleutnant*	Horst Uphoff	26	
IXC	518	22/10/1943	10	*Kapitänleutnant*	Friedrich-Wilhelm Wissmann	28	
VIID	214	23/10/1943	2	*Oberleutnant zur See*	Rupprecht Stock	27	
IXC/40	530	09/11/1943	5	*Kapitänleutnant*	Kurt Lange	29	
XIV	488	11/11/1943	5	*Oberleutnant zur See (R)*	Erwin Bartke	33	
IXC/40	193	15/11/1943	10	*Fregattenkapitän*	Hans Pauckstadt	27	

27/09/1943	2nd	Lorient	Lorient	Knights Cross	12	60,107
Alive	2nd	Lorient	Lorient	U-boat War Badge 1939	1	7,015
13/08/2000	2nd	Lorient	Sunk: Virginia	Knights Cross	3	19,551
Alive	2nd	Lorient	Lorient	Knights Cross	13	74,067
20/10/1997	10th	Lorient	Sunk: Azores	0	1	5,242
24/08/1943	3rd	La Pallice	Sunk: Biscay	U-boat War Badge 1939	0	0
Alive	1st	Brest	Brest	0	1	2,265
Alive	9th	Brest	Brest	German Cross in Gold	1	2,868
07/08/1943	1st	Brest	Sunk: Bermuda	German Cross in Gold	6	29,905
Alive	2nd	Lorient	Lorient	0	8	52,346
Alive	9th	Brest	Brest	German Cross in Gold	1	200
15/06/1995	10th	La Pallice	Lorient	German Cross in Gold	2	12,063
29/03/1945	12th	Bordeaux	Bordeaux	U-boat Front Clasp	0	0
14/08/1984	2nd	La Pallice	El Ferrol	0	1	10,172

IXC	129	16/11/1943	19	*Oberleutnant zur See*	Richard von Harpe	26	
IXC/40	170	16/03/1944	9	*Kapitänleutnant*	Gunther Pfeffer	29	
VIIC	541	04/04/1944	14	*Kapitänleutnant*	Kurt Petersen	25	
IXC	505	14/06/1944	6	*N/A*	US Navy	N/A	
IXC/40	539	26/07/1944	3	*Kapitänleutnant*	Hans-Jürgen Lauterbach-Emdem	24	
IXC	518	24/08/1944	6	*Oberleutnant zur See*	Hans-Werner Offermann	23	

02/03/1945	2nd	St. Nazaire	Lorient	German Cross in Gold	3	17,362
25/01/1966	10th	Lorient	Lorient	0	4	22,304
Alive	10th	Lorient	Lorient	German Cross in Gold	1	2
N/A	2nd	Brest	Captured	N/A	N/A	N/A
Alive	10th	St. Nazaire	Flensburg	German Cross in Gold	1	1,517
22/04/1945	2nd	Kristiansand	Flensburg	German Cross in Gold	1	3,401

Details of Fifteen Allied Merchant Mariners Buried in Bermuda in World War Two

#	STEAMSHIP NAME	DATE	NAME/S	BURIED
1	*Peder Bogen*	14-Jul-40	James Dowsen	St. George's
2	*Ninamac*	20-Aug-40	James Clarke	Paget
3	*Karamer*	08-Apr-41	Colin White	St. George's
4	*Magician*	19-Apr-41	St. Clair Cummings	Paget
5	*Alcoa Leader*	29-Apr-41	Carl Olafsen	Paget
6	*British Tenacity*	05-Jun-41	Sidney Barter	St. George's
7	*Wiopaina*	02-Aug-41	Robert E. Miller	St. George's
8	*Laguna*	29-Aug-41	William Pigett	Paget
9	*British Tenacity*	31-Jan-42	Harold Ransom	Paget
10	*British Tenacity*	31-Jan-42	William Kelley	Paget
11	*British Tenacity*	31-Jan-42	J. McIntosh	Paget
12	*British Tenacity*	31-Jan-42	Joshua Brewer	Paget
13	*Herman Winters*	25-Jan-43	Charles Davis	Paget
14	*Ocean Vesper*	16-Jun-43	John Wilkin	Paget
15	*Sangara*	20-Feb-44	Norman Leslie Lakey	Paget

Endnotes

Introduction

1 Zuill, W. S., *The Story of Bermuda and Her People* (Macmillan Education: Oxford, Oxfordshire, England, UK, 1999).
2 Gannon, M., *Operation Drumbeat* (Harper Perennial: New York, USA, 1991).
3 Land Evans, J., *A Colony at War: Bermuda in the Global Fight Against Fascism, 1939-1945* (Lulu Press, Inc: Releigh, North Carolina, USA, 2016).

Chapter One

1 Jordan, R., *The World's Merchant Fleets 1939.* (Naval Institute Press: Annapolis, Maryland, USA, 1999)
2 Hague, A., *The Allied Convoy System 1939-1945: Its Organization and Operation* (Vanwell Publishing Limited: St. Catherine's, Ontario, Canada, 2000).
3 The National Archives (TNA), TD/DEMS/139, ADM/199/2139 (Public Records Office [PRO], London, United Kingdom).
4 '34 Survivors of Sunken Ship Reach Bermuda,' *Galveston Daily News*, 1 November 1940.
5 Jordan, *op. cit.*
6 'Crew of Torpedoed Ship Landed at Bermuda: Captain and 2nd Officer Lost; Vessel 5 Days from England,' *The Royal Gazette and Colonist Daily*, 29 October 1940.
7 'Torpedoed Crew Rescued: 21 Britons Reach Bermuda—Captain Lost with Ship,' *The New York Times*, Oct. 29, 1940.
8 Brown, Warren, of Hamilton, Bermuda; email to author 2013.
9 Wrecksite.eu.
10 Uboat.net.
11 Forposterityssake.ca/Navy/HMCS_Margaree_H49.htm.
12 '34 Survivors of Margaree Soon to Be Returned Home: Have Now Arrived at Bermuda, Navy Statement Discloses,' *The Lethbridge Herald*, 1 November 1940.
13 'Forecastle Apparently Sheared Off When Margaree Rammed as Disaster Story Reconstructed,' *Canadian Press*, 2 November 1940. 'Tells How Survivors Pulled on Ropes to Move Floating Half of Margaree Near to Rescue Vessel,' *Ibid*. 'Margaree Survivors Tell of Disaster: Floating Stern Sunk by Gunfire to Remove Menace,' *Ibid*.
14 'Margaree Was Cut in Two by Bow of Large Freighter as Ships Ran Without Lights: Survivors, Now in Bermuda, Will Be Returned to Canada,' *The Lethbridge Herald*, 1 November 1940.
15 'Prime Minister Voices Grief in Canada's Sea Losses,'—an entire page dedicated to the losses of the Margaree and its impact on the Winnipeg community and Canada at large. *Winnipeg Free Press*, Monday, 28 October 1940.

Chapter Two

1 Uboat.net.
2 Gannon, M.,, *Operation Drumbeat* (Harper Perennial: New York, USA, 1991).
3 Gentile, G., *The Fuhrer's U-boats in American Waters.* (Bellerophon Bookworks: Philadelphia, Pensylvania, 2006)
4 Hickam, H., *Torpedo Junction: The U-boat War off America's East Coast, 1942* (Naval Institute Press: Annapolis, Maryland, USA, 1996).

Chapter Three

1 Jordan, R., *The World's Merchant Fleets 1939* (Naval Institute Press: Annapolis, Maryland, USA, 1999).
2 Information on the *West Ekonk* by Jonathan Kinghorn at atlantictransportline.us/content/88WestEkonk.htm.
3 Uboat.net.
4 Hague, A., *The Allied Convoy System 1939-1945: Its Organization and Operation* (Vanwell Publishing Limited: St. Catherine's, Ontario, Canada, 2000).
5 '34 Survivors of Ship Torpedoing Land Here,' *The Royal Gazette and Colonist Daily*, 31 January 1942.
6 Details of Carmelo Fenech found on chapter on Maltese Merchant Seamen found at website.lineone.net/~remosliema/maltese_merchant_seamen.htm.
7 Uboatarchive.net.
8 'British Cargo Vessel Sunk, Part Crew Saved,' *Maryland Cumberland Times*, 1 February 1942.
9 The World War Two Action Report of the USS *Lang* (DD 399) are compliments of the *Pemberton Southard Papers*, Collection No. 551, East Carolina Manuscript Collection, J. Y. Joyner Library, Greenville, NC. The report is dated 1 February 1942 and is entitled Serial 18, 'Report of the Rescue of Survivors of S.S. *Empire Wildebeeste*.'
10 Captain Southard's obituary is at Findagrave.com.
11 Details of Erskine Austin Seay were found on the USS *Lang* Association website, usslangassoc.webs.com.
12 Fold3.com has an entry from 24 January 1942 relating to the *Empire Wildebeeste*.
13 '34 Survivors of Ship Torpedoing Land Here,' *The Royal Gazette and Colonist Daily*, 31 January 1942.
14 Capt. Brown's email to the author in 2012. A multi-generation Bermudian, he lived from 1929 to 2014.
15 'Nazis Claim 6 Ships Sunk,' *San Antonio Light*, 6 February 1942.
16 '4 Engineers Buried at Mass Funeral Saturday—Died From Burns Following Explosion Aboard Vessel,' *The Royal Gazette and Colonist Daily*, 2 February 1942.
17 The National Archives, Shipping Casualties, London, UK, PRO: TD/DEMS/139/1243.

Chapter Four

1 Uboat.net, U-boat Commander and U-boat Patrol sections.
2 Kurowski, F., *Knight's Cross Holders of the U-boat Service* (Schiffer Military History: Atglen, Pennsylvania, USA, 1995).
3 Wynn, K., *U-boat Operations of the Second World War, Volumes 1 and 2* (Caxton Editions: Chatham Publishing, London, United Kingdom, 1997).
4 Uboat.net, *op. cit.*
5 Kurowski, F., *op. cit.*
6 Gannon, M., *Operation Drumbeat* (Harper Perennial: New York, USA, 1991).

Chapter Five

1   Jordan, R., *The World's Merchant Fleets 1939* (Naval Institute Press: Annapolis, Maryland, USA, 1999).
2   The National Archives (TNA), TD/DEMS/139, ADM/199/2139.(Public Records Office [PRO]: London, United Kingdom).
3   Wrecksite.eu
4   Hague, A., *The Allied Convoy System 1939-1945: Its Organization and Operation.* (Vanwell Publishing Limited: St. Catherine's, Ontario, Canada, 2000)
5   Uboat.net, *San Arcadio* page under Allied Merchant Ships.
6   *Survivor's Statements* (1941-1942) Series: Papers of Vice Admiral Homer N. Wallin, compiled 1941—1974. Record Group 38: Records of the Office of the Chief of Naval Operations, 1875—2006 Entry P-13. (National Archives at College Park: Textual Reference (Military) 8601 Adelphi Road, College Park, MD, 20740, USA).
7   Uboatarchive.net.
8   The National Archives, *op. cit.*
9   researcheratlarge.blogspot.com/2013/09/random-photo-pbm-mariner-rescue-1942.html, comment by Jaap's son aka 'a widower,' 13 October 2014 at 9.32 a.m.
10 *Life Magazine*, Bermuda – 'Floyd Davis paints US forces on Hospitable Isle,' Published by Time Inc., Chicago, IL, Vol. 13, No. 12, 21 September 1942, p. 90.
11 researcheratlarge.blogspot.com/2013/09/random-photo-pbm-mariner-rescue-1942.html
12 'Rescued Sailors from Torpedoed British Ship,' *The Lethbridge Herald*, 13 February 1942.
13 Fold3.com, British Admiralty War Diary for Foreign Stations, 11 February 1942.
14 'Plane Rescues U-boat Victims,' Canadian Press, *Winnipeg Free Press*, 14 February 1942.

Chapter Six

1   *The Royal Gazette and Colonist Daily* ran a detailed piece entitled '4 Engineers Buried at Mass Funeral Saturday—Died From Burns Following Explosion Aboard Vessel,' 2 February 1942.
2   Information was kindly provided by Doreen and Mr. Lee of St. Paul's Parish Church in Paget. Also Dr. Derek Tully of the Guild of the Holy Compassion, founded before the war in Bermuda by Dickie Tucker, who also founded the Sailor's Home. Together they provided concrete proof of the burial sites of these men as well as names of the ships (censored in the news), with photos of the graves, burial records, etc.
3   Dr. Tully of The Guild of the Holy Compassion, founded by Dickie Tucker, *op. cit.*

Chapter Seven

1   Uboat.net, U-boat Commanders section.
2   Kurowski, F., *Knight's Cross Holders of the U-boat Service* (Schiffer Military History: Atglen, Pennsylvania, USA, 1995).
3   Wynn, K., *U-boat Operations of the Second World War, Volumes 1 and 2* (Caxton Editions, Chatham Publishing, London, United Kingdom, 1997).
4   Kurowski, F., *op. cit.*
5   Wynn, K., *op. cit.*
6   Suhren, T., and Brustat-Naval, *Ace of Aces, Memoirs of a U-boat Rebel.* (Chatham Publishing: London, United Kingdom, 2006)
7   Uboat.net, U-boat Commanders section.
8   Alexiades, P., private correspondence with author, 2012-2017, including translations of Italian patrol logs.
9   Mattesini, F., *I sommergibili di Betasom 1940-1943.* (*Ufficio Storico della Marina Militare*: Rome, Italy, 1994)

10   Maronari, A., *Un sommergibile non è rientrato alla base* (BUR, Rizzoli: Rome, Italy, 1999).
11   RegiaMarina.net, Christiano d'Adamo.
12   Gannon, M., *Operation Drumbeat* (Harper Perennial: New York, New York, USA, 1991).

Chapter Eight

1   Jordan, R., *The World's Merchant Fleets 1939.* (Naval Institute Press: Annapolis, Maryland, USA, 1999)
2   Hague, A., *The Allied Convoy System 1939-1945: Its Organization and Operation* (Vanwell Publishing Limited: St. Catherine's, Ontario, Canada, 2000).
3   The National Archives (TNA), TD/139.1604. (Public Records Office [PRO], London, United Kingdom).
4   Uboat.net, Merchant Ship pages, Crew List.
5   Uboatarchive.net, KTB of *U-124.*
6   The National Archives, *op. cit.*
7   Uboatarchive.net, *op. cit.*
8   The National Archives, *op. cit.*
9   Uboatarchive.net, *op. cit.*
10   The National Archives, *op. cit.*
11   Shipsnostalgia.com/showthread.php?t=4826; detailed thread for survivors and KIA.
12   Fold3.com War Diary for NOB Norfolk, 15 March 1942
13   'War Diary, US Naval Operating Base Bermuda,' on HMS *Clarkia,* 14-16 March 1942.
14   'War Diary, NOB Bermuda,' *op. cit.*
15   Uboat.net Allied Navy Ships, information on commander of HMS *Clarkia,* F. J. G. Jones.
16   The 'Lloyd's War Medal for Bravery at Sea' are listed at Wikipedia. N. M. Coleman and F. R. Clark of the *British Resource* are listed on page 7.
17   In 'Third Supplement to *The London Gazette* of Friday the 26th of March, 1943,' on pages 1-2, there is a citation to Kennedy and Coleman.
18   The Coventry (UK) *Evening Telegraph* of 1 February 2003 has an article by Fiona Scott entitled 'Brother marks kindness of former enemy' online about Ronald Jordan of the *British Resource.*

Chapter Nine

1   Kurowski, F., *Knight's Cross Holders of the U-boat Service* (Schiffer Military History: Atglen, Pennsylvania, USA, 1995).
2   Uboat.net, U-boat Commanders section.

Chapter Ten

1   Jordan, R., *The World's Merchant Fleets 1939.* (Naval Institute Press: Maryland, USA, 1999)
2   'Beat Four Subs, Sunk By A Fifth,' Zanesville, Ohio Times Recorder, 6 April 1942.
3   Uboatarchive.net, ESF Enemy Action Diary, 20 March 1942.
4   Uboatarchive.net, *op. cit.*
5   The National Archives (TNA), TD/DEMS/139, ADM/199/2139. (Public Records Office [PRO]: London, United Kingdom).
6   *Survivor's Statements* (1941-1942) Series: Papers of Vice Admiral Homer N. Wallin, compiled 1941—1974. Record Group 38: Records of the Office of the Chief of Naval Operations, 1875—2006 Entry P-13. (National Archives at College Park: Textual Reference (Military) 8601 Adelphi Road, College Park, MD, 20740, USA).
7   'Ship Is Sunk After Flight From U-boats,' *Frederick Maryland News,* 6 April 1942.
8   'Beat Four Subs, Sunk By A Fifth,' Zanesville, *Ohio Times* Recorder, 6 April 1942.
9   Wrecksite.eu

Chapter Eleven

1   Uboatarchive.net, ESF Enemy Action Diary, 1942.
2   Uboat.net, U-boat Commanders section.
3   Gannon, M., *Operation Drumbeat* (Harper Perennial: New York, USA, 1991).
4   Uboat.net, U-boat Commanders section.
5   Wynn, K., *U-boat Operations of the Second World War, Volumes 1 and 2* (Caxton Editions, Chatham Publishing, London, United Kingdom, 1997).
6   Kurowski, F., *Knight's Cross Holders of the U-boat Service* (Schiffer Military History: Atglen, Pennsylvania, USA, 1995).
7   Uboat.net, *op. cit.*
8   *Ibid.*

Chapter Twelve

1   Jordan, R., *The World's Merchant Fleets 1939* (Naval Institute Press: Maryland, USA, 1999).
2   'Freighter From Atlantic Making Good Time Here,' *Oakland Tribune*, 28 April 1925.
3   'Freighter Returns After Long Absence,' *Oakland Tribune*, 21 March 1927.
4   Fold3.com, ESF Enemy Action Diary, 12 November 1942.
5   *Survivor's Statements (1941-1942), op. cit.*
6   'Torpedo Victims Rescued,' Joplin Missouri *News*, 28 April 1942.
7   Uboat.net, Merchant Ships, Crew List.
8   USS *Greer* war diary for 23 April, 1942, as found at fold3.com
9   'Navy Lands Score of Ship Survivors,' *Oakland California Tribune*, 25 April 1942.
10 '26 Survivors Reach Bermuda,' *The New York Times*, 25 April 1942.
11 '3rd Torpedoed Crew In Two Days Landed Here,' *The Royal Gazette and Colonist Daily*, 25 April 1942.

Chapter Thirteen

1   Uboat.net U-boat Commanders section.
2   Kurowski, F., *Knight's Cross Holders of the U-boat Service* (Schiffer Military History: Atglen, Pennsylvania, USA, 1995).
3   Wynn, K., *U-boat Operations of the Second World War, Volumes 1 and 2* (Caxton Editions: Chatham Publishing, London, United Kingdom, 1997).
4   Uboat.net U-boat Commanders section, *op. cit.*

Chapter Fourteen

1   *The Singapore Free Press and Mercantile Advertiser* of 4 April 1942 announced the launch of *Agra* for the Swedish East Asiatic Company.
2   Areschoug, R., *Dödlig Resa: Svenska hendelsflottans förluster 1939–1945* (*Svenskt Militärhistoriskt Bibiliotek*: Stockholm, Sweden, 2008).
3   'Eighth Army Drives Keep AFS Lieut. Atkins on Go,' *Wisconsin State Journal*, 25 June 1944, about *Agra* survivor Lt. W. James Atkins of the American Field Service.
4   American Field Service, Roll of Honor, 1939-1945 – very detailed; ourstory.info/library/drivers/WW2/RH.html.
5   Harvard University *Crimson*, Excerpts kindly provided by archivists of Harvard University, Cambridge Massachusetts, 2013.
6   American Field Service history site, afs.metarhythm.com/archon/index.php?p=collections/ controlcard&id=62.
7   Skiold, R., translated pages from the book *Swedish Sailors in War and Peace*, relating to the *Agra*.

8   Adam, C. H., 'A Copy Desk Saga,' AFS Volunteer, World War Two, ourstory.info/library/
     4-ww2/Adam/edit.html.

9   Uboatarchive.net KTB of *U-654*.

10   *Survivor's Statements* (1941-1942) Series: Papers of Vice Admiral Homer N. Wallin,
     compiled 1941—1974. Record Group 38: Records of the Office of the Chief of Naval
     Operations, 1875—2006 Entry P-13. (National Archives at College Park: Textual Reference
     (Military) 8601 Adelphi Road, College Park, MD, 20740, USA).

11   *Ibid.*

12   'Survivor Arrivals Here Elicit Wide Sympathy,' The *Royal Gazette and Colonist Daily*, 9
     May 1942. The article is sub-titled 'Two Groups Over-Crowding All Available Facilities.'

13   Lundberg, L., *Lejdtrafik och kvarstad: Den svenska lejdtrafiken och de norska kvarstad
     båtarna under andra världskriget* (*Marinlitteraturföreningen*: Karlskrona, Skane, Sweden,
     1999).

14   'Survivors of Swedish Ship Landed Here,' The *Royal Gazette and Colonist Daily*, 24 April 1942.

15   Uboatarchive.net KTB of *U-654*, *op. cit.*

16   '33 Survivors of Torpedoed Ship Are Safe,' *Ohio News*, 24 April 1942.

17   *Survivors Statements*, (1941-1942), *op. cit.*

18   'Local Youth Describes Torpedoing of Freighter: Carl Adam, James Atkins Home Again;
     Ready to Go Back' a Wisconsin paper, Spring 1942 as found on newspaperarchive.com.

19   'Survivors in Bermuda,' UP, Charleston, *South Carolina Daily Mail*, 26 April 1942.

20   '33 Rescued,' *Mansfield Ohio News Journal*, 24 April 1942.

21   The neutral Swedish paper *Aftonbladet* named the *Agra* in a 25 Apr. 1942 article from
     Stockholm and circulated by Domei.

22   'A Man from Faro among *Agra* rescued crew—Has already signed on again,' from news
     agency TT, Stockholm, Sweden, 4 May 1942, translated from Swedish.

23   W. H. Mitchell, L. A. Sawyer, L.A., *The Empire Ships. London, New York, Hamburg, Hong
     Kong* .(Lloyd's of London Press Ltd.: London, United Kingdom, 1995)

24   The National Archives, *op. cit.*

25   Hague, A., *The Allied Convoy System 1939-1945: Its Organization and Operation* (Vanwell
     Publishing Limited: St. Catherine's, Ontario, Canada, 2000).

26   The National Archives, *op. cit.*

27   *Survivor's Statements*, (1941-1942), *op. cit.*

28   Uboararchive.net, KTB of *U-572*.

29   Uboatarchive.net, ESF Enemy Action Diary.

30   The National Archives, *op. cit.*

31   Uboatarchive.net, KTB of *U-572*, *op. cit.*

32   The National Archives, *op. cit.*

33   Uboat.net, Merchant Ships section, *City of Birmingham* entry.

34   The National Archives, *op. cit.*

35   'Survivor Arrivals Here Elicit Wide Sympathy,' The *Royal Gazette and Colonist Daily*,
     9 May 1942.

36   Uboat.net

37   *London Gazette*, Supplement, 11 May 1943, Rixham's citation, london-gazette.co.uk/
     issues/36007/supplements/2093/page.pdf.

Chapter Fifteen

1   Wynn, K., *U-boat Operations of the Second World War, Volumes 1 and 2* (Caxton Editions,
     Chatham Publishing, London, United Kingdom, 1997).

2   Uboat.net, U-boat Commanders section.

Chapter Sixteen

1 Sommerville, I. of Burntisland Heritage Trust wrote an article at burghbuzz.org.uk in May 2006, entitled 'The Loss of the *Derrycunihy*', in which he cites all sister ship's losses, including the *Derryheen*.

2 The National Archives (TNA), TD/139/1328, R/JMK. (Public Records Office [PRO]: London, United Kingdom).

3 *Survivor's Statements* (1941-1942) Series: Papers of Vice Admiral Homer N. Wallin, compiled 1941—1974. Record Group 38: Records of the Office of the Chief of Naval Operations, 1875—2006 Entry P-13. (National Archives at College Park: Textual Reference (Military) 8601 Adelphi Road, College Park, MD, 20740, USA).

4 Uboat.net, U-boat Patrols section.

5 The National Archives, *op. cit.*

6 *Ibid.*

7 'U.S. Navy Plane Saves Eight Ship Survivors', *The Royal Gazette and Colonist Daily*, 24 April 1942.

8 'More Survivors Landed Here After Torpedoing', *The Royal Gazette and Colonist Daily*, c. 27 April 1942.

9 Clydebuilt Ships Database, clydesite.co.uk/clydebuilt/viewship.asp?id=6227, MV *Lobos* information.

10 *Survivor's Statements (1941-1942), op. cit.*

11 Telex from Alusna Havana Cuba dated 1 May clarifying that 'the Captain and seven survivors' were landed by the *Lobos* in Cuba; only 8 men from the small boat landed in Havana.

12 Uboatarchive.net ESF Enemy Action Diary, 25 April; evidence the *Roode Zee*, a Dutch tug, was looking for *Derryheen* survivors, and five (in fact, four) boats were sighted at 1.31 p.m., 22 April.

13 'Scores of Nazi Subs Lurked Off North Carolina, SS Derryheen Torpedoed', Burlington *Daily Times News*, 1 August 1945. Note the year 1945; the name *Derryheen* could be used post-war.

14 Fold3 document from the ESF: this gives details of Ensign K. R. Peachee sighting 16 *Derryheen* survivors and vectoring a PBY aircraft which landed and took them to NAS Banana River.

15 Uboat.net for details of HMS *Polyanthus* and other vessels involved in the rescue.

16 '12 surivors of a British merchant ship, SS *Derryheen*', Aiken South Carolina *Standard* of 1 August 1945, cites survivors landed at Parris Island and treated for sunburn, etc.

17 *Ibid.*, ESF diary 2 May 1942—at 3.40 a.m., the *Polyanthus* picked up twelve survivors from the *Derryheen*. They did not land in Charleston till the next day, 3 May, hence the news article dated 4 May and also the captain saying one of the boats had a voyage of eleven, not ten days. There is a poignant request for clothing to be ready.

18 *Supplement to the London Gazette*, 5 January 1943, commendation for Harold Ingledew and John Stuart Burgess of the *Derryheen*, awarded the Most Excellent Order of the British Empire (OBE).

19 Fold3.com, 6 May 1942 entry USS *Umpqua* searching for *Derryheen* survivors.

20 'Sub Sinks Vessel on Maiden Voyage', Bradford, Pennsylvania *Era*, 5 May, 1942, after all survivors were landed. The passenger is described as a diplomat or government official.

21 Fold3.com, 6 May 1942 entry cites USS *Umpqua* searching for *Derryheen* survivors.

Chapter Seventeen

1 Uboatarchive.net, ESF Enemy Action Diary, 1942

2 Kurowski, F., *Knight's Cross Holders of the U-boat Service* (Schiffer Military History: Atglen, Pennsylvania, USA, 1995).

3 Uboat.net, U-boat Commanders section.

4 Wynn, K., *U-boat Operations of the Second World War, Volumes 1 and 2* (Caxton Editions: Chatham Publishing, London, United Kingdom, 1997).

5 *Ibid.*

Chapter Eighteen

1 Uboat.net, Merchant Ships section.

2 Ellisisland.org for an entry on the *Modesta* carrying emigres in 1921.

3 *War Cabinet Weekly Resume* (No. 92) of the Naval, Military and Air Situation, 29 May to 5 June 1941, in which *Modesta* appears having been intercepted in the North Sea.

4 The National Archives London, Shipping Casualty, TD/139/1302, PRO: London, UK.

5 Uboatarchive.net, KTB translated by Prof. Stephen Aranha of Nassau, Bahamas.

6 The National Archives, *op. cit.*

7 Fold3.com ESF Enemy Action Diary for 26 April 1942 shows planes finding lifeboats, directing *Belgian Airman* to scene.

8 Uboat.net Merchant Ships section for information on the *Belgian Airman*.

9 '67 Reach Bermuda from 3 Lost Ships,' The *Herald-American*, Syracuse New York, 26 April 1942.

10 'Survivors Landed,' Bradford, Pennsylvania *Era*, 28 April 1942.

11 'More Survivors Landed Here After Torpedoing,' *The Royal Gazette and Colonist Daily*, 27 Apr. 1942.

12 Information on the *Durban Castle* at bandcstaffregister.co.uk.page186.

13 Photo of Lewis Waldron at caribbeanrollofhonour-ww1-ww2.yolasite.com. The same site has information on Clemen Sealy, Fireman on the *Modesta* and Cyril Lashley. In the photo of Waldron in Trinidad, the shadow of his expectant wife watching on, with hands clasped appears.

14 'Greenock Men Who Lost Their Lives While Serving in the Merchant Navy During the War 1939-1945,' in which Robert Borthwick, Cabin Boy perished on the *Modesta* is memorialized.

Chapter Nineteen

1 Wynn, K., *U-boat Operations of the Second World War, Volumes 1 and 2* (Caxton Editions, Chatham Publishing, London, United Kingdom, 1997).

2 Uboat.net U-boat Commanders section.

3 Kurowski, F., *Knight's Cross Holders of the U-boat Service* (Schiffer Military History: Atglen, Pennsylvania, USA, 1995).

4 Högel, G., *U-boat Emblems of World War Two 1939–1945* (Schiffer Military History: Atglen, Pennsylvania, USA, 1999).

5 Johnson, R., *Different Battles: The Search for a World War II Hero* (Sunshine University Press: Vero Beach, Florida, USA, 1999).

6 Wynn, K., *op. cit.*

7 *Ibid.*

8 Gentile, G., *The Fuhrer's U-boats in American Waters* (Bellerophon Bookworks: Philadelphia, Pensylvania, 2006).

9 Hickam, H., *Torpedo Junction: The U-boat War off America's East Coast, 1942* (Naval Institute Press: Annapolis, Maryland, USA, 1996).

10 Gannon, M., *Operation Drumbeat* (Harper Perennial: New York, USA, 1991).

11 Kurowski, F., *op. cit.*

Chapter Twenty

1 'Along the Waterfront,' about the *Newsom*, appeared in the Boston, Massachusetts *Post*, 25 Aug. 1919, two days after her launch.

2 *The Boston Post* of 20 January 1921 recorded the *Newsom* leaving Moss Point, Mississippi for San Juan.

3 Grenon, I., *Lost Maine Coastal Schooners: From Glory Days to Ghost Ships* (The History Press: Arcadia Publishing, Stroud, United Kingdom, 2010).

4 'Schooner With Lumber Pounding to Pieces,' *The Salt Lake Tribune*, 19 February 1926.

5 'British Ship Pulled Free,' a Reno Nevada paper, 30 April 1935 based on an Associated Press article from New London, Connecticut.

6 'Runaway Ship Captured,' Williamsburg, Indiana *Press Pioneer*, 29 July 1921.

7 Beaman, J. S., 'A Mystery of the Sea: An Unmanned Ship that Sailed Itself.' Also Sonny Williamson of Bern NC submitted a letter dated 29 November 1939 by J. S. Beaman to a USCG officer in the Core Banks Station.

8 'Captain Acted As Doctor,' Glensboro *Western Prairie Gazette*, Manitoba Canada, 12 September 1937.

9 Mozolak, J., *New York Ships to Foreign Ports* database, http://janda.org/ships/.

10 Wynn, K., *U-boat Operations of the Second World War, Volumes 1 and 2* (Caxton Editions: Chatham Publishing, London, United Kingdom, 1997).

11 Uboatarchive.net for the KTB of *U-69*'s eighth War Patrol.

12 Uboatarchive.net *op. cit.*

13 'Nine Ship Survivors Landed Yesterday,' *The Royal Gazette and Colonist Daily*, 8 May 1942.

14 'U-boat Activity, Atlantic Coast Sinkings,' Montreal, 11 May 1942, trove.nla.gov.au/ndp/del/article/47332141.

15 Uboat.net, U-boat Commanders section.

Chapter Twenty-One

1 Wynn, K., *U-boat Operations of the Second World War, Volumes 1 and 2* (Caxton Editions, Chatham Publishing, London, United Kingdom, 1997).

2 Uboat.net U-boat Commanders section.

3 *Ibid.*

4 Wynn, K., *op. cit.*

5 Kurowski, F., *Knight's Cross Holders of the U-boat Service.* (Schiffer Military History: Atglen, Pennsylvania, USA, 1995)

6 Wynn, K., *op. cit.*

7 *Ibid.*

8 Uboat.net, *op. cit.*

Chapter Twenty-Two

1 'CNS Part In War Effort,' *Daily Gleaner*, Kingston, Jamaica, 18 April 1946 about the Canadian National (West Indies) Steamship fleet.

2 'The Lady Boats,' and article by John Boileau, 1 January 2007 in *Legion Magazine*, legionmagazine.com/en/2007/01/the-lady-boats.

3 Uboat.net, Merchant Ships and U-boat Commanders sections.

4 Hanington, F., and Kelly, P., *The Lady Boats: The Life and Times of Canada's West Indies Merchant Fleet* (Canadian Marine Transportation Centre: Dalhousie University, Halifax, Nova Scotia, Canada, 1980).

5 Fold3.com for secret war diary of USS *Owl*.

6 Wikipedia.org for details of USS *Owl*, including photos.

7 'Survivor Arrivals Here Elicit Wide Sympathy,' *The Royal Gazette and Colonist Daily*, 9 May 1942.

8 'Bermudians Help Ship Survivors,' Mansfield *News Journal*, 9 May 1942.

9 '250 Reach Safety After Sub Attack,' Joplin, *Missouri Globe*, 17 May 1942.

10 'U.S.O. Club News,' *The Royal Gazette and Colonist Daily*, 13 May 1942.

11   *Survivor's Statements (1941-1942)*, Series: Papers of Vice Admiral Homer N. Wallin,
     compiled 1941—1974. Record Group 38: Records of the Office of the Chief of Naval
     Operations, 1875—2006 Entry P-13. (National Archives at College Park: Textual Reference
     (Military) 8601 Adelphi Road, College Park, MD, 20740, USA), extraordinary for the
     lengthy list of every item carried in its cargo.
12   The National Archives London, Shipping Casualties, TDS/139/1460 PRO: UK.
13   'Torpedoed Seamen Land Here Yesterday,' *The Royal Gazette and Colonist Daily*, date
     unclear, May 1942.
14   'Offers House for Use of Shipwrecked Officers,' *The Royal Gazette and Colonist Daily*, 20
     May 1942.
15   Uboat.net, Merchant Ships section.
16   Uboat.net, U-boat Commanders sections.

Chapter Twenty-Three

1   Kurowski, F., *Knight's Cross Holders of the U-boat Service* (Schiffer Military History:
     Atglen, Pennsylvania, USA, 1995).
2   Wynn, K., *U-boat Operations of the Second World War, Volumes 1 and 2* (Caxton Editions,
     Chatham Publishing, London, United Kingdom, 1997).
3   Kurowski, F., *op. cit.*
4   Uboat.net, U-boat Commanders section.
5   Wynn, K., *op. cit.*
6   Uboat.net, *op. cit.*
7   Wynn, K., *op. cit.*
8   Kurowski, F., *op. cit.*
9   *Ibid.*
10   'Werner Hartenstien and the Laconia Incident,' wernerhartenstein.tripod.com/
     U156Laconia.htm.
11   Wynn, K., *op. cit.*
12   Uboat.net, *op. cit.*

Chapter Twenty-Four

1   Jordan, R., *The World's Merchant Fleets 1939* (Naval Institute Press: Annapolis, Maryland,
     USA, 1999).
2   Uboat.net, Merchant Ships section.
3   The National Archives London, Shipping Casualties, TD/139/1443, PRO: London, UK.
4   *Survivor's Statements (1941-1942)*, Series: Papers of Vice Admiral Homer N. Wallin,
     compiled 1941—1974. Record Group 38: Records of the Office of the Chief of Naval
     Operations, 1875—2006 Entry P-13. (National Archives at College Park: Textual Reference
     (Military) 8601 Adelphi Road, College Park, MD, 20740, USA)
5   Uboatarchive.net, KTB of *U-506*/Würdemann.
6   Uboat.net, Merchant Ships, Crew Lists sections for lists of survivors.
7   fold3.com, USS *Ludlow*, USS *Bernadou*, and USS *Texas* war patrol diaries, including descriptions
     and drawings of the U-boat by survivors and details of injuries, and lists of survivors.
8   Uboat.net, Merchant Ships, Crew Lists sections for lists of survivors.

Chapter Twenty-Five

1   Jordan, R., *The World's Merchant Fleets 1939* (Naval Institute Press: Maryland, USA, 1999).
2   'Freighter Has Rich Cargo From South America,' *Oakland Tribune*, 16 July 1926.
3   'Freighter Brings First Shipment of Brazil Nuts,' *Oakland Tribune*, 18 August 1926.

4   Pedas, T. 'Captain Loren McIntyre, South America Circumnavigation,' pedasfamily.com/
    AssociatesMcIntyre.html, from a series of lectures which Mr. Pedas delivered on cruise ships.
5   'Hawaiian Confesses to Sabotage Attempt,' Maryland *Cumberland Times*, 18 August 1940.
6   Kingston, Jamaica, *Gleaner*, Shipping Section, 25 March 1938.
7   'Ship Strike at Seattle Settled,' The Oakland, California *Tribune*, 20 September 1940.
8   Mozolak, J., *New York Ships to Foreign Ports, 1939–1945*, database, janda.org/ships.
9   Coman, E. T., and Gibbs, H. M., *Time Tide and Timber: A Century of Pope and Talbot*
    (Stanford University Press: First Pope & Talbot Printing edition, San Jose, California,
    USA, 1978).
10 Uboatarchive.net, KTB for *U-404*. Translation by Prof. Stephen Aranha, Bahamas.
11 *Ibid.*
12 Mackenzie, J. G., *Ahoy—Mac's Web Log* has interviews of von Bülow regarding his
    attack on the *West Notus* on p. 8 at ahoy.tk-jk.net/macslog/ConvoyRB1.html including
    photographs of the U-boat skipper in and after World War Two.
13 *Post Mortems on Enemy Submarines*, US Navy, excerpts of interviews of Horst Degen in
    which he talks about von Bülow receiving an award for his sinking of West Notus and
    four other ships, history.navy.mil/library/online/u701sunk.htm.
14 *Survivor's Statements (1941-1942)*, Series: Papers of Vice Admiral Homer N. Wallin,
    compiled 1941—1974. Record Group 38: Records of the Office of the Chief of Naval
    Operations, 1875—2006 Entry P-13. (National Archives at College Park: Textual Reference
    (Military) 8601 Adelphi Road, College Park, MD, 20740, USA).
15 swissships.ch/schiffe/saentis_007/schiffsberichte_saentis/Rescue%20Operation%20 North%20
    Atlantic for information on MV *Saentis* and other Swiss ships like the *Jagersfontein*.
16 Fold3.com, 5 Jun. 1943; ESF Enemy Action and Distress Diary; discovery of 17 *West Notus*
    survivors on the MV *Saentis* on her arrival in New York.
17 For photo of the *Constantinos H.*, diaressaada.alger.free.fr/j-Marine/5-Cargos/CBVN/
    Nanceen_800.jpg
18 Wrecksite.eu
19 Hague, A., *The Allied Convoy System 1939-1945: Its Organization and Operation*. (Vanwell
    Publishing Limited: St. Catherine's, Ontario, Canada, 2000)
20 theshipslist.com/ships/lines/horn for details of the *Constantinos H.*
21 Tashimoro, B. H., *Honolulu Herald*, 19 September 1986, 'Charles Toguchi—Living Through
    Three Wars,' 100thbattalion.org/archives/newspaper-articles/ben-tamashiro/charles-toguchi/

Chapter Twenty-Six

1   Niestlé, A., *German U-boat Losses During World War Two* (Frontline Books: London,
    United Kingdom, 2014).
2   Vause, J., *Wolf: U-boat Commanders in World War II* (Naval Institute Press: Annapolis
    Maryland, USA, 1997).
3   Uboat.net, U-boat Commanders and Merchant Ships sections.
4   Uboat.net, U-boat Commanders section.
5   Wynn, K., *U-boat Operations of the Second World War, Volumes 1 and 2* (Caxton Editions,
    Chatham Publishing, London, United Kingdom, 1997).
6   *Ibid.*
7   Uboat.net, U-boat Commanders section.

Chapter Twenty-Seven

1   Uboat.net, Merchant Ships section.
2   *Reports from the Office of the Commandant*, US NOB Bermuda, James Report of Loss by F.
    E. Nuessle filed 17 June 1942 in New York City.

3   Uboat.net, Merchant Ships section.
4   RCNVR List, 1960, digital.nls.uk/british-military-lists/pageturner.cfm?id=93488946 &mode=transcription.
5   Morgan, D., and Taylor, B., *U-boat Attack Logs: A Complete Record of Warship Sinkings from Original Sources 1939-1945.* (Seaforth Publishing: Barnsley, South Yorkshire, United Kingdom, 2011). Detailed original documentation from both sides relating to the casualty.
6   *Ibid.*
7   'Dakota Captain Went Down With Ship But Lives to Tell Heroic Tale,' The Billings, *Montana Gazette*, 29 June 1942, by John A. Moroso.
8   Bureau of Personnel Information Bulletin citing Pettingell in April 1943, navy.mil/ ah_online/archpdf/ah194304.pdf.
9   Harvard University *Crimson*, citing Winslow L. Pettingell, including a photograph, and numerous reports on the Class of 1938. Compliments of the Harvard University Archives.
10 Morgan, D., and Taylor, B., *op. cit.*
11 Fold3.com, Action Report of USS *Hamilton* entitled 'Rescue of Survivors of USS *Gannet*,' 9 June 1942, DMS-18, Serial 022.
12 *Ibid.*
13 Morgan, D., and Taylor, B., *op. cit.*
14 'Old Times, July 1948,' Supplement to *The College Times*, archive.org/stream/ oldtimesjul1948ucco/oldtimesjul1948ucco_djvu.txt, newspaperarchives.com

Chapter Twenty-Eight

1   Uboat.net, U-boat Commanders, U-boat Patrols sections.
2   Wynn, K., *U-boat Operations of the Second World War, Volumes 1 and 2* (Caxton Editions, Chatham Publishing, London, United Kingdom, 1997).
3   Wynn, K., *op. cit.*
4   Uboat.net, U-boat Commanders section.

Chapter Twenty-Nine

1   Holm-Lawson, S., *Norwegian Merchant Marine and Ships* (warsailors.com: Sackets Harbor, New York, 2013).
2   Uboat.net, Merchant Ship section.
3   Holm-Lawson, S., *op. cit.*
4   *Survivor's Statements (1941-1942)*, Series: Papers of Vice Admiral Homer N. Wallin, compiled 1941—1974. Record Group 38: Records of the Office of the Chief of Naval Operations, 1875—2006 Entry P-13. (National Archives at College Park: Textual Reference (Military) 8601 Adelphi Road, College Park, MD, 20740, USA)
5   'Survivors' Group Landed,' *The Royal Gazette and Colonist Daily*, 13 June 1942.
6   Holm-Lawson, S., *op. cit.*

Chapter Thirty

1   Uboat.net, U-boat Commanders, U-boat Patrols sections.
2   Wynn, K., *U-boat Operations of the Second World War, Volumes 1 and 2* (Caxton Editions: Chatham Publishing, London, United Kingdom, 1997).
3   Uboat.net, U-boat Commanders section.
4   Wynn, K., *op. cit.*
5   Kurowski, F., *Knight's Cross Holders of the U-boat Service* (Schiffer Military History: Atglen, Pennsylvania, USA, 1995).
6   *Ibid.*

7   Uboat.net, U-boat Commanders section.

Chapter Thirty-One

1   Wrecksite.eu
2   Jordan, R., *The World's Merchant Fleets 1939* (Naval Institute Press: Annapolis, Maryland, USA, 1999).
3   'More Dutch Ships To Call Here,' *Singapore Free Press and Mercantile Advertiser*, 25 October 1939.
4   'Adds Another Ship,' *Oakland Tribune*, 28 November 1939 about the fleet.
5   *Port Director's Report*, Fold3.com, the *Jagersfontein* arrived in Honolulu at 9.30 a.m. the day of Pearl Harbor.
6   *Survivor's Statements (1941-1942)*, Series: Papers of Vice Admiral Homer N. Wallin, compiled 1941—1974. Record Group 38: Records of the Office of the Chief of Naval Operations, 1875—2006 Entry P-13. (National Archives at College Park: Textual Reference (Military) 8601 Adelphi Road, College Park, MD, 20740, USA).
7   Uboatarchive.net, KTB of *U-106*.
8   *Nasha Gazeta* (Moscow, Russia), for a description of Captain Gerber, nashagazeta.ch/news/12148, in Russian.
9   Wikipedia, *St. Cergue*'s 1941 voyage, en.wikipedia.org/wiki/Peter_Tazelaar
10   Swiss-Ships.ch, for details of the *St. Cergue* and her rescue of both *Koll* and *Jagersfontein* survivors, swiss-ships.ch/schiffe/st-cergue_005/fr_st-cergue_005.htm.
11   Uboat.net, on USS *Bernadou*.
12   Navsource.org, for the photo of the USS Bernadou, navsource.org/archives/05/0515310.jp.g
13   Coone T., for complete personnel list of the ship from the logs of the USS *Bernadou*. history.navy.mil/danfs/b5/bernadou-i.htm.

Chapter Thirty-Two

1   Uboat.net, U-boat Commanders section.
2   Kelshall, G., *The U-boat War in the Caribbean* (Naval Institute Press: Annapolis, Maryland, USA, 1988).
3   Kurowski, F., *Knight's Cross Holders of the U-boat Service* (Schiffer Military History: Atglen, Pennsylvania, USA, 1995).
4   Uboat.net, *op. cit.*
5   Niestlé, A., *German U-boat Losses During World War Two* (Frontline Books: London, United Kingdom, 2014).
6   *Ibid.*
7   Wynn, K., *U-boat Operations of the Second World War, Volumes 1 and 2* (Caxton Editions: Chatham Publishing, London, United Kingdom, 1997).
8   *Ibid.*
9   Uboat.net, U-boat Commanders section.

Chapter Thirty-Three

1   Zuill, W. S., *The Story of Bermuda and Her People* (Macmillan Education: Oxford, Oxfordshire, United Kingdom, 1999).
2   Land Evans, J., *A Colony at War: Bermuda in the Global Fight Against Fascism, 1939-1945* (Lulu Press, Inc: Releigh, North Carolina, USA, 2016).
3   'Sunset Heights Resident Who Escaped from Torpedoed Ship Back in Bosom of His Family,' *Titusville Herald*, 29 May 1943, about Stanley Matuszewski.

4   *Survivor's Statements* (*1941-1942*), Series: Papers of Vice Admiral Homer N. Wallin, compiled 1941—1974. Record Group 38: Records of the Office of the Chief of Naval Operations, 1875—2006 Entry P-13. (National Archives at College Park: Textual Reference (Military) 8601 Adelphi Road, College Park, MD, 20740, USA)

5   US Merchant Mariner's website, article about Mary Cullum Kimbro, usmm.org/women.html

6   'More than a footnote,' by David Ballingrud of the *St. Petersburg Times* on 3 July 2000, eulogized Evelyn Parker, a survivor.

7   Navsource.org, USS *Stansbury*.

8   'Dictionary of American Naval Fighting Ships,' USS *Stansbury*, ibiblio.org/hyperwar.

9   Uboararchive.net, KTB of *U-202*'s 6th War Patrol.

10   Fold3.com, references to the *City of Birmingham* on 1 July 1942.

11   'More than a footnote,' *op. cit.*

12   'Sunset Heights Resident Who Escaped from Torpedoed Ship Back in Bosom of His Family,' *op. cit.*

13   Fold3.com, 'Brief History of USS *Stansbury*,' 24 September 1945.

14   Fenbert, J., and Fenbert, R., (daughter of John Frederick Guests, Jr.), email to author, 4 Aug. 2014 provides granular details about the survival, Bermuda stay, and repatriation by air of many of the officers, men and passengers of the *City of Birmingham*, as well the men of USS *Stansbury*.

15   Fold3.com, Lieutenant Commander Maher, in his official report filed 11 July 1942.

16   'Ship Survivors Get $1,500 From US Base,' *The Royal Gazette and Colonist Daily*, 6 July 1942.

17   Uboat.net, U-Boat Patrols section.

18   US Navy Office of Naval Intelligence, Interrogation Report, debriefing of *U-128* survivors, uboatarchive.net/U-128A/U-128INT.htm.

19   Niestlé, A., *German U-boat Losses During World War Two* (Frontline Books: London, United Kingdom, 2014).

20   Morgan, D., and Taylor, B., *U-boat Attack Logs: A Complete Record of Warship Sinkings from Original Sources 1939-1945*. (Seaforth Publishing: Barnsley, South Yorkshire, United Kingdom, 2011)

21   Kahn, D., *The Codebreakers: The Comprehensive History of Secret Communication from Ancient Times to the Internet.* (Scribner: Simon and Schuster, New York, USA, 1996)

22   Niestlé, A., *op. cit.*

23   'Plane Rescues U-Boat Victims,' CP Cable, 14 February 1942.

24   White, T., researcheratlarge.blogspot.com/2013/09/random-photo-pbm-mariner-rescue-1942.html.

25   *Life Magazine, Bermuda – Floyd Davis paints US forces on Hospitable Isle* (Time Inc.: Chicago, Ilinois, Vol. 13, No. 12, September 21, 1942, p.90).

26   *Ibid.*

Chapter Thirty-Four

1   Kurowski, F., *Knight's Cross Holders of the U-boat Service* (Schiffer Military History: Atglen, Pennsylvania, USA, 1995).

2   Wynn, K., *U-boat Operations of the Second World War, Volumes 1 and 2* (Caxton Editions, Chatham Publishing, London, United Kingdom, 1997).

3   *Ibid.*

4   Uboat.net, U-boat Commanders, U-boat Patrols sections.

5   *Ibid.*

6   Wynn, K., *op. cit.*

7   *Ibid.*

8   Uboat.net, U-boat Commanders, U-boat Patrols sections.

9   Kurowski, F., *op. cit.*

10   *Ibid.*

11   Uboat.net, U-boat Commanders, U-boat Patrols sections.

12   Wynn, K., *op. cit.*

Chapter Thirty-Five

1   Uboat.net, Merchant Ship section.

2   Jordan, R., *The World's Merchant Fleets 1939.* (Naval Institute Press: Annapolis, Maryland, USA, 1999)

3   Uruguayan research site dedicated to their Merchant Marine, marinamercanteuruguaya. blogspot.com/2010/05/ss-maldonado-anp-1941-1942.html, in Spanish.

4   Wynn, K., *U-boat Operations of the Second World War, Volumes 1 and 2.* (Caxton Editions, Chatham Publishing, London, United Kingdom, 1997)

5   'Uruguayan Captain is Prisoner On U-boat,' *The Royal Gazette and Colonist Daily*, 8 August 1942.

6   'More Survivors Rescued,' *The New York Times*, 9 August 1942.

7   'Mongrel Pup Has First Taste of War,' Associated Press, 17 August 1942, about a dog on board.

8   'Nazi Sub Kidnaps Captain of Neutral Uruguayan Ship,' Racine, *Wisconsin Journal Times*, 8 August 1942.

9   *Survivor's Statements (1941-1942)*, Series: Papers of Vice Admiral Homer N. Wallin, compiled 1941—1974. Record Group 38: Records of the Office of the Chief of Naval Operations, 1875—2006 Entry P-13. (National Archives at College Park: Textual Reference (Military) 8601 Adelphi Road, College Park, MD, 20740, USA)

10   'Uruguay Ship Sunk; Captain Taken Prisoner,' Muscatine, Iowa *Journal and News-Tribune*, 8 August 1942.

11   *Ibid.*

12   'Uruguayan Ship Captain Captured,' *Kennebec Daily Journal*, 17 August 1942.

13   'Uruguay Envoy Phones Survivors Landed Here, Ship's Sinking Brings Sharp Demonstration in Montevideo,' *The Royal Gazette and Colonist Daily*, 10 August 1942.

Chapter Thirty-Six

1   Lundberg, L., *Lejdtrafik och kvarstad: Den svenska lejdtrafiken och de norska kvarstad båtarna under andra världskriget* (*Marinlitteraturföreningen*: Karlskrona, Skane, Sweden, 1999).

2   Suhren, T., and Brustat-Naval, F., *Ace of Aces, Memoirs of a U-boat Rebel* (Chatham Publishing: London, United Kingdom, 2006).

3   Uboat.net, U-boat Patrols sections.

4   Wynn, K., *U-boat Operations of the Second World War, Volumes 1 and 2* (Caxton Editions, Chatham Publishing, London, United Kingdom, 1997).

5   *Ibid.*

6   *Ibid.*

7   *Ibid.*

8   *Ibid.*

9   US Navy war crimes in the Atlantic during WW2, forum.axishistory.com viewtopic.phpt=56631 (9 Aug. 2004), uboatarchive.net.

10   *U-511 and Missiles: U 511, U 1063 and plans for U-boats armed with seabased missiles*, German U-boat Museum, dubm.de/en/u-511-and-missiles/.

11   Steinhoff's burial spot, ww2gravestone.com/people/steinhoff-friedrich/.

12   Milner, M., *Legions Magazine, Over the Side: The Courageous Boarding of U-94*, 15 January 2015, legionmagazine.com/en/2015/01/over-the-side-the-courageous-boarding-of-u-94/.

13   Kurowski, F., *Knight's Cross Holders of the U-boat Service* (Schiffer Military History: Atglen, Pennsylvania, USA, 1995) .

14 *Ibid.*
15 Uboat.net, U-boat Commander and U-boat Patrol sections.

Chapter Thirty-Seven

1 Shipbuildinghistory.com, Smith & Rhuland, shipbuildinghistory.com/canadayards/smithandrhuland.htm.
2 *Survivor's Statements (1941-1942)*, Series: Papers of Vice Admiral Homer N. Wallin, compiled 1941—1974. Record Group 38: Records of the Office of the Chief of Naval Operations, 1875—2006 Entry P-13. (National Archives at College Park: Textual Reference (Military) 8601 Adelphi Road, College Park, MD, 20740, USA)
3 Uboat.net, Merchant Ships and Crew Lists sections.
4 '4 Schooner Survivors Rescued by Fisherman,' *The Royal Gazette and Colonist Daily*, 19 September 1942.
5 Fold3.com, ESF Enemy Action and Distress Diary, 21 September 1942.
6 'Fisherman rescues survivors,' The *Bermudian*, Arthur Mann Purcell, Editor, October 1942, p. 11, in the *Landlubber's Log* section. It says Lamb had been 'attending his nets.'
7 Pitcher, G., of St. David's Bermuda, wrote online about his relative Gilbert Lamb, 15 November 2015. He subsequently sent the author photos of his relative, Mr. Lamb, in May 2017.

Chapter Thirty-Eight

1 Uboat.net, U-boat Patrol section.
2 Uboat.net, U-boat Commander section.
3 Wynn, K., *U-boat Operations of the Second World War, Volumes 1 and 2*. (Caxton Editions, Chatham Publishing, London, United Kingdom, 1997)
4 How, D., *Night of the Caribou*. (Lancelot Press Ltd.: Hantsport, Nova Scotia, Canada, 1988)
5 Wynn, K., *op. cit.*

Chapter Thirty-Nine

1 Wikipedia.org, HMCS *Prince David* towing the *St. Margaret* into Bermuda, 3 September 1942.
2 Hague, A., *The Allied Convoy System 1939-1945: Its Organization and Operation* (Vanwell Publishing Limited: St. Catherine's, Ontario, Canada, 2000).
3 The National Archives, London, Ship Casualty Division, TD/139/1757, PRO: London, UK.
4 Capt. Davies' diary account of the loss of SS *St. Margaret*, 39-45war.com/stmargaret.html.
5 Uboatarchive.net, KTB or war diary of *U-66*.
6 The National Archives, *op. cit.*
7 Fold3.com, USS *Ellyson*, USS *Corry* and USS *Ranger* corroborating rescue.
8 Fold3.com, USS *Hobson* rescuing a raft from *St. Margaret*, 2 March 1943.
9 Uboat.net, USS *Hobson* and partial list of *St. Margaret* officers and men.
10 'Group Of Survivors Is Landed Yesterday,' *The Royal Gazette and Colonist Daily*, 6 March 1943.
11 'Dare Of Friends Yields Results For 1st Sweater,' Fitchburg, *Massachusetts Sentinel*, 4 May 1944.
12 *Sinking of the USS* Hobson, Cold War Museum, coldwar.org/articles/50s/sinkingoftheUSSHobson.asp, researched by intern Megan Overman.

Chapter Forty

1 Wynn, K., *U-boat Operations of the Second World War, Volumes 1 and 2* (Caxton Editions, Chatham Publishing, London, United Kingdom, 1997).
2 Kurowski, F., *Knight's Cross Holders of the U-boat Service* (Schiffer Military History: Atglen, Pennsylvania, USA, 1995).

Chapter Forty-One

1   Jordan, R., *The World's Merchant Fleets 1939* (Naval Institute Press: Annapolis, Maryland, USA, 1999).
2   Uboat.net, Merchant Ship and Crew List sections.
3   White, J., 'MV *Melbourne Star*, Blue Star Line,' melbournestar.co.uk/Attack.html, nephew of survivor Leonard White.
4   *Survivor's Statements (1941-1942)*, Series: Papers of Vice Admiral Homer N. Wallin, compiled 1941—1974. Record Group 38: Records of the Office of the Chief of Naval Operations, 1875—2006 Entry P-13. (National Archives at College Park: Textual Reference (Military) 8601 Adelphi Road, College Park, MD, 20740, USA).
5   bluestarline.org/melbourne1.html, amplifying information on the *Melbourne Star*.
6   *Survivor's Statements (1941-1942)*, op. cit.
7   Finch, T., comments posted on the *Melbourne Star* casualty at Ancestry.com.
8   Fold3.com, War Diary of NOB Bermuda, 9 May 1943.

Chapter Forty-Two

1   Cervera, G. P., *Sinking of the German Submarine U-176*, historianaval.org/1903_1958/II%20Guerra%20Mundial/hundimiento_submarino_u_176/sinking_submarine_u176.htm, Sept. 2005, in Spanish.
2   Wynn, K., *U-boat Operations of the Second World War, Volumes 1 and 2* (Caxton Editions, Chatham Publishing, London, United Kingdom, 1997).
3   Kurowski, F., *Knight's Cross Holders of the U-boat Service* (Schiffer Military History: Atglen, Pennsylvania, USA, 1995).
4   *Ibid.*
5   Niestlé, A., *German U-boat Losses During World War Two* (Frontline Books: London, United Kingdom, 2014).
6   Wynn, K., *op. cit.*
7   White, J., *The Milk Cows: The U-boat Tankers 1941-1945* (Pen and Sword: Barnsley, United Kingdom, 2009).
8   Wynn, K., *op. cit.*
9   *Ibid.*
10 *Ibid.*
11 Uboat.net, U-boat Commanders section.
12 Stubblebine, D., *The Capture of U-505, 4 Jun 1944–17 Jun 1944*, ww2db.com/ battle_spec.php?battle_id=329.
13 Uboat.net, U-boat Patrol and U-boat Commanders sections.
14 *Ibid.*

Bibliography

Areschoug, R., *Dödlig Resa: Svenska hendelsflottans förluster 1939–1945* (*Svenskt Militärhistoriskt Bibiliotek*: Stockholm, Sweden, 2008)

Bercuson, D. J., and Herwig, H. H., *Long Night of the Tankers: Hitler's War Against Caribbean Oil* (University of Calgary Press: Calgary, Alberta, Canada, 2014)

Blair, C., *Hitler's U-boat War: The Hunted, 1942-1945* (Random House: New York, New York, USA, 1998)

Busch, R., Röll, H. and Brooks, G., *German U-boat Commanders of World War Two: A Biographical Dictionary* (Naval Institute Press: Annapolis, Maryland, USA, 1999)

Coman, Edwin T., and Gibbs, Helen M., *Time Tide and Timber: A Century of Pope and Talbot* (Stanford University Press: First Pope & Talbot Printing edition, 1978)

Cremer, P., *U-boat Commander: A German Sub Commander's View of the Battle of the Atlantic* (A Jove Book, Berkley Publishing Group: New York, New York, USA, 1986)

Cressman, R., *The Official Chronology of the U.S. Navy in World War Two* (Naval Historical Center: Contemporary History Branch, Washington District of Columbia, USA, 1999)

Edwards, B., *The Quiet Heroes: British Merchant Seamen at War 1939—1945* (Pen & Sword Military: Barnsley, South Yorkshire, United Kingdom, 2003)

Gannon, M., *Operation Drumbeat* (Harper Perennial: New York, New York, USA, 1991)

Gentile, G., *The Fuhrer's U-boats in American Waters* (Bellerophon Bookworks: Philadelphia, Pensylvania, 2006)

Goebeler, H., and Vanzo, J., *Steel Boat, Iron Hearts: A U-boat Crewman's Life Aboard U-505* (Savas Beatie LLC: New York, New York, USA 2008)

Hague, A., *The Allied Convoy System 1939-1945: Its Organization and Operation* (Vanwell Publishing Limited: St. Catherine's, Ontario, Canada, 2000)

Hanington, F. and Kelly, P., *The Lady Boats: The Life and Times of Canada's West Indies Merchant Fleet* (Canadian Marine Transportation Centre: Dalhousie University, Halifax, Nova Scotia, Canada, 1980)

HarperCollins, *Atlas of the Second World War* (Borders Press: Ann Arbor, MI, 1999)

Hickam, H., *Torpedo Junction: The U-boat War off America's East Coast, 1942* (Naval Institute Press: Annapolis, Maryland, USA, 1996)

Hill, J., Editor, *The Oxford Illustrated History of the Royal Navy* (Oxford University Press: Oxford, Oxfordshire, United Kingdom, 1995

Högel, G., *U-boat Emblems of World War Two 1939—1945* (Schiffer Military History: Atglen, Pennsylvania, USA, 1999)

Holm-Lawson, S., *Norwegian Merchant Marine and Ships* (warsailors.com: Sackets Harbor, New York, 2013)

Hulse, A., *This Blood Red Sea* (secondworldwar.org.com: England, United Kingdom, 2014)

Johnson, R., *Different Battles: The Search for a World War II Hero* (Sunshine University Press: Vero Beach, Florida, USA, 1999)

Jordan, R., *The World's Merchant Fleets 1939* (Naval Institute Press: Annapolis, Maryland, USA, 1999)

Kahn, D. *The Codebreakers: The Comprehensive History of Secret Communication from Ancient Times to the Internet* (Scribnter: Simon and Schuster, New York, New York, USA, 1996)

Kelshall, G., *The U-boat War in the Caribbean* (Naval Institute Press: Annapolis, Maryland, USA, 1988)

Kurowski, F., *Knight's Cross Holders of the U-boat Service* (Schiffer Military History: Atglen, Pennsylvania, USA, 1995)

Land Evans, J., *A Colony at War: Bermuda in the Global Fight Against Fascism, 1939-1945* (Lulu Press, Inc: Releigh, North Carolina, USA, 2016)

Lindbaek, L. and Solum, N., *Norway's New Saga of the Sea* (Exposition Press: New York, New York, USA, 1969)

Lundberg, L., *Lejdtrafik och kvarstad: Den svenska lejdtrafiken och de norska kvarstad båtarna under andra världskriget* (*Marinlitteraturföreningen*: Karlskrona, Skane, Sweden, 1999)

Maronari, A., *Un sommergibile non è rientrato alla base* (BUR, Rizzoli: Rome, Italy, 1999)

Mattesini, F., *I sommergibili di Betasom 1940-1943* (*Ufficio Storico della Marina Militare*: Rome, Italy, 1994)

Morgan, D., and Taylor, B., *U-boat Attack Logs: A Complete Record of Warship Sinkings from Original Sources 1939-1945* (Seaforth Publishing: Barnsley, South Yorkshire, United Kingdom, 2011)

Morison, S., *The Battle of the Atlantic, September 1939-May 1943* (Little, Brown & Co.: Boston, Massachusetts, USA, 1948)

Morison, S., *History of United States Naval Operations in World War Two, Volume 1, The Atlantic Battle Won, September 1943-May 1945* (Little, Brown & Co.: Boston, Massachusetts, USA, 1948)

Morison, S., *The Two Ocean War* (Little, Brown & Co.: Boston, Massachusetts, USA, 1963)

Mozolak, J. *New York Ships to Foreign Port, 1939 – 1945* (janda.org/ships/)

Miller, N., *The War at Sea* (Scribner, New York, New York, USA, 1995)

Niestlé, A., *German U-boat Losses During World War Two* (Frontline Books: London, United Kingdom, 2014)

Noli, J., *The Admiral's Wolf Pack* (Doubleday& Co., Garden City, New York, USA, 1974)

Rohwer, J., *Axis Submarine Successes of World War Two: German, Italian and Japanese Submarine Successes, 1939-1945* (Naval Institute Press: Annapolis, Maryland, USA, 1999)

Roskill, S., *The War at Sea* (Her Majesty's Stationers Offices: London, United Kingdom, Three Volumes, 1954-1961)

Russell, J., *The Last Schoonerman—The Remarkable Life of Captain Lou Kenedy* (The Nautical Publishing Company: Far Horizons Media Co., Rockledge, Florida, 2006)

Savas, T., Editor, *Hunt and Kill: U-505 and the U-boat War in the Atlantic* (Savas Beatie LLC: El Dorado Hills, California, USA, 2004)

Solly, R., *Athel Line, A Fleet History*, (The History Press: Gloucestershire, United Kingdom, 2009)

Spector, R., *At War at Sea* (Scribner, New York, New York, USA, 1995)

Stigloe, J., *Lifeboat* (University of Charlottesville Press, Charlottesville, Virginia, USA, 2003)

Stern, R., and Greer, J., *U-boats in Action*, (Squadron/Signal Publications, Inc.: Carrollton, Texas, USA 1977)

Stranack, I., *The Andrew and the Onions: The Story of the Royal Navy in Bermuda 1795–1975* (Bermuda Maritime Museum Press: Old Royal Navy Dockyard, Bermuda, 1990)

Suhren, T., and Brustat-Naval, F., *Ace of Aces, Memoirs of a U-boat Rebel* (Chatham Publishing: London, United Kingdom, 2006)

Survivor's Statements (1941-1942), Series: Papers of Vice Admiral Homer N. Wallin, compiled 1941—1974. Record Group 38: Records of the Office of the Chief of Naval Operations, 1875—2006 Entry P-13. (National Archives at College Park: Textual Reference (Military) 8601 Adelphi Road, College Park, MD, 20740, USA)

Syrett, D., *The Defeat of the German U-boats: The Battle of the Atlantic* (University of South Carolina Press: Columbia, South Carolina, USA, 1994)

The National Archives (TNA), TD/DEMS/139, ADM/199/2139 (Public Records Office [PRO], London, United Kingdom)

Tod, G., *The Last Sail Down East* (Barre Publishers: Barre, Massachusetts, USA, 1965)

Vause, J., *Wolf, U-boat Commanders in World War Two* (Naval Institute Press: Annapolis, Maryland, USA, 1990)

Werner, H., *Iron Coffins: A Personal Account of the German U-boat Battles of World War Two* (DeCapo Press: Cambridge, Massachusetts, 1969)

White, J., *U Boat Tankers 1941-45: Submarine Suppliers to Atlantic Wolf Packs* (Naval Institute Press: Annapolis, Maryland, USA, 1998)

Williams, A., *The Battle of the Atlantic: The Allies' Submarine Fight Against Hitler's Grey Wolves of the Sea* (Basic Books: Perseus Books Group, New York, New York, USA, 2003)

Vause, J., *Wolf: U-boat Commanders in World War II* (Naval Institute Press: Annapolis Maryland, USA, 1997).

Wynn, K., *U-boat Operations of the Second World War, Volumes 1 and 2* (Caxton Editions: Chatham Publishing, London, United Kingdom, 1997)

Zuill, W. S., *The Story of Bermuda and Her People* (Macmillan Education: Oxford, Oxfordshire, United Kingdom, 1999)